Anthropology and Literature

Anthropology
and
Literature

Edited by

Paul Benson

Introduction by Edward M. Bruner

UNIVERSITY OF ILLINOIS PRESS
Urbana and Chicago

Library of Congress Cataloging-in-Publication Data

Anthropology and literature / edited by Paul Benson :
introduction by Edward M. Bruner.
    p. cm.
    "An incarnation of a special issue of the Journal of the
Steward Anthropological Society," with the title:
Conversations in anthropology : anthropology and literature.
    Includes bibliographical references (p.) and index.
    ISBN 0-252-01944-X. —ISBN 0-252-06261-2 (pbk.)
    1. Ethnology—Authorship. 2. Ethnology–Methodology. I.
Benson, Paul
GN 307.7.A58 1993
305.8′001—dc20
                                         92-4206
                                           CIP

After all, the boundaries between fiction and nonfiction, between literature and nonliterature and so forth are not laid up in heaven.

—Mikhail Bakhtin

For Kim and Hunter

Contents

Preface and Acknowledgments

The fusion of anthropology and literature is one in which the language of the science employs the aesthetics of art. Ivan Brady has called it artful-science. It is a discourse where the beauty and the tragedy of the world are textually empowered by the carefully chosen constructions and subjective understandings of the author. The product is one that simulates the situation under study with all the imaginative advantages of poetically crafted prose. It is my hope that this literary and poetic anthropology will not only contribute to anthropological canon but will be useful to those in other disciplines in this interdisciplinary moment.

This book is an incarnation of a special issue of the *Journal of the Steward Anthropological Society*. I am indebted to Peter Heinricher who coedited the journal with me for four years and to Thomas Riley, my department head, for help in sustaining the journal and for making this volume possible. I am also indebted to the contributors for their wonderfully crafted essays and to Edward Bruner for his interpretative and perceptive integration of them.

I also would like to thank the American Anthropological Association for the use of the essay by William Rodman and work by Philip K. Bock; the University of Chicago Press for the use of the article by Frances Mascia-Lees, Patricia Sharpe, and Colleen Ballerino Cohen; and Lika Mutal and the Nohra Haime Gallery for use of the reproduction of her sculpture on the cover.

Certain individuals have been indispensable to this project. In their own unique and powerful ways, they are in their various works opening anthropological writing to new avenues of enhancement. Special thanks go to Ivan Brady, who has worked closely with me on the anthropology and literature project since 1984. Dan Rose has contributed to understanding the necessity of the expanding and transforming anthropological writing to broaden our perspective while simultaneously nurturing our communicative ability across disciplines and across cultures. I also would like to thank Janet Dixon Keller, Norman K. Denzin, Judith McCulloh, and the anonymous manuscript reviewers for their input, insight, and assistance.

On a personal note, I owe my deepest gratitude to my family: to my wife, Kim Weborg-Benson, and to my son, Hunter, for the great enrichment of the life we share and to my parents, Margaret and Donald Benson, for their faith and support.

Introduction: The Ethnographic Self and the Personal Self

Edward M. Bruner

The essays in this volume are concerned with ethnographic writing. The chapters by Turner and Ridington experiment with new ways of describing other cultures; the essays by Angrosino, Rodgers, and Fox deal with how to interpret the cultural accounts produced by other peoples about themselves; Rodman discusses how the people we study respond to the anthropologist; Grindal and Shephard trace the textual transformations in the telling and retelling of a story; Rose, Mascia-Lees, Sharpe, Cohen, and Brady focus on radically innovative theoretical issues involved in the production of ethnography.

All of the essays are caught up in the current reflexive, sometimes painful, always critical, and still evolving self-examination of the eth-nographic enterprise (e.g., Marcus and Cushman 1982; Bruner 1984; Prattis 1985; Clifford and Marcus 1986; Turner and Bruner 1986; Marilyn Strathern 1987b; Clifford 1988a; Geertz 1988; Renato Rosaldo 1989; Brady 1991; Lavie, Narayan, and Rosaldo 1993). As such, this volume is a product of its times, of the late 1980s/early 1990s "experimental moment" (Marcus and Fischer 1986) in anthropology and of the postmodern turn.

The challenge is not to produce yet another critique of ethnography. We know the objections to the traditional stance of the ethnographer as an objective, authoritative, politically neutral, usually white male observer standing somehow above and outside the text. We already know that ethnographers are historically positioned and locally situated all-too-human recorders of the human condition. We know that culture is contested, always in production. We know that meaning is radically plural, always open, and that there is politics in every account. Over the past decades in anthropology we have responded to the same intellectual currents of the various poststructuralisms, Marxisms, continental philosophies, feminist and critical theories that have had such a profound influence on literary criticism and the other humanities and social science disciplines. We have read Derrida, Foucault, Barthes, Bourdieu, de Certeau, and Baudrillard, and many have been influenced by the English cultural studies tradition. Anthropology, in turn, has influenced postmodernism.

The problem now is twofold: on the one hand we have to continue and deepen the critique, to correct its excesses, to explore and conceptualize new facets of our predicament as ethnographers in a postcolonial postindustrial era, and on the other hand, we have to get on with our work of writing about other cultures and to move ahead with the common ethnographic enterprise. The essays in this volume are contributions to both of these objectives.

Although these chapters respond to our historical moment, the questions dealt with have long been among the most fundamental in anthropology and have deep roots in the discipline. The basic issue is how best to describe and understand other peoples and cultures, which is a very old anthropological issue indeed. What I find so fascinating are the changing reconceptualizations of the relationship between subject and object,[1] between ethnographic observer and the native peoples studied. The problem is often phrased as a question about the extent to which the personal and the poetic should be inserted in the scientific scholarly text, as if there were an opposition between the scientific and the humanistic, between the academic and the poetic, between the scholarly and the literary. I reject these binaries (Bruner 1990), but acknowledge that each historical epoch has had its own answers to these questions, with limits set by the dominant discursive practice of the era, and of course there have always been individual exceptions.

The idea of a scientific, supposedly objective, ethnographic report that left the individual observer out of the account is not only a cliche, it is an impossibility. Every ethnographer inevitably leaves traces in the text. Despite conscious attempts to mask a presence, a close reading of any ethnography would reveal the persona of the author not only in the text but especially around the edges and the margins. Prefaces to monographs are particularly revealing. Presented first but usually produced last, the preface or introduction provide a space where the ethnographer is permitted a modicum of personal biography and intellectual indebtedness. Evans-Pritchard's famous (or infamous) introduction in 1940 to *The Nuer* is a classic case in this regard, where the author thanked military intelligence officers, described his hostile reception by the Nuer, and even discussed recent incidents of warfare between the Nuer and their British colonial masters and then proceeded to write an "objective" ethnography. The acknowledgments, however brief, are another space where the anthropologist may choose to locate himself or herself in relation to others in the discipline, and the bibliography has always been a wonderful source of information in this respect. The bibliography, as much political statement as scholarly reference, cites some authors and omits others, thereby positioning the writer within particular networks, schools, and traditions in the academic discipline. The politics of the bibliography has yet to be written. Prefaces, acknowledgments, introductions, and bibliographies are personally revealing spaces within the traditional monograph, windows to an inevitable subjectivism invariably duplicated in the body of the text.

The personal, the humanistic, and the literary have entered even the most realist of ethnographic accounts. The decision to remove the persona of the ethnographer from the text is itself as much a "literary" decision, a strategic one, as the opposite, the choice to include the ethnographer as a character in the events described. Until the past few decades, however, the majority decision was to sharply segment the ethnographic self from the personal self. This was accomplished in various ways. Edward Sapir and Ruth Benedict published realist ethnography in anthropology journals and published subjective poetry in literary journals. The one kind of writing was for them unrelated to the other (Rose 1991b). Others have used different publishers or pseudonyms to segregate more personal accounts from their ethnographic writing. A well-known example is Laura Bohannan, who did traditional African ethnography but published a separate, more personal book, *Return to Laughter,* under the pseudonym Elenore Smith Bowen (1954). Still others, such as Paul Rabinow, David Maybury-Lewis, and Jean-Paul Dumont, have published two separate books, each in their own name, one a standard ethnography and the second a field memoir or confessional.[2]

The question is why the separation of the ethnography from the memoir, why the pseudonym, why the two publishers? It was a distortion that emerged as a historical response to rigid canons of what was then assumed to be proper scientific practice. Personal memoirs, "literary" writing, poetry, and any work that inserted the Self in the account of the Other deviated from the standard realist mode and was considered inappropriate. As a protective mechanism, the personal and the literary were disguised, kept secret, or separated from the ethnographers' scientific publications. Make no mistake; to use pseudonyms or different publishers is not a benign gesture, it is a serious political act.

The split between the ethnographic self and the personal self was also a split between anthropology and poetics (Brady 1991:217). Those of an earlier era who used two different names, their real name for their anthropology and a pseudonym for their poetry, were also rupturing the discipline. This contrasts with the contemporary generation of anthropological poets, including Stanley Diamond, Dennis Tedlock, Dell Hymes, and Paul Friedrich, whose anthropological and poetic selves seem more compatible. They feel free to combine anthropology and poetics in the same manuscript, which they submit to the same publisher, and there is less of the uneasy segmentation between anthropology and poetry. I would much rather have these materials within the discourse of anthropology, where they can be utilized and criticized, than outside the discourse, where these texts are effectively lost to the profession.

It could be argued that the ethnography is designed to present the data on other cultures, whereas the memoir is a personal record of a field experience so it is appropriate to publish the two accounts separately, and some may simply prefer to do so.[3] Separate publication protects the objective ethnography from "contamination" by the highly subjective. It is true that the memoir describes the conditions under which the data were gathered; the ethnography presents those data. The memoir deals with processes of production; the ethnography with the product. But the processes of production are part of the product, just as the mechanisms of construction of the text are part of the text. To separate the memoir from the ethnography is to create a false dichotomy, which only makes sense if one believes that the data are independent of how those data were acquired. Further, in the field, the two are a unified experience. The events of the memoir and the events of the ethnography occur simultaneously in experience, and to separate them in the later writing stage takes some considerable mental gymnastics and does violence to the lived experience.

Here is a letter I received from a former student, now doing graduate work at another university, after she had been in the field for a few months:

> Your comments and advice helped alleviate some of my anxiety about fieldnotes. I had been advised . . . to try and keep a record for data and another journal for more "personal" notes, and was concerned that I was not doing a very good job at this because I couldn't separate these two aspects of research (or, as you write, my personal self from my ethnographic self). In reading your paper from the perspective of "being in the field," it struck me how incredibly rigid are the conventions of traditional ethnography—how powerful the authoritative discourse—

to suppress such a major element of the ethnographic experience. In actual fieldwork practice, the personal is foregrounded because the knowledge acquired is largely experiential. It is through the daily events, interactions, even struggles, in fieldwork that I learn and gather data; these are the very processes of production that I experience subjectively, personally, sometimes emotionally. And they shape the direction of research. Not only are the processes of production and the product, the personal and the ethnographic self a unified experience, but there seems to be a dynamic interplay between the two. Anyway, I enclose a copy of a first field report that I sent to my committee.[4]

There must be many failed ethnographers who went to the field but who never completed a thesis, an occurrence often attributed to a "writing block." This attributes failure to a flaw in the person, whereas it may have been, at least in part, a failure in the discourse, a consequence of the vast gap between the personal field experience and the impersonal conventions of the standard ethnographic monograph. In an earlier era of anthropology, not only was the self removed from the ethnography, but the culture was presented as integrated, the social structure as functionally consistent, and all in the hypothetical ethnographic present. Under these impossible conditions, the wonder is not that we have failed ethnographers but that we have any good ethnography at all. Of course, the stakes were high. A young anthropologist aiming to get on with a career and to achieve status in the discipline would be highly motivated to accept the prevailing conventions. The ethnographer would also have reason to present a fieldwork persona in the text as a rational, academic, task-oriented, objective scientist.

In that previous era, the personal and the literary were considered soft, lacking in rigor, too subjective, even emotional, and, yes, "feminine." It is no accident that women married to anthropologists, who were themselves anthropologists (Marjorie Wolf, Marjorie Shostak, Edith Turner, Elizabeth Fernea, Laura Bohannan), have produced rich accounts of the field experience—possibly it was the only space available to them in a discourse dominated by masculine conceptions of the discipline. Husbands would do the ethnography and wives would tell the story of the field experience.[5]

The distancing of ethnographic subject from native object was essential to an older model of ethnography, for how else could we be the impersonal authoritative voice empowered to represent the Other? If we were too much like them, if both we and they had active voices, then the distinction between the ethnographer as theorizing being and the informant as passive data would dissolve. Traditional ethnography required a sharp separation between subject and object if it was to retain its authoritative voice.

It is now so clear that writing is a political act. Those who claim that what is literary is not political or that humanistic interpretive anthropology does not deal with political issues are dead wrong, as any act of representation of the Other is inherently political.

The danger is in putting the personal self so deeply back into the text that it completely dominates, so that the work becomes narcissistic and egotistical. No one is advocating ethnographic self-indulgence. The challenge is to return the ethnographer to the text but not to the extent of squeezing out the object of study. The aim is a balance that reduces the gap between subject and object, that presents both ethnographer and informant as having active creative selves. The ethnographer can engage in a dialogue with the informant, just as there is a dialogue in the field between persons. The informants may be seen as sophisticated, knowledgeable, cosmopolitan beings, even as coauthors, and not just as folk persons with primitive knowledge. Further, the writer may speak through a narrator, directly as a character in the work or through multiple characters, or one character may speak in many voices, or the writer may come in and then go out of the work, may change in the course of it, or whatever. In the text as in the field, we can engage our informants as persons and write about how anthropological information is acquired at the same time that we present that information. No longer does the anthropologist and the informant have to inhabit the separate worlds of science and religion. In the text as in life, there is no need to be consistent or to speak with one voice. Today, it is possible to be evocative, to express feelings, ours and theirs, and to capture the drama of social life. That ethnography contains narratives or stories means that it is constructed, not that it is fictional in the sense of being false or not real, or that it avoids accountability. As contemporary ethnography is more true to life than old-fashioned realist ethnography, it is easier for the writer to accept political responsibility for the account.

In the traditional mode the ethnographer had to suppress, segment, and disguise part of the self, whereas now the ethnographer may reclaim all parts of the self, can unify the personal and the professional, can be both literary and scientific, or can use one in the service of the Other. The previously segmented self may come together, as the personal and the professional become aligned. There is no need to separate the memoir from the ethnography, no need to falsify, repress, and distort part of the ethnographic self, to be a hero or a mechanical recording machine. We can discard disguises and falsifications, and in so doing regain a unified self and a freedom to be oneself, *one self.* Or at least we can work in that direction. Ethnography can be liberating.

I should like to pursue further the question of the ethnographer as subject in relation to the native object by examining three recent ethnographic monographs, *Storytellers, Saints, and Scoundrels* by Kirin Narayan, *Crafting Selves* by Dorinne Kondo, and *The Poetics of Military Occupation* by Smadar Lavie. Others equally appropriate could have been selected.[6] Each of the three does what an ethnography is supposed to do: it tells about another culture, about Hindu religious teaching, the Japanese workplace, and Bedouin identity. But what is most fascinating in these books is how in each case the ethnographer positions herself in relation to her object of study.

Narayan, Kondo, and Lavie do not speak as objective outsiders who stand above the fray, nor do they adopt the authoritative professorial voice of the *distinguished scientist.* These ethnographers do not speak as *science* and *theory* who position the native object as *data.* The ethnographers here are not *above* the text, nor simply *in* the text, they *are* the text, but they do not dominate the text. In these works, the ethnographer becomes part of the text that she is producing as she interacts with the people studied at the same time that the role of the ethnographer is itself produced by the discursive practices of postmodern anthropology. But the people studied emerge clearly as persons with names and identities and personalities.

These ethnographers merge with their subjects because of their personal predicaments, and they blur the distinction between subject and object. Kirin Narayan studies Swamiji, a Hindu holy man. Narayan had a Gujarati father and a German-American mother; she is half Indian and half American. She was brought up in India but has lived in the United States since she was sixteen. As a Berkeley graduate student she came to India as a foreign observer, but she has known her informant, Swamiji, since she was a child of ten, so she also returns to India as the daughter of a local family. She dresses in a sari with a red dot on her forehead but she reports that she doesn't look quite right — she is too fair and too tall.

Kondo is a Japanese American who, from the perspective of her informants, was a "living oxymoron, someone who was both Japanese and not Japanese . . . [a] conceptual anomaly (1990: 11) . . . who looked like a real human being [a Japanese] . . . [but] who simply failed to perform according to expectation (12)." She started out as foreign but during the course of her fieldwork became more local, more Japanese-like.

An Israeli, Lavie is an Arab Jew. Her father was a Lithuanian Ashkenazi and her mother was from Yemen. "As a Jew of both European and Arab descent, [she was] someone conjoining Self and Other in herself" (1990:288). "Each half of me is the Other of my other Self. I am able to be an Other both to European Israelis and to Bedouin Mzeinis" (308). Lavie speaks of herself as a "metaphor of bifurcation, of unity in division, of a paradox without resolution" (308).

I ask, in these accounts, who is the Self and who is the Other? Where is the boundary between subject and object? How do we distinguish between ethnographer and native? Where does the personal end and the scientific begin? What counts as science and what as data? Narayan writes, "Rather than being a discovery of the exotic, this work is in many ways a deepening of the familiar" (1990:9).

I have selected these three works because they clearly transgress boundaries and they call into question our comfortable binary oppositions. The point is not that these three exceptional ethnographers are of mixed origin or that they are women. We have had anthropologists in the past of mixed origin who have not taken a reflexive position about their fieldwork, and we have also had objectivist female ethnographers. What we have here is also the right historical moment, an appropriate time to maximize the theoretical potential of these ethnographers' marginal position. But to call them "marginal" is not really appropriate, for it suggests that the rest of us are part of an orderly straight world of clearly defined categories, without ambiguity, which is not the case. As I know the world, all anthropologists are like Narayan, Kondo, and Lavie in terms of the struggles and paradoxes of fieldwork. All ethnographers are decentered subjectivities confronting the field more like half Indians or Japanese Americans than as objective internally consistent scientists speaking monolithically about their people, the data. We ethnographers are all Arab Jews. In its practice, ethnography is both science and humanism, and to separate the two, and to oppose one against the other, is a gross distortion.

Thus far, I have set the stage for the essays that follow by characterizing the historical moment in which they were produced. In the remainder of this Introduction, I will do a brief summary of the major thrust of each essay and occasionally shift to a discussion of some of the larger comparative issues suggested to me by my reading of them. My aim is to give a sense of coherence to the separate contributions by focusing on common themes.

• In the first essay, Edith Turner describes an event that took place in January 1988 in the Eskimo community of Point Hope, Alaska. An Eskimo hunter named Jimmie Nashanik was lost for three days and was finally found by a rescue team using snowmobiles and a helicopter.

To describe bounded events is not new, for it was prominent in the work of Max Gluckman and the Manchester school, but what is fresh is how Turner handles the descriptions. The key point is that the events are described sequentially as they emerged in the field—the first news of the missing hunter, the speculation about his chances for survival in the extreme cold, the mounting tension of the rescue effort, the discovery and final rescue, and the emotional religious response of the community as they welcomed Jimmie upon his return. That the order of the events in the written ethnography parallels the order that occurred in the field has the consequence that the ethnography retains the sense of life and drama of the original event. The ethnography takes the form of a story, of an unfolding narrative, so that the meaning of the events to the participants is retained in the written account. We are also reminded that in the harsh Arctic environment, despite snowmobiles, helicopters, television, and other modern technology, survival remains a tenuous life and death matter.

Certainly every ethnographer is aware of the gap between the richness of lived experience in the field and the paucity of the written professional product, but the breach may be minimized to the extent that the ethnographer interprets her own experiences in the field at the same time that she interprets the experiences of others, and to the extent that these separate interpretations are retained in the written ethnography. This is the crux of Edith Turner's field methodology. One's own experiences are known by looking inward, by being sensitive to one's own reactions to the external events as they unfold. To say that the ethnographer must "interpret" her own experiences suggests that one's own feelings are sometimes inchoate, that they are not always obvious or apparent, and that it is so easy to disguise one's true feelings or to respond as the stereotypic model of the idealized anthropologist, as hero or victim, rather than as a frail all-too-human being. Possibly even more important is the necessity to interpret how the Eskimo experience the same events, and here the ethnographer can only do her best. We have only faint clues to how others experience the world, but in Turner's methodology one has the responsibility to attempt such characterizations. It is essential that the ethnographer keep separate her accounts of her experiences from her accounts of *their* experiences. In this respect, Turner's account is exemplary. Turner, for example, does not presume to report on how Jimmie experienced the three days lost in the Arctic wilderness, for she was not there and had no opportunity to observe. She was in Point Hope throughout the three days with the women of the village who waited and prayed for his safe return. What Turner does then is to report on the speculations of the people of the community on how he may have felt alone and lost in the Arctic cold.

The result is a true sense of "being there" that preserves the drama of the lived event and conveys a striking impression of the integrity and the honesty of the ethnographer (Geertz 1988). The reader comes to trust the account of the community reaction to the lost hunter of Point Hope, for Turner is scrupulous in separating her account of her reactions from her account of their reactions. In her own terms, Turner is more witness than analyst. In so many older ethnographies it is almost impossible to separate subject and object, to know if the ethnographer is reporting on her own or on the peoples' perceptions and attitudes. Turner's account rings true, and it is paradoxical that she achieves this not by taking on the role of objective superscientific detached observer, but rather by taking the role of what she is, an involved and courageous ethnographer who braves the Arctic winter to explore her ideas on an anthropology of experience (cf. Turner and Bruner 1986).

• Robin Ridington tells an amazing story of how a sacred object, tribal traditions, and ethnographic authority have each circulated over a period of a century from the Omaha people to ethnography and then back to the Omaha. In 1888, Yellow Smoke, the keeper of the Sacred Pole of the Omaha, gave the Pole to Francis La Flesche to take back East for safekeeping. La Flesche was an Omaha and a professional anthropologist employed by the Smithsonian Institution. He was coauthor with Alice Fletcher of the monumental monograph *The Omaha Tribe*, published by the Bureau of American Ethnology in 1911. La Flesche placed the Pole with the Peabody Museum of Archaeology and Ethnology at Harvard University, where it remained for 101 years until July 1989, when the Sacred Pole was formally returned to the Omaha homeland in Macy, Nebraska. The Pole was used in ceremonies on the Omaha reservation in 1989 and 1990, and subsequently has been stored temporarily with the University of Nebraska State Museum until the tribe develops its own museum and cultural center.

Thus, the Pole, an object that was traditionally used by the Omaha people in an annual ceremony of renewal, went on a journey for safekeeping from the Omaha to a bastion of institutional anthropology, the Peabody Museum at Harvard, then back to the Omaha people, and then temporarily to the University of Nebraska State Museum. Omaha tribal traditions went on a similar journey from Yellow Smoke and other elders to Fletcher and La Flesche, where they were incorporated for safekeeping within the pages of *The Omaha Tribe*. The traditions were returned to the Omaha in August 1988, when Robin

Ridington, who had been asked by the Chairman of the Omaha to make a speech at the annual tribal powwow, used the occasion to tell the Omaha people about Omaha traditions, which he did primarily by quoting Fletcher and La Flesche. My retelling in this introduction oversimplifies the story but the essentials are correct, for both a sacred object and tribal traditions have made a similar 101-year journey, circulating from the Omaha to ethnography and then to the Omaha. Tracing ethnographic authority, however, is a bit more complex.

The issue is who has the authority to tell the story of the Omaha, to what audience, and in what context? As we know, the power to tell the Omaha story, to be recognized as having a legitimate right to describe Omaha culture, is the ultimate power because it constructs the Omaha in the sense of describing and representing their culture (Bruner 1993). Before 1888 it was clear that Yellow Smoke and other tribal elders had the authority, but that in giving sacred objects and knowledge to Fletcher and La Flesche that authority was transferred to the ethnographers and to their institutions, the Peabody Museum, the Bureau of American Ethnology, and the University of Nebraska State Museum.

Where is the locus of that authority now? In one sense it has returned to the Omaha just as the Pole is now is the hands of the proper Omaha clan in Macy, Nebraska. The transfer of authority was manifest when the Pole was officially returned to the Omaha by the powers that be at the Peabody Museum in Cambridge. But in 1988, the Omaha replicated history when they once again turned over authority to the ethnographer to talk to them at their annual powwow about Omaha traditions relating to the Pole. History repeats itself, for just as Yellow Smoke gave away for safekeeping the most sacred Omaha object to ethnography, so does Doran Morris, the present Tribal Chairman and great-great grandson of Yellow Smoke, give away to ethnography what may possibly be an even more sacred right, the right to tell the Omaha story. It could be argued that although Ridington was asked to make a speech the power was still with the Omaha, as they simply extended an invitation they could rescind. It is the Omaha Tribal Council and the Tribal Chairman who have the power to decide who will speak at their powwows. Possibly the Omaha were just being courteous and appreciative of the help given to them by the ethnographer Ridington, and they showed their respect for his scholarship and his specialized knowledge of Native Americans by asking him to talk. My view, however, is that ethnographic authority has passed to Ridington, and, further, that although the content of the narrative may be about the Omaha, it is Ridington's story. After all, Ridington is telling the story here, in the pages of this volume, and it was he who decided where to begin the story, where to end it, what to include in the middle, and where to publish it.[7]

In a sense, Ridington is also the hero of the story, just as Turner is the heroine in her essay on the Eskimo. In contemporary anthropology, we want the ethnographer to be included in the text and we want to separate the ethnographer's speech and reactions from the people's speech and reactions. We want to know whose voice we are hearing in the text, and in this respect, both the Ridington and Turner essays are models of ethnographic reporting. Both identify their sources of information and keep the time levels straight, which until recently has been relatively rare in Native American ethnography. Ridington goes so far as to transcribe audio cassettes and to include the transcription in the text. The dilemma, however, is that insofar as the ethnographer describes events sequentially, as they emerge to his or her consciousness, then inevitably the ethnographer will be prominent in the text, the main character, as it were. But the real issue could be phrased this way: in these essays, do we learn more about the Eskimo and the Omaha than we do about Turner and Ridington? The answer is unequivocally yes. These are ethnographic contributions as well as experimental methodological essays.

Of course, the portraits of Turner and Ridington that emerge in the text are clearly an ethnographic construction. We must separate the ethnographer as a *person,* Turner and Ridington as individuals or subjectivities, from the ethnographer as *writer,* how Turner and Ridington choose to represent themselves in their essays. To give just a superficial surface reading, Turner emerges as a compassionate sixty-seven-year-old grandmother who jogs in the Arctic cold, whereas Ridington presents himself as a poet who has spiritual sensitivities, who resonated with the power of the Omaha Sacred Pole while still a graduate student, and who even writes using Omaha-like language and expressions. He is a modern La Flesche. The "real" Turner and the "real" Ridington are not revealed to us, for all the reader has is how they are represented in the text.

I trust it is clear that the issues raised in this introduction are Ed Bruner's questions and reflections based on his understanding of the essays and are not to be confused with the essays themselves. The construction placed on the story of the Omaha in my retelling is certainly not the way Ridington chooses to tell the story. But one function of an introduction is to be suggestive and provocative, and the reader is invited to compare my retellings with the originals.

• Angrosino's West Indian dub poets are performing artists who recite their poetry to music. The tradition started by removing the words but retaining the music from standard records, and the dub poets would "rap" to the music, substituting or dubbing their own words for the original lyrics. It is now serious poetry and the performers are artists who have a following. Dub poetry is performed in reggae clubs, and the movement was influenced by the Rastafarians. The content of the poems is anti-establishment and revolutionary, calling for the liberation of lower-class urban blacks. Live performances are multimedia events, with the poetry delivered with biblical overtones and evangelical fervor, all to the pulsating reggae beat.

The artists have the opportunity to publish their poetry, which brings money and prestige and is an indication that they are being taken seriously, for they are then "in print," but their dilemma is that the printed words are decontextualized, removed from the spontaneity of the multimedia live performance, and the printed poems are in standard English as opposed to West Indian "nation language," or folk speech, the usual language of dub poetry. Angrosino presents the data in convincing and lively fashion. He casts the problem as one of the transition to literacy, as a movement from oral to written forms and refers to the work of Jack Goody, which is somewhat reminiscent of the oppositions of folk-urban or Gemeinschaft-Gesellschaft. Readers might also find relevant Derrida's work on speech versus writing, which denies the priority of any one term in the opposition over the other, or the work on performance by Richard Bauman, which examines each individual expression.

What I find most exciting in Angrosino's work is that the dub poets are confronting a predicament similar to the one confronted by ethnographers everywhere, including Turner and Ridington, of how to make the transition from rich lived experience in the field, or in the reggae clubs, to writing. All ethnographers in the field find themselves in the middle of an ever-changing multimedia event, with everything happening simultaneously, in all sensory modes, and they try to reduce this complexity to conventionalized fixed writing. Ethnographic writing has its long-standing conventions of form and style, and what postmodern ethnography is now fighting against, the stylized anthropological voice, detached, objective, scientific, and above the fray, is similar to what the dub poets are fighting against, the conventions of standardized poetic writing. Does it stretch the imagination too much to regard the dub poets as indigenous ethnographers, writing about their own culture, providing a metacommentary on the urban poor in Kingston, holding the elite white establishment up to ridicule and satire?

The West Indian poets may be ethnographers with a point of view, but then aren't we all?

• It may be questionable to regard one of Angrosino's dub poets, or his main consultant Lumumba, as an indigenous ethnographer, but there is no question that Susan Rodgers's Angkola Batak informant named Siregar Baumi is explicitly and consciously an ethnographer of his own culture. Rodgers reports that since 1977, Sutan Tinggi has published a total of eight books, nearly a book a year, enough to get tenure anywhere, on such topics as clan histories, marriage, kinship, brideprice negotiation, inheritance, social life and social class, art forms, funerals, and other rituals. He does not describe the total culture, whatever that may be, but rather he makes a particular construction of his culture that reminds me of British social anthropology, of Radcliffe-Brown, Evans-Pritchard, and Fortes, in that he focuses primarily on social and ceremonial organization. Further, Siregar Baumi presents his culture as functionally integrated, as consisting of parts that fit together neatly, forming an organic whole, another characteristic of British structural-functionalism, but I don't want to push this perceived similarity too far.

Rodgers's key point is that many amateur ethnographers in many areas of the world are writing about their culture, and it would be useful for us "to begin to collect such texts, interview their authors, and analyze such folk sociologies." It is an important point well taken, although Rodgers would be the first to acknowledge that some cultures are more reflexive than others. But when cultures do write about themselves, all too often in the past such indigenous ethnographies have been ignored or incorporated into our own texts without proper acknowledgment. Part of the problem has been that we have not known how to handle indigenous texts written primarily for a local audience that do not fit our already established categories. We do, for example, pay attention to locally produced Third World novels, an accepted Western genre, even *art,* but we are not as confident about how to handle productions such as Siregar Baumi's ethnographic writings about his own culture. His is an ambiguous genre, which is what makes it so fascinating. We cannot quite regard Siregar Baumi as an equal, as a fellow ethnographer, for that would be too threatening, as it would blur the distinction between us and them, between anthropologists and natives, between scientific accounts and folk narratives, but there is no doubt that his enterprise is similar to our own.

As Rodgers makes clear, the Batak have been writing about their own culture for the past seventy years, since the 1920s, and Siregar Baumi is only one in a long line of adat experts writing adat handbooks.[8]

The term *adat* is often translated as custom, but this is misleading as the adat is a Batak conceptualization of aspects of their social and ritual organization, part of a sacred tradition handed down to them from the gods. To violate the adat is to invite supernatural sanctions, and even though the adat has changed drastically in the century since European contact, most Batak even today strive to "follow the adat." If this is the case, then why the proliferation of articles, guides, and books about Batak adat and custom?

Rodgers gives us insight here when she tells us that Siregar Baumi and the other adat authors tend to classify, organize, reconcile, and reduce their culture to fixed schemata, often presented as diagrams, charts, and outlines, a "schoolmaster's array of subjects." Rodgers sees Batak writing as a transition from orality to literacy, sacred to secular, myth to folklore. Readers might consider under what conditions a people would want to record their own culture and hold it up for examination. Sometimes they do so when the culture is threatened, during periods of very rapid change, when the disparity between the explicit cultural premises, in this case the adat principles, depart too greatly from everyday practice and experience. Readers might then wonder if Batak writing also represents a means of controlling a world that is moving too rapidly, of fixing a culture in print that is actually in continual flux. To classify, categorize, and synthesize is an effort to gain a kind of control in writing that eludes one in life. Perhaps the Batak can no longer control their real world so they construct an imaginary one in their adat books, a world that never existed even in the past, so that the flow of experience is safely contained, categorized, and fixed within the pages of a book.

This supposition, too, can be only partial, for there are many factors at work, as Rodgers indicates. In multiethnic Indonesia, with its three hundred ethnolinguistic groups, to write about one's own culture is to establish one's ethnic identity, particularly in opposition to the Javanese, with their reputed claim to cultural superiority. Indigenous ethnographies are also inherently political documents that may arise particularly when formerly tribal peoples find themselves incorporated into nation-states. In any case, Rodgers has made an admirable contribution in analyzing an indigenous ethnography and in specifying the conditions that have led to its production.

• Turner and Ridington are experimenting with ethnographic writing, with how we describe the culture of others; Angrosino and Rodgers examine native experiments with the way people describe and inscribe their own culture; Fox takes as his text *Antigone* by Sophocles, a classic tragedy from fifth-century Greece first produced in 440 B.C. What Fox does is precisely what Edith Turner does—to interpret how members of another society experience their culture. The information available to Fox, however, is limited to texts, scraps of history, and a mountain of secondary sources from Hegel to George Steiner, but what he does with these materials is extraordinary. After these many years in the discipline, I am continually amazed at the power of the anthropological paradigm to provide new insights.

The basic drama in Sophocles' *Antigone* has long been seen as a conflict between the individual versus the state, which Fox shows is really based on a limited seventeenth-century Anglo-Saxon view of the world. In the play, Antigone, the daughter of Oedipus, buries her deceased brother, Polynices, in defiance of the ruler Creon. As Polynices had committed treason, Creon decreed that his body should not be given a formal burial but should be left to the elements as a punishment for his crime against the state. Antigone's actions in burying her brother, which led to her own death, have been misinterpreted as an individual heroic act, a particular conscience-driven exploit. Fox demonstrates that Antigone's behavior may be better understood not as a challenge to the state but rather as the responsibility of a daughter of the patrilineage to bury her kin. It is less a personal sacrifice than a kinship obligation. Patrilineal ideology has been neglected in previous commentaries because we have been obsessed with individualism and with the assumed war between the freedom of the individual and the constraints of the authoritarian state.

Fox places it all in the larger context of the evolutionary transition from tribalism to the formation of the state. Tribal societies based on kinship and descent give way to state organizations based on citizenship and government. This is an old distinction in anthropology, but what has not been recognized in the literature on Greek drama is that the world depicted in the play is itself in transition between the era of tribal Homer and state-based Athenian democracy. An embryonic Greek *polis* is in the process of formation but the old kinship-based loyalties have not yet disappeared. Toward the end of his chapter, Fox extends his analysis to reinterpret the basic crime of Oedipus as less an incestuous marriage to his mother, Iocasta, and more as the murder of his father, Laius. In a patrilineal system, incest is a less severe crime than patricide, as we learned from Radcliffe-Brown.

The conflict between kinship groups and the state is an ongoing struggle that continues to this day. As Fox puts it, the state abhors kinship and would much prefer to deal solely with the nuclear family and the individual. The state works against such powerful American families as the Kennedys, the Rockefellers, and the Du Ponts by estate laws that mitigate against the inheritance of large fortunes. Illegal groups in various parts of the world that cannot count on the protection of the state organize themselves in terms of kinship, as we know from the American Mafia, from terrorist units in Lebanon, and from drug traffickers in Colombia. Kinship also flourishes in the Third World urban centers of Africa and Asia, especially where the state is new and weak. In these emerging nations where the state is still struggling to establish itself, kinship groups fulfill many of the political, economic, and social functions of protection, welfare, and help provided by the state in the more developed industrial societies. Such nineteenth-century sociologists as Tönnies, Maine, and Marx were correct in identifying the direction of world change from status to contract, but they certainly overlooked the many pockets of resistance.

• Where Fox interprets a classic text, the essay by Grindal and Shephard not only constructs their own text but discusses the processes of the production of texts. Where Fox presents a more conventional anthropological essay in the "appropriate" style, Grindal and Shephard's is a nonconventional experimental work tracing the telling and the retelling of the "same" story in a postmodern journey from experience, to a letter, to a short story, to the script of a play, to a performance in a theater, to a videotape shown at a meeting of the American Anthropological Association, to their piece in this volume, to my retelling in this introduction, ending I suppose with the readers' own interpretations of the text. The essential transition is from experience to writing to performance to video and then back to writing. When I refer to retelling of the "same" story, the quotes acknowledge that each new telling, although based on the previous telling, is different because the context and audience are different and also because each genre has its own conventions of expression.

The story began in 1982 in an encounter between Grindal, the ethnographer, and the informant on a bus traveling to Tallahassee in north Florida. Grindal met a young Southern woman who at the age of sixteen ran away from home after her parents were divorced; had a sleazy life as bartender, waitress, and singer in a band; and eight years later at the age of twenty-four was returning home. In the anonymity of the monotonous bus ride, the woman tells the ethnographer about personal details of her present life, her grim early childhood experiences in Pascagoula, Mississippi, and her aspirations for a better future. Grindal was so struck by the chance meeting that he sent a letter to a friend about his experience and finally in 1985 wrote a short story called "Redneck Girl," emphasizing the working-class proletarian southern background of the woman on the bus. Grindal then sent the story to his friend and theater director Shephard, who collaborated with Grindal to turn the story into a play that was performed in a theater in 1986. In 1987, a video of the play was shown at the annual American Anthropological Association meetings.

What is the anthropological relevance of this sequence of events? As stated in the first paragraph of this essay, the most fundamental problem in ethnography is how to describe a culture, and Grindal, an ethnographer of southern culture, is here describing a slice of life in the American South. That he chooses to report his findings in the form of a short story rather than a standard ethnography is in part what makes it so interesting. After all, Turner describes a slice of life in the Arctic, Ridington in Macy, Nebraska, and Angrosino in the reggae clubs of south Florida, so they share with Grindal the basic descriptive mission of ethnography. But according to the somewhat dogmatic conventional wisdom, isn't the difference that ethnography is FACT, whereas a short story is FICTION; that one tells the TRUTH whereas the other is FANTASY; that ethnographers are SCIENTISTS whereas writers are ARTISTS? I reject these binaries as too simplistic, but the story does change in the telling.

The difference between ethnography and fiction is more apparent if we compare Grindal's short story with Shephard's rewrite as a play. For me, the most fascinating aspect of the essay is the contrast between the short story and the play. Grindal's story was more true to his direct experience on the bus and more true to his own personal experience as a resident of the South and as an ethnographer of the culture of the American South. Shephard, on the other hand, saw the problem as one of enhancing the dramatic values of the short story and of adapting the story to live theater. Shephard made a number of changes in the content of the story, in that he reduced the ambiguity and amplified the role of the ethnographer, but more significant were the changes in the plot structure.

Shephard turned Grindal's story into a more stereotypic master narrative of the American South, a Tennessee Williams drama where the heroine's father is discovered to be part African-American and there is an early history of sexual abuse. These data were not part of the short story, although there were veiled hints in that direction. As Shephard tells us, the plot becomes "Leaving Home," "Painful Reflections," and "Finding the Self." These are not merely dramatic embellishments, they add a psychoanalytic cast to a familiar plot structure, where a bus journey becomes a metaphor for an inner journey. Shephard utilized his professional knowledge and imagination in casting Grindal's story into a play, but as it becomes more dramatic it becomes less ethnographic.

Grindal also lost control over his own image as an ethnographer in the play, an image other ethnographers, including Turner and Ridington, take pains to protect. For Grindal the loss became a source of embarrassment at the American Anthropological Association showing. It is permissible these days to introduce a note of sexual desire or to acknowledge uncertainty and insecurity, but the character in the play who portrayed the ethnographer did not meet Grindal's expectations of how he saw himself. In Shephard's initial rendition, redneck girl touched Grindal, suggesting a sexual relationship, which Grindal had to edit out. Even then, the fictional characterization placed him in an awkward predicament in front of his colleagues at a professional meeting.

The transformation of Grindal's story into a play may have highlighted the fictional dimension of the final work, but is not Grindal's original story also exposed to the same critique? It may be one thing to employ literary techniques in the construction of ethnography, but it is another to present "ethnographic" data as fiction. After all, Grindal chose to write fiction, not ethnography. Given the fleeting nature of the meeting on the bus combined with Grindal's extensive personal and professional understanding of the South, I find the short story to be useful, part of a new genre called ethnographic fiction. If I were teaching a course on the culture of the American South, I would assign stories and novels to supplement the standard ethnographies, and I would also include ethnographic fiction.

• Rodman's paper led me to think back to Geertz's (1973) early papers on interpretive anthropology. Ethnography for Geertz is a second-order interpretation; it is our own interpretation of their interpretation (15) of their experience. The Balinese cockfight, for example, is a Balinese reading, a first-order interpretation of their culture; in our ethnographic descriptions we are looking over the shoulder of the Balinese, reading their culture as an ensemble of texts, and we make a second-order interpretation, our reading of their interpretation of their cockfight. But we have learned in the twenty years since Geertz wrote *The Interpretation of Cultures,* as Rodman's paper shows, that the situation is more complex.

Not only is the ethnographic subject interpreting the native object but the native people are interpreting the ethnographer.[9] More significant, their interpretation of their own culture is influenced, sometimes in profound ways, by their interpretation of us. What is the meaning of the ethnographer's questions, and more significant, what is the message of anthropology? How do they perceive us? In a subtle and elegant way, Rodman shows that the interpretive process is a two-way street, that both we and they are creative beings with active selves. While we are interpreting them, they are interpreting us. The interplay is truly dialogic, for as he says, "We are not just observers observed; we are interpreters interpreted." Ethnographic description is thicker than Geertz had anticipated.

It is so difficult to evaluate or even to understand the impact of anthropology on the people we study, as frequently the impact manifests itself only after we have left the field. I know that in Indonesia, in Java and Bali, the attention shown to certain dance dramas and art forms by high-status foreign professors has lead the Indonesians to privilege those forms within their own culture (Becker 1979; Vickers 1989; Bruner n.d.). What interests us takes on added importance to them, or, to overstate the case, they become what ethnography studies. If we selectively value certain aspects of their culture while ignoring others, they too come to appropriate what we value, not universally, or even necessarily frequently, but in enough instances to become worthy of study.

A critical issue, as Rodman describes so well, is that each people have their own language, their own means of communication, and their understanding of us must be viewed in the context of their symbolic system. Rodman says the people of Ambae in Vanuatu teach by indirection, by parable, in a form of hidden talk based on implicit meanings. Their talk is disguised, and as every ethnographer learns, it is essential to understand their talk. It is not only a question of the content of the message but the form within which that message is enveloped.

Further inquiry into native peoples' interpretation of anthropology would take us in some fascinating directions. In some Native American groups, among Southwest Pueblos, for example, many generations of anthropologists have relied on the same informants. What for the ethnographer, fresh from graduate school, with foundation grant in hand, first approaching "native" peoples, a new and exciting undertaking for the neophyte anthropologist, is for some native peoples a familiar event, repeated season after season, something they have experienced many times before.[10] They have already learned how to interpret and take account of anthropologists. Whatever we learn about field methodology pales by comparison with the knowledge they have acquired by experience with anthropologists.

Rodman's point is important. We have to learn more about how they interpret us, about the consequences of anthropology for native culture and how this changes over time, through the colonial era to independence. What we study — customs, tradition, and culture — may in certain historical circumstances be something to be ashamed of, a source of embarrassment, a mark of primitiveness, whereas in other times it may be a symbol of national pride and identity. Their view of what we study, and hence of us, may change over time.

Having said all this, the fact remains that Rodman is still telling his story of the people of Ambae, Vanuatu. It is still his interpretation, despite the unexpected outcomes and exciting story he has to tell, which I shall let the readers discover for themselves. Rodman describes the reactions of the people to the ethnographer and he presents their view of the message of anthropology, and his account is convincing, but it remains *his* account since there is no unmediated narrative or naive experience.

• Rose calls for a revolutionary reexamination not only of subject-object relations but of the larger institutional and structural context within which ethnography is produced. The lives we live as anthropologists, in and out of the field, reflect and are shaped by academic subculture. We need to explore the links between what we do as ethnographers and the corporate organizational forms within which we work. This proposition is not as surprising as it may appear, for after all, standard ethnographic method tells us to view the content of knowledge within the social context of its production, and this is precisely what Rose does, not to primitive peoples located elsewhere, but to ourselves.

Rose states that the main context of ethnographic inquiry is the capitalist corporation, that is, the university and the discipline, the institutional framework that envelops us. We carry within us the disciplined self, the work ethic, and the established conventions for appropriate conduct in the corporation. We live this life, we are this life, and we carry it to the field. Labor within the academy shapes us at the same time that it shapes the discipline. The classic texts we read in graduate school provide models for the texts that we will produce when our turn comes to go to the field. Whatever else ethnographic fieldwork may be, it is the texts that we produce based on fieldwork that become the markers of our anthropological careers, the basis for our advancement within the academic corporation.

To support his position, Rose demonstrates that adventurer's and merchant's texts, explorer's accounts, traveler's reports, ship captains' logs, and other materials from the late sixteenth and early seventeenth centuries that led eventually to the Dutch East India Company and the London-based East India Company were in effect "intelligence" reports designed to provide information necessary to the establishment of profitable trade. The emerging capitalist corporation needed to know about the peoples and cultures of the world. These early accounts have multiple "resonances" with our ethnographic accounts. Both travelers' accounts and ethnography are two of the genres within capitalist society designed to provide knowledge about the Other. Indeed, the *Notes and Queries on Anthropology,* first published in 1874, which influenced generations of ethnographers, including Malinowski, follows a form strikingly similar to the older questionnaire for travelers produced by the British Association for the Advancement of Science in 1841, and this in turn probably has deeper roots. Rose's point is that accounts of other peoples of the world that arose from Western sources, since the 1700s, reflect a striking historical continuity, despite the obvious differences. Ethnography has been a stable genre.

It is difficult to summarize Rose's contribution, for his is arguably the most radical in the volume. Parts of it are wild and outrageous; it begins as prose and ends as poetry; it contains a manifesto for future ethnography and ideas for the transformation of graduate education in anthropology. The title of his last section is "After the Death of Ethnography." Not only does Rose suggest that ethnography should use multiple genres but his work does what he suggests, it employs multiple genres.

Readers will respond to this work in their own way. My feeling after reading the final version was a sense of exhilaration. He invites us to experiment with texts, to take risks, to be more experimental, to use literary forms, to place ourselves in our accounts, and to move in new directions. In 1984 I wrote an essay on the "opening up" of anthropology (Bruner 1984b), then more of a wish than an actuality, and in my introduction to this volume I wrote that the new ethnography was liberating. Rose is liberating.

• Whereas Rose unmasks the global and academic politics that constitute the conditions of possibility of the new ethnography, the contribution by Mascia-Lees, Sharpe, and Cohen[11] follows in a similar vein, except they argue that the new critical self-reflexive ethnography would be better off taking feminist theory as a model rather than postmodernism. They point out that key insights of the new ethnography — that culture is contested, that it entails relations of domination, that language and politics are inseparable — have been considered in feminist theory for the last forty years. Their point is that the native is to the anthropologist as women are to men, the female is the "Other," and feminism has much to offer the new ethnography. Anthropology may write for the Other but feminism speaks from the position of the Other.

The problem, again, is when does reflexivity become narcissism, when does ethnography turn inward so that it becomes oblivious to the politics of the world? A case could be made that in postmodern ethnography, as well as in Clifford and Marcus's *Writing Culture: The Poetics and Politics of Ethnography*, the poetics is stronger than the politics, or rather that there is a tension between the two.[12]

The feminist scholars' position has always been inherently paradoxical, in that as feminists, as women, they are the "Other," but as scholars they remain authoritative speakers, who may unwittingly preserve the dominant power relations that they explicitly aim to overcome. We have seen this paradox at work in this book, particularly in the work of Turner, Ridington, and Rodman. The feminist solution is to frame the research questions according to the desires of the oppressed group. As Mascia-Lees, Sharpe, and Cohen state in their last sentence, they want us to "merge our scholarship with a clear politics: to work against the forces of oppression." Their chapter is more than a caution, it is a challenge.

Postmodernism pictures a world that is multivocal, fragmented, decentered, with no master narratives or central texts, a world in which meaning is radically plural. Mascia-Lees, Sharpe, and Cohen, however, suggest that this characterization of the postmodern world, what many of us had accepted, is actually a construction of Western white males. We want to undermine the subject just when our authority is being undermined by women and by non-Western peoples who have found their own voice. Postmodernism is a defense devised by white men to deny anyone a mastery which they "are losing the privilege to define." Or as Mascia-Lees, Sharpe, and Cohen suggest, referring to Lennox and others, when we white Western males can no longer define the truth we claim there is no truth. This is provocative stuff, at least for this white Western male, but the argument makes sense. Their central point is that postmodernism is blind to its own politics and that multivocality may disguise hidden power relations.[13]

In the past, feminists have questioned the universality of psychoanalytic theory, which was so male centered, as well as the applicability of Marxist theories, which were so focused on class as opposed to gender, and now they caution us against an uncritical acceptance of postmodern theory. Mascia-Lees, Sharpe, and Cohen want us to move in the direction of a more open, multivoiced, contested, plural, and humane theory of culture, but they suggest that we draw on feminist theory to do so, examine our own political presuppositions, and our institutional structures. Feminist theory in many ways is echoed by postmodern theory—possibly because both are responding to similar epistemic forces in our historical era—but what feminist theory offers is a politics for dealing with domination, power, and oppression. Mascia-Lees, Sharpe, and Cohen aim not just to describe the world, they want to change it; they want us to listen to the desires of oppressed groups; they want to go to the lived experiences of the oppressed.

• The final contribution by Brady is a sophisticated discussion of many of the key issues considered in the previous essays, and thus it is appropriate as a kind of epilogue. Brady's takeoff point is an evaluation of the work of James A. Boon, especially his *Other Tribes, Other Scribes* (1982). Boon, one of the more stimulating thinkers in anthropology, deals with fundamental questions in a delightful, witty manner. Brady lays the issues out clearly, and the basic issue is that in ethnography we need to consider both order and meaning, simultaneously. In pursuit of both "sense" and "event," of organizational logic and action in the world, Boon exploits the tensions between structuralism and hermeneutics. There are no abstract structures expressed without performance, just as there are no performances without some prior pattern, even if that pattern is only the memory of the last performance. The sin of excessive structuralism is to reduce everything to universal structures of the mind; the sin of excessive performance theories is the belief that the world is reinvented anew with every enactment. Boon avoids excesses, arguing that while pattern and meaning can be revealed by extremes they are not in opposition, and in the process he gives us a sensible reading of structuralism and hermeneutics.

Sherry Ortner (1984) has noted that in anthropology we move from one intellectual fashion to another, from structuralism to symbolism to Marxism to practice, and all too often in our critiques of a theory, especially as the tide is turning in another direction, we sometimes move to such extremes that we seemingly discard an entire theoretical perspective, as if structuralism were now over and currently we are all doing interpretation. But it doesn't work that way. We have very few pure psychoanalytic practitioners in anthropology, but all of us have been informed by Freud's work on the unconscious and on the mechanisms of defense, just as we have all been informed by the Marxist stress on inequality and domination. So too with structuralism. Too often eager critics have misread Lévi-Strauss, simplified and condensed his work to a cliche, and later readers accepted the critique as if it were the original. This is one of the good reasons for returning to the originals of out-of-fashion texts. In Boon's work structuralism lives, with hermeneutics.

But make no mistake; this is Brady's essay, not Boon's. Brady reflects on a series of problems and paradoxes in ethnography and uses Boon as the medium for his own commentary. The work is Brady's reading of Boon, hence it is Brady's own, his retelling.

The chapter is an exemplar of what the contributors to this volume are doing: experimenting with the fire of fieldwork and the ice of ethnographic writing; struggling with pattern and performance; realizing that we, as authors and as readers, are always culturally and historically situated; acknowledging that our ethnographies are embedded in relations of domination and recognizing our implicit politics; separating our accounts of our experience from their accounts of their experience; examining carefully the processes of production of texts, ours and theirs; accepting more genres of our writing from poetry to short stories to ethnographic fiction at the same time that we accept more genres of their writing from dub poetry to local ethnography to classic Greek tragedy; living with the inevitable tension between seeing each culture as a uniquely poetic manifestation of human potential at the same time as it is seen as just another unit in a comparative science of society. Anthropology will thrive to the extent that we continue to live with our ambiguities and paradoxes.

NOTES

Parts of this paper were presented at the 1988 meeting of the American Anthropological Association in a session on narrative ethnography; other sections were given in 1990 at the symposium "Scientific and Humanistic Ways of Understanding in Anthropology." I am indebted to Barbara Tedlock, Cary Nelson, Nina Baym, Kirin Narayan, Margaret B. Blackman, and Ann Anagnost for helpful suggestions.

1. The same issues, of course, arise in many other fields, such as folklore and literary criticism.

2. Barbara Tedlock (1991) has an excellent bibliography on these issues and also good examples of early precursors of each genre. Her aim is to discredit the notion of an "experimental moment" and to show a continuity in literary anthropology from the past to the present. I, however, see discontinuity and a shift in dominant modes. Her list of anthropologists who have published poems, short stories, or novels is impressive, but I read it as further evidence of the segmentation of the ethnographic self from the personal self. Her exceptions are an affirmation of the irrepressibility of the human spirit, but I focus more on the authoritative discursive practices. See also Stewart (1989:1–13).

3. Some contemporary ethnographers, fully aware that they can now combine the ethnographic and the personal in one account, may choose to write a monograph and a memoir as two separate accounts simply because they have different things to say to different audiences. See, for example, Gottlieb (1992) and Gottlieb and Graham (1992).

4. The letter is from Daphne Berdahl, 2 May 1991.

5. This is an oversimplification of the working relationship between anthropological couples in different historical eras, a complex topic that merits extended study. It is important if we are truly interested in the conditions of the production of the text, because in the past many couples collaborated in the research yet the results were published in the husband's name alone. Two examples that come to mind are Ruth Lewis and Edith Turner, both brilliant women. Ruth collaborated with her husband, Oscar Lewis, and Edith with her husband, Victor Turner, for decades, yet their contributions and creativity were mostly given mere mention in the acknowledgments while the husbands maintained sole authorship and hence received the public honor and recognition. The University of Illinois conferred belated recognition to Ruth Lewis in 1988 by giving her an honorary doctorate. These days, many anthropological couples do field work together and publish separately, under their own names, but this is a relatively recent phenomena.

6. For example, ethnographies by Ruth Behar, Barbara Bode, Vincent Crapanzano, Virginia Dominiguez, John Dorst, Michael Jackson, Karla Poewe, Dan Rose, John Stewart, Paul Stoller, Barbara Tedlock, and Dennis Tedlock.

7. For an alternative journalistic account see the *Wall Street Journal*, 27 August 1991, p. A10. Along with the Pole, 280 other artifacts were returned from the Peabody Museum to the Omaha, and the sacred white buffalo hide was returned from the Smithsonian. The Omaha will also reinter 92 Omaha remains, which were returned by the University of Nebraska.

8. From my own fieldwork among the Toba Batak, a related group, I can affirm that they too have produced many adat books, both published and unpublished.

9. Geertz knew this, of course, but he did not emphasize it in his 1973 book.

10. See Don Handelman's contribution in Lavie, Narayan, and Rosaldo (1993).

11. In the interest of intellectual honesty, I report that Macsia-Lees, Cohen, and Sharpe were dissatisfied with my treatment of their essay in my original introduction to the articles that appeared in the *Journal of the Steward Anthropological Society,* from which this book is derived. They felt my summary of their essay was a "gallant dismissal," that I had missed the main point, and that as a Western white male, my introduction reflected precisely what they were criticizing. They had some good points, primarily that I underestimated the political dimension, and I have revised my remarks accordingly, but hope that I did not go so far in the other direction that I have become politically correct in not criticizing a feminist position.

12. The tension between the poetic and the political emerges more strongly in the preliminary report of the conference than in the final book, but the preliminary report is rarely cited (see Marcus and Clifford 1985).

13. The relationship between multivocality and power was Bakhtin's main point.

Experience and Poetics in Anthropological Writing

Edith Turner

The well-known problem of writing in anthropology is as yet only half solved. It is basically how to impart serious information about the social behavior and culture of human beings and how to interpret that behavior without adopting an anti-humanistic stance or style. Until recently this was not seen as a problem because anthropology took as its model either distancing from the subject matter as it is accepted by academic scholars in the humanities, such as historians, or the model of the hard sciences—for which the coldness of absolute zero would seem a desirable state, as in the technology of superconductivity. Superobjectivity, if not superconductivity, has been the virtue of the social sciences since their birth, and for many anthropologists it is still their goal. They believe that what they produce must not be in any way fed by their own roots, infected as it were with their own culture's biased "common sense," but must be cool enough to be abstract, and thus available to similar researchers in the high cultures. To accomplish this the structures of society, codes and laws, high myths, and the like have to be distilled and freed from the dross of actual life and contemplated in their pure form. This project, which we call structuralism, has achieved the first real step toward universalism and indeed confirmed the suspicion that "there are no simpler societies"—that all societies reveal complex structures at some level.

However, as is known this enterprise is outrunning its true purpose, leaving behind a whole world of living action. Structuralism is appearing to the peoples studied like elitism, a kind of imperialism. A powerful school of critical anthropology has risen (Clifford and Marcus 1986; Marcus and Fischer 1986; Tyler 1987; Geertz 1988; Clifford 1988; pioneered by Wagner 1981 and Fabian 1983), radical and sometimes Marxist in character, defending the ethnic peoples from the imposition of Western theories from outside, and concerned with justice in the relation of the authority of the ethnographer to that of the field person, the consultant. This movement has promoted, as opposed to cognitive analysis and structural-functionalism, other modes of authorial convention—the experiential, interpretive, dialogical, and polyphonic (Clifford 1988). In this essay I adapt these modes and try out their use where they would naturally occur. They can be traced in the content of a dramatic field event I give below. I believe that without examples of actual events in which the anthropologist took part (not just texts) many of the attempts to describe the new "interpretive anthropology" tend to become confusing and obscure. The problem exists of how to produce a new subtlety and honesty in fieldwork and conclusions and yet remain within some kind of normal human range of understanding.

This latter is a serious objective, because a major function of anthropological writing may not be only for other anthropologists to read but as an outlet for, to give a voice to, some of the conscious minds among the field people, for example Ernest Frankson, my Eskimo consultant at Point Hope, Alaska. Just as folklore through the good offices of the folklife programs of the Smithsonian Institution actually conserves, stimulates, and nourishes the folk cultures and their arts, so anthropology may enrich and be enriched by its so-called subjects. Anthropology can be looked at as a kind of getting in down and behind people, learning many details about their lives, about their intentions, their techniques and ways, and at the same time gradually demonstrating that you do know and understand those ways; and then reflecting them back to the people, as innocently as possible, like the moon reflecting the sun, nonjudgmentally. You choose the good (though not sentimentally and not politically) but as a person's own lifeblood chooses what it needs. There is a kind of kidney process going on, naturally making innocent the bloodstream of the society while acknowledging the existence of the excreted substance, and a kind of oxygenating process, adding another human being's vigor to it—a simple social process, the social interaction of the anthropologist in the field and afterwards, her function of giving reflexivity. This is reflected in the vital rule: that the anthropologist will have to interact with her community, breathe with it, that the relationship must not be cold—as far as is commensurate with the fieldworker's capabilities. This is the least one can do. And in reply, one receives a stimulus to one's own reflexivity. For example, in the following discussion Ernest Frankson, my Eskimo consultant, was able to put what I wanted to say about the destructive effect of analysis better than I could.

Ernie was sitting on his beat-up sofa, watching the TV out of one slit eye. We were talking about the Inupiaq language teaching at the local high school, where I had been attending the ninth grade language class.

He said, "How do they teach language? They teach words—which are parts of words and mean nothing by themselves. Nothing." He eyed me through the smoke of his cigarette.

It was true. We had been learning lists of words, written down in my language notebook.

"They've set out the way to learn it using the English way of speaking. The children are made to learn English Eskimo."

I asked, "Was it Mary Smith who decided that?" (the author of my own grammar book).

"Yes. She speaks Eskimo like a second grader." Ernie's voice grew soft and sad and his eyebrows rose. "She's an Eskimo but she never spoke her language properly. She was at Fairbanks, with the university, speaking English all the time. She speaks like a second grader."

We walked into the kitchen where he filled the electric water heater for tea. "Like 'running' in Eskimo. Eskimos have all sorts of ways of running, fast, slow, easily, with a dog sled, and enjoying it." I was thinking too of "wanting to run, being able to run, going to run," all those postbases you hear about, not called postbases except by Mary Smith.

Ernie said, "You can't learn what to say just using one word, then adding one other word, and then another word." He stopped and gave an Eskimo phrase. I couldn't say it. "You learn by saying things."

I could see that the language form was indeed quite different from that of English; in fact it had the same rolling connectedness as the Point Hope genealogical "strings"—strings of kinship connections, of siblings, half-siblings, cousins, siblings-in-law, adoptive siblings, other children of divorced parents, even pseudo-kin namesake relations—that ran all through the village and around again, not in power pyramids of lineages but in strings, on a here-and-now level.

"The children don't learn anything at all at the bilingual class—how can they?" Ernie looked around in wonder, showing his gappy teeth. I interpolated agreement.

He suddenly remembered a ballet dancer who had come to Fairbanks to make a study of Eskimo dancing.

"She said to the Eskimo dancer who was supposed to go to her for an interview, 'Let's take each action separately.' " Ernie put out an arm straight from his side and the other across toward it, Eskimo style.

"She said, 'Let's see one action at a time and learn what each one consists of.' " Ernie's arm jerked again and he gave up.

"Analysis!" I said—and myself remembered a New York University performance studies dancer who wanted to analyze Ndembu African ritual dancing in the same way—it had annoyed me at the time. I had tried to persuade that analyst that if you neglected to look at the whole ritual you missed the meaning—but the meaning of the ritual didn't interest her.

Ernie was laughing wryly at the error of the experts.

What has this passage to do with anthropological writing? Several things. What Ernie was saying agreed with what Dorcus Rock, the healer, said about language learning. One should learn, not from books, but from people's facial expressions. She would look at me intently, trying to transmit the meaning of what she was saying in Inupiaq. (I couldn't catch the clues, because I had been such a short time in the culture.) It is the same with hunting training. Eskimos don't *tell* a young boy how to catch, say, a walrus. The boy *watches*, then after some time tries it himself. Then if he makes mistakes he must ask his elders— that is, if he wants to elicit comments and advice—and the comments usually consist of laughter, not anger; and he will then watch again.

In a roundabout way I am showing the seamlessness, the connectedness of everything that surrounds the person of an Eskimo. Learning is without analysis, without breaking down the subject matter. In a sense it has the form of a mystery, in the theological sense; it enters the realm of the sacred. A child learns speech this way. The result is an unbroken awareness of the whole—holism, a philosophy of the Eskimo and Indian awareness of the connectedness of all living things— of animals and humanity—which is the circle of life.

The tribal healer will say about her first training, "I wasn't taught. I *knew*."

Here we come back around to the problem of anthropological writing. It is of course possible to make a composite picture of Eskimo culture, by adding a "word" to another "word" and to another "word," as Ernie put it. An apparently coherent picture can be obtained, based on many experiences, numerical surveys, and reported events. We could break down the material into the Environment, Subsistence, Social Structure and Kinship Rules, Economic Exchange, Religious Change, Conflict and Maladjustment, and end by deploring the imminent disappearance of the old culture—our one emotional statement. Nowadays this method is known to have serious defects. It is the way an adult learns a language from a grammar, and the method clearly derives from left-brain thinking. The grammarian fragments the language to classify its regularities, searching for structural rules. But, as D. H. Lawrence said, "Analysis presupposes a corpse." And the result of anthropological writing performed according to such a method is dullness, lifelessness. This is because the field material came into being stage by stage and connected in time in its own unique way. So the flavor of an event in its context depends on all sorts of imponderable hints and traces that themselves need to be imparted for the material to live. Thus, some sense inherent in the piecemeal origin has to be conveyed. Art, the art of writing, is the tool for this. It can be used to more closely approximate the living truth and to help the reader to touch on the mysteries that do exist, that, as it were, need their orange peel taken off to be tasted properly.

When a child learns to speak, or when an ethnographer begins to "get" her society, the buildup of regularities takes place much as the brain forms in the fetus, from a blueprint inherent in the growing system. One thing sheds light on another, the "word" accretes to itself—as with the Eskimo verb—the style of the act, "*running fast in pursuit of an animal*," is conceived all as one thought. In the adult rationalist method, all this has to be done from without, there is no alternative (as there was no alternative for me as I did not seem able to *receive* from Dorcus's intent eyes the meaning of the long words). My learning of the language had to be done from a grammar book, a mechanical blueprint that could never be other than an approximation of the real thing, no matter what. This disadvantage exists for most adult students of a foreign language unless they are immersed, alone, among monolingual speakers of the language. Anthropological writing must then immerse, and it starts with anthropological experience, happenings before words, experience before meaning and objectified mind, as Dilthey said. From the inside of a living culture, even happenings that have a more-than-human-character, as long as they occur in their own idiom, are luminously true, visible as solidly there, lit up, revealed, highlighted by the viewpoint, their factual nature clearly demonstrated. Seen from the outside looking in, as through a church's stained-glass windows from the outside, the same events appear dark and featureless, with no evidence that they have any importance at all.

Dealing with Field Material

There are many possible ways to deal with the results of a year's anthropological fieldwork. Here I have a diary, written to myself at the end of each day during my fieldwork among Alaskan Eskimos from 1987 to 1988. Do I start to systematize my notes? I read in a recent book by Stephen Tyler, *The Unspeakable: Discourse, Dialogue, and Rhetoric in the Postmodern World*, that "the idea of system is only

nostalgia for the wholeness that analysis has killed and thinks to re-
suscitate by reinfecting the corpse with the germ that killed it. 'System'
is another name for the great spider goddess" (1987:54). Then should
I start right in and let that diary rip, just as it is? The reader would
be puzzled, understandably. I would like to map the social and physical
terrain first, for I like maps—visual things that are very useful. Maybe
after that I should line up the *dramatis personae* acting in the events
I plan to recount, give their genealogies, and prepare the reader for
their acts by showing the cause of those acts in their structural position.
Perhaps it would be best to tell the bare facts of those events, becoming
cool and objective so as to avoid bias or even ethnocentrism. (My
dilemmas are beginning to show.) The bare facts method would need
commentary and analysis *after* the account; analysis could well pick
away the whole mystery of the events until everything was cleaned up
with no loose ends at all. The other extreme, the confusing one of
the raw diary, would hardly be anthropology, even though some commentary does exist in those pages. Should I read my notes through,
go into a kind of trance, and come out with the pure metaphysics of
my experience? I cannot resist quoting Tyler again:

> Why not rid ourselves of the fetishisms of space [he means overorgani-
> zation, totalitarianism] whose only teachings are separation, displace-
> ment, and alienation? When men shall roll up space as if it were a piece
> of paper, then there will be an end to evil, and we shall know the
> magician who creates the illusion of the universe [the Wizard of Oz?].
> And the Great Noun, the thing called language, the *maya* of the gram,
> that placate creature of the grammarian and grammatologist—let all
> speak of it as the unspeakable plexiform illusion it is, and turn to
> discourse without the metaphors of space and light, of *potentia* and
> *actus*. Discourse is being time without the end, honey without the
> honeycomb or the bee. And this might be the postmodernism whose
> coming has been foretold and whose arrival is still awaited.
>   Beneath the glimmering boreal light, mirrored polar ice groans and
> heaves, the flame flickers feebly on the altar hearth, in the alter heart,
> into the holy, breathing darkness of the antipodeal night. (1987:59)

All this makes me long to go back to Point Hope and help my friend
Annie skin a seal.

There is truth in what Tyler, Clifford (1988), and Clifford and Marcus
(1986) say about the inevitable distancing that takes place, the feeling
of unreality when an ethnographer tries to systematize her work. However, the literary style of these very interpretive anthropologists who
are so much on the side of the masses would be incomprehensible to
those masses.

What do *I* want to do? I too am someone who loves to think, talk, and write about the reality of my anthropological experience. Indeed I do need to give a map of the physical and social terrain, then start straight in with a fully felt tale of the events, reliving and fleshing out the diary from memory even more than was written in it, then branching out periodically to follow living lines of association where they insist themselves. These may be an emotional intuiting of another's feelings—resulting in not only polyphony or heteroglossia, the speech of different protagonists, but polypsychy, as one might say—the use of one's own spirit to intuit their different spirits (different from psychology, the word-science of the mind); also some historical elucidation may be useful, about Christianity, or about family sagas of the past; or jerking to a stop to marvel at some manifestation of Eskimo "connectedness"—already a favorite theme of mine.

The result would be a body of writing in a tree form, or rhizome form as the postmodernists call it, articulated in the way the tale itself seems to ask—rather as if an inquisitive interrupter kept prodding for relevant details. Then at the end it would be possible to replay the key points, showing the "heartbeats," as it were, of the society and even how that heart beats.

What is behind this method? The communication of a series of activities as resonant music, alive itself, connected to the reader, saying the unsayable. This method cannot subsume all of anthropology, of course, but in the end anthropology will die without any of it. By means of it anthropology can reach, participate in, and experience levels it could not otherwise encompass, because such writing corresponds to the way a human being is articulated; it is not a logical construct. But neither is it fiction or a novel or journalism, though it may look like these. The culture, the entire society, is the protagonist, not an individual. The aim is understanding, not entertainment. So here is an attempt to realize my aim, using the diary. The way events occurred or were told to me is retained, and the comments I made at the time are included because they had an effect on my viewpoint as things moved along. Religion enters the picture to a considerable extent because it was there.

When Jimmie Nashanik Was Lost on the Tundra

The setting of the events of 17–22 January 1988 was the Eskimo village of Point Hope Alaska, 125 miles north of the Arctic Circle, on the extreme west of the northern slope which descends toward the Arctic Ocean and the Chukchi Sea. The people, numbering about six hundred, obtain 60 percent of their food from subsistence hunting, an occupation they pursue on ice, sea, and land. This January the temperature went down to −30°F, with strong winds. The people are members of the tough Inupiaq tribe; they still speak their own language.

When I arrived the previous fall I was struck by the flatness of the landscape — then realized how appropriate was the gravel spit around me in view of the people's livelihood, because the sea mammals have no choice but to swim around the point on their migration east. In the village itself that was set in a grid system of streets directly on the gravel I was assigned a very small frame house. The people of Point Hope didn't much like anthropologists, some of whom had incompletely interpreted their culture; in fact in a neighboring township the Eskimo authorities refused all but their own appointed researchers because they had experienced certain vicious slurs from unauthorized writers in the past. Moreover my interest in precontact customs aroused the ready factionalism of the village — there were those who were satisfied with Christianity and those whom the satisfied ones labeled "dissidents," who were satisfied with little of what the whites did. However, by dint of smiling a lot, and trying to behave with the courtesy and sharing behavior of Eskimos, I was gradually accepted as a familiar harmless figure, an elder of sixty-seven after all, with quite a lot of children and grandchildren of her own.

And I made it a habit to go to church.

On Sunday, 17 January there were forty in church. It was a frustrating day throughout, because when I later toiled over the gravel and snow to visit Irene, my language instructor, she wasn't at home. I went on to the house of the healer with whom I'd been having discussions, but she was in bed, turned away from the world, just as she had been on my previous visit. I sent in a present of ripe pears, feeling somehow guilty — had I done something to annoy her?

The day was bad for Jimmie Nashanik, as we shall see. Even the next day was bad; I had a dinner guest who forgot to come. There was much activity on the Citizen's Band radio. "Dora . . . Mum and Dad . . . Cape Lisburne . . ." What was going on? Dora was the huge and glorious wife of Robert Nashanik, the most respected whaling captain in town, a quiet small man gifted with a personality that made him look tall.

The next day Annie, my neighbor, came around to see me; she used to call me her "buddy," and so I was. She was a multiple grandmother and a great cook. "It's Dora's son Jimmie," she told me. "He's lost, out on his snowmobile."

"Why that's terrible, Annie. Where?"

"Up Cape Lisburne way, they think. There're a lot of people out searching for him. B. B., Joel, Bill, and them. He's been lost for a whole day." She sighed and sat down. I went to put on the kettle.

Annie was afraid about the cracks in the mountains hidden by snow. A snowmobile could fall far down in one of those and be trapped. Jimmie was twenty-three and had gone out hunting alone on his snowmobile. Annie and I looked at each other. Her round face and black eyes were restless with worry. We drank up our tea and decided to visit Dora.

I was very upset by this. Dora and Robert were the epitome of Eskimohood; I loved them, as everyone did. As Annie and I toiled across the village gravel and snow to Dora's house we were beginning to pray for them in that coming-and-going, frantic-in-parts way you do about someone else's kid. Molly pushed into the house. It was crammed. Old Tigluk (Robert's uncle), Vera Tuzroyluk, Irma, Aileen, Dora's daughters, Pikuq Tuzroyluk (the Tuzroyluks were related to Dora), Millie (Jimmie's girlfriend), faint with fear, Nelda and her small adopted son Richard, and many others were there. Irma, Aileen, and Nelda were related to Millie. Dora was in the middle of them, hollow-eyed and weeping, then laughing with her old courage. She handed around tea. Annie whispered to me, "She's always generous"—this was the prime Eskimo virtue. Young Richard had injured a muscle in his arm. Nelda told him to go to Robert in the back room, for Robert was a healer. Robert healed the injury—like Jesus, I thought, healing the soldier's ear in the midst of his own passion. Robert looked taller than ever, collected. Was his animal counterpart a snowy owl, like the one I'd seen high on the lookout tower? Dora and Robert loved each other—I caught their faces signaling to each other in love.

I was murmuring my fears to those standing near me, then thought of B. B., the nephew of Dora. B. B. had raped Millie, Jimmie's girlfriend and mother of Jimmie's son. B. B. entered the house when Jimmie was away, forced Millie out of doors in front of her small son—leaving the child alone in the house screaming—and raped her on the gravel outside. Now B. B. was at this moment out in the growing darkness and extreme cold hunting for—perhaps—the body of Jimmie. B. B. was a burly character, resembling the idiot thug in *The Grapes of Wrath*. I frowned. This present circumstance was beyond my anthropology.

There were further horrors in the family history. Dora was from the Lowe family, and Maurie Nashanik, her son, had raped and brutally murdered the estranged wife of Dora's brother, Tommie Lowe. Maurie was now in jail, and in a later incident Tommie committed suicide. B. B. was the son of Tommie, adopted to another of Dora's brothers, Joel, a great whaling captain and a deeply respected charismatic personality. In the past, then, there was more than a hint of feud. Now the story must move on.

The men had been up to the Cape Lisburne cliffs forty miles to the north, men who knew each hill and dip of a tract that was altogether confusing and wild. Through Dora's window we watched and watched the village trails outside—maybe this gliding light was Jimmie coming back, maybe that sound of an engine. We saw two snowmobiles arrive. Two older men got off and entered stiffly.

"See anything?"

"Nope. There's no light now, so we're giving up 'til eight in the morning. They're sending the planes from Barrow and Kotzebue, and they'll send the Search and Rescue chopper too."

"See any tracks?"

"There were some near Lisburne and some near the upriver camp. But new snow is coming down." It would be obliterating those tracks at this moment.

Three more snowmobiles came in; but there was nothing. The tracks were obliterated. Dora began to weep; then Jimmie's sister, Catherine, burst into great sobs, and they both wailed, they wailed. I hadn't heard that sound since Africa—that high, great, and wondrous weeping.

"Lost! Lo-ost!" cried Catherine, fetching tears from us all. One woman, an Episcopalian, said, "Stop it Catherine, just quit that."

Writing my notes that night I said, "O God, why do I write notes and not cry all the time? *But I do.*" And began to think about what I'd seen. The women in that house: they as a body were the balancing factor, antinomic to the searchers out on the tundra. Were they impotent to do anything about the tragedy? Yes and no. In the area of practicality, yes, they were impotent because they never moved from the house, while the searchers were all motion, all effort. But at another level, no. We were praying. Irma the seamstress gave a testimony of faith—she knew God would save Jimmie; old and ugly Vera Tuzroyluk likewise. Annie was beside me and before she left at midnight she led prayers and a final grace in which everybody joined—we were an interlacing body of women yet not touching, a counterweight system, just as the whaler's wife assists when her husband is out there after a whale—she is quiet and slow in the house to quiet and slow down the whale. In the old days many of these women would have been shamans and would have been able to quiet and clear the weather also; maybe they could do it still.

All that evening in Dora's house the TV had been on, as ever. It was 18 January, Martin Luther King Day, the twentieth anniversary of his death. And between the crises in the house we heard those heartfelt speeches come flaming out of the ordinary round-faced black man on the screen. What came through was honor to the non-whites, it sounded like honor to Eskimos. As Annie and I were walking home she suddenly said to me: "I had a dream. I dreamed about that, him."

"Martin Luther King?"

"Him. King. I dreamt we were in the old town site, in our sod house, and his face was in the skylight. I could see it. Saying something . . . something . . . and then his face turned into God's face." Annie's eyes squeezed at the memory, her voice became soft and gravelly with emotion, like warm brown sugar.

After writing this in my diary I remembered what Annie had recently told me about whaling. The whaling captain's wife raises an empty pot to heaven, to bring the whale. What comes into it? It is a "ping," a drop from above, a golden "ping." It is the whale saying, "I am coming to you." What did these utterances of Annie's mean?

The next day was Tuesday. At midmorning I went out into the darkness and in the distant southeast saw morning "break"—I saw a gap low in the sky "break" with a faint gray. I looked at it for a full minute. Later on I went to see Irene, my language teacher, and we talked about Jimmie and the snow.

"My husband was out there once, in the mountains in the snow," she said. "He drove down a slope, then he saw a light ahead. Why a light, there? He stopped, then he found a big hole in front of him. If he hadn't stopped he'd have fallen into it and been killed. God sent that little light," said Irene.

I went on afterward to Dora's and found even more people there, including Annie. The atmosphere—it is hard to describe now—stunned, glum, but gradually taking on the nature of deep interior seriousness, until I knew we were in a sacred event. Robert looked taller again, carrying himself with great fortitude. "He has *faith*," Annie said to me. Old, mad Grace Lisbourne was there, Irma again, Catherine, Millie and her two children, her sister Grace, old Ella Lisbourne, Tigluk the uncle, Ruth who was a Lowe and her husband Timothy Nashanik, Robert's brother, all backing him up as the news—simply because more time had gone by—got worse. All, all of us, were thinking of the cold. Nelda, Sophie who had seen the Satan man in November, Bernard Nash the solid citizen, Aileen, and her niece Leona cuddling her own niece of two months in age, Catherine weeping loud. Which made all of us weep and made Dora weep. The window watching went on, people continually going up to see if anyone was coming.

A young woman from the Search and Rescue headquarters entered the house smiling with a deliberate smile. She passed through the crowd and went to Dora and Robert.

She told them, "They've found fresh snowmobile tracks, made on Monday, out by Kivalina in the south," and continued talking beyond my hearing. Everyone began to look more cheerful. Tracks!

Around me I heard, "He was alive on Monday. He's driving."

Out of the corner of my eye I noticed that the TV was showing a story about the survival of two Eskimo children lost and wandering on the tundra. Now in the room everyone's eyes became riveted on the screen as the story unfolded. The eyes grew tender at the familiar scenes, the familiar animals, lemming, duck, wolf, caribou, wolverine, polar bear, the too-familiar predicament of the lost children. More and more people shifted to sit on the floor facing the TV. And they saw that the children did survive, they saw how the parents turned up in the nick of time, they saw the rejoicing and special gifts for the children, including an ivory whale charm, regarded with awe by our viewers. I myself was carried away by the enthusiasm, though still dreading that a mere TV program was no indication of Jimmie's safety. Mere TV? I forgot that Oral Roberts on the TV had healed Tigluk's son.

Robert came over to me (he's so slight in build: and a *big* man, an umialik). He said, "They've seen new tracks and followed them. The helicopter spotted them but lost them again later. The snowmobiles followed the tracks as far as there was gas enough to get home. They'll go back there tomorrow and follow them again."

"How much gas did Jimmie have?"

"Seventeen gallons—a lot."

"What's the weather like there?"

"Good. It's not snowing, and there's not much wind." But it became cold overnight, to −22°F.

I smiled at Robert and said, "I'm praying."

He said, "I think I'll go in the helicopter tomorrow."

"Yes," I said with a rush of hope, for Robert had saved people before in a certain strange way of his. "Do that! It would be good."

People told me that Jimmie had taken with him a cigarette lighter, a thermos, a tarp, and a good fur parka and mittens. However, he was wearing rubber Sorel boots that were not warm. Still, he was young and strong and was not at that time overly disturbed by the rape as I thought he might be, because it had occurred some time before. He had simply gone out after wolverine, which makes a valued ruff—just to emulate his brother, Bill.

Now a prayer was said and we all bowed our heads. Afterward Robert smiled. Dora smiled a little, though she stayed grim and patient. We thought of Jimmie's feet. Could he avoid frostbite? I had an awful private thought: would he lose both his legs? No, no. But his hands would be OK. *If* they find him.

Annie said, "He could wrap a caribou skin over his legs. We try to tell the young ones that, when they go out to hunt. They don't do it. They should let us know where they're going—and they should go out with someone else, two of them together. I tell Barbara, 'You should make Gordon take food with him, put food up for him to take.' " Barbara was the girlfriend of Annie's hunter son, Gordon. Annie was thinking, what if the same thing should happen to her son? I was thinking, what if my son Rory were in a car accident—it could so easily happen.

Annie told me a story about one of the snowmobile trips she and her relatives made to Kivalina, the next village. On the way back there was a 25 mph wind and thick snow. They heard the sound of rattling bones. They stopped at this mystic warning and tried to turn back—but they had to hole up, the weather was too bad for traveling. They made a deep cave in the snow and covered the top with their sled, and there they stayed. When they were found they were so starved that they couldn't eat much at first, for their stomachs couldn't stand food.

We went home at about 1 A.M. Annie slept the night with me because I was all on my own. In the morning the propane was frozen. I had some activated hot pads, and after a lot of work unfreezing the propane with the hot pads I gathered them up, reactivated them, and took them to the Search and Rescue headquarters at the firehouse, along with my big binoculars. It was dark, with a faint pale line in the southeast. Eight snowmobiles hitched to sleds stood outside the firehouse, and inside I found fifteen men, muffled up and ready to go. I gave my friend Rex the pads and binoculars to distribute, hoping they might help. The men went out into the night and lined up beside their snowmobiles. I moved to let them go, but instead one of them spoke, I couldn't see who. The heads went down. I stood still with my head bowed. We prayed, eyeing the sleds that were loaded with survival equipment, well tied down. The long loads—they were un-coffins. This scene again was sacred and there was no question about it, it just was.

One by one they started up and sped off down the wide, dark road toward the mountains. I watched until their lights grew small and finally disappeared—I was going along with them as far as I could.

This was Wednesday. At the post office I spoke with Steve Lisbourne, the postmaster. He said, "If they don't find him they'll go to that place in the summer and find him" ("the bones," I thought). He bent over the window counter. "The trouble is, young people don't bother to go to the elders and ask to be taught. The elders could show them all right, they'd teach them how to hunt safely."

That afternoon when I went jogging I was in a bit of a tough mood. As I ran I was addressing God severely. "God, it just doesn't do to let Dora and Robert suffer. C'mon, three days! Enough is enough, you've made your point. You didn't even make your own son suffer longer. God, it doesn't *do*."

On the way home as I approached Annie's house her husband, Samuel, appeared on the outside porch in his singlet (the temperature was −20°F).

"Come on in," he hollered.

"What's he want?" I thought.

Once in at the door, it was IT: "He's found!"

God, a glorious moment. I rushed at Samuel, hugged him, drew Annie in, we all hugged, we had the kids all smiling up, I was sweaty from running, crying and laughing—we all were, Annie raising her eyes in half-comic fashion toward . . . up there (Annie's way of referring to the one up there I had been telling off half an hour before).

"Job. It was the trial of Job," said Annie. I nodded. I had been thinking the same myself. We had a lot in common, those two and me.

Well, he was found. And alive. After a few moments the helicopter was heard arriving. I looked out but couldn't see it. I went back in, then went home, then heard it again—it sounded as if it were in the village, where? East? Echoing west? By the dome? (The pilot was actually flying low over us in triumph before he took Jimmie on to the airstrip.) At home I couldn't stay put, thinking of the helicopter and the young man. By the time I had put on my parka and hood the sound had ceased. I went to Dora's. Outside her house in the snow it was all quiet save for a parked snowmobile and a boy on toy skis. I knocked— and entered a room crammed with people, who turned toward me.

"Congratulations, everybody," I exclaimed. "You did it!" They laughed delightedly.

"And Him up there," I nodded upward quickly before I could be theologically faulted.

There stood Catherine. I hugged her *big*, the huge crying sister. Then went over as Dora came to me and we had a big hug—we were so happy; and I stood back in the glorifying crowd, which had become quite a gospel scene. "Praise *God*," they said, and "*Thank* you Jesus." In a moment they burst out singing to the tune of "Amazing Grace," "Praise God—" over and over. Surely the Christian church is alive and well and living in Point Hope.

I said to Irma, "You see, it took the men out there and the women in here to do it." That bit of structuralism left her cold, as structuralism always does here in Point Hope.

Dorcus came over and hugged me, and explained that she'd been having flu and had a bad time as her husband was away. She thanked me for the pears. "I hid them in my room, away from the kids," she said. "And I ate them myself, every bit, they were so juicy." So that was all right.

"He's here!" hollered the children who had been watching at the window. Everyone crowded to look. The pickup from the airstrip was halted outside and we saw people getting out.

"Where is he, where is he?" they asked. Then laughter. "He's getting his gear out. He's there." A young man appeared in a white hunting parka carrying something and surrounded by a little crowd.

Dora rushed out in her thin emerald blouse. The watchers hushed. Two were hugging, the green and the slight form in white. A hug. We all stood and looked toward the door. People came in, and kept coming in, Dora charging forward to the kitchen to put on food for *him*— in her green blouse, her face buoyant and red with tears. The younger brother Bill came in, also Catherine's boyfriend, Millie the girlfriend, and after them a young figure with long black hair—Jimmie. There came an explosion of joy, a terrific clap and a cheer.

"He's walking, he's *walking*." That was a surprise. The young man walked limber and cool to the kitchen—for food, obviously.

"Welcome home, Jimmie!" "He's been walking since Monday." Robert entered, his eyes lit up in a controlled face. He went to the far end of the room and sat at the table. His older sister was at the table too; Ruth entered, and many others. There was an expansion of spirit; this was the resolution of our troubles.

Tigluk asked for silence. He took up the Citizens Band microphone and spoke to the village. "Godiq . . . " praying in Eskimo with spontaneous thanks, though his emotion created gaps in his old voice. Messages came back on the CB: "Thank you Jesus." This was Annie's voice. Afterward she asked me, "Did you hear me?" "Sure thing."

Instantly Dora grabbed her parka and went out on her three-wheeler, shopping for food. It was known that later that evening she and Millie went to Bingo and won two hundred dollars—because their karma was good, said Ernest's wife.

People were leaving. I went up to Robert and said, "Thank God. And you were right to go in the helicopter. That had something to do with it. You the father." He thanked me—why?—and I left.

When I visited Annie next door Samuel said: "When Jimmie heard the chopper fly over he set fire to his mittens and tarp and made a big smoke"—which saved his life. Jimmie didn't look as if he had frostbite—these boys were tough. What had happened was that his snowmobile broke down out there, toward Noatak, five-sixths of the way upriver, about a hundred miles from Point Hope or any other habitation.

Samuel's son Gordon who had been out with the rescuers now came back with frostbite on his cheeks. He had in fact taken meat and sausages with him. He showed me knowledgeably on the map where Jimmie had been, a region with nothing in it but rivers and mountains blanketed with snow. Because of the fog Gordon had used a compass, one that I'd given him, and his companion had used another.

"Did you follow your own tracks back?"

"No. You have to head toward the beach going back, then follow along the beach home."

This was at 10 P.M. Gordon was sitting at table hungrily devouring a roast leg of caribou. He and Samuel cut pieces from it and dipped them into seal oil. Samuel gave me a piece. That was strong seal oil. Annie gave me trout from Kivalina, which I liked very much, just as it was, frozen. I myself had been over to Dorcus's with a joint of caribou because her daughter said they hadn't any. I had a shee fish from Irene to eat the next day. Always there was food.

During this evening Annie kept harping on the murder of Marjorie Lowe by Maurie Nashanik—very slightly indicating her own crotch and wrinkling her eyes. It was a sexual murder. She also pointed out to me that another of Dora's sons had broken up with his wife, in spite of a lavish wedding complete with the wedding photographs that now dominated the Nashanik walls. She was thinking the present scare was somehow fate's revenge on the Nashaniks.

My diary comments that many stories pop up from the past as a reflexive reaction in this kind of drama, their importance heightened now, the old meanings clearer—as we even saw in the reaction to the TV showings. A religious bent nourishes the playing of past against present and it also triggers gossip, which constitutes criticism by means of a comparison of the actual situation with a continually presented ideal. Drama in the life story is savored by fundamentalists like these—the drama of fall and salvation, the wonder of miracle and synchronicity—as James Peacock has shown in a study of fundamentalist conversion (1984:95–116). As I wrote this diary I commented that I was right in the midst of the religious events myself, my makeup in process of being modified back to the Protestantism of my childhood, gladly falling into step with local ways, moving as it were into the traffic flow, up the ramp of Eskimo life to reach its own speed. I wanted my writing to be close to the body, just like the "feeling" of the interior body sought by the healers (see Edith Turner 1989).

The CB was full of speeches. You could hear the Search and Rescue squad ordering the rescuers home. Robert came on the CB and thanked the squad and the National Guard and all those who prayed. It appeared there had been seventeen snowmobiles out on the search.

By now everyone was acting cheerful and funny and expressive— almost everyone. Later that evening the following was heard on the CB.

Woman's voice: "When's the movie?" (Sylvester Stallone was on in the school gym.)

Child's voice: "I think they canceled the movie."

Woman: "How come?"

Silence.

Woman: "How come?"

Silence.

Child: "How should I know?"

Man's voice: "Sure it's an earthquake on . . ."

At midnight the CB announced: "All the Search and Rescue members made it home."

What had been Jimmie's own experience out there? Pikuq, whose mother-in-law was a Lowe, told me the next day, "Jimmie's leg was swollen, and his jaw was too. When he went to sleep on the snow he wrapped himself in his tarp, but one arm got wet; he turned over, and the other arm got wet. These boys are tough." And when Pikuq's husband, Rex, came back from the search he told me, "The first day Jimmie was out the oil seized up, so he tried to walk to the beach; but he got mixed up, see, and walked into the mountains by Noatak. The snow was one foot deep up there in the mountains, and Jimmie was very tired from walking through it. Those snowmobile tracks down by Kivalina got covered with snow and the rescuers had to brush it off in order to find what direction he'd been going in. In fact the fog was so bad that all the rescuers had to use compasses. Jimmie used gas to make a fire of willow twigs; that was for warmth when he rested. He had signal rockets with him all right. He set one of them off when he heard the plane that first day, and two on the second day. No one saw the rockets go up because of the fog, and then there were none left. He had a blowtorch with him and that's what he used to set fire to his tarp and mitts when he heard the helicopter come over."

Others have told me in soft, awed voices of the dread attending the experience of being lost or of being stranded on an ice floe. During such an ordeal these men would continually wonder if they were going to make it.

Now on Thursday the weather was vile; it was −16°F with a wind chill up to −50°F along with blown snow. I didn't run that day. During the morning Dora came on the CB with her voice full of tears, to say thank you. She was quoting Psalm 130:

> Out of the depths have I cried to thee, O Lord.
> Lord, hear my voice: let thine ears be attentive to
> the voice of my supplications.
> If thou, Lord, shouldst mark iniquities, O Lord, who
> shall stand?
> But there is forgiveness with thee, that thou mayest
> be feared.
> I wait for the Lord, my soul doth wait, and in his
> word do I hope.
> My soul waiteth for the Lord more than they that watch
> for the morning: I say, more than they that watch for the
> morning.
> Let Israel hope in the Lord: for with the Lord there
> is mercy, and with him is plenteous redemption.
> And he shall redeem Israel from all his iniquities.

We know the source of those tears, Dora, the deepest fountains from which they rose—supposedly rare in our day, but never rare; we too are bathed in them as in every age.

Commentary

It can be seen how I partly entered under the skin of various people— Annie and Dora, for instance, but failed to do so directly in the case of Jimmie himself. At the time I was trying not to think of Jimmie in the whiteout, horribly aware how far he was from home, trudging down some deceptive slope that seemed to lead to the beach but never did, only toward high slopes further on—where am I?—that totally frightened feeling. And this going on for days and days. No. You need to be among that mass of women to endure the knowledge. What I had been exploring was where in a familiar social environment these barriers to consciousness exist and by what means they are resolved.

When the gathering became stunned, glum, and gradually entered into that sacred place—was it the courts of death?—the knowledge could now exist at that blind level, where all of them were held—as they would say—in God's hand. Robert, Annie told me, never lost the faith that his boy would be found. Robert was known for special Eskimo gifts that were his own private affair—powers of finding and saving. Here was a level of consciousness that none of us others had entered—but the big drama showed where that level was. My argument is that anthropological writing can well live around these levels of human experience and need not ignore them. For after all, nothing human is alien to us, as our motto says.

The above account is not intended to array a number of "voices" uttering "texts"; that is, I am not using "polyphony" as such as my basic method but different living viewpoints or loci of consciousness; the prime end product of the experience being not a text but witness—a word related to "witting," knowing—and the acceptance of subjectivity. There is nothing wrong with the visual or a viewpoint—each of us had a viewpoint during the events—but only with "single vision," as Blake called it, the positivist's measuring eye. And the other, seeing Blake's "fourfold vision in my supreme delight," truly is given to some.

So the insights of Jimmie's finding remain with us; and the reader may get inside my experience and my witness as one who was present, may get inside Dora's agony, inside the circumstance of Annie and I exchanging our own vision of the events (for we had developed a habit of exchange), also our playing a counterpoint of viewpoints with each other; Annie and Irene remembering past miracles—the emphasis being not on that they said the words and uttered a text, but on their actual memory alive with the miracle itself, alive too in Annie's case with the dream of Martin Luther King and God. Then Annie and Steve Lisbourne sore with the young for their failure to attend to the advice of the elders, the "if only they would listen they would not get into such danger" complaint. Then suddenly the entering in of the practical—the woman from the firehouse saying that tracks had been seen and Robert's decision to go in the helicopter. This was the heart of the matter—a practicality of that sure-handed kind that *knows* the future is OK. By contrast my own reproach to God while jogging was slight—funny at best, showing my peripheral position, yet with a burst of personal feeling. The boy had already been saved, anyway. The practicality of the burning mitten and of the helicopter containing the powerful miracle worker being the answer to the longing, to the "if onlys," to the time in the world of prayer and of past miracles; it became too the reply to the appearance of the sacred realm, a realm powered by antipower, that curious power-of-the-weak of us women — which I should warn is of all power the least easy to measure, for where it operates is beyond words. Enough to repeat that that world was seen as solid when you were within it as contrasted with how it looked when you were outside it — showing the palpable existence of different modes of being.

Further signs of the double nature of the events are also seen in the resolution, in the work of the finding on the one hand and the announcements and response on the other, the first practical and the second open-ended to the Almighty, exploding outward until they culminated in Dora's psalm.

As in most Eskimo events the two levels wove in and out of each other continually, with a fusion of them at the center, at the finding, in the situation of Robert's unuttered powers.

Curiously enough Michael Jackson, a reviewer of Victor Turner and Edward Bruner's edited volume *The Anthropology of Experience,* drew attention to a passage from Geertz's epilogue to the otherwise positive volume. Geertz says: "We cannot live other people's lives, and it is a piece of bad faith to try [Why? Apparently this doubter is one of those who would taboo such an attempt, perhaps because it would imply a kind of shamanism]. We can but listen to what, in words . . . they say about their lives. . . . Whatever sense we have of how things stand with someone else's inner life, we gain it through their expressions, not through some magical intrusion into their consciousness. It's all a matter of scratching surfaces" (Geertz 1986:373). Jackson shows how prevalent is this image of the world as text, and he calls such a view both logocentric and ethnocentric, demanding instead "an empiricism which embraces both thought and feeling . . . and includes in its account of the experiences of others an account of our experience of ourselves" (1987:457).

To conclude, I have presented this piece as testing material for the method of multilevel, even polypsychic, writing, where the movement in and out of levels can be gauged as if the boundaries of those levels were perforated screens, "nets" as Richard Schechner (1988) called them in preference to the word *frame.* Such concepts as "net" may well mark a more flexible and intelligible era of ethnography as we approach the end of the twentieth century.

The first need then, as ever, is to sink oneself in the society, in action and converse. Then note the circumstances when one slips in and out of familiarity; use all possible means to situate and contextualize others as they experience feelings about each other and about oneself — get behind them; reflect back all that one feels and sees, an important role of the anthropologist; write one's own story by means of a narrative of action, along with other people's accounts of the events and how those accounts affect one, one's own memories and knowledge, their memories and knowledge, following the arabesque of interpersonal thought, action, and conversation; be faithful to the order in which things occurred to one, so that the whole will have organic coherence and so that insights will be true ones. Thus the art of writing will render the instrument transparent so that all concerned will have a sense of recognition, both those who originally experienced those events and the readers.

NOTES

My thanks are due to my sponsors, the Wenner-Gren Foundation for Anthropological Research and the University of Virginia, and to James and Mary McConnell for further help. I am particularly grateful to Ernest Frankson and Molly Oktollik, who were guides and educators in their different ways. Ernest declined coauthorship, though he was the theoretician behind this piece. Theodore Mala, Rosita Worl, Lori Krumm, Karlene Leeper, Ann Riordan, and others assisted the research plan at various stages. The people of Point Hope gave me unstinting encouragement and affection that I remember with much gratitude. It should be noted that certain names in the narrative have been changed to protect the privacy of individuals.

A Tree That Stands Burning: Reclaiming a Point of View as from the Center

Robin Ridington

> My son has seen a wonderful tree.
> The Thunder birds come and go upon this tree,
> making a trail of fire
> that leaves four paths on the burnt grass
> that stretch toward the Four Winds.
> When the Thunder birds alight on the tree
> it bursts into flame
> and the fire mounts to the top.
> The tree stands burning,
> but no one can see the fire except at night.
> —Alice C. Fletcher and Francis La Flesche, 1911

Anthropology in the 1980s began to develop a critical perspective on its own traditions of writing. In an article that is a touchstone of the genre, James Clifford identified ethnographic authority as a central problem of ethnographic writing in the twentieth century. "Ethnography," Clifford argued, "is from beginning to end enmeshed in writing." By translating experience into textual form, Clifford wrote, "ethnographic writing enacts a specific strategy of authority." He suggested that "a rather different economy of ethnographic knowledge prevailed ... before Malinowski, Radcliffe-Brown, and Mead had successfully established the norm of the university trained scholar testing and deriving theory from first-hand research" (1983:120-21).

While university training may have established fieldwork as a normative basis for testing and deriving theory, it also imposed the authority of its own institutionally defined "economy of knowledge" upon ethnographic writing. One pre–university-based system of knowledge that resonates sympathetically with the contemporary interest in shared ethnographic authority (Clifford 1983; Buckley 1987) may be found in a remarkable collaborative ethnography called *The Omaha Tribe*, published in 1911 by the Bureau of American Ethnology. Its authors, Alice

C. Fletcher and Francis La Flesche, himself an Omaha, present the authority of Omaha traditions as a system of knowledge and power through which "all things are related to one another and to man, the seen to the unseen, the dead to the living, a fragment of anything to its entirety" (134).

"A Tree That Stands Burning" is a narrative ethnographic sketch of moments in the life of a living object from that tradition, the Sacred Pole of the Omahas. It is a montage of perspectives surrounding what Fletcher and La Flesche called "a point of view as from the center" from which to understand the life of the Tribe. In Omaha tradition, the Sacred Pole is a living being, a "Venerable Man." The narrative brings together stories about its origin in a young man's visionary moment long ago, with accounts of its traditional keeping by members of the Omaha Leader Clan and its later transfer for safekeeping to the traditions and institutions of anthropology. The narrative combines the following sources of information:

1. an account of events in the life of the Pole I experienced directly (written from memory and fieldnotes);

2. an account of events in the life of the Pole experienced by Fletcher and La Flesche (in Fletcher and La Flesche 1911);

3. written versions of oral traditions relating to the Pole and its origins (in Fletcher and La Flesche 1911);

4. transcriptions of modern Omaha speeches relating to reclaiming the pole (from audio actualities);

5. transcriptions of speeches by academics relating to the transfer of their authority over the Pole (from audio actualities);

6. transcriptions of readings from all of the above as incorporated into a speech about the Pole the Omahas asked me to give at their 184th Annual Omaha Tribal Powwow (from audio actualities).

"The ability of a text to make sense in a coherent way," Clifford wrote, "depends less on the willed intentions of an originating author than on the creativity of a reader." He cites Barthes's observation that a text is "a tissue of quotations drawn from innumerable centers of culture" (1983:141). My intention in writing "A Tree That Stands Burning" has been to bring together "a tissue of quotations" drawn from experiences Omahas and anthropologists have shared during the past century in relation to the Sacred Pole. Alice Fletcher and Francis La Flesche intended their ethnography to provide "a point of view as from the center." The Pole itself, they knew from Omaha tradition, represented one visionary image of such a center.

The quotations I have brought into this narrative will make sense to the reader only if they actualize a creativity that the Omahas call Wakonda, "a power by which all things are brought to pass." Both the reader and the Venerable Man possess the authority of persons in the narrative. Like the Venerable Man, the reader must imagine a center where "four paths . . . stretch toward the Four Winds." Like him, she or he must connect "the seen to the unseen, the dead to the living, a fragment of anything to its entirety." Like the reader of any text, written or spoken, a person must focus intelligence upon "innumerable centers of culture." Intelligence permeates all things, seen and unseen. It is the ultimate authority, "a power by which things are brought to pass." It exists simultaneously in a text and in our readings of it. My narrative braids Omaha stories with those of anthropology. It will be up to the reader to discover the intelligence coded within that braiding. Within that intelligence are the "actions of mind and body" that a common Native American blessing refers to as "all my relations."

Flight of the Thunders

At 8:30 in the evening of 25 June 1988, Jillian Ridington and I were boarding Delta Airlines flight 810 from Cincinnati to Boston, the last leg of our journey from Vancouver, British Columbia, to Cambridge, Massachusetts. We were on our way to witness an important event in the braided history of contact between members of the Omaha Tribe and the Peabody Museum of Archaeology and Ethnology at Harvard University. For the first time in exactly one hundred years, Omaha hands would touch their Sacred Pole. The idea of the Pole has been at the center of Omaha identity for hundreds of years, but the Pole itself has been at the Peabody since its last Omaha Keeper, Yellow Smoke, handed it to Francis La Flesche, an Omaha anthropologist, in 1888. As he promised Yellow Smoke, La Flesche sent the ancient tribal emblem to the "great brick house" in the East for safekeeping. When La Flesche received the Pole from Yellow Smoke he wrote, "This was the first time that it was purposely touched by anyone outside of its hereditary Keepers." Returning the Pole to Omaha hands would complete a cycle in its life and in that of the People.

The flight to Boston also completed a cycle in my own life. I did graduate work at the Peabody from 1962 to 1967. The Pole was then on public display in a glass case just around the corner from the anthropology department office. I found myself drawn to it. Nearly every day I spent in the museum I would break from my studies in the museum's wonderful old library. I would visit the Pole and wonder at the world from which it came. Although I saw it regularly, I did not understand then how to penetrate its mystery. I knew it simply as an object of power that had touched me in ways I would only begin to understand in the years to come. I knew that it spoke to me. It spoke to me first and foremost of the Native American presence in this land to which my ancestors had come as immigrants not so many years ago. It spoke to me through its physical presence. It spoke about a tribal history of which I was as yet unaware. It spoke of stories I would learn and tell in years to come.

Omaha history began to take shape for me when I read the Twenty-seventh Annual Report of the Bureau of American Ethnology and discovered a very different ethnographic language from the one I was being taught was normative. I learned that Fletcher and La Flesche had used the Sacred Pole as a centerpiece of their ethnography, just as, they said, the Pole itself had provided "a point of view as from the center" from which to understand the ceremonies that held the Omaha Tribe together during their buffalo hunting days.

The flight to Boston took me further into the unfolding story of that center. It took me further into "a trail of fire that leaves four paths on the burnt grass that stretch toward the Four Winds." It took me toward the motionless star, the Pole Star of the North. Flying into Cincinnati, the checkered prairie fields were an unnatural sickly yellow as we looked down on them across our tiny perfect microwaved airplane dinners. They looked as though a trail of fire had burned into the heart of the continent. The captain announced that the temperature in Cincinnati was 101 degrees. A heavy haze burnished the slowly setting sun to a shimmering spot of brilliant color above an indistinct horizon. North America was in the midst of a heat wave that was to become a terrible crop-destroying drought. A hundred years ago the Plains Indians were learning to live without the buffalo. I wondered how the Whitepeople would cope with a land in which corn and wheat and barley could no longer grow. I wondered if they could learn from the experience of the Indian people.

The Omaha Sacred Pole was also on my mind. Three weeks before this flight, I had been in Macy, Nebraska. Their tribal historian, Dennis Hastings, had introduced me to Tribal Chairman Doran Morris and former Chairman Edward Cline. I had come to Macy to talk with tribal leaders about arrangements for a visit to the Peabody. Doran is the great-great grandson of Yellow Smoke, the Pole's last Keeper. Like Yellow Smoke, Doran belongs to the Leader Clan. When I saw Doran and Eddie in Macy, Eddie told me that he had been to the Peabody in the 1970s. He had been upset at seeing the Pole on public display there. He was upset that the Whitepeople to whom Yellow Smoke gave it for safekeeping in 1888 did not understand or respect it. He spoke to Stephen Williams, the museum's director, and requested that it be removed from public display. Williams complied with his request. Since that time the "Venerable Man" has been in repose in the great brick building's cavernous basement vaults.

Flight 810 was climbing swiftly through the shimmering haze and into a clear sky-world such as visionaries sometimes know in the most powerful of their dreams. We reached a cruising altitude of 41,000 feet and leveled off. The wide-body aircraft was half empty. It looked cavernous. We flew north and east along a line of towering cumulus thunderheads whose tops boiled up above our flight level. A golden light flooded in from the west and crossed the vacant seats in the plane's wide center section. A few passengers moved about as if in a dream of flying. Mottled beams of sun and shadow streamed from port to starboard. I felt a warm mask of light upon my face. On a larger scale, this same visionary light illuminated the white tops of the thunderheads that walled the eastern edge of our flight path. Tongues of forked lightning snaked in and out of the clouded turbulent atmosphere from which the thunderheads rose. A passenger asked me nervously, "Do you think there is any danger?" "No," I answered smiling. "Just sit back and enjoy the passion of the elements."

I glanced toward a waxing gibbous moon that hung high above this passionate but strangely silent show of elemental power. I knew that the moon would become full soon after Doran and Eddie touched their Sacred Pole. I knew that the Omahas refer to the moon following this one as "the moon when the buffalos bellow." This moon is the one in which Omahas traditionally conducted their ceremonies of renewal. In 1888, the Tribe gave up its Sacred Pole to the keeping of anthropology. In 1988 Omahas were asking me to witness their renewal of contact with the Pole. That purpose had now led me to this spectacular and visionary encounter with the thunder beings. It led me to think about how a fragment of anything is connected to its entirety.

At 41,000 feet I could see the Thunder birds come and go upon their cloud world, making a trail of fire that stretched toward the Four Winds. I could look directly into their home. The thunderheads mushroomed aloft from a dark mycelium of rain and wind-streaked storms. As we flew north and east, the system became more intense. The white towering thunderheads had become incandescent with the golden light that streamed toward them from the setting sun. I thought about the story Yellow Smoke told Alice Fletcher and Francis La Flesche in a small house in Macy a century earlier. I could almost hear the tapping of the old Keeper's stick as he told them,

> When the Thunder birds alight on the tree
> it bursts into flame
> and the fire mounts to the top.
> The tree stands burning,
> but no one can see the fire except at night.

Fletcher and La Flesche wrote that

> While the old chief talked
> he continually tapped the floor with a little stick
> in his hand, marking with it the rhythm
> peculiar to the drumming of a man
> who is invoking the unseen powers
> during the performance of certain rites.

They recalled that

> His eyes were cast down,
> his speech was deliberate,
> and his voice [was] low,
> as if speaking to himself.

Within a few minutes the scene changed entirely. The sun had set. The thunderheads became white with moonglow. The forked lightning tongues suffused the cloud world with power. Each shocking flash reached out to illuminate the entire cloudscape. Each lattice of lightning revealed to me, momentarily, a visionary sky-world. Each vision flickered across my eyes in perfect silence. These miraculously glowing clouds reminded me of the tree that stands burning, the tree that stood in a glass case in the Peabody museum, the tree that stands for Sky People and Earth People who, together, are the Omaha Tribe. Fletcher and La Flesche wrote that the proper form of address when speaking to the Tribe as a whole was "Aho Instashunda, Hongashenu ti agathon kahon" (Hello Instashunda, Sky People; Hongashenu, Earth People, I greet you as both sides of a single house joined here together). I thought about Yellow Smoke and the story he told to Fletcher and La Flesche a hundred years before. I thought of Doran and Eddie and the Omaha People of Macy. I thought of the Pole, the Venerable Man, waiting in silence to feel the touch of sun and air and Omaha hands after a century of seclusion.

Touching

On the afternoon of 27 June 1988, Jillian and I witnessed Joe Johns, a Creek artist-in-residence at the Peabody, present the Pole to Doran

Morris and Eddie Cline. Doran wept as Eddie spoke to the people assembled in the little courtyard outside the museum:

> I'm going to say a few words to Our Creator in our Omaha language and I hope that you might forgive us. We hope in a very short time, that we can take it [the Pole] home where it belongs—among the People. This is a living tree. This is a living person—as far as we're concerned. Maybe, to some of you, it's just an old piece of wood, but the teaching . . . it was there for the People to see, to become a part of, to touch, and to be tied to it—what kept the Tribe together—that's the teaching. And so, we would like to have this at home—so that our People could have the opportunity to look upon it and to maybe even—to touch it. So, I'm going to say a few short words to Our Creator on behalf of our Tribal Chairman and this living tree that we look upon this day.

Eddie's prayer was in Omaha, but its meaning was understood universally. Then, Ian Brown, associate curator of North American Collections, spoke about the trust relationship anthropology has to the Pole:

> Today is truly an honorable day. It has been over a hundred years since proper respect has been paid to the Venerable Man, the Sacred Pole of the Omaha. No object embodies so much of the soul of the Omaha. It represents the authority of their leaders, the unity between man and woman, and the binding element that has held the Omaha People together for so many centuries. Many hundreds of years ago, the Sacred Pole came to the Omaha. The layers of paint encrusted on its surface are testimony to the respect offered yearly to the Venerable Man. The last time this event occurred was in 1875—a very long time ago, but a short episode in the rich history and promising future of the Omaha. Since 1888, the Sacred Pole has rested in the Peabody, protected from the ravages of time, studied by several generations of anthropologists, but certainly not revered. Over this past century, it has failed to play the role it was meant to serve among the Omaha, but it should be emphasized that the Sacred Symbol of the Omaha has still survived. It is our hope that the Ceremony which has occurred here today will, once again, be an annual event, and that someday, in the not-too-distant future, the Ceremony will be held where it should be held—among the Omaha themselves. Thank you for coming.

When the Pole had returned to its place of repose in the museum basement, we assembled in the museum's Bowditch Room for refreshments. Eddie Cline spoke again:

> Well, Dr. Ridington, you visited with us and we had a visit up at Dennis's place, and we talked about this—coming here. And you indicated that,

and appreciated that the approach to the Pole would be with a sincere heart and mind, and I guess that's—as Indians—that's the way we are. Regardless of what kind of day-to-day people we are, we have a very strong feeling about the things that were meaningful to the Tribe— some of the culture that still exists—very meaningful to us, and I guess the Sacred Pole, you indicated—and I hope that we've satisfied your thoughts along those lines.

Before we came, we went and visited with my sister, I call her, as the keeper of the good things that belong to the families and the Tribe, and we, the Chairman and I, and her—we sat and cried. We talked about the Pole. And you see the reaction of the Chairman out there. I hope that, as an interested person, as a trained person along the lines that we're looking at here, we're hopefully returning to our village— you've seen our village—very humble, very small, insignificant in comparison to some of the Tribes across this country. But, to us, it, it was a way of life—the Pole. It was a living tree. And they went even further, and said it was a living person, according to the People that made up our Tribe. They held onto it, and they done things together . . . and so we come as simple and humble people—not as a great leader or former leader or anything like that.

We come as humble people, and in comparison to us, the significance of the Pole, we don't even rate consideration with the Pole—as people. You know we look up to it and, our people at home will, hopefully, will have the opportunity to regain their ties, to revitalize [the Tribe]. Maybe this Pole will inspire us, will get us together so that we can talk as one person, think and do as one group of people. We have high hopes for it. . . . Doran said, "Maybe that Pole will give us strength. Maybe it will bring something to us." I'm sure he's talking about land.

So, we appreciate your reaction, your interest, and on behalf of our People at home, we thank you. Each of you had some thought, some— done all of the work getting this together. We appreciate that. We couldn't, we wouldn't have been able to do anything, and so our thanks to you on behalf of the People at home. And, we have—we're anxious for this to happen. We're anxious—to send someone to take that home. And, hopefully, it will reside in the center—be the centerpiece again of our Tribe—to bring good things to them. We look at the youngsters. We want them to have a good way of life. We look at the old people. We want them to have a good ending to their lives. Hopefully those all in-between will have something good and this, this I pray someday— maybe this will help us—so, we feel good.

So we say thank you on behalf of the Chairman—he talks better than I can. I'm older so he expects that I will say these things. With all our hearts we thank you for being here, you know—for your participation. I know that Dr. Ridington there has very much interest in what we saw today. The teaching is that they put food for that living person—the old ways. And, I'm sure that if you take a microscope and shave some of it off, you'll find the remains of food on there yet, that they fed that person, wanting him to continue to live. So, we feel good. We feel humble in front of it and the significance of the meaning. A hundred years, it's been here and we prayed for this building. We prayed for all the other things that you have here that belong to other people that saw fit to bring them in and put them here for safekeeping. We prayed that way today. We prayed for the people who work here in this building, so we had that opportunity so we took advantage of it, and said those things to God and it makes us feel good. We can go home and tell—the Chairman will report to the People that the reaction was good here, and that they support the ideas that the Chairman has for the People—so we'll leave you with a good feeling in our hearts— and I just wanted to say thank you, all of you.

I replied:

When the People renewed the Pole in the old days, the Seven Chiefs selected a reed from a bundle of reeds that represented every man of the Tribe, and then they—those People who were selected—they [the Chiefs] sent them back into each of the lodges that was in the camp circle when they were on the buffalo hunt—and the person who'd been selected would go and touch one of the poles—in one of the lodge poles—and touch it as counting coup on it—touch it, he would touch it. And that pole would then be brought by members of your clan to the center where they'd make a Sacred Lodge, and that was the beginning of the Renewal Ceremony—that's where it took place. And I see the two of you here today, as being like members of your Tribe whose, whose sticks have been chosen—and you're going to go back and you're going to be touching the lodge poles of other People back home—all of the Omaha People who are interested in this—and, this is the beginning of building another Sacred Lodge—a Sacred Lodge where the Tribe will continue to renew itself.

When we were flying up here, we flew up via Cincinnati, and it was very, very hot, and we flew at 41,000 feet, and we flew up along a line of thunderheads, and we could see them even above us. They were even higher than 41,000 feet, and we were looking off to the side and the sun was setting on one side and the moon was almost full—a waxing moon getting bigger, but right towards full—above them, and so there was this golden glow on the clouds, and then, looking down at the bases of all the clouds, we could see they were connected to one another by this dark storm mass. And then, as it got dark, we could see that—that lightning was flashing between all the clouds.

And, I've just never seen anything like that before. It made me think, "Well, I'm seeing something in a very elevated and spiritual way," but it also reminded me that in the story of the Pole, the boy who found it saw it as something that was—was spiritually endowed, that was glowing, as if it was on fire, but it wasn't consumed. And when he told that story—took that story back to the Chiefs, they told him, "That's the Thunder birds. That's the place where the Thunders come to rest, and they come from the four directions, and all of the animals come together at that place as well." And so I thought, that was a very good sign—to be able to look across to those Thunder Beings and when what was in my mind was, was the Pole and this meeting that was going to be taking place.

I gather from the book by Fletcher and La Flesche that the Renewal Ceremony took place in the moon that would be the one following this full moon. It was the moon "when the buffaloes bellowed." I don't know how you say that in Omaha, but I think that would be the one that we're just coming into after this full moon.

Following the speeches, we left the Peabody and went to a Mexican restaurant with Doran, Eddie, Bette Haskins, director of Harvard's American Indian Program, and Emma Featherman-Sam, volunteer co-ordinator with the Job Corp's Women in Community Service program. The Omahas had been delayed in getting to Cambridge because of mechanical problems with the plane. They had not made hotel reservations. It turned out that accommodation in Cambridge was very expensive and almost unobtainable on short notice. Finally, Jillian noticed a listing in the yellow pages that said "reasonable accommodation for transients." It gave an address within walking distance. Six of us, four Indians and two Whitepeople, walked the few blocks to what looked like a haunted house on Kirkland Street. Yes, they had a room, not in this house but in another, a block away. It would be forty-five dollars a night plus a key deposit of five dollars. When we finally found the place, it turned out to be humble indeed. Their lodging was a clean but otherwise bare room, a glorified flophouse. Doran and Eddie were tired and happy to have a place to lay their heads before going on to testify before Senator Daniel Inouye's committee on Native American affairs in Washington.

A few weeks after Jillian and I had returned to Vancouver, I got a call from Doran. He asked if I could give him the proper titles and addresses of Bette Haskins and Emma Featherman-Sam. I had the information and gave it to him. Then I reminded him of the speech Eddie had given after touching the Pole. I reminded him that Eddie said they had "come as simple and humble people—not as a great leader or former leader or anything like that. We come as humble people, and in comparison to us, the significance of the Pole, we don't even—we don't even rate consideration with the Pole." "Maybe," I told Doran, "the Great Spirit was listening to what Eddie said. That is why he sent you that flophouse to stay in." Doran laughed. Then he came to the main point of his call. "We would like to invite you, Dr. Ridington, to speak to the Tribe at our powwow in August, about what you have learned of the traditions relating to the Pole."

So it was that on 13 August 1988, I found myself speaking in the sacred circle of oak trees that is the Omaha powwow arena in Macy, Nebraska. I found myself giving breath to words that had long been locked between the covers of a book. I found myself breathing the words of a story that Yellow Smoke told Doran's great-great grandfather a century earlier. Some said that Yellow Smoke is buried on the little hill just overlooking the arena. I thought I could feel the old Keeper supporting the breath I brought to his words.

A Speech to the 184th Annual Omaha Tribal Powwow Macy, Nebraska—13 August 1988

Dr. Robin Ridington

I feel very honored and very humble at being given the opportunity to speak in this sacred arena here today, and I pray that the words that I say will receive the blessing of this circle. Your arena is open to the East like a single lodge. It's open to the East like the great camp circle, the Huthuga in which your elders used to come together for ceremonies of renewal during their annual buffalo hunt. And, it's open to the East like the earth altar of long ago—a place called Uzhin'eti—where long ago they offered meat and buffalo fat to feed your Sacred Pole. So I will begin my words of greeting to you in the manner of these elders, as they used to say long ago (I hope my pronunciation is reasonably good), "Aho Instashunda, Hongashenu ti agathon kahon." That means, "Hello Instashunda, Sky People; Hongashenu, Earth People, I greet you as both sides of a single house joined here together as one people"—one Tribe in the sacred arena, just as they did, long ago, in the Huthuga—the camp circle.

You may wonder, as I sometimes do myself, what business I have, a non-Indian, speaking to you, a great nation that is native in this land to which my ancestors came as strangers not so many years ago. And the answer, I will try to give you, in the form of a story, and in the form of a teaching. My story is simple. The teaching, from your tradition, is more complex—and I hope that you will bear with me as I try to convey what I have learned of your traditions—and I hope those of you among you who know a great deal more than I do will come forward to me, as time goes on, and give me the benefit of your wisdom and your understanding. The story goes like this. In January 1962 I began to study anthropology at the Peabody Museum of Harvard University in Cambridge, Massachusetts. And there, your Sacred Pole (whose name I later learned is Waxthexe, or Washabe-gle) it was on public display. At first, I didn't know what this stood for. I didn't know what it meant. I didn't even know whether the Omaha People were still together on their lands. But I did know, even then, that the Pole must have represented a power of life, and a power of motion—a power of unity—for the People who once carried it with them from place to place. I knew also that the Pole had touched and moved my own life. I'll give you an example of this. Nearly every day that I studied in the Peabody Museum library I did what student scholars usually do—you get bored, you get restless, you get tired, you want to go for a walk—and somehow I got drawn toward that Venerable Man— the Sacred Pole—when I was on my little walks away from the library I would go up to the Pole and I'd stand by it and look at it. It was on public display at that time. And I'd just contemplate it. I'd think about the times that this Pole represented, even though I didn't know very much about it at the time. Being close to your Venerable Man—to your Sacred Pole—has turned out to be as important to my education as the courses I took in anthropology at Harvard University. So that's the story of how my life came into contact with your sacred symbols. Now I want to tell you some of what I have learned about the Pole, and most of what I'm going to tell you is what I've learned from what is on record, in writing. I look forward to learning more from you, from the oral tradition, from the elders who have passed on information and knowledge and teachings from generation to generation. So, what I'm giving you today is simply the benefit of what has been written down about your traditions. I think that's something that, if you haven't come into contact with, it's useful for you to know what people have written down about your traditions.

As a formal part of my education, my teachers introduced me to the Twenty-seventh Annual Report of the Bureau of American Ethnology. This is an enormous book. It weighs about ten pounds. It's 660 pages long, and was published in 1911. Its title is simply *The Omaha Tribe,* and its authors are Alice C. Fletcher (whose name, in English, means "puts feathers on arrows") and Francis La Flesche, or Frank La Flesche (whose name, in French, means "the arrow"). And, as you know, Frank La Flesche, Francis La Flesche— was part Omaha. He belonged to the Elk Clan—of this Tribe, and also— he was one of the very first native Indian people to become a professional anthropologist. He wrote a number of books in addition to *The Omaha Tribe.* For many years he worked at the the Smithsonian Institution in Washington, D.C.

From this book I learned that the name for the Pole, which they said was Waxthexe, means "wa," a sacred thing—like in Wakonda—"a sacred and powerful object with the power of motion—the power of life," and "xthexe," which they said means "mottled as by shadows." Mottled is a pattern of light and dark—a sort of blending of light and dark—shadow and sunlight. Mottled makes me think of the pattern I see out here today as sunlight streams through the trees of your sacred arena here and marks this circle—some places in shadow, some places in light. And it also makes me think of you as a People—you Instashunda, you Hongashenu—here together—Earth People, Sky People as one People—one People celebrating this powwow as you've celebrated it for many, many years in the past.

The name *Xthexe,* they say in the book, also "has the idea of bringing into prominence to be seen by all the people as something distinctive." That means something that is beautiful, is unusual, is striking—something that's an emblem—something like the flag—that you look up to. And the book says, also, that Xthexe is also the name given to the blue spot or the Mark of Honor that women among you have worn with pride and with dignity throughout the century when the Pole was at rest in the Peabody Museum. The elders told Fletcher and La Flesche that the name *Waxthexe* means that the right to possess the Mark of Honor was controlled by the Pole. The Pole and the Mark of Honor were related to one another. This Mark of Honor (many of you, I'm sure, have seen it—you have relatives who bear it, or have borne it in their lives)—this blue spot was tattooed on a young woman's forehead. And the book says that this signifies the sun at its highest point in the sky—when the sun makes its passage at noon time, the very highest point that it ever reaches—the blue spot stands for that. And they said that the Mark on the young woman's throat was a star sign—was a four-pointed star—radiating out to form a perfect circle—and that that stood for the star of the night time.

In 1984 I returned to this book, which I hadn't studied for some years, and I began to look at it again and to write about some of the teachings that it contained as a way of trying to find out how to make sense of all this information in the 660 pages of this big book.

The authors of the book believed that a book was important because it was one way of preserving the memory of traditions that might otherwise be lost—and I think we have to honor them for that objective. Some of the things they said may have reflected the point of view of only particular people that they talked to—they talked to people from some clans, perhaps, and not from others—but I think we have to respect that the information in that book is information that we can now study, we can now make our own opinions of, and perhaps we wouldn't have today, if they hadn't done that. So I honor them, the authors of that book.

They also believed, and I think this is true as well, that the Sacred Pole itself carries memories—many memories. It is a Person. It is alive. And, like a person, it carries memories. They understood that when they wrote the book, and they said that the Pole and its teachings would provide "a point of view as from the center" from which to understand how the Tribe had been able, for many, many years, up until 1888, to keep itself together as it moved from place to place and from generation to generation. They also wrote that everything that we can see or perceive in this world is created and maintained by a spiritual power known as Wakonda. And, this is what they have to say about it—I'm quoting now from the book [134].

> An invisible and continuous life
> permeates all things, seen and unseen.

This life manifests itself in two ways.
First, by causing to move:
All motion, all actions of mind and body,
are because of this invisible life.
[And] second, by causing permanency
of structure and form:
As in the rock, the physical features
of the landscape, mountains, plains, streams,
rivers, lakes, . . . animals and [lastly of] man.
This invisible life
Is similar to the will power
of which [a] man is conscious
within himself.
[It is] a power by which things are brought to pass.
Through this mysterious life and power
All things are related to one another
and to man.
The seen to the unseen,
the dead to the living,
A fragment of anything
to its entirety.
[And] this invisible life and power
[is] called Wakonda.

Wakonda is the spirit of life in the universe. It shows itself in the moving winds, and the resounding Thunders. It shows itself in the clans that have knowledge of these, and all the other powers. It shows itself in the sun's path across the daytime sky, as it reaches the highest point, and it shows itself in the fixed star at the center of the night sky, the star around which all the other stars turn. It's the star that in English we would call the Pole Star. Wakonda has the authority of cause and effect. Wakonda is a blessing, but it is also a powerful force of nature. The person who fails to keep sacred vows, the person who lies, or the person who fails in pity and compassion, will be touched by Wakonda in the same way that the forces of nature come back upon a person who ignores or disrespects them. When the people of today violate our mother the earth, they will discover that they are turning against the creative power of Wakonda itself.

In 1985, I came to know Omaha People in person as well as through the writings about the past, when the Tribe invited me here to the 1985 powwow. And I learned, at firsthand, that here in Macy the idea of the Sacred Pole, the idea of the Venerable Man is still very much alive—just as I knew from 1962 that the Venerable Man in the Peabody Museum was still alive when it touched my own spirit then. The IDEA of something spiritual is "similar to the will power of which a [person] is conscious within himself." It is "a power by which things are brought to pass." The idea of something is also a power that keeps things in control. An idea must keep control of one's life through knowledge, and through ceremony. We have ceremonies to give us the forms by which we can apply our knowledge in a meaningful and correct way. That's why we have the sacred arena here. That's why it is considered sacred. That's why when I see a feather drop, or I see a child walking around without knowing where it's supposed to be—I see people pay attention to that—because this is a place of ceremony. I also know that the story of the Sacred Pole is as important as the physical object itself. The Pole's last Keeper was a member of the Honga called Shudenachi (Yellow Smoke). His name, I understand, means that (it's more like a title) his title means that his very person was smoked yellow—like the sacred tent in which the Pole was kept.

In September of 1888—almost exactly a century ago—Yellow Smoke agreed to tell Frank La Flesche the Pole's sacred story so that it could be recorded for safekeeping in the book that we now know as *The Omaha Tribe*. And I'll just quote you the description that the authors give of that moment. They say:

> While the old chief talked he continually tapped the floor with a little stick . . . in his hand, marking with it the rhythm peculiar to the drumming of a man who is invoking the unseen powers during the performance of certain rites. His eyes were cast down, his speech was deliberate, and his voice [was] low, as if speaking to himself [224].

That story that Yellow Smoke told is part of Omaha tribal history. Many of you already know this history better than I ever could, but I would like at least to summarize for you the version that Fletcher and La Flesche wrote down from Yellow Smoke's words on that September afternoon a hundred years ago. I hope that those of you who know—and are able to tell other details to me—or to other people of the members of your Tribe, will do so. So, this is a summary of the story:

> The son of an Omaha Chief was hunting alone in the forest at a time when the elders were in council. They were in council to deal with a problem that the Tribe still has. That is—how to keep the People together. How to keep the People together and the Tribe from becoming extinct. That's not a new problem. That's one they had hundreds of years ago—according to this story. And, on his way home, as the Chiefs were deliberating, that young man became lost in the forest at night, and didn't know where he was. So, he stopped to rest and take his bearings. And, the only thing he could take his bearings from was (they didn't have compasses in those days) was the Pole Star—that "motionless star" at the center of the night sky around which all the other stars turn. And as he was looking at that Pole Star, and taking his bearings from it, finding the north, he looked down at the earth—and just below where the Pole Star was shining in the sky—he was attracted by a light. And as he approached that light he saw that it was "a tree that sent forth light." That young man went up to the tree, and he saw that the whole tree, its trunk, its branches, its leaves, were alight, and

yet they were not burning up. It was not consuming itself. It was simply glowing throughout the night.

And he watched that luminous tree all night. Stared at it. It was a powerful vision. Until finally, as the sun came up, the tree resumed its normal appearance. It became an ordinary tree. And he remained by that tree throughout the entire day—so that he wouldn't lose it. And, the next night, he looked again and sure enough the tree began to glow again. And when the young man returned home, he told his father of this wonder that he had beheld. And together they went to see the tree, and they saw it—all alight, as it had been before. But his father, who was an older and more knowledgeable man, observed something that had escaped the notice of the young man. This was that the paths of—four animal paths—led up to the tree. One for each of the four sacred directions. These paths were well beaten and as the two men examined the paths and the tree, it was clear to them that the animals had come to the tree and had rubbed against it—and they looked and they saw that the bark was all polished from the bodies of the animals coming from the four directions.

The young man's father went back and he reported what he had seen to the Chiefs. He said, "My son has seen a wonderful tree. The Thunder birds come and go upon this tree, making a trail of fire that leaves four paths on the burnt grass that stretch toward the Four Winds. When the Thunder birds alight on the tree it bursts into flame and the fire mounts to the top. The tree stands burning, but no one can see the fire except at night."

When they heard this, the men went to the tree in turn. They stripped, they painted themselves, they put on their ornaments—just as I see people here wearing regalia. They painted themselves, and they ran toward the tree in a race as if "to attack the tree as if it were a warrior enemy." The first man to reach the tree struck it as he would an enemy. And then they cut the tree down "and four men, walking in a line, carried it on their shoulders back to the village." They made a tent for the tree and they set it up at the center of the circle of lodges, just like the flagpole is set up here at the center of this powwow arena.

The Chiefs worked upon the tree; they trimmed it and they called it a human being. They made a basketwork receptacle of twigs and feathers (a kind of woven—twigs and feathers woven around with—and tied this around the middle) and they placed a large scalp lock on top of the Pole for hair. Then they painted the Pole and they set it up before the tent, and they leaned it on a crotched stick which they called "the staff" because they called it their "Venerable Man" and they had to lean it on a stick. When all the People were gathered the Chiefs stood up and they said, "You now see before you a mystery. Whenever we meet with troubles we shall bring all our troubles to Him (the Pole). We shall make offerings and requests. All our prayers must be accompanied by gifts. This (the Pole) belongs to all the People, but it shall be in the keeping of one family (in the Honga) and the leadership shall be with them. If anyone desires to lead and take responsibility for governing the People, he shall make presents to the Keepers of the Pole and they shall give him the authority." When all was finished the People said, "Let us appoint a time when we shall . . . paint him and act before him the battles we have fought." So the time was fixed, and it was to take place in "The Moon When the Buffaloes Bellow," which will be the moon that's full in July. This was the beginning of the Ceremony of Renewal—the Ceremony called Waxthexe xigithe—which means (I'm probably not saying this right), but it means "to paint the Pole, to anoint the Pole with red."

La Flesche describes how the Pole actually left Macy and how it came to the Peabody Museum. He says—these are his words:

After dinner, . . . we sat smoking in the shade of the trees, [and] we spoke of the past life of the Tribe and from time to time [and] in our conversation I pleasantly reminded [Shudenachi of the times when] within my own knowledge, and of others of which I had heard, where his knowledge guided the actions of the people. This seemed to please him very much and he spoke more freely of the . . . customs of the Omaha. He was an important man in his younger days and quite an orator. I have heard him deliver an address on the spur of the moment that would have done credit to almost any speaker in either branch of our congress. He was one of the signers of the treaty entered into between the Omaha and the United States.

As my visit was drawing to a close, without any remarks leading thereto, I suddenly swooped down upon the old Chief with the audacious question: "Why don't you send the 'Venerable Man' to some eastern city where he could dwell in a great brick house instead of a ragged tent?" A smile crept over the face of the Chieftain as he softly whistled a tune and tapped the ground with his pipe stick before he replied, while I sat breathlessly awaiting the answer, for I greatly desired the preservation of this ancient and unique relic. The pipe had cooled and he proceeded to clean it. He blew through it now and then as he gave me this answer: [He said] "My son, I have thought about this myself but no one whom I could trust has hitherto approached me upon this subject. I shall think about it, and [I] will give you a definite answer when I see you again."

The next time I was at his house [La Flesche writes] [Yellow Smoke] conducted me to the Sacred Tent and delivered to me the Pole and its belongings. This was the first time that it was purposely touched by anyone outside of its hereditary Keepers [248–49].

At the beginning of the Moon When the Buffaloes Bellow this year (27 June 1988), Omaha hands once again touched the Venerable Man for the first time in a hundred years. My wife and I were witness to that event that took place in a little courtyard outside the Peabody Museum to which I was returning myself for the first time in more than twenty years. As the Ceremony began, I remembered the words that Fletcher and La Flesche quoted from an elder of long ago who told them:

> Tears were made by Wakonda as a relief to our human nature; Wakonda made joy and he also made tears! . . . From my earliest years I remember the sound of weeping; I have heard it all my long life and [I] shall hear it until I die. There will be partings as long as man lives on [this] earth; Wakonda has willed it to be so! [598].

The Keeper of a particular ceremony, the elders say, wept whenever there was a break in the ritual order for which he was responsible. He wept because he trusted that the compassion of Wakonda will always send someone to wipe away the tears. On 27 June I watched as Mr. Joe Johns, a Creek Indian artist-in-residence at the Peabody Museum, carried your Venerable Man out into the life-giving winds beneath a great round summer sun for the first time in a hundred years. I saw your Tribal Chairman, Yellow Smoke's great-great grandson Mr. Doran Morris, weep as it came into Omaha hands again. I saw him weep as he and your former Tribal Chairman, Mr. Edward Cline, had wept with elders of your People before coming to visit the Pole for the Ceremony. They wept for the break of a hundred years in the life of your Venerable Man. They wept for the compassion of the night. They wept for you Instashunda, you Hongashenu, to come and wipe away the tears. As Edward Cline said following this beautiful Ceremony, he hoped that renewing contact with the Pole would inspire us to "talk as one person . . . [to] think and do as one group of people."

The elders told Fletcher and La Flesche that the Sacred Pole stands for emotion as well as for intelligence. The power it represents is both compassionate to people, but it is also a reflection of the compassion that exists within them. The Venerable Man today represents the compassion that night has for day. It represents the intelligence of a single fixed point in the night sky, as the young man saw it long ago. It represents the sense of direction that he found, and the sense of direction that the Omaha People have always had—to keep them together to this very moment, as I see you here together today. It represents the proper coming together of people in ceremony, in families—acting in the right way—the coming together of man and woman, the proper coming together of day and night, of sky and earth, of Instashunda and of Hongashenu. It represents your survival. You have survived as a People, Instashunda, Hongashenu, because you have kept the ideas of your traditions alive. One of these traditions is the blue spot that I mentioned earlier—the Mark of Honor.

Women among you have worn the blue spot for all these years. They have worn it as part of themselves. They have worn it because of the compassion their fathers showed for needy people of your Tribe. They have worn it as people blessed by the night. They have worn it as an emblem of the night's compassion for the son of a Chief who discovered the tree on which the

Thunder birds came to earth, many centuries ago. They have worn it as a reminder of the balance between day and night. Vision came to that young man long ago when the dark of night showed him that the stars circle around a single point of light among their multitude. Even today, the Pole that came from his vision rests on a staff so that it points at a 45 degree angle toward where its Keeper knows that the Pole Star will be. And when Mr. Joe Johns carried it out of the Peabody Museum, he carried it out at the correct angle—45 degrees—up to where the Pole Star will be, when you see it, when you can see it again at night. The vision of the young woman receiving the Mark of Honor comes as a gift of the sun—comes as a gift of the sun as it passes through the highest point of the sky during the day.

During the buffalo hunting days, your People fed the Sacred Pole and they painted it with buffalo fat and red paint. That Ceremony of Renewal they called "the Sacred Pole to tinge with red." You no longer travel as a People from place to place on the buffalo hunt but you do continue to travel together in time. You do come together each year in this sacred arena to renew yourselves as a People. I will conclude my talk today with a brief description of this Renewal Ceremony which, I think, will give you some ideas to think about as you continue the renewal that you are participating in now.

The Ceremony of Renewal traditionally takes place in a large tipi—a tipi that was like the house of all the People—a tipi that was like this arena—a circle open to the East where all the People could come, and they could find life together. The Chiefs met in council before the Renewal Ceremony. They decided that a certain group of men should go out among them and secure the tipi poles to build the ceremonial tipi that would be the house of renewal. Each of the Seven Chiefs took a reed—a stick from a bundle of sticks that they kept throughout the year in a sacred tent. There was a reed in this bundle (a stick in this bundle) for each man of the Tribe. The Chiefs then called out the names of the men whose reeds they had chosen. They chose them in the same way that, that when you have a raffle and you choose a raffle ticket, and then you call out the name of the person. They called out the names of the men whose sticks had been chosen. They then called out the accomplishments of each man—his honors, his names. The tribal herald then took the reeds out into the camp circle and gave them to the men who had been chosen. That was a responsibility to that man. Each man then took his reed, his stick, back to the Sacred Tent, and that was a sign that he had accepted both the honor, and also the responsibility, of being chosen. He placed his stick back into the bundle kept by the Keeper. Then he had to fulfill his obligation.

Each of the men whose sticks had been chosen went out among the People, and instead of being an arena with bleachers around it, it was a sacred circle of tipis—of tents—of lodges, with all of the People camped according to their clans. The People—the men whose sticks had been chosen—went to every single one of these lodges, and they went into each lodge and they selected a single lodge pole—a single tipi pole—and they touched it. They touched that pole in the same way that your Tribal Chairman touched the

Sacred Pole, in the same way that the men of the Tribe long ago touched it when they found it. They touched that pole, and it became sacred. And then, members of the Tribe brought back these poles, one from each lodge, and used those poles to create a tipi in which the Renewal Ceremony would take place. A single stick stands for a single man of the Tribe. A single lodge pole stands for a single family of the Tribe. The lodge that they made from all of these lodge poles stands for the possibility of the Tribe renewing itself. And the Sacred Pole stands for the Tribe as a whole.

Throughout the Ceremony of Renewal, the Honga support the Tribe in the same way that the Keeper physically supports the Pole, as he carries it from camp to camp, but that support—whoever it is who supports the Pole—is not possible without the support from the Tribe itself. They have to support him, in the same way that he supports the Pole. They have to be there. Everyone in the Tribe has to be there together—to wipe away the Keeper's tears—whoever it is who has touched that Pole. They take that burden from him. They take it because it is theirs. It is their responsibility.

Frank La Flesche describes what he calls a "boyhood memory" which illustrates some of the power in the Pole. He describes that one day he and some friends of his got a little tired and reckless, and they cracked a whip at a couple of the horses they were driving. One of these horses took off, and it nearly ran down the old man who was carrying the Sacred Pole. This is when they were moving from one camp to another. And the young boy then (Frank La Flesche), went back to his dad and he told him. First he was scared to tell him, but then he thought, "Well, I've just got to say something," so he told him what had happened, and his dad said, "You have to go to the Pole and talk to Him," so that the young man, who became Frank La Flesche, the author of the book, went to the Pole and he said, "Venerable Man! We have, without any intention of disrespect, touched you and we have come to ask to be cleansed from the wrong that we have done." The old man "took from [him a] scarlet cloth [which he had brought], said a few words of thanks, and [then] re-entered the tent; soon he returned carrying in his hand a wooden bowl filled with warm water. He lifted his right hand to the sky and [he] wept, then [he] sprinkled us [he says] and the horses with . . . water, using a spray of [sweet sage]. This act washed away the anger of the 'Venerable Man' " [245].

In the Ceremony, the Ceremony is completed when the wife of the Keeper of the Pole takes seven arrows—one for each of the Seven Chiefs—and she shoots the seven arrows through the wickerwork bundle that is called the wrist shield, or the wrist guard of the Pole, like it was the wrist guard that an archer, a bowman, would wear. She shoots these through the wrist guard of the Pole and directly into the earth—and if each one of these seven arrows goes into the earth, and sticks in there firmly, it is a sign that the People will be blessed throughout the year—that they will be successful in their buffalo hunting, that they will be successful against attack by enemies. The Ceremony is no longer done—it hasn't been done for over a hundred years—because it was involved in the buffalo hunt, and your People are no longer buffalo hunters. But you People are alive, you have survived, you have survived together as a People.

This summer, Omaha hands once again touched and held the Venerable Man. Following the Ceremony, Edward Cline said a few words of thanks on your behalf to the directors and curators of the Peabody Museum. He said that he and Doran Morris had come as "simple people," not as great Chiefs, and his words reminded me that in the Renewal Ceremony, the Seven Chiefs selected a reed from the bundle of reeds that represented each man of the Tribe. As I said, these men would then go out among the lodges of the People and select a single pole from each one with which to build the Sacred Lodge of renewal. When it was my turn to speak I said, "I see the two of you here today as being like members of your Tribe whose sticks have been chosen. You're going to go back and you're going to be touching the lodge poles of other People back home—[of all] the Omaha People who are interested in [your traditions, and the Sacred Pole]—and this is the beginning of building another Sacred Lodge, a Sacred Lodge where the Tribe will continue to renew itself." The idea of renewal is still strong among you. I look out upon you Instashunda, Hongashenu, with the wistfulness of a child waiting for some good thing to happen, as the elders said People looked out upon the place where the renewal would take place. I thank you for giving me an opportunity to share in the renewal that is continuing to take place in this sacred arena. I thank you for allowing me to be witness to these events that have taken place, and I hope that I will continue to witness the renewal that you are undertaking. I will conclude this with a simple blessing that we can all share: "All my relations." I would also like to thank you, to thank Doran Morris for inviting us here, to thank you all for the hospitality you have shown us, and I finally would like to contribute a small sum, a gift of twenty dollars to the powwow committee. Thank you.

Conclusion: A Point of View as from the Center

The Venerable Man of the Omaha Tribe is alive. He is a person. He is a person with a long history. He is a wonderful tree.

> The Thunder birds come and go upon this tree,
> making a trail of fire
> that leaves four paths on the burnt grass
> that stretch toward the Four Winds.
> When the Thunder birds alight on the tree
> it bursts into flame
> and the fire mounts to the top.
> The tree stands burning,
> but no one can see the fire except at night.

Alice Fletcher and Francis La Flesche placed Omaha words and images within the pages of the Twenty-seventh Annual Report of the

Bureau of American Ethnology. They placed the Sacred Pole in the "great brick house" in Cambridge, Massachusetts. The words are alive as the Pole is alive. Together, they provide "a point of view as from the center" from which to understand the meaning of Omaha identity. But no one can see the fire except at night. No one can see it without a vision of the center, a point of view.

There are many ways of keeping traditions alive. Yellow Smoke was a Keeper within the authority of his Leader Clan. He kept the Pole and its words as others had done before him. During the years that the Venerable Man rested in the Peabody Museum, Instashunda People and Hongashenu People continued to come together in ceremony. They came together as man and woman. They came together in family life. They came together as a Tribe. Thunders rolled over the hills of Macy, Nebraska, as they have always done. Women bearing the Mark of Honor continued to take pity on those among the People who were weak and in need of care. Few of these women are left now, and they are very old. A young man's vision will renew the life that slips away from their bodies. More than a hundred winters have come and gone over brick house and sacred arena alike. The time has come now for the Venerable Man to move among the People once more.

The Story Continues

When I first began to write about the Sacred Pole of the Omaha Tribe in 1984, I imagined that his story had come to a definitive end in 1888. I remember wondering as I wrote whether Omahas might still be living somewhere in Nebraska. I recalled that Margaret Mead had described them as a "broken culture" in 1932. She said they were "culturally deprived" (xiii–xiv). Then in the spring of 1985, I went to the National Anthropological Archives in Washington, D.C. I wanted to see the fieldnotes or other unpublished material that Fletcher and La Flesche might have left behind. While there, I discovered that other scholars had recently been through the same material. One was Joan Mark, who was then in the process of writing a biography of Alice Fletcher (Mark 1988). The other was an Omaha tribal historian, Dennis Hastings. I phoned Joan at her home in Cambridge, Massachusetts, to find out what she knew about Dennis and the Tribe. She told me to write Dennis at the tribal office in Macy. "Macy," I said. "Where's that?" "In eastern Nebraska," she replied. "It's on the Omaha reservation." So began my first contact with the Omaha Tribe.

Following Joan's advice, I sent the first draft of a paper about the Sacred Pole to Dennis. Soon after, I received a phone call from him at my office in Vancouver. "I liked what you wrote," he said, "but you should really come down and visit us here. Why don't you come down for our powwow?" Jillian and I were pleased to take Dennis up on his invitation. Our first Omaha powwow was in the summer of 1985. To our astonishment, we learned that there were still women alive who bore the blue spot, the "Mark of Honor." We were taken to meet two of them, Maggie Johnson and Helen Grant Walker, by Marguerite La Flesche, the granddaughter of Francis La Flesche's brother. My relationship to the Tribe deepened over the next few years until I found myself taking part, at the request of the Tribal Chairman, in negotiations with the Peabody Museum for the Pole's return. It was as if I had suddenly discovered a continuation of the story that I thought had broken off a century before. Astonishingly, I found that I was a character in the story. My thoughts about Omaha tradition that had begun as an exercise in the history of anthropology had grown into a relationship with the Pole himself. I recalled what Fletcher and La Flesche said about the power of thought in Omaha philosophy. I realized that by thinking seriously about the Sacred Pole, I had become responsible to an idea that is still alive among the People. Fletcher and La Flesche report:

> The Omaha estimate of the value of thought is strongly brought out in their Sacred Legend, which briefly recounts their experiences from the time when they "opened their eyes and beheld the day" down to the adoption of the Sacred Pole as an emblem of governmental authority. Every acquisition that bettered the condition of the people was the result of the exercise of the mind. "And the people thought" is the preamble to every change; every new acquirement, every arrangement devised to foster tribal unity and to promote tribal strength, was the outcome of thought. The regulation of the tribal hunt, wherein the individual was forced to give way for the good of the whole people; the punishment of murder as a social offense; the efforts to curb the disintegrating war spirit, to bring it under control, to make it conserve rather than disrupt the unity of the tribe—all were the result of "thought." So, too, was the tribal organization itself, which was based on certain ideas evolved from thinking over natural processes what were ever before their observation. The Sacred Legend speaks truly when it says "And the people thought." (1911:608–9)

The story you have been reading describes how "the people thought" in order to renew contact with the Sacred Pole. On 12 July 1989 in the moon when the buffaloes bellow, the Venerable Man came home to the Omaha reservation. Doran Morris rested him on a forked stick at the western edge of the powwow arena. Elders of the Tribe prayed

over him and burned cedar in his honor. They referred to him as
Umoⁿhoⁿti, the "real Omaha." The meaning of this title is that he is
a person who stands for all the People, a tribal metonym, a part that
stands for the whole. He returned later that summer for the powwow,
or We'wachi Ceremony, and again for the same Ceremony in 1990.
The Tribe hopes in time to develop a cultural center and museum on
reservation land overlooking the Missouri River. Until that plan is
realized, they have asked the University of Nebraska State Museum at
Lincoln to provide temporary storage for the Pole and other sacred
objects that the Peabody Museum returned to the Tribe.

The generations of Omahas who grew up with little or no knowledge
of the Tribe's buffalo hunting days now have an opportunity to center
their thoughts on *Umoⁿhoⁿti,* an enduring and living symbol of Omaha
identity. His return has compelled both Omahas and non-Indian anthropologists to think about the Pole. Omaha opinion is divided on
the meaning of his return. Many of the elders welcomed him as a
blessing from the past. Others are ambivalent or even fearful because
they no longer practice the ceremonies through which the Tribe honored him long ago. The Tribe wishes to relieve those fears by education.
Through the efforts of Dennis Hastings, Omaha tribal members have
joined scholars and administrators to form the Omaha Tribal Historical
Research Project, which is now incorporated as a nonprofit corporation
with the following objectives:

1. to promote and encourage research regarding the history, heritage,
language, religion, and other aspects of the culture of the Omaha for
the purposes of encouraging the preservation of the materials and
information collected

2. perpetuating the Omaha culture and traditions, and to serve as
an educational resource for Omaha People and other people who may
be interested in the culture and traditions of the Omaha Tribe of
Nebraska.

On 14 January 1991, the tribal council passed the following resolution:

> NOW THEREFORE BE IT RESOLVED THAT the Omaha Tribal Council
> hereby authorizes and pledges its support for the Omaha Tribal His-
> torical Research Project to facilitate academic and cultural preservation
> projects pursuing another five and ten year strategic plan for the gen-
> erations of the Omaha Tribe.

All My Relations

The time has come for the anthropologists who have been keeping
and caring for the Pole to discover a language in which to communicate

with him and with members of the Tribe. The Omaha Tribal Historical Research Project provides an opportunity for scholars to join with tribal members in thinking about the Tribe's past in relations to its future. Participants in the project are discovering a center for their thoughts that is like the motionless star under which a Chief's son long ago discovered a tree that stands burning. I am glad to be a part of that discovery. The story continues. All my relations.

Dub Poetry and West Indian Identity

Michael V. Angrosino

Expressive forms (poetry, fiction, drama, music, oral history) have often been mobilized to enhance the ethnic or national consciousness of West Indians. The need for such symbolic affirmation of identity has deepened in the past two decades as the pace of migration—from smaller to larger islands/territories and from the Caribbean itself to Europe and North America—has increased.

In the city in southern Florida where I live, the small but growing group of migrants from various parts of the English-speaking Caribbean is finding a sense of community in several social clubs where traditional distinctions between, for example, Jamaicans and Trinidadians are less important than their shared identity as West Indians. Although the West Indians can and do make common cause with the indigenous African-American community on a variety of political and economic issues, they like to think of themselves as black people with a distinctive culture and social tradition.

The clubs are, therefore, not only places where West Indians can socialize but are also centers of the active promotion of pan-Caribbean culture. They sponsor appearances by performers from the West Indies, as well as by authorities who lecture on current political, economic, and artistic affairs. The clubs further function as centers of an active communications network linking the West Indian diaspora; newsletters and other correspondence are regularly exchanged with clubs in Britain, Canada, and New York, as well as with relatives and friends back home. A few of the clubs also see themselves as having a public relations function. To that end they encourage the participation of non–West Indians in the hope of disseminating knowledge about and sympathy for Caribbean culture. "We want them to forget the 'Day-o' image," one club leader told me (chuckling ruefully as he did so because of the newfound popularity of "The Banana Boat Song," which was featured in a recent hit movie). This goal is fostered by the proximity of several of the clubs to the campus of a large state university where there is an active and vocal Caribbean Student Association; several of the faculty are also engaged in West Indian research.

During the past several years, club patrons have learned about a new movement, "dub poetry," from people in touch with happenings in Jamaica and Britain. One of the clubs has sponsored regular appearances by a dub poet from Jamaica. His stage name, like that of many of the dub artists, was chosen to evoke a "revolutionary African" image. I will refer to him as Touré Lumumba. He became my main informant about this new artistic direction.

The dub phenomenon is intimately related to one of the most pressing politico-cultural issues facing contemporary West Indians — the question of the "nation language." West Indian English has long been considered a debased dialect, and West Indians who have aspired to any sort of advancement at home or abroad were forced to adopt the standard language. Since the advent of a Black Power consciousness in the early 1970s, West Indian intellectuals have denounced this subtle, but damaging, form of imperialism. They have upheld the validity of West Indian English as a language in its own right (echoing the arguments of proponents of Black English in the United States) and have taken to calling it the "nation language." As such, it is a potent symbol of a nascent consciousness of an identity separate from that of the old colonial "metropole."

Dub poetry, among other things, is an attempt to use the nation language as the vehicle for the expression of political and social values of non-elite West Indians and to do so in terms of what Lumumba calls "serious verse—not just song lyrics." Lumumba, however, is keenly aware of the dangers inherent in translating the fluid, demotic "parole" into a deliberately composed poetic "langue." The vernacular is threatened to the extent that it achieves standardization. Can the voice of the people, Lumumba asks, retain its "revolutionary potential" if it goes the way of formalization? On the other hand, can it be taken seriously, even by non-elite people, if it does not achieve the legitimization of the written form?

Lumumba's concern parallels a set of issues prominent in the anthropological study of literacy and the symbolic expression of identity in the shift from an oral to a literate social system. It should be kept in mind that my point of view in this analysis will be that of the politically conscious social clubs in one (perhaps atypical) corner of the West Indian diaspora. The people among whom I have studied dub poetry have sharp concerns about assimilation that may not trouble dub poetry's audience in the West Indies, or in very large, somewhat self-contained West Indian communities such as those in Britain. Moreover, the consciously sought ties to the university reflect my informants' general inclination to think of their art forms in critical, conceptual terms. I do not in any sense presume to represent the views of the larger audience for dub poetry either in the Caribbean or abroad. My bias is also shaped by the views of my key informant, whose point of view is admittedly a minority opinion even among dub artists. I am willing to suggest, however, that my informants may only be articulating concerns that are felt but not directly addressed by others involved in the dub movement, either as performers or as audience.

The Consequences of Literacy: A Conceptual Overview

According to Goody (1968:1), writing is not simply a convenience — it is a new medium of communication, one that *objectifies* and *preserves* speech by encoding it in visible signs. In Goody's view, language in preliterate societies developed in "intimate association with the experience of the community" and was learned through face-to-face communication (1968:30–31). In oral discourse, consciousness of the word as a separate entity is limited. But in the written form, words "may take on a life of their own" (53), a process also referred to as the "decontextualization of discourse" (Scollon and Scollon 1981:48). More broadly, writing preserves not only the act of speech but the entire cultural tradition from which the individual speech act derives. That tradition can thus be recorded for later reference. Such an act of cultural preservation has obvious advantages, but it also serves to divorce the individual from the immediate expression of that tradition. The individual can analyze the tradition at a dispassionate distance, rather than be personally involved in its transmission. Because it lends itself to analysis, the written tradition tends to become more heterogeneous and idiosyncratic through time. The oral tradition, by contrast, tends toward formalized, even stereotypical, communication as an aid to the transmission by memory (Goody 1968:63).

Despite the formalization of oral *literature,* the oral language is subject to fairly rapid change because it is constantly being created in the act of interpersonal communication. By contrast, the written form of a language achieves formal standardization even as the written literature develops great diversity. Written literature can generate a body of "classic" works, but since the survival of new ones is not dependent on anyone either understanding them or passing them on (they can be printed and then sit on the shelf indefinitely until an audience for them emerges), new writings can and do vary considerably from the original classics in both form and content.

In the preliterate folk society, everyone can be engaged in the transmission of the oral tradition. But in a literate society, people are "faced with permanent, recorded versions of the past and its beliefs" (Goody 1968:67). In other words, the objective, physical presence of the written word encourages skepticism about received ideas, since the reader does not necessarily have a personal stake in the creation or the maintenance of "the word." As a result, literate cultures come to value the possibilities of alternative explanations more than they do the sense of permanence and continuity embodied in the oral tradition.

With writing it becomes possible, in the ideal at least, to "perfect" language so that it conveys every conceivable nuance of personal meaning. Such an end can only be thought possible if language is treated not as subject to the vagaries of interpersonal interaction, but as inherently lawful and orderly. Discourse that can convey meaning because of paralinguistic cues available in face-to-face communication must become more formally grammatical and rule-bound if it is to be precise when divorced from that interactive context. Initial translation of the vernacular to a written literary form seeks to preserve all the ungrammatical, contextualized meanings of the original speech, but since oral discourse looks confusing on the printed page, the written form moves toward a regularized standard. According to Scollon and Scollon (1981:91), decontextualization is accompanied by the creation of "an explicit, grammatically and lexically marked information structure which is high in new information, and the fictionalization of the roles of author, audience, and in the autobiography of the self." To put it more simply, the written word may *evoke* the sound of the vernacular, but it cannot recapture the sense of real people conveying meaning to each other within the context of a shared set of assumptions about the nature of the world. The writer is inevitably tempted in the direction of a *personal* expression achieved through the skillful manipulation of grammatical form. This meaningful and worthwhile aesthetic aim separates the resulting text from the immediate vernacular exchange the writer originally set out to evoke, or even to celebrate.

Oral Traditions in West Indian Literature

The English-speaking Caribbean has produced an extensive and impressive body of prose and poetry, and the region has nurtured a vibrant literary community that includes several writers of international stature. This literary circle has historically been linked to the artistic life of "metropolitan" centers of English literature, such as London or New York, but anglophone West Indian writers have not been unaware of the irony of their position. On the one hand, they have tended to see themselves as spokespersons for (and sometimes as leaders of) their people, giving voice to the inchoate aspirations of the dispossessed colonial masses. Indeed, Brown (1984:9–10) has stated that the strength of West Indian literature, especially poetry, has been in its "capacity to transform the 'nothingness' of the past into the source of creative self-consciousness." But to the extent that the artists have viewed themselves as *writers* ("authorship," in the colonial milieu, having no other legitimate form), they have known that to secure publication— not to mention a serious readership—they would have to write in a style that would be comprehensible, and even pleasing, to their metropolitan audiences. The result was the creation of an elite literature "appreciated" by metropolitan literati as evidence of the emerging sophistication of "the colonies," and yet purporting to speak to the feelings, views, and even grievances of the people back home—people who had very limited access to the printed word.

There have always been West Indian writers who used local dialect in their work to keep up their connection to the people for whom they spoke. But their solution was, until the 1960s, mostly limited to dialogue passages involving "folk" characters embedded in narratives written in standard English. Over the years poets and playwrights— followed at some distance by novelists—debated the merits of composing complete selections in the vernacular. Such a choice would have political as well as aesthetic implications, since it would be an overt statement of solidarity with those outside the political establishment and far from the literary mainstream. Artists who decided in favor of the vernacular felt that they had a message to convey and a consciousness-raising role to play in the political development of their region. But, of course, they could not convey that message to the audience most in need of having its consciousness raised. They used the nation language of the people—but they *wrote* it and hence alienated it from people who may not have been technically illiterate, but who were rarely in a position to obtain books printed in Europe or North America. The political aims of these artists might have been more immediately achievable had they employed the nation language in oral media. But since they were products of the metropole-oriented colonial education system, they could not really feel themselves to be validating that language *unless* they transferred it to writing. One way out of this dilemma seemed to be the union of oral expression with other art forms, especially music. The development of a performance-based oral literature seemed a more valid and aesthetically serious aim than "simple story-telling."

West Indian Nation Language

The demotic speech of non-elite West Indians is a very diverse phenomenon, the result of a complex interplay of historical circumstances. For one thing, British colonists were themselves a mixed lot, so there was no single standard of the "King's English" to be heard. This diversity was accentuated in places such as Barbados, where Irish people predominated among the colonists, and Jamaica, where many of the white settlers originally came from Scotland. At the same time, the slaves were being taken from various parts of Africa and did not share a unified linguistic background. Slave trading moved gradually eastward along the West African coast during the colonial period, so islands populated early on, such as Jamaica, received many Ashanti-speaking slaves, while islands colonized later on were dominated by people from Dahomey and then the Yoruba-speaking areas. The English of various territories was further influenced by the other Europeans who happened to be prominent in those areas—Jamaica, the English-speaking enclave in the Greater Antilles, was surrounded by Spanish-speaking islands, while the islands of the Lesser Antilles were more in contact with the French, and the Guianas with the Dutch. To complete the mixture, certain territories (notably Trinidad and the Guianas) were heavily influenced by plantation labor imported from India following the abolition of slavery. Still other territories, such as the British Windwards, were relatively late in exterminating their native populations and so were influenced by Amerindian languages as well (see Le Page 1969 for elaboration).

Despite this mixed linguistic heritage, there are some distinct characteristics of phonology, grammar, lexicon, intonation, and stress pattern that are typical of all West Indian English varieties. Taken as a whole, West Indian English is clearly different from the English of England, the United States, and Canada. For example, West Indian English tends to use more open, less nasalized vowels than does standard English, and there are relatively more palatalized than dentalized consonants as compared with standard English. West Indian English tends to omit endings for the plural and past tense (see Le Page 1969:4; Le Page and Tabouret-Keller 1985).

There is a temptation to treat these distinctions as if they were "merely" quirks of speech and not significant dialectical variants on standard English. But the intent of the current proponents of the nation language is to demonstrate that West Indian English is sufficiently different from standard English so as to constitute an essentially distinctive way of encoding—and hence of reacting to—the world (Moore

1974:69). This argument is similar to that which surrounded the Black English controversy in the United States (Gumperz 1976).

If we provisionally accept the status of the nation language as a distinct language, then we must address the cultural consequences of "reducing" it to writing. There is no inevitability to such a "reduction." Dub poetry, as we shall see, began as another form of oral expression and, in the minds of at least some of its practitioners, that is what it should remain. But various factors have led many dub poets to follow the lead of *writers* of poetry, as distinct from performers thereof.

Performance-based Oral Literature

Calypso, the Caribbean art form that achieved international popularity in the years following World War II, began as an expression of political social protest. Its language was drawn from that of the urban lower class of Port of Spain, Trinidad. As Rohlehr (1972:13) has noted, it was "the language of the small-time confidence trickster... whose method is to spin words fast enough to ensnare his victim, or, in the case of the calypsonian, to 'captivate' his audience." While the calypso has, in some places, been turned into an officially sanctioned "folk art" for the tourist trade, it still retains the flavor of protest. Its essential method is to employ the exuberant vernacular to embody the good sense of the common people as they mock the pretensions of the elite. (The tourists, infected by the peppy, "jump-up" beat, rarely pay attention to the lyrics.) Nevertheless, no matter how clever calypso lyrics are, or how widely they are quoted, the calypsonians rarely think of themselves as writers of poetry. Their lyrics are inextricably tied to their songs and to their performance.

Reggae, despite its diverse roots as a musical form, flowered as the vehicle of social consciousness among lower-class West Indians at home and abroad at a more recent time of deepening economic malaise and political violence. Reggae has a large and heterogeneous international audience, but it is still thought of as the legitimate voice of dissent by many politically conscious lower-class West Indians. Reggae is composed almost exclusively in the nation language, the most appropriate vehicle of dissent. One explanation of the origin of the name is that it is the lower-class singers' parody of the way middle-class people disparagingly say "raga," short for "ragamuffin," the label applied to the poor of the Kingston slums (Plummer 1978:41).

Some reggae artists have therefore come to feel that their message is of sufficient political import that it transcends the act of performance. A few, led by the late Bob Marley, have had their lyrics published in anthologies of poetry in England. This precedent set the stage for the emergence of dub poetry and for the paradoxical situation in which the poets find themselves. The paradox, then, is that in attempting to reproduce the nation language in written form, West Indian authors inadvertently move away from the coherence of the folk tradition that they profess to celebrate. Their attempted evocation of social solidarity thus becomes a factor in the eventual subversion of that solidarity. Although literacy has been encouraged in the Third World as a means to "empower" the masses (a notion given its most passionate support in the writings of the Brazilian theorist Paulo Freire), it really only has revolutionary impact when it is promoted by a revolutionary regime already committed to the empowerment of the masses. Literacy fostered by moderate regimes serves mainly to push the masses into the mainstream and away from their folk traditions (Smith 1986:271). When a theory of revolutionary empowerment is united with a literary movement that extols the folk tradition, the effect is even more ambiguous. The resulting literature is supposed to be a mirror of the experiences and aspirations of the masses, and yet by objectifying their experience, it renders it subject to criticism and revision.

Dub Poetry

Dub poetry began in the Jamaican reggae clubs and was fostered by reggae artists who, while not necessarily Rastafarians, were heavily influenced by Rasta "style."[1] During the 1970s, disc jockeys in the Kingston clubs emerged as celebrities in their own right, offering commentary on the music they played, as well as on political events of the day. As their influence spread, they were able to persuade Jamaican record producers to publish records with a "dub side," that is, the instrumental backing of popular dance numbers with the vocal tracks removed ("dubbed out"). The DJs would play these "dub sides" and improvise their own "raps" to fit the rhythms. These raps were half-sung, half-spoken, and soon acquired choreography as part of the number. The "dub lyrics" thus improvised were usually topical and satirical in nature (Burnett 1986).

Burnett suggests that the DJs' raps were merely unions of the old Afro-Caribbean tradition of rhythmic oral expression (see Abrahams 1983) with a new technology. It was not long, however, before people whom Lumumba considers "serious poets" realized the potential in the mingling of oral expression with a compelling musical beat. They then began composing "serious" poems that were specifically designed to be recited to music in live performance—a move in the direction of formal poetry and away from the purely extemporaneous "rap" of the first DJ-dubbers. Thus was born "dub poetry" as a consciously created art form, and by the late 1970s there were dub poets appearing in England, as well as in Jamaica and Trinidad.

There is a difference of opinion among the dub poets about the role of music. Some prefer to consider themselves as poets in a very traditional sense; they seek publication for their verse and do not account themselves successful unless they have appeared in print, despite the "revolutionary" diction of their nation language. Others feel that the music, which may or may not be specifically composed for the occasion, is still more than just incidental—they see theirs as a performance art in which words, the musical beat, and electronic techniques such as reverberation are thoroughly integrated. Lumumba is a partisan of this latter position, and he makes a convincing case that the future of dub poetry as an art form is in performance, not in words on a printed page, because the performance is unique and capable of capturing the nuances of changing mood and vibrant emotion that have revolutionary potential. He adds that recording, while important for prestige, tends to "fix" both the text and the delivery as much as a printed version does. Therefore a true dub poet will try to make each live performance as different as possible from all others. A performance of dub poetry must never be reduced to a script, he insists, for the poet must respond to the beat of the music at the time of the performance, as well as to the temper of the specific audience gathered for that performance. Many dub poets would agree with Lumumba's purism in theory, but few are in a position to disdain attractive publishing and recording contracts. They thus continue to perform numbers that have already been "fixed" in a standard form. No matter how hard they try to keep the spontaneity in those performances, they must at some point respond to the expectations of an audience that knows the number from a record or from having read it in a book.

The dub poets who have worked extensively in Jamaica before emigrating have tended to be trained as actors and so have distinctive stage presences; a number of them studied at the Jamaica School of Drama and so are far from naive folk artists. Many of the leading dub poets currently working in England emerged from the several "cultural cooperatives" that were active throughout the United Kingdom in the 1970s. These groups of musicians, poets, and actors presented multimedia consciousness-raising programs for predominantly black, urban, lower-class audiences. The most influential of these groups was the Radical Alliance of Poets and Players (RAPP). RAPP composed both its poems and its music collectively, but some members have gone on to become solo performance artists.

The best known solo performer to have emerged from the cultural cooperatives is Shango Baku, whose lengthy prose poem "From the Dread Level" was probably the first "dub lyric" to be transferred to print; it has become the political manifesto of the dub movement in its call for the liberation of the emigrant urban black poor through the power of such symbols of prideful consciousness ("dread" in the Rasta phrase) as the use of the nation language. Shango Baku wrote:

> I write for the fool. His actions are near to my heart. For the wanderer, the tramp, the misfit. They know the sweetness of despair. They have known true joy. I write for I. It is a flow . . . not premeditated. I write for the singers of songs. . . . I write for you who pass me in the thoroughfare of life.
>
> I am more myth than reality, more legend than life. No one knows where I am coming from or that my life is a ritual wherein I lose myself in layers of silence. I am unknown and terrible.
>
> Therefore am I contentious and without friends. Yet in every angle of the earth are men who believe in me and will further my work if I wish it. . . . Always I am at a crucial stage. (Berry 1984:xxvii)

The dub poets generally follow Shango Baku in his revolutionary messianism by adopting the cause of the urban poor. There are two levels on which poetry may work to achieve revolutionary goals: on the level of content and on the level of the form, which itself conveys a symbolic message. In this essay, I will be concerned only with the latter formal aspects of the poetry, so as to illustrate the linguistic problems in the translation of oral expression into writing.

First, it should be noted that in print versions of the poems, there is a tendency to make orthography conform to standard usage; a perusal of anthologized dub poetry, such as that edited by Berry (1984) from which the selection by Shango Baku cited above was taken, would not indicate to the casual reader what the language sounded like in live performance. In performance, however, the *sound* of the nation language is all important. The nation language of the dub poets is imbued with Rasta style in addition to more generalized lower-class West Indian argot. The Rasta influence is heard in the poets' frequent lyrical celebrations of African sounds and images. They often employ the richly biblical-sounding phraseology of the Rastas, and they have adopted the Rasta practice of using "I" words.[2]

One of the finest examples of a Rasta-influenced dub poem is Michael Smith's "I an I Alone," which begins:

> I an I alone
> Ah trod tru creation
> Babylon on I right
> Babylon on I left
> Babylon in front of I
> an Babylon behine I
> an I an I alone inna de middle
> like a Goliath with a sling shot. (Burnett 1986:91)

Even dub poets who are not Rastas like to use the Rasta style because it is such an effective, explicit form of antiestablishmentarianism, and one garbed in religious significance to boot; it is indisputably black and of Third World provenience, and it symbolically thumbs its nose at "standard English." The melding of this indigenous ideology with the new multimedia form of dub poetry creates a potent revolutionary ambience that is very appealing to audiences of the downtrodden. The political message is delivered in sonorous pulpit tones, and yet the medium of delivery is as up-to-date and as accessible as the nearest dance club or radio station.

It bears noting that Rastafarians disdain the "club scene," as it is offensive to their values of personal dignity and morality. I therefore do not mean to imply that Rastas themselves are part of the bar culture to which their style has been imported. I am also not suggesting that the kind of dub performance that is most typically found in club settings is the only, or even the dominant, form of expression. It is, however, the context in which my main informant (who is not a Rasta) functions, and so my analysis is colored by the experiences of his particular career.

In addition to Rasta imagery, a vernacular sound is achieved by use of the idiom derived from Jamaican folk speech. The dub poets borrow that idiom in three main ways. First, there is the use of proverbs and allusions to local lore, such as folk songs and children's rhymes, as in Linton Kwesi Johnson's "Song of Rising," with its refrain, "dere'll be peace in da valley some day," which is triumphantly transformed at the end to "dere'll be peace in da valley forever." Second, the specific reggae beat is translated into the meter of the poetry. That beat takes the form of a slightly syncopated dactylic meter: a stressed beat, a pause, two unstressed beats. When performing, the poet will often deliberately alter the natural pattern of speech emphasis to achieve this dactylic beat, although no particular effort is made to synchronize the meter of the poetry to the beat of whatever music happens to be playing in the background. The result is of the same strong, pulsating pattern of intonation chasing itself in two parallel, independent streams. This effect is completely lost in the written form. Third, phrases borrowed directly from the songs of major reggae artists will often be inserted into the dub lyric. Particularly popular is Bob Marley's "Trenchtown Rock," with its oft-quoted lines "one good ting about music / when it hits, you feel no pain." The repetition of set phrases has always been a characteristic of oral literature, so this borrowing fits into a most ancient tradition, despite the newness of the source material. On the other hand, printing such lyrics can pose copyright problems, so there is a tendency for the published versions of dub poems to omit these citations, even if they continue to be used in live performances of the same poem.

The emphasis on the spontaneity and uniqueness of the performance is reflected in the fact that dub poetry is essentially "imagistic." Careful attention is paid to clusters of description or evocations of emotion, but there is little concern with the overall structure of the poem. Certainly no "serious" dub poet composes in set, classical forms such as sonnets or quatrains. And while the meter can be very regular, there is no standard metric line. There is often rhyming, but there is rarely a discernible rhyme scheme that follows through the whole of the poem.

The Jamaican literary critic Mervyn Morris offers some insights into the relationship between performance and print versions of dub poetry. He was a particular friend and champion of the late dub artist Michael Smith, of whom he says, "In spite of — or because of — his immense success as a performing poet, Mikey was anxious also to be in print" (1985:52). But Smith had little or no training in the formalities of poetic writing. His manuscript drafts of his own poems were difficult to read, partly because of "inconsistent spelling and punctuation," but mostly because "Mikey . . . had little idea how a poem might be made to work on the page" (52). As a result, the written poems were set out in lines that were "often very much at odds with the rhythms as he performed them" (52). Morris suggested a procedure whereby Smith read his poems into a tape recorder and then Morris set out the versification for print. "Then Mikey would look carefully at what was suggested, and would make decisions. Ultimately the choices would be his" (53). Smith's desire to be true to his own voice and yet to be "correct" in poetic form reflects an important characteristic of the dub poetry movement that, although derived from extemporaneous street "rap," has become a self-consciously "artistic" production. It also raises an interesting point: is the resulting printed poem, "fixed" forever on the page (all the more so since Smith's untimely death brought an end to the evolution of the text through live performance), the work of the oral performance artist or of Morris, the conscious scholar? It bears mention that Morris is a respected poet in his own right, but he is a rarity among contemporary West Indian poets in that his works remain "generally faithful to the iambic pentameter and to a general stanzaic regularity" (Moore 1974:71).

I discussed Morris's article with Lumumba, who knew Smith and has met Morris. He refused to criticize Smith for going along with Morris's plans, although it was clear that he felt Morris (whom he respects as an academic, but certainly not as a dub poet) to have done Smith a disservice. For his part, Lumumba remains in the minority of dub poets who refuse to write down their poems. I asked him if he'd mind my trying, as an experiment, to do for him what Morris had done for Smith. He bemusedly agreed. Enlisting the aid of a colleague in the English Department, I set about to transcribe one of Lumumba's most popular numbers, one entitled "Turn Away," about the plight of the homeless. Lumumba took our typescript under consideration, and during his performance the next weekend he said, "I would now like to do a number written by my two professors." He proceeded to read the poem, as we had carefully typed it and set it out metrically, in a flat, pedantic voice. The audience howled appreciatively, and even we had to agree with the assessment of another patron who told us, "It ain't *bad*, you know, but it ain't Lumumba."

Conclusions

The dub poets are committed to having their nation language taken seriously. They would agree with Moore (1974:74) that "the poet is no longer a kind of putative Rhodes Scholar, learning his craft, his language, and his references by way of 'English literature.' " But there is poignant irony in the defiant cry of the poet Knolly La Fortune: "We've seen through / the writing on the wall." The implication is that the poets have recognized the danger to their own culture in thinking that standard English and classical metrical form are the only acceptable vehicles of expression, particularly when it is the views of non-elite people they wish to convey. But the poets have only been able to achieve a political breakthrough (a validation of their own "seriousness") by publishing their poems as words on a page, products of a conscious aestheticizing of the raw, kinetic live performance. They have seen through the writing on the wall—and have opted to write their own words on the same wall.

Such aestheticization is not inherently bad, and these vigorous and impressive poems can still be read to great effect. It may also be true that the prestige derived from publication lends the poets greater authority even among the non-reading public. On the other hand, once one had heard dub poetry in performance, one misses the "multimedia" effect when one is left simply with the decontextualized words.

The atmosphere in the clubs where Lumumba performs, for example, is far removed from that of a literary salon or a university seminar— although not a few university people are among his most enthusiastic fans. Lumumba works with a local reggae band whose leader he considers an equal partner in the creation of his art. But in performance it is definitely Lumumba who is at center stage. A self-proclaimed "health nut," Lumumba refuses to come out on stage if people are drinking or smoking, and the audience by and large goes along with his prohibitions for the duration of his set. He seeks, in fact, to create an aura of religious catharsis not unlike that fostered by those he calls "gospel shouter preachers." His poems are secular in content, of course, but he recites them with the fervor of a man of the pulpit. (He did, in fact, study for the ministry during "an earlier incarnation.") He begins at a podium, but as his passion rises, he takes to roaming the small stage. Sometimes he will circulate among the audience and encourage patrons to fill in a line here and there. Lumumba will often incorporate these variant lines into later performances of that poem. He is often at pains to keep up his image as simply the articulator of the people's interests—never as a litterateur who has set himself above them or who knows better than they. To that end, he rarely uses a microphone, claiming that he doesn't want anything artificial between his voice and "the masses." (He only uses a mike to make special sound effects.) There is thus a sense of shared community, a sort of evangelical fervor, an easy spontaneity in his presentation of dub poetry.

But when other dub poets commit themselves to publication, they achieve standardization and fixity of expression and have objectified an essentially subjective, fleeting experience. The verve of the poetry is then purely in objective language, no longer in the interplay between performer and audience. The performed dub number directly invites the audience to a kinesthetic response to the message; it is a medium of direct, sensual involvement. The written poem, by contrast, may be quite revolutionary in its content. Indeed, some poets explicitly heat up this revolutionary rhetoric to compensate for the loss of the kinesthetic charge of performance. The poet Oku Onuora, for example, explains his aims as follows:

> You ask me: Why do you write
> so much about blood, sweat, and tears?
> Don't you write about trees, flowers,
> birds, love?

Yes

I write about trees—
trees with withered branches
and severed roots

I write about flowers
flowers on graves

I write about birds—
caged birds struggling
I write about love—
love for destruction
of oppression. (Berry 1984:xxvi)

The poets may also compensate in terms of structural innovation, as in Linton Kwesi Johnson's evocation of a musical beat as an aural metaphor for revolutionary movement:

Shock-black bubble-doun beat bouncing
rock-wise rumble-doun soun music:
foot-drop find drum blood story;
bass history is a moving
is a hurting black story. (Berry 1984:53)

But in the last analysis, the poetry now exists in fixed space, to be reread, studied, analyzed, and criticized. It can be enjoyed as pure form even by those who are not partisan to its political message, who are not part of the vernacular communication act that gave rise to it in the first place. The revolutionary potential of the oral vernacular is in danger of becoming just another tame artistic tradition.

NOTES

1. Rastafarianism is a millenarian movement originating in West Kingston. It traces its inspiration to Marcus Garvey's Back to Africa movement in the 1920s and 1930s, but received its spark with the accession of Haile Selassie to the Ethiopian throne—an internationally recognized, courageous black king in the African homeland. Rasta doctrine is based on the following points: (1) black men are remnants of the ancient Israelites, exiled to the New World (Babylon) because of their sins; (2) white men are wicked and inherently inferior to blacks (although they have been used in recent history as instruments of chastisement); (3) life in Babylon is hopeless—there can be no accommodation with its evil, for Ethiopia is the true home of the exiled black man; hence Rastas reject ordinary work, styles of dress, and standards of good grooming and hygiene as marks of oppression; (4) Haile Selassie (one of whose titles was Ras Tafari) is the living God; (5) Haile Selassie will arrange for a

return to the homeland; (6) then black people will get revenge by compelling whites to serve them (Simpson 1970:208–28).

Some of this theology has been tempered over time; the death of the emperor has led some Rastas to believe that rather than a unique black messiah, Haile Selassie was simply the "first manifestation" of true divinity. He was not a black "second coming" of Christ; he was the inauguration of something entirely new. Modern-day Rastas have also toned down their anti-white racism in favor of a rhetoric of universal brotherhood and peace, although there is no doubt that the blacks, purged of their sins through their sojourn in Babylon, will be the dominant force in the coming millennium.

Originally scorned and reviled for their unconventional lifestyle and harassed by the police because of their fondness for ganja (marijuana), the Rastas have come to be a major force in contemporary Jamaican society. They anticipated the wave of black pride that swept the West Indies in the 1970s and have come to represent the most outrageous and successful challenge to the officially sanctioned mores and political institutions of the West Indian elite. They have style, they have an attitude of easy superiority and dignity, and they have remained uncorrupted by Babylon. They are unashamed of their circumstances and hold out the hope of a reversal of the fortunes of the suppressed lower classes. Hence, even lower-class West Indians who do not subscribe to the Rastafarian theology like to identify themselves with the Rasta outlook. As Rex Nettleford, the Jamaican artist and critic, has noted, Rastafarianism "suggests itself as a viable alternative to that dominant body of beliefs which inheres in the operation of a political, social and economic system that renders the mass of people not only unemployed but unemployable, without a sense of place or a sense of purpose" (in Joseph Owens 1976:vii).

2. The syllable *I* has special significance for Rastas. It apparently originated from a mistaken reading of the Roman numeral in the title Haile Selassie I. Since then it has been treated as a symbol of reversal. Lower-class West Indians traditionally used the pronoun *me* even in constructions that call for the nominative *I*. Rasta theoreticians speculate that under the slave system they internalized their status as objects and could not even bring themselves to speak of themselves as if they were active players. Using *I* even in constructions where *me* would be grammatically correct (such as "He spoke to I") reverses this process—it becomes an affirmation of the undefeated active principle. For Rastas, the use of *I* thus symbolizes black pride, and unique forms have been adopted to reinforce this view, such as *I and I* instead of *we*—expressive of the solidarity of strong individuals rather than the submerged collective mass. Even common words that begin with other vowels have been replaced by an initial *I*, such as in the pronunciation "Ithiopia" instead of "Ethiopia" (Joseph Owens 1976:64–68; Pollard 1985).

A Batak Antiquarian Writes His Culture: Print Literacy and Social Thought in an Indonesian Society

Susan Rodgers

This essay presents a case study in the rapidly changing social history of print literacy in Indonesia, a country of great communications systems complexity. Print can introduce new ways of categorizing knowledge in any country, but in modernizing multiethnic nations, such as Indonesia, which often have sturdy oral heritages as well as long traditions of script literacy, the changes are often dramatic and rapid. Today, and in fact since the 1920s, writers in certain highly literate Indonesian ethnic cultures are vigorously rethinking their public imagery of society, the human person, speech, and time. Authors do this on a public stage, through the commercial, private, and sometimes government publication of books and pamphlets on local "traditions and customs," or *adat,* through textbooks, and through articles in mass media forms such as newspapers. In the most general terms, print literacy seems to be pushing many of the country's 350 ethnic societies away from the mythic worldviews of oral village life (where the social world was often conceptualized in relation to cosmological models highlighting fertility and regeneration) toward more secular, specifically historical modes of understanding. In printed works, once literacy is deeply entrenched in a society, Indonesian ethnic minority worlds tend to emerge as social rather than cosmological phenomena and as human entities open to study and comparative inquiry. In this process their ontological claims are greatly reduced from an earlier, preprint vision in which local society was conceptualized as paralleling the very order of cosmological reality. With print, such large claims often emerge in more modest form as "things our ancestors used to believe."

This formulation, however, puts the matter in overly generalized terms. This is especially true in politically complex nations such as

Indonesia, which have both growing national cultures and a variety of competitive local ethnic cultures. Many of these ethnic cultures are at different stages of experience with literacy; they also interacted in different ways with the Dutch colonial state and (since the 1945–49 national revolution) with the Indonesian nation. Detailed case studies of the ways in which individual Indonesian cultures are transformed through print within Indonesian national political culture can offer a more nuanced view of the conceptual changes involved in the transition from orality to literacy in developing nations outside the West.

Drawing on my fieldwork and archive research in the Angkola Batak culture of South Tapanuli, North Sumatra[1] I would like to take a rather narrow focus here on these large matters of communication systems, politics, and oral and print aesthetics. I shall examine not that entire society's use of print to rethink the social world (too large a task for anything shorter than a book) but shall focus rather on one individual Angkola writer's efforts to do so, as seen in an extraordinary set of "ethnic culture" books this man has been publishing since 1977. The author is a Muslim school principal and freelance newspaperman named G. Siregar Baumi. Since that date, at a rate of about a book a year, he has been writing a series of descriptive volumes on what he bills as "all aspects" of his home culture. So far, his books have covered Angkola inheritance traditions, courtship practices, marriage customs (including a separate small book on how to negotiate a brideprice), kin term usage, new house construction and dedication, funerals, and Angkola art forms. He is also tireless in describing Angkola society, in terms of its social classes, as he puts it. Siregar Baumi clearly sees these topics as "subjects" in a sort of curriculum of Angkola culture. He approaches his descriptive task with seriousness and an air of scholarly endeavor, styling himself a perspicacious recorder of his own culture for three principal audiences. He writes, that is, for Angkola young people who live in multiethnic Indonesian cities purportedly "far from their ancient village traditions," for future generations of Angkola who he imagines may only be able to recover their ethnic traditions by reading about them, and for a more diverse audience of Indonesians of other ethnic groups and foreigners such as (he writes) Malaysians, Australians, and Americans[2] who might have a comparative interest in world cultures. Typically, he addresses this last audience with an air of firm certainty that any evenhanded student of comparative culture would surely recognize the inherent "excellence" of Angkola culture and "rank" it highly in relation to other ethnic traditions. In conversations with me in 1986–87, the writer made it clear that he sees Angkola to be as fine a culture as that of Java or Bali, two court-centered cultures whose "high civilizations" and palace arts are promoted by the Indonesian national government as the epitome of cultural development in the country. As Atkinson (1984) and Hoskins (1987) have noted, Outer Island Indonesian ethnic societies are currently engaged in imaginative and politically quite resourceful efforts to redefine local traditions in such a way that the latter can compete forcefully with Javanese and Balinese high culture and with the national culture itself. For instance, the national state has demanded that every "respectable," patriotic ethnic group must profess an *agama,* or an organized world religion such as Islam or Christianity (Kipp and Rodgers 1987). Acceding to this demand in an astute way, some ethnic societies in remote regions are refashioning their ritual knowledge into entities that resemble *agama* religions, with set doctrines and book-based rituals. Similarly, local heroes are sometimes redefined as "national heroes" in terms that are flattering to the local ethnic society and provide the latter with the raw materials for fashioning a hidden rhetoric of resistance against total national state control of local thought. In sum, efforts to record ethnic cultures are deeply political statements in contemporary Indonesia.

Given Siregar Baumi's vaunting ambitions to record "all" of his ethnic culture and his evident avocational zeal in pursuing his goals, this Batak writer presents students of literacy with a good opportunity to study, in miniature, some of the major ways in which print can transform folk knowledge in an Indonesian culture like this one. In this Angkola case, the culture as a whole is still located quite near an oral world: until about the 1870s literacy was largely restricted to village priests, village social order was coded into such forms as mythic chants and verbal duels between marriage alliance partners, and knowledge of outsider societies was limited to traveler's tales and vague stereotypes of "dangerous societies of poisoners" over the next mountain ridge. Mission schools and Dutch-run public elementary schools introduced print literacy in the 1870–1920 period. A flood of books by Angkola men on Angkola "ways" followed. In Siregar Baumi's case, his burgeoning encyclopedia of Angkola culture has the effect of reducing myths, ritual speech forms, and "old" ideas about society to the status of folklore, which is then given an origin point in the distant past. This is set in counterpoint to the lives of contemporary Batak readers, who learn about such old cultural forms during their leisure time or at school, through books. Their own culture, located in the here and now, is portrayed as more enlightened and "progressive" (*maju*) than the old culture, but is presented as being less refined and complex than the old ways. Siregar Baumi styles himself a translator of the intricate, subtle old customs for an audience of somewhat culturally deracinated contemporary Batak. Thus, his works offer outside observers an opportunity to study all the major epistemological claims of the Angkola "culture and customs" literature.

I shall examine several excerpts from Siregar Baumi's books to demonstrate how this important conceptual reduction from myth and oratory to folklore and "custom book" culture has taken place. I will pay special attention to the way this particular format of print (that is, this author's attempt to document and preserve his entire culture, in book-by-book form) has fostered peculiarly secular and almost social scientific ways of imagining society, speech, and time. Also of crucial importance is the way that Siregar Baumi's efforts at writing his culture have led him to imagine Angkola traditions as *culture* (as *kebudayaan,* in Indonesian). He uses the concept of culture in an antiquarian sense of "ancient, ethnic ways." This culture of his, as we shall see, is portrayed as an entity made up of subparts, such as Angkola language, literature, art, music, law, and religion. Such an imagery of culture as a systematic phenomenon made up of separate, functionally interlocking parts has intriguing comparative implications, for it resembles the visions of writers of other societies just entering an age of mass literacy and producing their own folklorists, grammarians, and antiquarians. I shall discuss some of these implications briefly in the conclusion to this essay.

Writing, Print, and Angkola Batak Social Thought

As is true of many Indonesian ethnic cultures, Angkola has retained many genres of ritual speech, such as verbal duels and traditional political orations, as rural people and city migrants have entered an era of print literacy at a time when they are making increasing use of mass media forms such as Indonesian-language radio, television, and commercially produced tape cassettes (the country has a single national language, called Indonesian, and then about three hundred separate ethnic languages; Angkola Batak, unintelligible to Indonesian speakers, is one of four main Batak dialects). These tape cassettes are used for entertaining radio-serial-like dramas (Rodgers 1986) as well as for performances of supposedly ancient-form gong and drum music. The cassettes are also used for popular songs, which are based in part on village songs, in part on church music (Angkola is 10 percent Protestant and 90 percent Muslim), and in part on international music forms, such as American rock and roll. Contemporary communication in Angkola is obviously a melange of traditions that reach far beyond

North Sumatra to an international arena of print and mass media entertainment forms.

I have already examined this complex, composite literacy and mass media situation in several publications (1978, 1979a, 1979b, 1981, 1983, 1984, 1986, 1987, 1988, 1989, 1991). The main theme of that work is that each major communication form in Angkola, such as printed books or newspapers or tape cassettes, tend to "work back" on the other forms, such as ritual speech, and define them in the conceptual terms of the media at hand. Thus, Batak folklore collections from the 1930s present the *turi-turian* oral mythic chants as oral *literature,* worthy of serious scholarly study. As part of the same process the chants in their new printed form enter an arena of interethnic and national political discourse. In another common example, the city newspapers (in the Indonesian language) present Angkola ritual dances and their associated oratory as colorful ethnic folklore.

In addition to this, each of Angkola's major communication forms (oratory, still practiced in village and market town ceremonies; printed genres; mass media forms) carry somewhat different images of person, society, and time. As these communication forms interact, qua communication forms, they also work to mutually influence each other's imagery of human life. So, for instance, the vision of "village social order" that one gets in printed, folkloristic versions of the *turi-turian* chants is not a fully mythic imagery of human society (about a group that lives in a Middle Continent under an upper Spirit Kingdom), but rather a view in which the narrator of the *turi-turian* notes, in print, that "this is the way our ancestors used to see the world" before this current age of enlightenment. In sum, the Angkola are editing and conceptually redacting their older mythic world through print and relativizing its significance for an audience of "cultured readers," who sample it during their leisure hours or at school. Such invented ethnic traditions, however, are useful for carving out modest conceptional territories for these ethnic minority societies within Indonesian national political space.

Literacy in the old Batak syllabic script (similar to the Sanskrit-derived writing systems of the courts of south Sumatra) was limited to village priests, oratory experts, and perhaps some segments of the long-distance Batak trader population until the mid-1800s. At that time, German and Dutch Protestant missions in the Sipirok highlands region established village Bible schools, where reading and writing was taught through scripture lessons. For the first ten to twenty years of their work, the European missionaries offered literacy instruction in the old Batak script, but by the 1870s they had converted many of their primers to the Latin alphabet. By that date too a thin network of Dutch colonial government public schools had been established in some of the larger market towns in Angkola and its southern neighbor, Mandailing. These public schools also used the Latin alphabet as their medium of instruction, and the Batak script began to retreat to a status of a special subject in school. It is today little more than a curiosity. The script is taught in South Tapanuli junior high schools as a special subject but very few people can read or write it fluently. Even *rajas* (ceremonial experts) rarely use the script.

Angkola and Mandailing's first generation of writers (men like Willem Iskandar, Radja Goenoeng, and Sutan Martua Raja) came to prominence as the authors of primers for children. Between 1910 and 1920, the region had developed into one of Sumatra's centers for newspaper publishing, book dealing, and textbook writing. Novels, based in part on Dutch models and in part on Chinese Indonesian pulp fiction, were published in profusion in Sibolga and Medan in the twenties and thirties; some of these were in the Angkola language while others were written in Indonesian (Rodgers 1981, 1991). The thirties also saw a flood of publication of nonfiction works by Angkola school principals and reporters. These books deal with folklore, clan history, and *adat,* or custom (Rodgers 1991).

The last sort of work is particularly important to note since it was the precursor to Siregar Baumi's books on Angkola ways. *Adat* means "ancient, genuine village customs" and in Angkola is often set in contradistinction to *agama* (or, as noted, organized religion). Adat includes rite of passage ceremonies, the ideal marriage arrangements involving alliances between wife-giver houses and their wife-receivers, and pronouncements about village government, which people say is based on this marriage alliance tradition. In anthropological terms, the Batak peoples have patrilineal clans (*marga*), asymmetrical marriage alliance of the Kachin type, and preferred mother's brother's daughter marriage. Through the end of the Dutch period the southern Batak societies were organized into chiefdoms centered around noble houses. There was a high degree of social class stratification in the larger market towns, with nobles, commoners, and slave descendants.

Angkola writers began to publish adat guides in the twenties, with titles such as *Haronduk Parmanoan* ("Rattan Ancient Memory Satchel") and *Adat Batak*. Some of these books[3] offered narrative overviews of adat ritual practice; others offered glossaries of difficult oratory terms; others dealt with arcane domains, such as the old Batak astrological calendar and its augury uses. Some guides, such as *Haronduk Parmanoan,* argued for a modification of old adat practice to bring it into line with modern life in the Indies. Other books were more conservative, not to say hidebound: they offered their readers strict compendia of rules and regulations that all good people were urged to follow. Many of the same sorts of adat guides in shorter form were published in Angkola newspapers in the twenties and thirties.

After the Japanese invasion of 1942 and the fall of the Dutch colonial government, the noble houses in Angkola also fell. Adat ceremonialism and its attendant publications went into a temporary eclipse. By the late fifties, however, a few prominent aristocratic families who also happened to have impeccable nationalist credentials began to stage a few large-scale adat rituals, called *horja*. Adat guides also began to make a comeback. This trend has accelerated over the last fifteen years, until now a man such as Siregar Baumi finds himself in a hotly competitive publishing world of southern Batak adat aficionados. The writers (most of whom are men, in their forties, fifties, and sixties) are school officials, newspaper reporters, or, more rarely, government officials working for the Ministry of Education and Culture. Though highly literate, most authors are unaware of the long history of adat guide publication in North Sumatra. None that I have interviewed know of the extensive collections of prewar Angkola adat books in the national library in Jakarta and in the Netherlands. In general, these authors remain antiquarians, not scientific scholars. Most of these writers are accomplished adat orators in their own right and tend to come from noble families. Some claim special access to the old customs through their family connections, in fact. This is the case with Siregar Baumi: he hails from the noble lineage of the Siregar clan from the village of Marancar, and his presentation of Angkola ways is slanted toward Marancar historical memories and ritual practices. However, he protests that he is writing of a generalized Angkola culture applicable to all areas from the Sipirok region through Padang Bolak and Angkola Jae and Angkola Julu. These are South Tapanuli's major chieftaincy domains north of Mandailing.

Sutan Tinggi and His Curriculum of Culture

Siregar Baumi normally publishes his works under his honorific chieftaincy title, Sutan Tinggibarani Perkasa Alam.[4] This translates roughly as "Sutan Bold and Exalted Resolver of Great Matters of the World." Few (if any) Angkola chiefs today sport so prepossessing a title as this; several I talked to about the title thought it rather funny. However, the writer is proud of the *gelar* (title) as an old lineage name and he uses it to help assure his readers that they are dealing with a true adat expert. In line with that I shall use it here in referring to the man for the rest of the essay, although for simplicity's sake I shall abbreviate the title to Sutan Tinggi.

As background to Sutan Tinggi's work it should be noted that his personal circumstances may well have shaped him as a writer. He leads an unusually divided life in what is today a fragmented Batak society. Contemporary Angkola spans the physical and social territory from rural South Tapanuli to multiethnic cities such as Medan and Jakarta. Sutan Tinggi himself commutes between these two locales, largely because he owns and manages Muslim schools for young children in both Padangsidimpuan (the South Tapanuli administrative seat) and the large city of Medan, a ten-hour bus ride from that part of Tapanuli. He also has two wives (an unusual circumstance in Angkola), and each helps him run one of his schools. The elder wife teaches in the institute in Medan and the younger wife is an instructor in his Padangsidimpuan Madrasah school (an after-hours school for Arabic language and theology instruction, for young children). Both institutions are financially fragile, and Sutan Tinggi clearly sees his publications on Angkola culture as a way to earn supplementary income. His occasional freelance articles for Medan newspapers, which are usually on adat subjects or about the old Batak script, also provide his households with extra income, although it would be a mistake to see his books and articles as hack work done from exclusively pecuniary motives. Sutan Tinggi seems to have a genuine commitment to documenting and preserving old Angkola ways "before they disappear," as he puts the matter. He certainly does write his books for sale (from his homes, from Tapanuli bookstores, from stalls on South Tapanuli culture at Medan Fair, a yearly ethnic culture exhibition), but he also sees himself as something of a gentleman scholar. Appropriately enough, given this, he keeps voluminous handwritten and typewritten files on his field research (he does extensive interviews with Tapanuli rajas). He has many new writing projects planned for the future, and he is constantly seeking a commercial publisher for his works, most of which are circulated now in roughly bound, mimeographed fashion.

Let me summarize his eight books to date, to give an indication of the scope of his work. Like most Angkola men of his age, Sutan Tinggi is fully fluent in both Angkola and Indonesian. He writes his books in a combination of these languages, for he fears that many Angkola young people do not understand a great deal of their home language. He is correct in this assumption.

Before describing the volumes it is interesting to note that Sutan Tinggi rarely attempts to reconcile adat to Islam or to any abstract idea of world religion in any of these volumes. At several junctures he does mention Islam in passing (for instance, he notes that the religion has been used as a reason to allow marriages within a single clan in some areas, although this goes against adat [Sutan Tinggibarani Perkasa Alam, Rukiah Siregar, and Paruhuman Harahap 1977]). In addition to this he also conforms to the general Angkola convention of framing any statement about "Those-Not-Seen" (vengeful, especially powerful anthropomorphic spirits) with the caveat that "people today no longer believe in these" in this present age of monotheistic enlightenment. Beyond these mild and expected pieties, Sutan Tinggi engages in no extended exegetical attempts to reconcile adat and Islam.

The first book Sutan Tinggi published is a broad-focused volume entitled *Unfurled Betel Leaves: A Study Book of South Tapanuli Adat, Presented to the Public, to Young and Old* (Burangir na hombang: Buku pelajaran adat [Tapanuli Selatan] siulaon sepanjang adat dipersembahkan untuk masyarakat dan naposo/naulibulung). The last phrase about "young and old" is an adat saying, which literally means "the young leaves and the old leaves," with the metaphor of human society as a tree. This book appeared in 1977, in Padangsidimpuan; it was privately published and uses the Angkola language for most of the text. The volume has three authors: Sutan Tinggi; his sister, Rukiah Siregar (a lecturer at the main Islamic theology college in Medan); and Paruhuman Harahap, the head of the South Tapanuli office of the Ethnic Culture Bureau of the national government's Ministry of Education and Culture. *Unfurled Betel Leaves* is a general work that describes "the shape of society" and "family connections" before going on to set out all the major Angkola adat rituals. The authors accomplish this latter task by including sample orations of the sort that the different chieftaincy and kinship factions would deliver to each other at weddings, birth rituals, new house dedications, and funerals (wife-givers speaking to wife-receivers, and so on). The speeches are often introduced by short narrative descriptions of what sort of activity would be occurring as the oration was delivered (e.g., presentations of textiles or special goods). The book ends with a glossary of arcane words from the oratory the authors explain in simple terms.

The second book, published in 1978, is the work of Sutan Tinggi alone entitled *Measuring Out the Brideprice/Negotiating a Brideprice (The Congress for Negotiating a Brideprice according to South Tapanuli Adat)* (Mangampar ruji/mangkobar boru [musyawarah perhitungan mas kawin menurut adat Tapanuli Selatan]) (Siregar Baumi 1978). This one is in the Indonesian language and is intended for urban readers who are presumed to know so little of their traditional culture that they cannot be trusted to conduct the marriage ceremonies of their young people with ritual accuracy and financial astuteness. The book describes the various stages of the "standard" brideprice negotiation session, for various types of brides (according to traditional social class); it also offers a sort of how-to guide, with fill-in-the-blank charts for practice purposes.

The third, (Siregar Baumi 1980a), published in Padangsidimpuan, is entitled *A New Method for Learning How to Read and Write the South Tapanuli Batak Letters.* The small publication, in Indonesian, is a workbook intended for home use, for Angkola young people or adults who wish to become fluent in the old script on their own. The "new method" here consists largely of Sutan Tinggi's use of numerous practice drills, inserted in the text after new combinations of syllabic signs are introduced.

Book four, in Angkola except for an Indonesian language introduction, is entitled *Great Celebration for the Arrival of a Bride: May Souls Be Cool and Secure until All Reach Old Age* (Horja godang mangupa di na haroan boru, horas tondi madingin sayur matua bulung). This 107–page book (Siregar Baumi 1980b) repeats much the same subject matter covered in *Unfurled Betel Leaves* but maintains a sharper focus on adat ritual over descriptive accounts of Batak society. A traditional, lengthy wedding of the sort once staged by wealthy noble families is described in step-by-step fashion, with sample speeches.

The fifth book (1981), again a relatively short one, is an extraordinary how-to guide to Angkola and Mandailing kin term usage entitled *The Tree Stem Basics of Kin Terms (The Way to Trade Terms for Relatives with Proper Respect and Politeness in Family Relationships according to South Tapanuli Adat)* (Bona-bona ni partuturan cara-cara bertutur sopan santun dalam hubungan kefamilian menurut adat Tapanuli Selatan). It provides narrative and chart-form information on which relative says which kin term to whom. There are also glossaries and narrative discussions of related matters, such as kin term usage between pairs of speakers, which anthropologists would call joking relationship partners and avoidance partners. Sutan Tinggi has two co-authors here: his sister and Drs. Bahasan Siregar.

The next book (Siregar Baumi 1984a), offers a comprehensive description and enthusiastic praise of "all" the major forms of art in South Tapanuli. *Art* is Sutan Tinggi's word. This Indonesian language book is called *The Arts of the Traditional Culture of the South Tapanuli Region of the Angkola-Padanglawas Mandailing and Coastal Batak Peoples* (Seni budaya tradisional daerah Tapanuli Selatan suku Batak Angkola-Padanglawas Mandailing dan Pesisir). The work includes sections on songs, dances, "Musik/Instrument," carvings and decorations, literature, games, and the martial arts. Each of these is presented in a separate chapter.

Book seven (Siregar Baumi 1984b), at 294 typescript pages, is Sutan Tinggi's most massive work to date. It is also his most all-encompassing work, as it treats all the topics covered in his separate books in a single volume. Entitled *Hidden Messages in the Old Leaf Letters: The Adat of the Angkola-Sipirok-Padangbolak-Barumun-Mandailing-Batang Natal-Natal Bataks* (Surat tumbaga holing, adat Batak Angkola-Sipirok-Padangbolak-Barumun-Mandailing-Batang Natal-Natal), the book includes the chapters "The History of the Population and the Clans," "Language and Letters," "Religion and Beliefs," "Society and Daily Life," "Adat Government," "Public Meetings and Adat Congresses," "Adat Ceremonies" (this is an especially long section), "Adat Instruments" (that is, things used in rituals), "Art," "Astrological Charts," "Adat Chieftaincy Powers," "Adat Law," "The Influence of Religious Law on Adat" (one of Sutan Tinggi's few excursions into the subject, as noted), and "Establishing a New Village."

His latest book is a more modest work called *Pabagas boru,* or *Getting a Daughter Married.* Published in 1986 (under the name Siregar Baumi), this Angkola language work repeats much of the material covered in *Hidden Messages in the Old Leaf Letters.*

Taken as a group, these books present the reader with a welter of ceremonial detail and social observation about, as Sutan Tinggi says, "the shape of society." His portrayals of human speech, time, and society shed light on his construction of Angkola "culture."

Images of Speech

In Sutan Tinggi's books, human speech emerges as a part of human life that is broken down into different genres. Among those he lists and then describes are *ende,* or songs; *marosong osong,* or verbal duels between wife-givers and wife-receivers; and *markusip* speech, or "whisper courtship" verses that girls and boys would trade at night during secret trysts, "in the past" (see, for instance, Siregar Baumi 1984b:184–224; 251–57). Some of these genres fit into a more exalted generalized category, "The Arts of Literature and Language" (Siregar Baumi 1984b:251–57). Under this rubric come Adat Language (the speech of rituals); *Andung* Language, which is the speech of mourning and leave-taking occasions; the Language of the Camphor Gatherers, which has a secret vocabulary for plants in the forest; Sorcerers' Language; the Language of Anger and Curses; Veiled Language, for fooling people;

the Language of the Turi-turian chants; and the Backwards Language of playful children and courting couples, who seek to cover up their messages by saying their words in reverse order. Sutan Tinggi gives sample texts for several of these varieties of speech. In other books he enumerates even more subtypes (in *The Arts of the Traditional Culture,* for instance, he deals with twenty-three named types of songs).

Throughout all of his work, Sutan Tinggi presents Angkola "literature" as one of a series of local arts, which also includes such things as ritual dances and ceremonial textiles. He sets out all of these arts in simplified, schoolbook form, in an easy-to-study manner; he makes heavy use of charts, outlines with Roman numerals, and lists of terms.

In his presentation of the secret speech of camphor gatherers and other esoteric genres Sutan Tinggi leads his readers to believe that these forms come to their speakers from "Angkola ancient traditions," rather than from any specific source of inspiration such as a clan ancestor. In villages, some orators do believe that particularly fine, well-modulated "flows of words" come to the speaker from lineage ancestors who were also expert orators; no hint of this theory is evident in Sutan Tinggi's presentation of the matter. Rather, he consistently attempts to domesticate oratory as literature and to portray the speechmaker as a folk artist drawing on old traditions. The reader is also provided with sample, high literature–form sample texts, so that the reader too can participate in the old village arts.

One additional general point should be made about Sutan Tinggi's portrayal of speech. He implies that its more secret precincts can and in fact should be "decoded" for the public, through books. Thus Sutan Tinggi takes care to unravel the "exact meaning" of riddles and proverbs. To this end, he often provides glossaries of difficult terms. This approach stands in sharp contrast to that of the village rajas, even today. These rajas hold ceremonial positions of great moral influence in their villages; the positions derive from lineage status and an individual man's oratorical abilities. The councils of rajas are separate from the civil service administration of the national government. They generally seek to keep their high oratory mystifying and secret and accessible only to their own number. In Sutan Tinggi's hands, through his books, the arts of language become accessible to all, through the study of literature. In the process, words lose their supernatural power to bless or curse and become simple human instruments for recording a reality external to themselves.

Images of Time

Sutan Tinggi places his summaries of Angkola customs within a specific time framework that is decidedly literate and even schoolbookish in conception. Angkola today can be located with exact dates; in fact, Sutan Tinggi sees that historical task as one of his main jobs.

In his books, Angkola customs derive from a vague, ancient past, which is in itself left undated. These customs were "influenced" and "modified" by a succession of exactly dated *jaman,* or ages. These include the Bonjol Age, when troops from Minangkabau stormed into the Angkola region and converted many people to Islam; the Colonial Age, under the Dutch; and the National Age, under the Indonesian government. When Sutan Tinggi narrates the history of an individual area, such as his home region of Marancar, he employs a modified version of the *tarombo* narrative, or clan genealogy (see, for instance, Siregar Baumi 1984b:3–10). In oral speech these *tarombo* trace the past of a village's founder lineage back many generations to a founding ancestor; they refer to spirit beings and supernatural wonders. In Sutan Tinggi's hands, however, *tarombo* emerge as "historical sources," whose veracity can be checked against other supposed historical materials for their factual accuracy.

It is also important to note that Sutan Tinggi attempts to reconcile different historical narratives into a single, true, "full" version of the human past related to events in Angkola. For instance, in the introduction to *Hidden Messages,* he combines Toba clan history, Islamic world history, European and Middle Eastern trade history, and Angkola *tarombo* clan histories from Marancar into a single framework, with himself as arbiter of the differing versions. Indeed, he sees differences of opinion about history as inevitable. In line with this he presents the writer's task as one of discovering the most valid version for his readers.

Images of Society

In his portrayals of human society, Sutan Tinggi gives his diagrammatic and classification impulses full rein. He presents a socially variegated world to his readers, a world divided into set social classes. These classes interact to make for smoothly working adat rituals and to make for a smoothly working human village in general.

His discussion of the three classes of brides involved in brideprice negotiation sessions is typical of his approach here (Siregar Baumi 1978:18 ff). He does make it clear that he is referring to the prewar period, when families still purportedly kept strict account of the class backgrounds of newlyweds. He writes that the three sorts of *boru,* or brides, are

A. *Halak Bujing,* all the daughters of the rajas and nobles and their lineage-mates. The basic brideprice payment here would be as large as 120 florins, which was once called 120 yellow-yellowest-glittering-goldpieces.

B. *Halak Hundangan,* all the descendants of the village chiefs and their lineage-mates. The basic brideprice payment would be eighty florins.

C. *Halak Parampuan,* all the daughters of the common people (the regular populace). The basic brideprice payment would be forty florins. (18)

Sutan Tinggi then proceeds to give a sample roster of supplementary brideprice payments for each class of bride. In other books he details other classes of social persons. In *Unfurled Betel Leaves,* for instance, he describes three main categories of brides according to whether or not they eloped or held various types of prewedding public ceremonies. At a more general level, he always places his discussions of weddings and other ceremonial gatherings within a social world made up of nobles, free commoners, and slave descendants. He places this society within Sumatra, with its other ethnic societies. In *Hidden Messages,* typically for his books, in a chapter called "Society and Mode of Life," Sutan Tinggi describes the constitution of a typical Angkola village. It includes a founder lineage, that line's wife-provider house, the founders' wife-receiving house, a raja, his official spokesperson (drawn from the ancestral wife-receivers), a Rajas' Council, a Council of Village Elders, a Village Military Commander, and some *hatoban,* or slave descendants (Siregar Baumi 1984b:58–60). Sutan Tinggi hastens to add that this last category of people "is no longer in existence" (60). He then goes on to describe six categories of village rajas and seven categories of wife-receiver aides-de-camp for those noblemen (60–62).

There are many more passages like these throughout his books, often set into chart or outline form. In general, Sutan Tinggi imagines society to be a stratified, organic entity made up of various mutually dependent classes of people. If each fills their proper role in society, all will prosper. Notably de-emphasized here is the more traditional imagery of human society as a collection of Three-Stones-on-the-Hearth, which work together to evenly balance a cookpot. This homely image (in Angkola, the *Dalihan na Tolu*) is repeatedly employed in ritual adat oratory and in adat chief's conversational descriptions of local society. In such statements, one balance stone is a man's close lineage-mates, a second stone is that group's wife-givers (*mora*), and a third stone is the focal unit's *anakboru,* or their subservient wife-receivers. Close cooperation and mutual dependence and indebtedness among the three marriage alliance partners lead (in this oral portrayal of things) to an orderly, productive village society. Sutan Tinggi does indeed sometimes refer to the virtues of the *Dalihan na Tolu,* but in general he seems to prefer a more scientific-sounding language of mutually dependent "sub-units of society" in his culture guides. In other words, he is more the wordy folk-sociologist than the aphorist.

Angkola "Culture" and the Encyclopedist's Vision

Sutan Tinggi "looks back" at an oral village world and reorganizes it in print into a schoolmaster's array of subjects, each one fixed neatly in its proper slot on his charts and outlines. In his minutely detailed volumes, Angkola customs emerge as things every bit as intricate and complex as Javanese palace ways or Balinese court dances (at least this is what Sutan Tinggi wants his readers to believe). The society that has this exemplary culture is divided into subsections, rather like that culture itself. That is, Angkola traditions consist of arts, law, mores, and village government practices, while society, for its part, has its separate classes. Other, neighboring societies, or new ages of history, can come into this system of people and traditional ways and influence them (in this view). These influences can be for good or ill: for ill if they disrupt the smooth working order of complete villages; for good if new influences bring helpful changes, such as literacy itself. Not surprisingly, for a school principal, Sutan Tinggi is an enthusiastic proponent of literacy in all its forms. He would have all adults and children read and write Indonesian in the Latin alphabet, Batak in the old script and in the Latin letters, and Arabic in the standard alphabet and in the Arabic letters. In this view, the home life of adults would be transformed into continual study sessions.

As noted, no other southern Batak writer today has quite so wide a reach in his treatment of local customs, nor so large an array of custom handbooks and guides to ethnic ways. In this, Sutan Tinggi stands out as an extreme case, at least in South Tapanuli. Other societies relatively new to literacy, however, have produced writers and writing conventions that are intriguingly similar to Sutan Tinggi and his modes of exposition.

For instance, as Ong (1982) notes, newly literate cultures often develop folk sciences of rhetoric, as they "look back" to their oral world and organize it into set, named systems of knowledge. He also makes the familiar point that newly literate cultures begin to discover that they have something called oral *literature,* which an educated elite among them set out to record and classify. Moreover, as the historian

Prys Morgan has noted in an insightful study of the rise of a folklore and "ancient customs" movement in eighteenth- and early nineteenth-century Wales (1983), local amateur scholarship on local culture can increase with particular intensity when an ethnic group finds itself being politically incorporated into a larger nation. The past becomes especially relevant in a politically troubled and vulnerable present for minority societies in powerful states. This is certainly the case with Angkola, as each generation of schoolchildren learn in their lessons that they must be patriotic Indonesians first and Batak second (if at all). Goody (1977, 1986) has also reported the particular fascination diagrams, charts, and outlines hold for writers in newly literate societies and how these forms are often used in nearly compulsive ways to describe local social life (through such forms as legal codes, sets of marriage rules, and rosters of ceremonial obligations). This penchant for the list, the chart, and the description can lead to profuse numbers of written works in newly literate societies.

The near-mania to cast social life into categories and then to build up great edifices of written knowledge about these has also been explored by the historian Robert Darnton (1985) in his studies of the spread of the literate imagination in seventeenth- and eighteenth-century France. Darnton writes of provincial bourgeois authors who write folk sociologies of their home cities, of police inspectors who invent a kind of rogue's gallery of certain writers they have under surveillance, and (most apposite here) of Diderot and his circle of encyclopedists who set down the entire world of knowledge in a series of books, covering reality from A to Z. Darnton recognizes the radical edge to this encyclopedia project. Writers emerge as the preeminent social seers. "Pigeonholing is . . . an exercise in power," he writes of Diderot's attempt to encompass all the proper subjects of human inquiry into a single set of books (1985:192). Further, Darnton goes on, "Setting up categories and policing them is therefore a serious business. A philosopher who attempted to redraw the boundaries of the world of knowledge would be tampering with the taboo" (1985:193). Diderot and his followers rearranged the accepted categories of science and theology, and in the process brought the sacred studies into the secular realm of humane letters. This was a particularly audacious attempt to "rearrange the mental furniture" (Darnton's phrase) of European thought, but it stood in a long line of such efforts. As Darnton notes, "Reordering the *trivium* and the *quadrivium,* the liberal and the mechanical arts, the *studia humanitatis* and all the branches of the ancient curriculum was a favorite game for schematizers and synthesizers during the Middle Ages and the Renaissance" (1985:193–94).

The Batak peoples seem to be in the midst of just such a reordering process at present. As we have seen, for Angkola this effort started in a significant way in the 1920s, with the publication of the first adat handbooks. Since that time Angkola writers have been inventing traditions for themselves and reconciling those historical narratives to other histories they encounter in print literature. They have also been inventing society as a secular entity made up of social classes that exist in secular space and time. As Darnton notes for eighteenth-century France, the creation of major new categories of thought can be both politically and conceptually disruptive. In the Angkola case, the sort of curriculum of culture Sutan Tinggi is proposing has by no means been politically accepted as yet. The national government is promoting its own versions of local Indonesian ethnic cultures, through its centrally controlled television station, through national museums, and through the mass media. Ethnic groups emerge in these public forums as rather quaint, colorful tourist attractions, in contrast to the more politically robust Angkola culture of some adat custom guidebooks (see Rodgers 1989 for further discussion). Sutan Tinggi's own position in this highly politicized arena of Indonesian public culture is ambiguous. He is actively seeking a commercial publisher for his works, but at the same time he has sent some of his shorter works to the national government's Ministry of Education and Culture for possible inclusion in their series on ethnic folkways (a series whose volumes are distributed to public and school libraries; authors are paid a modest fee for their works).

Beyond his immediate financial hopes, Sutan Tinggi's grand plans to set down his culture in words is important for two principal reasons. First, it may be that his vision of ethnic culture as a compartmentally organized, holistically integrated entity is simply one instance of a very general tendency of writers in newly literate societies to invent secular social worlds whose outlines conform to the logical contours of print itself. Secondly, there may be many more Sutan Tinggi's in the sorts of ethnic minority cultures that anthropologists typically study. These local writers may be constructing literate worlds much like Sutan Tinggi's Angkola. If so, in a methodological sense, it would be useful for fieldworkers to begin to collect such texts, interview their authors, and analyze such folk sociologies in local and national contexts. A particularly productive framework for examining these texts would be one in which researchers ask why local writers opt for the path of nostalgia and the exuberant invention of ethnic traditions (Sutan Tinggi's tactic). Other options exist, such as overt political resistance to the national state or full-scale nativism carried out in a ritualistic or militaristic key. Sutan Tinggi's more peaceable approach to an Angkola past and an

Angkola culture will probably only make full sense when his prodigious literary efforts are seen in the context of this larger range of political options as they have been played out in other ethnic minority societies in Indonesia and elsewhere in the developing world.

NOTES

1. The fieldwork on which this paper is based was conducted July 1974–Jan. 1977; Dec. 1980; May 1983; and Oct. 1986–Feb. 1987, with support from the Social Science Research Council, the National Endowment for the Humanities, and the Ohio University Research Committee. The research was sponsored by the Lembaga Ilmu Pengetahuan Indonesia. For basic ethnographic information on Angkola, see Rodgers (1978). On the Batak peoples in general, see the bibliography in Siagian (1966) and the Kipp and Kipp (1983) and Carle (1987) collections.

2. See, for instance, Siregar Baumi (1984b:ii).

3. The most complete collections of these books are to be found in the National Library in Jakarta and in the Koninklijk Instituut voor Taal-, Land-, en Volkenkunde in Leiden. Typical adat guides include Pane 1922, Soetan Pangoerabaan (1930) and Loebis 1922. A particularly fine folklore text by an Angkola author is M. J. St. Hasoendoetan 1941 (a *turi-turian* chant, collected by a prominent novelist). An excellent school primer is Soetan Martoewa Radja 1919. A related publishing phenomenon was also occurring in the Toba region in the 1930s (see, for instance, Siahaan 1937, 1938). The earliest adat guide I have found was published in Singapore under American Mission auspices (American Missionary Society 1899); I have never discovered any line of influence from this mission in Angkola.

More recent Angkola adat guides include Dalimunte and Pohan 1986, H. M. D. Harahap 1986, T. Mr. Tagor Harahap n.d., Marpaung 1969, and Marpaung and Sohuturon 1962. Sutan Tinggi's senior wife has written a small book on Angkola and Mandailing language (Rangkuti 1983). One of the only overtly social scientific works on southern Batak adat is Palti-Radja Siregar's book on inheritance law (1958); that book was based on his law thesis at Gadjamada University, and unlike most of the other Angkola adat writers he drew extensively on Dutch sources.

More recently, the national government has started to publish guides to local ethnic cultures through the Ministry of Education and Culture. One such book is *Ungkapan tradisional yang berkaitan dengan Panca Sila,* which attempts to draw parallels between Batak proverbs and the "Five Principles," or Panca Sila, the basic national ideology. The book's title can be translated as "Traditional Expressions Relevant to *Panca Sila.*"

4. Sutan Tinggibarani Perkasa Alam's works can be found in the Library of Congress.

The Virgin and the Godfather: Kinship versus the State in Greek Tragedy and After

Robin Fox

The clash of duties in ANTIGONE, which is not simply a clash between piety and civil obedience, or between religion and politics, but between conflicting laws within what is still a religious-political complex, represents a very advanced stage of civilization: for the conflict must have meaning in the audience's experience before it can be made articulate by the dramatist and receive from the audience the response which the dramatist's art requires.

—T. S. Eliot

Today it is Creon's secretaries who deal with the case of Antigone.

—F. Dürrenmatt

In a rhetorical flourish at the end of my preface to the revised edition of *Kinship and Marriage* (1983), I wrote: "The war between kinship and authority is alive in legend. In story and fantasy kinship struggles against bureaucratic authority, whether of church or state. It undermines, it challenges, it disturbs. The Mafia constantly fascinates because "the family" demands total loyalty and provides total security. When the state fails to protect, people look longingly at the certainty of kinship." Enough. I wrote a good deal more about the "resilience" and "subversiveness" of kinship, and so on in the same vein. But a point was made to me by several colleagues that struck home. We thought, they said, that the battle, in the occidental world at least, had been between the *individual* and the state or church. Indeed, the growth and origins of individualism have been a pretty constant theme in social science and historical literature. A recent distinguished contribution from anthropology itself is Dumont's *Essays on Individualism* (1986). In this growth of individualism, it was objected, kinship—in the form of clans or extended families and the like—has been as much an enemy as the state itself. The burgeoning individual has had to throw off the kinship yoke as much as the yoke of the state in order to be fully autonomous—the creature of "contract" as opposed to "status" in Maine's classic distinction. Do we not now, I was asked, live in a relatively "kinshipless" society in which the autonomous individual is the recognized unit, to the point where children can sue their parents for inadequate care and education and a fetus has rights against its mother?

I would answer two things. First: the extreme assertion of individualism seems to me to be a peculiarly Anglo-Saxon affair. It may not, as is commonly held, be a product of late Renaissance humanism, the Protestant Reformation, or the philosophy of John Locke, or of the industrial revolution, or any of the other claimed causes. It may well, as McFarlane (1978) and others have argued, go well back into Anglo-Saxon tribal custom, transferred to Britain and nurtured there with minimal Norman interference. There might never have been strong, relatively independent kinship groups in the Anglo-Saxon (Jute and Frisian) tribes; the tribe itself might always have been superior, and the individual warrior was its unit. Tacitus certainly thought so. Families there were (and always are), of course, but strong independent extended families there were not. Kinship was not unilineal but classically cognatic in these tribes, and the Sib (Sippe) was an ego-centered group, not a descent group (Fox 1983). Individual ownership of land, for example, goes way back in English history, when it was unknown among the continental peasantry. English laws of inheritance, by effectively disenfranchising younger sons, never allowed the build-up of huge aristocratic clans. The Tudors were among the first European monarchs to tame the noble houses and create a meritocratic bureaucracy. Although the great noble houses of the eighteenth-century Whig Oligarchy might have appeared to constitute a kinship system to counter state power, they were never serious challengers and disappeared in the rampant individualism of the nineteenth century, their younger sons constantly descending into the middle class. Once the Scottish clans were once and for all defeated at Culloden and broken by the Highland clearances, which sped most of the clansmen to Canada, that remnant of the kinship world was doomed (except in Sir Walter Scott–inspired sentiment that had even Queen Victoria and her German consort decked out in "authentic" Highland costume invented by canny cloth manufacturers anxious to cash in). Even so, the Duke of Argyll, as the head of the Clan Campbell, exercised an extreme influence on the English imagination with the thought that he commanded the allegiance of five thousand swordsmen; a fascination much like that a powerful Mafia chief exercises today in America. (Those who understood the situation knew it was the command of forty seats in the House of Commons that was his real power. But there were always those claymores ready in the background. . . .)

The second point, then, is that we tend, as a result of our peculiar history, to see the world in terms of the inevitable struggle of individual and state, with the individual, we hope, triumphing against the state (and state church), which is always trying to infringe on his autonomy. Dumont sees this as a gradual secularizing of a religious idea of the individual. But as we have seen, the "idea" may have been there in Anglo-Saxon institutions well before the religious theories caught up with it or the secularization (after Calvin) got under way. Locke, then, is our central political philosopher, not so much for any original contribution as for articulating this struggle and expressing the case for the individual. Spencer, Mill, and Marshall continued the intellectual battle against the collectivism of both left (socialists) and right (idealists) (see Parsons 1937 for what is still the best account). We have, of course, never wholly settled the issue and continue to agonize over the proper balance. It is *the* problem of our current political lives and our philosophers are obsessed with it. But—and this is the crux of my second point—can we wish this simplified view onto the rest of the world, and is it even so simple in our own world? For between the individual and the state there always stands at least the family, and for most of the world, much more. However individualistic our legal systems become, for example, they always recognize the family, however defined, as being a peculiar form of social institution within which the usual individualistic rules of contract do not apply in most cases. In other systems than the Anglo-Saxon the family is accorded a much larger role, even if the struggle I have spoken of is always present.

And there is a paradox here too. It is often put to me that the state in fact does a lot to promote the family rather than to destroy it. This is true. But it does not affect my argument, which is that the state abhors kinship—not the family. In promoting the self-sufficiency of the nuclear family unit, the state is in effect attacking the essence of kinship, which lies in the extension of consanguineal (or pseudo-consanguineal) ties beyond the family into strong and effective kinship groups. To put it another way, from the state's point of view, the highest level of kinship group it likes to see is the nuclear family, which is in fact the lowest level of operative kinship group possible that is compatible with effective reproduction and socialization of the young. To be exact, this could be done by the mother-child unit with the state as provider. But this is not the state's aim and in fact causes it a great deal of trouble—for example, the welfare system. The state (in reality as opposed to in utopia) prefers males to act as providers to the mother-child units and gets annoyed when this doesn't happen. The reasons are purely economic. But note also that the state usually dislikes intensely the idea of the male supporting several mother-child units, i.e., polygyny. One could ask why the state should be concerned as long as the male can provide for them. But, religious objections aside, the state frowns on the possibility of the growth of large kinship units and actively discourages it by breaking up large inheritances and hysterically pursuing the legal-military destruction of such deviances as the Mormon experiment. (Islamic countries are a special case since polygyny is allowed by the Koran—four wives. But before the fundamentalist revival, the "modernizing" leaders and parliaments of Islamic nations had actively discouraged the practice by law and example. Nevertheless, Islamic societies have still to be ranked among those where the individual acts toward the state essentially through the mediation of his kin group—[see Gellner 1981].) The paradox then is that in promoting the nuclear family, the state (or church) is paring kinship down to its lowest common denominator while appearing to support basic "kinship values."

I would argue that a lot of our intellectual life, from political philosophy to literary criticism, is biased by this late seventeenth-century Anglo-Saxon view of the world as a struggle between the state and the individual. It leads us to fail to see clearly what has been happening in history and the rest of the world as we impose this model upon it. As anthropologists, we should be skeptical of the model in the first place and open to the possibilities of reinterpreting certain classic examples of this supposed struggle.

As always, we should start with the Greeks. I am prompted to do so, since so many commentators have taken Greek tragedy as the first example of the literary recognition of the "individual versus the state" struggle. And indeed, the Greek *polis* was the first real example of a state organization that was not kinship and tribal based, so it is plausible that this is where the first evidence of ideological sensitivity to the struggle should emerge. Marx certainly thought so. The great classicist who did so much to introduce anthropological ideas into the study of Greece, E. R. Dodds, waxed passionate on the very issue we are addressing:

> It was a misfortune for the Greeks that the idea of cosmic justice, which represented an advance on the old notion of purely arbitrary divine powers, and provided a sanction for the new civic morality, should have been thus associated with a primitive conception of the family. For it meant that the weight of religious feeling and religious law was thrown

against the emergence of a true view of the individual as a person, with personal rights and personal responsibilities. As Glotz showed . . . the liberation of the individual from the bonds of clan and family is one of the major achievements of Greek rationalism, and one for which the credit must go to Athenian democracy. But long after that liberation was complete in law, religious minds were still haunted by the ghost of the old solidarity. (1951:34)

It was not only religious minds that were so haunted. But Dodds beautifully expresses the "progressive-individualist" notion that has dominated our thinking on this topic: the individual had to be freed from the "bonds" of kinship and family before becoming a true person who could participate in the "new civic morality"—and hence in the eventual struggle against the burgeoning morality which became the "individual-versus-the-state" theme we are pursuing. To Dodds, the persistence of "primitive" kinship values is a hindrance in this progressive struggle.

When looking for the origins of the new individualism, commentators have looked in particular at Sophocles' *Antigone*. This, we are to suppose, displays the prototype of the dawning individuated, almost existential, conscience in its struggle with the dominance of the *polis* and political necessity. Since this play is part of the famous Theban cycle—including *Oedipus Tyrannus* and *Oedipus at Colonus,* and since the Oedipus saga has been of much interest to anthropologists in other contexts—evolutionary, structural, and psychoanalytical—it seems a good place to start.

Let us look first then at *Antigone*. I am inspired to do this by reading and rereading George Steiner's remarkable *Antigones* (1984), which was finished in the same year as my previously quoted bold remarks on kinship (1983). No discussion of the play can ever be the same after this exhaustive analysis of all the "Antigones" that have followed, some closely, some loosely, Sophocles, masterpiece, and all the commentaries on them. The basic story as given in the "Argument" to the Loeb Classics edition is as follows:

Antigone, daughter of Oedipus, the late king of Thebes, in defiance of Creon who rules in his stead, resolves to bury her brother Polynices, slain in his attack on Thebes. She is caught in the act by Creon's watchmen and brought before the king. She justifies her action, asserting that she was bound to obey the eternal laws of right and wrong in spite of any human ordinance. Creon, unrelenting, condemns her to be immured in a rock-hewn chamber. His son, Haemon, to whom Antigone is betrothed, pleads in vain for her life and threatens to die with her. Warned by the seer Teiresias, Creon repents him and hurries to release

Antigone from her rocky prison. But he is too late: he finds lying side by side Antigone who has hanged herself and Haemon who has also perished by his own hand. Returning to the palace he sees within the dead body of his queen who on learning of her son's death has stabbed herself to the heart. (311)

The play was first presented around 440 B.C. and was the first of the "Theban Trilogy," but it is the last episode of the legend: the culmination of the tragedy of the House of Cadmus and the ultimate fate of the children of the doomed Oedipus and his mother-wife Iocasta. We must return to Oedipus himself, inevitably, for clarification (as we must take a side glance at the equally unfortunate House of Atreus), but for the moment let us look at some of the issues raised by the actions of his children: the daughters Antigone and Ismene, and the sons Eteocles and Polynices.

The plot is simple and as outlined above (except for the important information that Eteocles, the loyal brother, was also killed fighting against the rebel Polynices, and Creon has buried him with honor). What has excited the huge volume of commentary, adaptations, translations, and imitations from the 1530s on is the drama of the conflict between Antigone and Creon. Commentators and adaptators have sided with one or the other, but overwhelmingly, of course, with Antigone. Hegel, in his *Lectures on the Philosophy of Religion* (II.3.a), was perhaps the first to give Creon his due, but even he called it a tie with his famous formula that the "tragedy" lay in the fact that they were both right: Creon acted as a responsible ruler driven by "necessities of state," Antigone as a conscience-driven individual moved by deep family loyalties. In the most famous latter-day interpretation, Anouilh has Antigone as an existentialist heroine, acting out of individual "commitment," and Creon, again, as the reasonable representative of state authority. When the play was put on in occupied Paris, both the Resistance and the Germans applauded with equal enthusiasm.

But while attention has focused on the Creon-Antigone struggle, no one has seriously challenged the "individual versus the state" interpretation. Of course, a lot of baggage goes along with this. Steiner lists five antinomies that are "constants of conflict in the condition of man" and with some of which, therefore, every tragedy must deal:

men vs. women

age vs. youth

individual vs. society

living vs. dead

men vs. gods

He rephrases these later as "masculinity vs. femininity; aging vs. youth; individual autonomy vs. social collectivity; existence vs. mortality; human vs. divine." The greatness of *Antigone,* he avers, lies in its being the only tragedy to encompass all these oppositions. (If he were a disciple of Lévi-Strauss he might add that in doing so it "overcomes" the oppositions — or as they are puzzlingly described, "contradictions"; but Steiner is too canny for such easy overinterpretations). I think he is right, and this is a pretty good summary of the major themes of all tragedy and of *Antigone* in particular. But I want to call attention to his insistence that it is the "individual" that is at issue in the struggle with "the state"; or "individual autonomy vs. social collectivity." Like many other commentators, Steiner sees Antigone as standing up for "family values," but he sees the "issue" nevertheless as one of individual assertion of conscience in the face of the demands of "state necessity." As the most authoritative commentator on the text of *Antigone,* Sir Richard Jebb, puts it squarely in his introduction: "The simplicity of the plot is due to the clearness with which two principles are opposed to each other. *Creon represents the duty of obeying the state's laws; Antigone, the duty of listening to the private conscience*" (1902:xviii).

The early Hegel is interesting in that he does see this as an issue of male/state versus female/family. The dead, in Greek theory, pass from the power of the state to that of the familial gods. In this passage, the supreme duty lies with the women of the family to bury their dead thus ensuring the passage to Hades. But, says Hegel, there are times when the state does not wish to relinquish its rights, even over the corpse. This is the driving energy of the Antigone plot (Bradley 1909). Creon (the state) wishes, for sound political reasons, to make an example of Polynices, who has committed treason by bringing foreign armies against his native city. He here obeys the "law" that the *polis* must be preserved at all costs. But Creon chooses to do this by denying burial to Polynices, and thus runs up against a greater and more profound law: that kin must bury their own dead to ensure their passage to the afterlife. Let us not forget the fate of the Athenian commanders after the brilliantly successful sea battle of Arginusae. Faced with a storm that might destroy their fleet, they took it into safe harbor, and in doing so neglected to gather up the bodies of dead Athenian sailors. They were tried for this impiety and executed. Socrates, who, like Creon, always put prudence before divinity, presided in the council at the time of this trial. He boldly stood against the indignant tide and refused to put the matter to the vote. Later, ironically, he was put to death himself by the same council, on a charge of impiety. At his trial (see Plato's *Apology*) he cites this episode as an example of his unfitness for a political life (and as a further irony insists that he would not have been in office had it not been the turn of his *phratria, vide infra*). But there is no question that here we do have a clash of individual and state; what I am questioning is whether there is really such a clash in Antigone's case.

The case of the admirals at Arginusae should, despite what the famous commentators have said, tell us what Antigone is about; what Sophocles really meant. Naturally we are here on familiar if dangerous ground. How can we really know what a fifth-century Athenian really meant? But it is ground that anthropologists have often trodden. We have been trying to explain what the mythmakers of alien cultures really meant for a long time now, although we have not settled on a consensus regarding method and interpretation. But here we have some texts and some scraps of history, and this is close to all we ever have, so let us not be daunted.

That it is the kin who must do the burying, and in particular the female kin (a symbol of the "homecoming" of the warrior—his return to the womb-tomb) has been, as I have said, regarded as part of the "baggage" that helps us interpret the essential "individual versus the state" conflict. After all, Antigone had to have something to oppose the state *about,* and it had to be something about which she felt deeply. But one gets the impression from many of the commentaries that any issue would have done as long as she felt strongly enough about it. I am going to suggest that the commentators have the cart before the horse and that the burial of kin is the essence of the meaning; Antigone's or Creon's "individuality" is only manifested in the *style* with which they play their conflicting "kinship" and "political" roles. The commentators, in other words, have confused style with substance. Antigone is either an appealing and courageous heroine or an annoying, pig-headed religious fanatic, depending on the reader's sympathies. Creon, likewise, is either the embodiment of reason or a vicious sadist (although I feel there was no doubt that Sophocles meant us to understand that he was in the wrong, despite Hegel's authoritative opinion to the contrary). But these individual styles are not what is at issue. They provide a kind of dramatic subplot to the main theme. Thus, Sophocles brilliantly, from a dramatic point of view, pits Antigone's religious fanaticism against her sister Ismene's pragmatism: "Yes, it is terrible, but there isn't a lot we can do about it, so we'd better learn to live with it." Antigone will have none of this: Polynices *must* be buried. Now here there are interesting individual differences, but the play is not, as a modern play (say, *Long Day's Journey into Night*) might be, *about* these differences. They give color and point to the plot, but they are not the plot itself.

The issue is not Antigone's stubborn devotion to her own point of view, it is her stubborn devotion to *the divine law*. She is not an existentialist heroine before her time, given to some bloody-minded "commitment," nor is she the supreme individualist challenging the power of the state. Above all she is not, despite many comparisons of this kind, a sort of Joan of Arc listening to her own private voices, which she considers to have authority over all external voices. Antigone would have thought Joan a complete crackpot and paid her no attention. The truth is the contrary: Antigone is not challenging the state in the name of individual conscience; she is not challenging any law in the name of that conscience; she is upholding a law in the name of religious duty. She is, at least in my reading of Sophocles, the supreme example of the unwaveringly loyal kinswoman doing her utmost to fulfill her duties to her kin group. If this involves her in a struggle to the death with the political authorities, so be it. She knows she represents a higher law, and after the intervention of Teiresias (the blind hermaphrodite prophet who is the major catalyst of *Oedipus Rex* also) Creon admits this, but too late: Antigone; Haemon, his son and her betrothed; and his wife, Eurydice, are all dead.

In death Antigone is vindicated, but what is vindicated is not her right to her individual conscience, but her adherence to a supraindividual law—almost a law of nature, at least of divine nature. This is why, to Sophocles, she is a heroine and a tragic figure. It never ceases to astonish me that her repeated insistence that she is *not* acting "individually" or "rebelliously" but in strict accordance with divine law is taken as a manifestation of her instinct—or impulse-driven femaleness—in contrast, of course, to Creon's male "reasonableness." Although these commentators usually mean this as some sort of compliment to Antigone, they should be investigated for sexism! They amply illustrate my point that we are viewing the whole plot through our very particular "individual versus the state" spectacles, and hence are only left with Antigone's stubborn individual style.

But as I keep wearisomely repeating, this is not the issue. Ismene, despite her very different "style," in the end joins in Antigone's protest, not because she is convinced that individuals must assert themselves against the state but because she is stung by her sister's call to religious duty. She asks Creon to let her share her sister's fate. She doesn't often get much credit for this from the commentators, and Antigone is priggishly nasty to her, while Creon dismisses it as an idle gesture. But it helps to make my point. The "individual" issues for Sophocles are matter for personal conflict and dramatic effect; they are not what the play is about. Thus, the moment when Ismene tearfully asks Creon to bury her alive with Antigone is, for me, a supreme moment of the play. It must have drawn a gasp of relief, admiration, and approval from the seventeen thousand Athenians in the Theater of Dionysus. The other surviving female of the House of Laius had come back to her duty, despite her all-too-understandable individual and womanly fears. The kinship group had closed ranks against the state, and the beleaguered Creon was more than ever on the defensive after this.

Although the language of the *Iliad* echoes throughout the Greek tragedies, this theme could never have arisen there. There could not have been a conflict of individual or kinship versus the state because there was no state; there were only tribal groups and tribal loyalties. People could disobey their tribal rulers, of course, but this was more like a child disobeying a parent than a citizen defying a bureaucracy. Both rulers and followers were expected to keep divine laws. Antigone belongs to this world, which is why Creon, the embodiment of the *polis,* can't stand her. There could have been no Antigone in the *Iliad,* for there everyone was under the rule of the gods; the state did not stand apart with its secular purposes. Thus, there could be no Creon either. Students discover this when made to think about the difference between the two great quarrels: that of Antigone versus Creon and Achilles versus Agamemnon. The latter is often misinterpreted. Students are often angry with Achilles. While they recognize he had a legitimate personal complaint against Agamemnon they do not see why he went as far as he did in refusing to fight for "his fellow Greeks." It has to be pointed out that he had no "fellow Greeks" in any nationalistic sense. This notion is ours, and neither the protagonists nor the other Greeks shared it. They knew that the alliance of tribes that sailed for Troy was a loose agglomeration of (often related) tribal chiefs of whom Agamemnon, while more than simply *primus inter pares* was nevertheless no more than, say, the High King of Ireland: an almost ritual leader with limited powers over his territorial "kings." He could summon them to war, but he had no power to keep them there. The Greeks were not engaged in a "great patriotic war"—a nationalist struggle—but in a raiding expedition on the coast of Asia Minor in which the siege of Troy was one incident: the one that gets related in the *Iliad.* Thus Achilles was quite within his rights to behave as he did to force his point, even at the expense of "his fellow Greeks." Sir Moses Finley, as usual, puts it succinctly:

The fact is that such a notion of social obligation is fundamentally non-heroic. It reflects the new element, the community, at the one point at which it was permitted to override everything else, the point of defense against an invader. In the following generations, when the community began to move from the wings to the center of the Greek stage, the hero quickly died out, for the honor of the hero was purely individual, something he lived and fought for only for its own sake and his own sake. (Family attachment was permissible, but that was because one's kin were indistinguishable from oneself.) The honor of a community was a totally different quality, requiring another order of skills and virtues: in fact, the community could grow only by taming the hero and blunting the free exercise of his prowess, and a domesticated hero was a contradiction in terms. (1979:116-17)

But this "new community"—the incipient state—did not exist yet in the epics. So while the Greeks wanted their hero back, and even deplored his refusal of Agamemnon's overtures of peace, they never questioned his right to sail home, as he threatened to do several times. Even Agamemnon conceded that Achilles was right, and pleaded temporary insanity—"Zeus made me do it." Thus at this tribal stage of Greek society the issue does not arise, as it does not arise in any tribal society or in any conglomerate of tribes or even in primitive divine monarchies. Spencer, and Durkheim following him, may have been going a bit far when they said that at this stage of social evolution individuals did not exist, except for chiefs. But one knows what they meant. It is why only the doings of chiefs are reported in the *Iliad* and why Aristotle was led, therefore, to think that tragedy could only be about "noble persons." *Death of a Salesman* would have been incomprehensible as a tragic subject, and until the twentieth-century play, salesmen and their like were fit subjects only for comedy.

In the epics we *can* have a conflict of individual and *society*. This is often the essence of them. But "society" is here not understood as "state." (The failure to make this distinction, Dumont points out—following Sir Ernest Barker—vitiates much of the arguments of Locke and Rousseau.) Rather, society is the culture, the way of life, the "proprieties" in Havelock's terms (1978). The epic teaches the proprieties by showing the awful consequences of the breach of them. Thus, in the *Iliad*, it is Agamemnon himself who breaches the proprieties and brings about the disaster. Achilles only breaches them in the sense of overreacting, both to Agamemnon's insult and later in despoiling Hector's body. But in a sense both of these were "acceptable" behaviors in a hero when the "wrath" had come upon him (Redfield 1975; Friedrich 1977). And he mends both offenses: he makes up with Agamemnon and accepts his apology (and unbelievable oath that Briseis is still a virgin), and he restores Hector's body to Priam. Again, the assertion of the primacy of proper burial in the hierarchy of the proprieties (for an interesting account of burial as a clue to understanding Greek society and "state" see I. Morris [1987]).

But in no case of the "individual versus society" conflicts do we have a quarrel between individuals and the *state*. In Creon's case, however, he does not act as a tribal chieftain with a grievance against a subject but as the chief executive officer of a constitutional monarchy, answerable, in the end, to the citizens of the *polis*. He does not act purely for spite or personal gain, but out of Necessities of State. The cases are parallel only in that, in the wider context of the "proprieties," it is Creon, like Agamemnon, who is the offender, and Antigone, like Achilles, who is the offended party (and she too "overreacts"). But this is an appeal precisely to those more archaic values of the epic, and the audience would have well understood this. Antigone offended against the perceived necessity of "state interests": Creon offended against "what was done."[1]

If one does not distinguish between these cases, then much confusion is inevitable. It is one thing to offend against sacredly established custom, another to break a municipal ordinance. Creon understands this and hence the strength of Antigone's appeal, by trying himself to invoke the "gods of the city" or even the "divinity of kingship" (*Zeus Basileus*), almost contemptuously handing over to Antigone what he had hypocritically tried to claim for himself: the "Zeus of blood-kinship," or the "Zeus of the Family Hearth" (*Zeus Herkeios*). But his appeal is limited. Only one person can be a king, while everyone has a family. And to deny proper burial went even beyond what the divinities of the *polis* could plausibly demand.

What we must grasp is that at the tribal stage allegiance was personal, familial, based on kinship or pseudo-kinship. The war between kinship and the state had not begun because the tribe was, conceptually, a large kinship group and the "individual" was defined by his kinship status and kin group membership. There were tribal "assemblies" where all the warriors attended, and these have a superficial look of the *polis* assembling in the *agora* to debate. Indeed, the Homeric poets may have read certain practices of the town assembly back into the gatherings of the *Iliad,* and conversely, these assemblies of equal citizens might well have originated in the old tribal assemblies. But in the *Iliad* the assembled troops were essentially brought in as witnesses to the doings of the chieftains. In an oral culture, as Eric Havelock (1978) points out, decisions could not be written down, they had to be remembered.

And for truly important decisions, the collective memory was necessary as a witness. Also, the "sense of the meeting" could be taken, since it was important for the leaders to know how far they could carry the armies with them. But these gatherings were not assemblies of citizens for the purpose of taking votes. As Finley points out (1979:110), these assemblies were "passive spectators." "The defense of a right was purely a private matter." He adds that the poet "was composing at a time when the community principle had advanced to a point of some limited public administration of justice. But he was singing of a time when that was not the case, except for the intangible power of public opinion" (110).

By the time of the *Odyssey* the "limited public administration of justice" had not advanced much, but the idea was taking shape. The *polis* definitely existed in Ithaca. At the beginning, Telemachus takes his complaints against the suitors to a not very sympathetic assembly in the *agora*. At the end, when he and Odysseus have dispatched the suitors, their followers go to the *agora* and justify their actions—not without lively debate and dissension, especially since most of the citizens there were relatives of the suitors. Here a notion of the secular state and secular purposes emerges, and the characters of the *Odyssey*, even down to the lowly swineherd ally of our heroes, are that much more "individual." Odysseus has here been transformed from a tribal "king" to a very powerful nobleman, himself subject to the laws of the political community. At this stage, even a "king" was as often as not a *turannos*—a tyrant. This to the Greeks was not necessarily an evil kind of government (although in its bad form it could turn into that), but one which ultimately drew its legitimacy from the acquiescence of the governed, rather than from right of descent. Oedipus was, we must remember, as the correct title of the play (rather than its Romanization to "Rex," which we regularly use) insists, a *turannos* as far as Thebes was concerned. Had the Thebans recognized him from the start as their true "Rex" he would have been "Basileus." Creon too was a *turannos*, for although he had a shadowy claim by descent to the throne of Thebes, it was only in the "usurper" line. Nevertheless he was the chief official of a *polis* and was ultimately answerable to it; he was not a tribal chief or oriental despot. And while one can say with confidence that, by any definition, a "state" existed with the fully developed Greek *polis*, it can be argued that an equally fully developed idea of the autonomous individual was something that itself came even later—after Plato and Aristotle and with the the development of Hellenistic thought (Dumont, 1986). Even so, Socrates' quarrel was clearly that of an individual with the Athenian state, and as such was not like

Antigone's with Creon in this crucial aspect: Socrates had no mediating kin group that he represented in his quarrel; he stood alone and, indeed, like Joan of Arc, listened to his voices—his *daemon*.

To summarize: the "state" in Sophocles' mythical Thebes had a somewhat more advanced form than that of Homer's Ithaca but not as advanced as Athenian democracy. It was not yet at the point where all the free male citizens voted, but it was at the point where they assembled and voiced opinions and where a tyrant could not rule with impunity. But there was a rudimentary "public administration of justice." Creon had laws and police to enforce them, and everyone, including the royal family, was expected to obey them; definitely a step above the self-help system described by Finley for archaic society. Thus we can speak here of a genuine "individual/family versus the state" issue: there was a state because, in the classical formulation, there was a sovereign who claimed a monopoly of the legitimate use of force.

We shall return to this theme as well as looking at the reality of kinship and political institutions in Athens, but for the moment let us see what the raw text has to offer to support my thesis. A good place to start is the first line. *Totus locus vexatus* was an early despairing commentary, and this is puzzling since Sophocles was not one to waste an opening statement. This was not a theater where it was fashionable to arrive ten minutes late. It was a religious festival dedicated to the god Dionysus, and seventeen thousand Athenians had already sat in the hot sun to watch the comedy and the satyr play before settling down to the high point of the day: the prize-winning tragedy. And *Antigone* was to become the most popular tragedy of them all. This was a religious occasion, not a secular entertainment, and the audience expected a religious message not a humanistic moral. (This should help us in interpreting the "meaning.") So they were silent and even reverent, and totally expectant, when the masked male actor representing Antigone addressed his counterpart playing Ismene.

Would Sophocles have then fed them an unintelligible line? Of course not—see his other plays. The opening line of *Oedipus Tyrannus* clearly addresses the Thebans as members of the lineage of Cadmus:

> Ὦ τέκνα, Κάδμου τοῦ πάλαι νέα τροφή.

In the opening of *Oedipus at Colonus* he clearly states his old age, his blindness, and his relationship to Antigone:

> Τέκνον τυφλοῦ γέροντος Ἀντιγόνη, τίνας.

Why then the despair of the commentators and the confusion of the translators over the first line of *Antigone?* The line has been translated in wildly different ways, and the latest poet-translator, Stephen Spender, simply abandons the attempt and starts without it. Yet the line, which for me does what it is supposed to do and sets the theme of the play, is of great anthropological interest:

᾿Ω κοινὸν αὐτάδελφον Ἰσμήνης κάρα.

O koinon autadelphon Ismenes kara

Here is a sample of translations:

Own sister of my blood, one life with me (Campbell 1896)

Ismene, sister, mine own dear sister (Jebb 1900)

Ismene, sister of my blood and heart (Storr 1912)

O sister, Ismene, dear, dear sister Ismene! (Watling 1947)

Ismene, dear sister (Fitts and Fitzgerald 1949)

My sister, my Ismene (Wyckoff 1954)

Come, Ismene, my own dear sister, come! (Roche 1958)

My own flesh and blood—dear sister, dear Ismene. (Fagles 1984)

(I would have quoted Yeats, but he took it from the French, not the original, so it isn't helpful.)[2] Obviously "sister" and "Ismene" can be agreed on, but little else. There is, for example, despite the translators' predilection for it, no possessive pronoun in the line at all. As for Roche's invocation to "come" (twice), even his eloquent plea for poetic feeling and nuance over mere literal accuracy does not justify calling this a "translation." But if we look at it word by word we see that "translation" is impossible if we mean literal translation. It might look something like this:

O kinsperson, selfsame-sister, Ismene's head.

But even with the first noun we are in trouble. Thus *koinon* means "kindred person" and, according to Jebb, "refers simply to birth from the same parents" (1902:49). But it is also etymologically related to, for example, *koine,* the "vulgar" or "common" language, and can suggest "commonality" or "communality" as we use its English equivalent in expressions like "a kindred spirit." The second term is "sister" with an intensifier meaning "full" or "true"—literally "self" or "same." This is perhaps the least problematical term (except for the proper noun) but what are we to make of "Ismene's head"? Except in the eccentric translation of Hölderlin, the head never appears literally, and everyone takes it as a periphrasis. What exactly it meant to fifth-century

Athenians we just don't know. Even Jebb is driven to find Latin parallels. It "usu. implies respect, affection, or both," he says, and the translators have, with relief, taken this to heart (1902:49). But of course we often, in Indo-European languages, use body parts as kinship metaphors, speaking, for example, of the "head of a family." Steiner seems to suggest this in his proposed "literal" translation of the line:

O my very own sister's shared, common head of Ismene.

But it seems to me this both gains and loses at the same time. There is the intrusive possessive pronoun again, and there is nothing, grammatically or otherwise, to suggest that the head is common or shared. The probable relation of *koinon* to *kara* is that both may suggest "springing from the same source"—if we can have "godhead" then we can have "kinhead," if you like. Thus the idiom, which must have meant something forceful to Sophocles' audience, probably reinforced the opening word directly. It is not so much that the head is common, as that Antigone and Ismene share a common "source." Remember that Athena was born from the head of Zeus—a point to which we shall return—so this is not such a far-fetched idea in the Greek context.

But, we then might ask, why is Antigone saying this? If Ismene is her true (full) sister, then of course they are kin and share common descent. But surely this is the point. She knows this, Ismene knows it, and the audience knows it too. But Sophocles chooses to open the play with a line that trebly stresses their common blood—their relatedness by descent—because this is precisely what the play is about. And a failure to see this clearly as *the* theme of the play—not "Antigone as Joan of Arc"—leads often to an unnecessary overinterpretation of the line. Its plain unadorned statement is its strength. It says "this play is about kinship, folks, and the bonds that unite those of common blood—particularly siblings." It signals this issue as much as the opening line of *Oedipus Tyrannus* signals the unity and common curse of the people of Thebes as the lineal descendants of Cadmus (with the added irony, surely not lost on the sophisticated Athenian audience, that Oedipus does not believe himself to be of that line and hence not governed by its fate). With the first line of *Antigone* again we are immediately into the central action: the sisters, as the last living members of the line of common descent, have all the duties of the women of the line thrust upon them. It is their burden and they must share it totally and without reservation. Indeed this is what Antigone goes on to say in detail to Ismene (interestingly using the Greek dual form, which she drops after Ismene's demural).[3]

But it is all telegraphed in that first line, which alerts the audience precisely to the meaning of the *agon*—the struggle that is to follow. It is captured quite well in the paraphrase with which Don Taylor opened his BBC-TV production of the play in 1987:

> Ismene, listen, the same blood flows in both our
> veins, the blood of Oedipus.

Steiner (1984) and Knox (1984), for example, hover close to seeing this, and could be quoted at length for their many mentions of "kinship"—indeed it is inescapable if one looks at the words squarely. But ultimately they overinterpret, because still hanging in there is the Joan-of-Arc syndrome: the Antigone-as-supreme-individualist idea. For all its strangeness, Hölderlin's marvelous German coinage perhaps comes closest to the essence of the line:

> Gemeinsamschwesterliches, o Ismenes Haupt!

"A willed monster" Steiner calls it—and I cannot do it justice. But anthropologists will instantly recognize the *Gemein* as the root of *Gemeinschaft*—a word they are totally familiar with from Tönnies (1887) in its contrast to *Gesellschaft*. Tönnies was stressing the difference between the natural community based on kinship ties with the "association" based on individual contract. (It is Maine's distinction in another guise of course.) Thus it is the "kinship community of the sisters" that is captured in Hölderlin's word, while Ismene's head is left uninterpreted, which is just as well. (When I presented the word to a bilingual informant—my department chairman in fact—and asked for his spontaneous response he answered, "sisterly togetherness.") Goethe and Schiller might have laughed out loud at some of Hölderlin's seeming blunders, but his bold coinage here seems to hit the mark better than Goethe's weak "most sisterly of sisters." If I had to render the "head" into some English equivalent, I would try a first line something like this:

> O kinswoman, true sister-in-descent, Ismene.

Now this is not intended as a mellifluous "literary" translation, nor is it "literal," but it is directed at anthropologists who have their own idioms that others find hard to handle, just as the Athenians had theirs. By insisting on the jargon-word *descent* I should be flagging, for such an audience, an interpretation heavy with meaning, just as for his specialized audience Sophocles did the same with his in-group jargon-word *head*. The subconscious processes will be at work as I continue. So let them ferment while I try to make some sense of the most disputed passage in the play.

A way into this is perhaps via Hegel, who has been much criticized for his "two rights make a wrong" analysis but who always, to his credit, insisted that the struggle ultimately was between *the family* and the state—or rather between family values and civic values. But then Hegel too was protesting against the overindividualized interpretation of society. This does not prevent him, however, from falling back into it where *Antigone* is concerned. Thus Steiner points to Hegel's distinction between *Kriegstaat*—the "war state"—and the domain of *Privatrecht*—"private right"—which has to do with "the preservation of the family." But one still has the feeling that ultimately this "family" is really a kind of emotional resource for the individual who is the real point of the struggle. Thus Steiner summarizing Hegel: "The division between *polis* and individual itself reflects the engagement of the Absolute in temporality and in phenomenal contingencies" (1984:26). And so on in the same vein.[4]

The problem here is precisely with "The Family." What is it? Much that is eloquent about family values is said in the commentaries. Thus, for Hegel and those who follow him, the state only values a man for his actions, the family values him for himself. In this, the relationship of brother and sister is paramount, being a nonerotic valuing-of-another-for-the-self relation between man and woman, the two poles of the human dialectic. And so on. Actually, in light of modern genetics, one might quibble with Hegel's contention that because siblings have no reproductive interest in each other they are not "estranged by self-interest." Each has, in fact, an exact, measurable $(r = .25)$, inclusive-fitness-maximizing interest in the other. But be that as it may, it does not help us, any more than Hegel's "non-reproductive" formula, in understanding the real meaning of "family" or "kinsperson" in *Antigone*.

We are cursed, in a way, in English, in having the dual Latin and Germanic inheritance, since it has given us the two words *family* and *household*. Once a language has two words it will invent a conceptual distinction between them whether one was there originally or not. (Thus *cow* becomes the live animal and *beef* the consumable dead flesh.) Most languages do not make the "family/household" distinction that has led anglophone anthropologists sadly astray. The Roman *familia*, like its Greek counterpart, *oikos*, was not thought of apart from the household, and the latter could include other relatives, servants, and slaves. It is interesting that the Oxford English Dictionary still prefers as its primary definition: "Members of a household, parents, children, servants etc." Even etymologically the two words may be related in some proto–Indo-European *fa-* or *ha-* (Sanskrit *dha-*) meaning "neighborhood," their derivatives being diminutives of some kind (Partridge 1983). But between the household on the one hand and the *sib* or *Sippe,* the *curia* or *gens,* and the *phratria* or *genneta* on the other, their was no intervening "family" in either Germanic or Greco-Roman society. (The same is true in Celtic, the only other language/culture of this group with which I am thoroughly familiar.) There were "relatives" of course (*cognati* or *kind* or *muintir*) but these were not a social group; they were a category, of which the "family" was the coresidential unit.

House, of course, was often used metaphorically to refer to a noble line, as in "The House of Stuart." But again, this was not either a family or a household but a lineage. Even if our commentaries were to replace *family values* with *kinship values*—which would be more accurate perhaps—we still have to ask "what kinship values?" The particularistic values that Hegel and his followers describe most certainly apply universally to kinship; but as we all know, who is or is not kin, and even among that wide category what *kind* of kin, (no pun intended) is very variable. The values apply, but to whom? Simply to talk about "family values" in this universalistic fashion will not do, especially when one knows that it is some modern concept of "the family" that the commentator has in mind and that cannot even have existed for the fifth-century Greeks.[5]

Thus, for example, for the Hegelians, Steiner states that "in death, the husband, son or brother, passes from the domain of the *polis* back to that of the family" (1984:34). These males become the "familial" responsibility of "woman," and where the task falls upon the sister it "takes on the highest degree of holiness." Well, this may be true in a world where "absolutes engage in temporality" and the like; but was it true for the Greeks? And for the Greeks of all eras?

Actually, for the fifth-century Greeks of Sophocles' audience it may have approximated the truth, since the decline of kinship-based groups and their replacement with voluntary associations and territorial units (*demes*) was well on its way after the reforms of Cleisthenes (Murray 1986). Even so, membership more often than not passed from father to son, and women were excluded. Sophocles himself eloquently describes their fate in being "exiled" from their father's house on marriage (in a fragment [no. 583] from the otherwise lost play *Tereus*). A patriarchal, if not strictly patrilineal, ethos prevailed in Athens even when citizenship and contract had already displaced kinship and status to a large extent. But we must remember that Antigone and her people belonged to an older, aristocratic and monarchical age, when kinship, for the noble families at least, was more thoroughly patrilineal in the technical sense. This still remained in the Athens of Sophocles in the form of the *gennetai*—the aristocratic religious groups that monopolized the priesthoods and more important city cults. Sophocles' audience then would expect the *Antigone* to reflect the archaic and royal conceptions of kinship, not the vulgar democratic concept that dominated the lives of most of them. Antigone was, let us remember, not a daughter of the people. She was a princess of a royal house only a few generations removed from the gods themselves, being a direct descendant (in the male line) of Cadmus, through his wife Harmonia of Ares and Aphrodite, and through Cadmus' father, King Agenor, of the unfortunate Io and Zeus himself. She was also, through another of Zeus's alliances, a cousin of Dionysus at whose festival, and in whose theater, her story was being told.

Let us keep this in mind as we look at the disputed passage. It occurs during Antigone's sad and beautiful lament for her fate, so often quoted (ll. 891–928). She interrupts the lament with a passage of bitterness and casuistry that seems so at variance with her high ethical position that many who have loved the play, from Goethe onwards, have insisted that it is an interpolation by some other hand. Goethe prayed that some scholar would be able to prove once and for all that it was indeed an alien interpolation. None of the doubters, however, seem able to suggest why anyone should have wanted to insert the passage! But this lack of motive has not stopped the endless scholarly wrangling with the "experts" variously dismissing it as not worthy of Sophocles or praising it as the essence of Sophoclean brilliance. Aristotle did not doubt its authenticity, and had a high regard for Antigone's casuistry. This alone should give us pause. If Aristotle of all people regarded it as "logical" then who are we to question it? And remember that he was working with an earlier and more authentic text than we possess. But Goethe continued with his prayers, and several scholars obliged with *obiter dicta*. Jebb, perhaps the greatest of the textual critics, feels that Sophocles' son Iophon, or some other "sorry poet," must have been responsible, but again, he never says why (1902:182). And why did Aristotle accept it? Could it again be our modern sensibilities getting in the way of what was, for Sophocles and his audience, and for Aristotle, a very straightforward statement of archaic, aristocratic fact?

I will give the original here for accuracy of reference, and then quote the translation of Fagles (1984), since it seems to me true to the original and does not present the same problems of translation as the first line. Antigone speaks of how she performed the obsequies for her father and mother and for her brother Eteocles, but is now being punished for trying to do the same thing for Polynices. Then she launches into the disputed lines (905-12).

οὐ γάρ ποτ' οὔτ' ἂν εἰ τέκνων μήτηρ ἔφυν,
οὔτ' εἰ πόσις μοι κατθανὼν ἐτήκετο,
Βίᾳ πολιτῶν τόνδ' ἂν ᾐρόμην πόνον.
τίνος νόμου δὴ ταῦτα πρὸς χάριν λέγω;
πόσις μὲν ἄν μοι κατθανόντος ἄλλος ἦν,
καὶ παῖς ἀπ' ἄλλου φωτός, εἰ τοῦδ' ἤμπλακον
μητρὸς δ' ἐν Ἅιδου καὶ πατρὸς κεκευθότοιν
οὐκ ἔστ' ἀδελφὸς ὅστις ἂν βλάστοι ποτέ.

Never, I tell you
if I had been the mother of children
or if my husband died, exposed and rotting—
I'd never have taken this ordeal upon myself,
never defied our people's will. What law,
you ask, do I satisfy with what I say?
A husband dead there might have been another.
A child by another too, if I had lost the first.
But mother and father both lost in the halls of Death
no brother could ever spring to light again.

What has upset the whole line of commentators from Goethe on-wards is, in the first place, Antigone's seeming glaring inconsistency. Having been the high ethical defender of "familial values" she now seems to dump half the "family" she is supposed to be devoted to. Husbands and children don't count, it seems. Now, she has never said they *did* count; she has only insisted that she has to bury her brother. It is the commentators, bringing to the lines their own notions of "family" and "familial" who scream "inconsistent." They are even more outraged by the "casuistry" in which she appears to justify her "in-consistencies." One can get another husband, she says, other children, but since her parents are dead, there can be no more brothers. Aristotle thought this a good defense and cited it as an example to follow. Personally, I see it as unnecessary. She did not need to defend her position. I suspect, however, that Sophocles felt that some of his audience might not fully grasp what she was saying, or might need to be reminded what the "familial values" were that she was defending, and so put in the "casuistry" to make her position clearer.

Even those who believe the lines to be genuine do not seem happy to take them at face value. Sophocles certainly wrote them, they say, but the lines *are* inconsistent, so we must explain with great subtlety the nature of the inconsistency, thus rendering it intelligible. Watling (1947) in his notes maintains that these lines are "possibly a spurious interpolation," but he doesn't say why anyone would have interpolated them in the first place. Some editors, he says, have considered them "logically and psychologically inappropriate." However, he argues, "On the supposition that Antigone, in her last despair, gives utterance to an inconsistent and even unworthy thought, the passage seems to me to be dramatically right" (167). There we have it: the thought is inconsistent and unworthy, but Sophocles probably wanted us to realize that Antigone was breaking down under the stress. Why then, we might ask, did she utter such a seemingly cunning and casuistical argument that impressed Aristotle with its cogency? Other commentators often come closer. Thus Steiner, for example, stresses Antigone's "aloneness" and attributes her outburst to "shallow but momentarily dazzling rhetorical ingenuity which marked her father's style" (1984:280). It is her "extremity" that forces her into this "Herodotean plea." It is "the sophistry whereby she would prove the unique status of a dead brother as against all other losses" (280). But does she prove it against *all* other losses? Actually not: only against the loss of husband or children. She has already performed the lustrations for mother and father, and where it concerns males, she never excludes the father from consideration, only the husband and son. Even though Creon, for instance, is her mother's brother, it is clear she would never include him among those who deserve her "devotion unto death" in the matter of burial.

Unfortunately, her father, Oedipus, had no brothers or paternal nephews, or we could have clinched the argument if she had included (or not excluded) these. For if we assume that she is here asserting a strict aristocratic-patrilineal view of kinship, it is indeed totally logical to exclude the husband and son. Neither of these are members of *her* royal patriline—of her own patrilineage. The lineage—or in the Greek usage the "house"—in question is of course that of Labdacus and Laius (ultimately of Cadmus—back to the first line of *Oedipus Tyrannus* again), and Knox in one of the most perceptive contemporary commentaries recognized this: "It is her fanatical devotion to one particular family, her own, the doomed, incestuous, accursed house of Oedipus, and especially to its most unfortunate member, the brother whose corpse lay exposed to the birds and dogs" (Knox 1984:49).

He points out that her repudiation of husband and son is not wholly hypothetical, since she has indeed sacrificed her marriage to Haemon and the children that might have issued from it. But even Knox sees this declaration as a "moment of self-discovery" when she realizes she is "absolutely alone." She identifies "the driving force behind her action, the private, irrational imperative" and so on. Although he comes close, Knox still feels some elaborate explanation is required. He cannot take her words at face value, because, like the others, he does not know what that value is.

For those who are not anthropologists and for whom the transparency of patrilineal ideology may not be so obvious, let me simply diagram the relationships as they would appear patrilineally (see figure 1).

The line of Laius, going back to Cadmus (the brother of Europa), is in "balanced opposition" to the line of Menoeceus, going back to Echion of the Spartoi (who sprang from the Dragon's teeth sown by Cadmus). And indeed, the throne of Thebes has passed back and forth, by marriage and usurpation, between the two lines. As Bernal (1987) points out, in legend, accepted as based on historical truth by Hesiod and the Greeks generally, Kadmos (Cadmus) was a Phoenecian who founded Thebes, bringing with him the Canaanite alphabet, which he taught to the Greeks. If we wish, we could take the Cadmean line back at least to Agenor, King of Argos, one of the sons of Io and

Figure 1. Patrilineal Relationships

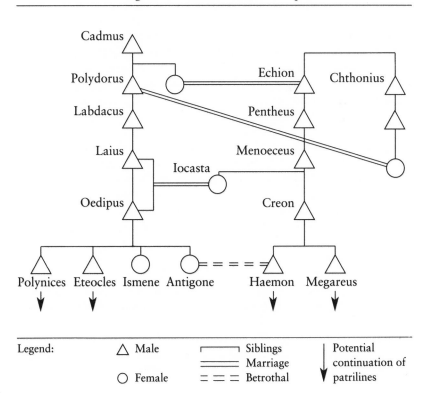

Legend: △ Male   ┌────┐ Siblings   │ Potential
                              ════ Marriage   ▼ continuation of
           ○ Female   ═ ═ ═ Betrothal   patrilines

Zeus. The Spartoi, springing from the ground, could well represent an autochthonous (Pelasgian?) lineage usurped by the immigrant line, or in turn usurping it.[6] There were a number of important intermarriages between the lineages, and the impending marriage of Haemon and Antigone would have been the last in the series; its failure brought the dynastic story to a close in a sense wholly appropriate to tragedy: it was consummated in death and entombment. (We don't know what happened to Ismene.)

On Antigone's theory (the ideology of patrilineal relatedness) she would have been responsible for the children of her brothers, for example (they didn't have any), but not for those of her husband (i.e., her own children). None of this means she would not have *joined in* the lustral rites; she obviously would have. As we have seen, a wife was thoroughly incorporated into her husband's household and would have joined the women of the household in mourning the death of a member. Thus Antigone had helped perform the rites for Iocasta, her mother. But what she is saying in her speech is that she would not have felt an obligation to defy the state unto death to perform such rites. That obligation she felt only for her patrilineal kin. In these matters, royal women in Greece were not nearly so isolated from their "houses" of origin as common women. No matter whom they married, they remained a "daughter" of their father's house first and foremost and continued their attachments to it. As an example, think of the behavior of Olympias, the mother of Alexander the Great, who was constantly returning to her father's house to plot against her husband, Philip of Macedon (Lane Fox 1973).

What Antigone is saying, then, in her casuistry, is in effect: "there is no way in which the royal line of Cadmus/Laius/Oedipus could be continued now that my brothers are dead. Polynices was the last male of that line and my duty was to him. Sons and husbands I could have had, but they would not replace him or continue the line; they would only perpetuate their own line. Therefore my duty to him was absolute and final." Thus, viewed as a statement of patrilineal ideology and its obligations, her "casuistry" is logical. It is a plain statement of the facts and can be taken absolutely at face value. And this patrilineal ideology, as we know, is deep-rooted not only in the Greek but in the general Indo-European past, as exemplified in the "Omaha" kinship terminology of proto–Indo-European (see Friedrich 1966; Benveniste 1969).

I was alerted to this issue in Greek tragedy by the more obvious case of Orestes in the *Eumenides* of Aeschylus. There Apollo defends Orestes against the charge brought by the Furies that in killing his mother (Clytemnestra) in revenge for the murder of his father (Agamemnon) he laid himself open to death at their hands as the avengers of murdered kin. This was their job—a dirty one, but someone had to do it—since parricide could not go unpunished. Many anthropologists from McLennan in his *Studies in Ancient History* (1886), to Kluckhohn and Firth and even Fox have been fascinated by this passage. Let me quote it here since it is of obvious anthropological interest. Apollo has brought Orestes to Athens where Athena has promised a fair trial. The Furies (Erinyes) are the accusers—the chorus in fact— and Apollo the defense counsel. Athena is the judge, and a jury of twelve Athenians has been impaneled. The Furies make their final accusation and Apollo makes his final clinching argument as follows (from the Loeb Classical Library Edition):

> Chorus: Mark now the meaning of thy plea for acquittal! Shall he who has spilled upon the ground his mother's kindred (*homaimon*) blood, shall he thereafter inhabit his father's house in Argos? To what altars of common worship shall he have access? What brotherhood (*phrateron*) will admit him to its lustral rite?

> Apollo: This too I will set forth, and mark how rightful shall be my answer. The mother of what is called her child is not its parent, but only the nurse of the newly implanted germ. The begetter is the parent, whereas she, as a stranger for a stranger, doth but preserve the sprout, except God shall blight its birth. And I will offer thee a sure proof of what I say: fatherhood there may be when mother there is none. Here at hand is a witness, the child of Olympian Zeus—and not so much as nursed in the darkness of the womb, but such a scion as no goddess could bring forth.

Smyth, the translator (1926), in a footnote makes two interesting comments. The Furies ask among what "kin," "clan," or "brotherhood" Orestes may perform the lustral rites. *Brotherhood* is the more correct translation of *phratria*, since, apart from its etymological connections with the Indo-European root for *brother* (e.g., Latin *frater*), as Smyth observes: "Kinsfolk, actual or fictitious, were united in *phratriai* with common worship, offerings, and festivals" (1926:334). But the *phratriai* were not descent groups in the anthropological sense. Kin of any connection could be inducted into them, and nonkin, upon adoption, became pseudo-kin—a kind of *compadrazgo* system. Thus the Furies here are asserting a kind of bilateral or cognatic or even fictive notion of kinship. This is interesting in view of Smyth's second note where he gives examples of the patrilineal ideology of procreation in other Greek authors (especially Euripides) and says: "This passage in the play has been invoked as evidence that the Athenians of the 5th-century

B.C. were upholding some ancient mode of tracing descent from the mother (the argument of the Erinyes); others, the patrilinear theory advocated by Apollo" (335).

He obviously had McLennan and others of the "matriarchal origins" persuasion in mind, and indeed this is still alive and well in the works of Mary Renault (suitably seasoned with Frazer) and Robert Graves, to say nothing of its resurrection by some feminists. But there is no historical evidence for this, and indeed the internal evidence suggests that the Greek playwrights and audience expected the Erinyes to avenge *all* murdered parents—not just mothers. Why, it is asked, did they not visit vengeance on Clytemnestra for killing Agamemnon? Obviously, a husband is not kin to his wife, they reply. And note that Antigone invokes the same principle. But Apollo counters with the argument that neither is a son kin to his mother, for example, Athena who sprang from the "head" (again) of Zeus without maternal intervention: a not-too-subtle attempt to sway the judge who had the deciding vote in the trial when the Athenian judges were deadlocked. Thus, according to Apollonian theory, it is only patricide, and not matricide, that has to be punished.

Looking ahead, we might note a peculiarity about interpretations of *Oedipus Tyrannus* that involve this point. Although commentators, and in particular Freud, have dwelt on the incestuous marriage of Oedipus and Iocasta, there is little in the original to suggest that this was nearly so important a "crime" as the murder of Laius; if indeed it was a crime at all as opposed to an unlooked-for disaster. What the oracle demanded in order to lift the plague from Thebes was the discovery of the murderer of Laius: the patricide. The incest was never mentioned. This is not to say that it was lightly regarded by the Greeks, but that it was not the cause of the misfortunes of the city, while the patricide was. In *Oedipus at Colonus,* we must remember, Creon, through the mediation of Ismene, begs Oedipus to return so that he may be buried just outside the boundaries of Thebes. This is in response to a prophecy promising victory in battle to those who honor the bones of Oedipus. But even though Thebes desperately wants to keep control of the tomb, it cannot allow it to be within the boundaries of the city because Oedipus' crime of patricide is too great. This is quite explicitly stated. It is not the incest, but the killing of his father, the Theban king, that prevents his native city from garnering the rich reward of burying him there. Oedipus, of course, refuses the offer, and Athens gets the honor of his bones and ultimate victory. He had not slain his father in Athens, so there was no danger for the Athenians.

The quarrel in the *Eumenides,* as I read it, is not between a matrilinear

(Erinyes) and patrilinear (Apollo) ideology, but between the aristocratic/royal/divine theory of the latter and a demotic notion of kinship based on the image of the *phratria*. After the reforms of Cleisthenes, the phratries took on greater importance, and the patrilinear *gennetai* declined. What Apollo, on Orestes' behalf, is saying, in essence, is what Antigone is saying on behalf of Polynices: whatever notions of kinship apply to the *demos* and are supported by the Erinyes, they do not apply to the royal/divine kinship, which is strictly patrilineal.

It is important to look back for a second to a point we flagged earlier. In all societies "kinship" is cognatic in the sense that kin through both father and mother are recognized as such (the Roman *cognati*). But, as I said, different kin count differently for different purposes. Thus Creon acknowledges that Antigone (as his sister's daughter) is his nearest kin except for his own family, but that brand of kinship does not count for purposes of succession, for example, or for the burial obligation. These are strictly a patrilinear matter, and that is what Antigone asserts. It is also what Apollo asserts; if you like to use the anthropological jargon, what they both assert is the aristocratic principle of *descent* as opposed to the Eumenidean/democratic principle of mere kinship.

While I had often referred to the Aeschylean passage in discussing similar ideologies of procreation in patrilineal societies, I had not thought of applying it to the disputed passage in *Antigone* until I read Philip Bock's (1979) comments on the Theban plays. He was criticizing Michael Carroll's (1978) criticism of Lévi-Strauss's (1958) rendering of the Oedipus myth. Lévi-Strauss in his structural analysis of the myth sees two of the elements in opposition as "overvaluation of kinship" versus "undervaluation of kinship." Thus, in marrying his mother, Oedipus overvalues kinship, while in killing his father he undervalues it. Carroll, after a careful analysis in which he rejects the other opposition of "autochthonous origins" versus "natural origins," retains the undervaluation versus overvaluation opposition, but makes it "affirmation of patrilineal ties" versus "devaluation of patrilineal ties." He thinks this points to an "ambivalence towards patriliny" in the fourth- to sixth-century Greeks.

It is interesting to me to see the stress put on patriliny, which is certainly there. But I am not so sure about the particular case Carroll wants to make. He claims that the main evidence, in the sagas, for the "ambivalence towards patriliny" is the frequent killing of patrilineal relatives that goes on: Oedipus and Laius are but one example; Eteocles and Polynices another. But does the killing of these relatives indicate an ambivalence toward patrilineal ties? Surely not. These killings occur in all patrilineal systems and in their legends where struggles for succession and power are the issue. Patrilineal descent legitimizes claims to power/authority, but at the same time stands between individuals "down the line" and those further up. Alexander Pope advised that any king who wished "to rule alone / Bear, like the Turk, no brother near the throne." (The Sultan on ascending the throne was reputed always to have his half-brothers by his father's other wives strangled.) The saga of the Zulu clan from even before Shaka to its eventual downfall (Ritter 1957; D. R. Morris 1965) is replete with murders of patrikin. But were any of those involved in the bloody histories and legends of patrimurder *ambivalent* about the principle of patriliny? I can't see this at all. The contrary if anything is true. The principle is so important that the principals are willing to kill for it. It is patrilineal descent that legitimizes their claim to authority: it is patrilineal kin who stand in their way. They never, never question the principle; to do so would be to question their own legitimacy. They simply object to the person of the incumbent and so get rid of him. (This is of course Max Gluckman's point [1963], in contrasting rebellion with revolution.)

In Greek (and other) legend kin kill each other all the time (thus reflecting a common trend in all societies where, like our own, 80 percent of murders are "family affairs"). Wives kill husbands, sons kill mothers, mothers kill their children, fathers their daughters. Does this represent a "devaluation of marriage and the family" in fifth-century Athens? I doubt it. There is certainly no evidence of it. And while there is evidence—and Carroll is quite right—that the aristocratic patrilineal groups were not so powerful after the much quoted reforms of Cleisthenes, it cannot be inferred that the Athenians were "ambivalent" about patriliny. They understood it to be a principle applicable to the nobility and particularly to the archaic/divine nobility represented in the dramas. (Much as we understand the principles of succession—e.g., from John of Gaunt—as central to the Shakespearean history plays, even though these principles have no part in our own democratic lives.) But the killings of patrikin in fifth-century B.C. dramas cannot be adduced as evidence for the average Athenian's "devaluation" of the principle that scarcely applied to him anyway, at least in its strict form. (Greek society was, as we have said, still overwhelmingly patriarchal if not strictly patrilineal.) As for Carroll's other point, one borrowed without acknowledgment from Sir Henry Maine, that "territory" was replacing "kinship" as the basis for social organization in the Athens of the time, this may have been to some extent true (the combination of *deme* and *phratry* that was the peculiar genius of

Cleisthenes) but it is not in any way reflected in the plays or legends. And in any case, the legends on which the plays were based long antedate these changes (see Murray 1986).

Thus, like Bock, I cannot see that replacing Lévi-Strauss's two "oppositions" with these two solves anything at all. It rather tends to confuse the whole matter and lose the point of the "patrilineal emphasis" in the plays. But there is a deeper principle at issue, and that is the nature and validity of any "structural analysis" of this kind. What guarantee do we have that any such analysis corresponds to any mental or social reality of the people who produced the plays and legends? It is claimed that the "real" message of the cycle, for example, is not something simple like "avoid incest and patricide at all costs," but rather the more subtle "do not overvalue or undervalue kinship." Now at one level Lévi-Strauss's point is well taken. The "surface" tale, he tells us, in a brilliant metaphor, is a jigsaw puzzle, and often appears jumbled and inconsequential, because the shapes of the pieces seem arbitrary. But what, he asks, if the shape of the pieces has been determined by some formula for regulating the cogwheels that turned the camshaft that drove the saw that cut the pieces that made up the final jigsaw puzzle? Then the only way we would know why the pieces had the shape they had would not be from studying the surface picture but from discovering the nature of the formula that produced it. Thus, in the Oedipus case, the "mythemes," that is, the jigsaw pieces, are produced not by some simple moral about not sleeping with one's mother, but rather by a complex interplay of camshaft formulae to do with "overcoming contradictions" between overvaluation and undervaluation of kinship and between autochthonous versus human origins.

This is all very ingenious, but it raises the problem: *how do we know that his definition of the jigsaw pieces is correct in the first place?* For that is the clincher. The pieces are not simply given to us as in a real jigsaw puzzle: we have to define them ourselves. And the argument that they are "sentences" does not inspire confidence. Whose sentences? They may be "sentences" in translation, but these may not relate isomorphically to the original. No. If we, the analysts, get to define the pieces, then this renders any determination of the camshaft formulae potentially tautological. And this can go back and forth forever. Thus, Carroll throws out one opposition, slightly amends a second, and suggests a third (kinship versus territory). Other structuralists have run it through their own imaginations and have come up with other dichotomies. There is no end to it. An embarrassing air of casual arbitrariness pervades the whole enterprise.

Bock, on the other hand, takes the patrilineal issue, which *is* there in the plays without a doubt, and looks for a "meaning" that is related to a solid social fact: the existence of two intermarrying patrilines. He is primarily concerned with how this affects the Oedipus myth, but we can see that his diagram is very close to the one I used to stress the patrilineal issue in *Antigone* (see figure 2).

What Bock asserts, simply, is that what the whole Theban saga is "about" is the rivalry and intermarriage between the two patrilines that we have identified. Commentators as astute as Knox have "diagrammed" the "genealogy of Oedipus according to Sophocles" as follows (see figure 3).

Figure 2. Bock's Patrilineal Diagram

Partial genealogy of actors in the Theban saga. (Numbers indicate order of succession; arrows show marriages between the two patrilines.)

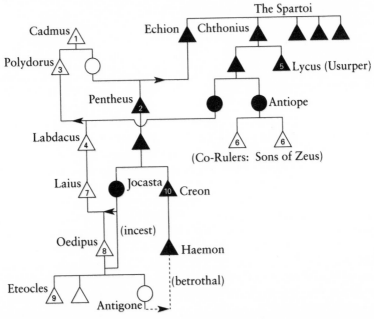

Source: Reproduced by permission of the American Anthropological Association from *American Anthropologist* 81:4, December 1979. Not for further reproduction.

Here, as you see, he has put Menoeceus as a direct descendant of Cadmus equal to Labdacus, making Laius and Creon equally his descendants. Such a genealogy might have suited the Eumenides, but it hides the fact that Menoeceus was descended from a *daughter* of Cadmus, the mother of his father, Pentheus. This makes Menoeceus and Creon scions of the house of Ethion of the Spartoi, not the house of Cadmus. Such a small slip can make a huge difference when it comes to interpreting just what "doomed house" it was that Antigone (in her extremity of self-discovery, of course) was identifying with, and the logic of her exclusions.

Figure 3. The Genealogy of Oedipus according to Sophocles

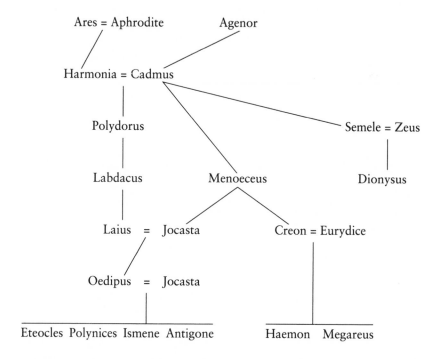

Source: *Three Theban Plays* by Sophocles, translated by Robert Fagles, translation copyright © 1982 by Robert Fagles. Used by permission of Viking Penguin, a division of Penguin Books USA Inc.

Bock is much more accurate. There are a few differences of emphasis between us, but since there are many different versions of the myths, it is hard to settle on a definitive version. Bock does not include Haemon's brother, Megareus, for example, and he is not relevant to the Oedipus story, certainly. But he is important in interpreting *Antigone,* since Creon is held responsible for his death, and this identification of Creon as "child-slayer" underlines his tyrannical nature and foretells his extermination of *all* the children, and hence of both lines. (Megareus appears in Euripides' *The Phoenician Women* as "Menoeceus"—named after his grandfather.) On the other hand I have not included the two sons of Antiope, who indeed ruled Thebes for a while in the legends, but do not appear in the trilogy. But if we take Bock's brilliant insight— that what we have here is a saga of two patrilines (houses) intermarrying and competing for the throne of Thebes and apply this to the argument we have been making, then our interpretation of Sophocles' first line, Antigone's "inconsistency," and Apollo's defense of Orestes, makes great sense. It introduces a coherence to the use of the argument from patrilineal ideology in Greek drama that was not there before, and that probably gets closer to the "meaning" of the plays than arbitrary "oppositions" between elements that have been equally arbitrarily read into them.

There is one loose end before we move on. We mentioned the importance of patricide and how it took precedence over incest as a polluting "crime." Brother could kill brother, wife husband, and mother children, but none of these had the same polluting effects. Orestes had not committed patricide, and the matricide was declared of no account. Oedipus, on the other hand, albeit unknowingly, had committed patricide and this was the source of the pollution. Although we have argued that the killing of patrilineal relatives (particularly brothers and half-brothers) is part and parcel of the patrilineal game and reinforces rather than "devalues" the patrilineal principle, nevertheless, the killing of the father by his son was reckoned as striking at the heart of the principle; it was the worst crime of all—far worse than incest with the mother, which was only a compounding of the offense against the father. But in the Oedipus story, as in all Greek tragedy, there is a theme of inevitability, of fate operating above and beyond the contingent affairs of mortals. Once the wheels are set in motion, fate grinds on to its grim conclusion. Somehow or other, Cadmus the Phoenecian, the originator of both lines, made the initial fatal error—perhaps his refusal to search further for his brothers and sister, Europa (which, contrary to Lévi-Strauss, we could see as an *undervaluation* of kinship), and his angering of Ares by the slaying of the dragon whose teeth gave rise to the Spartoi when sown in the ground. Whatever. The curse continued down the line. One gets the feeling that nothing these people did would ever result in anything but tragedy. There was no way out.

Thus, Oedipus was doomed to commit patricide. Laius brought this upon himself in the first place by abandoning his son with crippled feet on the mountainside, thus setting himself up for a reencounter at a later date. But more to the point, we must ask, why did Laius *deserve* to meet this terrible fate, which would then pollute the city of his fathers and lead to the further crime of incest and the products of incest, which would eventually end in the deaths of Antigone and Haemon? The legends never left such things to chance; there was no such thing as chance or accident in Greek theology, only fate (see Dodds 1951:6). If Oedipus met his father on a lonely road and killed him in a quarrel, it was fated, as the oracle declared. Thus Laius deserved to die, but in making his son the instrument of divine justice, fate contrived to compound the plot by making it inevitable that Oedipus himself would continue the saga of doom. But why the "punishment" of Laius and hence of his children and children's children? What had Laius himself done?

The answer to this "riddle of the Sphinx" is not to be found in Sophocles, but was always there in the texts. I was reminded of it by Velikovsky. He cites variations on the Oedipus legend that accuse Laius of the crime of introducing sodomy to Greece with his seduction of the youth Chrysippus. In one version, evidently, Oedipus kills his father while defending the youth from these unwonted advances. (He cites E. Bethe, *Thebanische Heldenlieder,* 1891:23, 26. Robert Graves in *The Greek Myths,* vol. 2, cites various classical sources to the same effect [1960].) This would indeed produce the cruel twist of fate the legend demands: in defending virtue, Oedipus commits the ultimate crime of patricide, for which he and the city and his offspring must then pay: not because of personal guilt, but because the taboo was broken and the inevitable punishment had to follow.

So it was with Oedipus. The original unnatural crime (not counting any of the offenses of Cadmus and his successors) was the sodomy of Laius. In becoming the instrument of the gods (fate) in avenging this crime, Oedipus unwittingly breaks the taboo on patricide and thus brings down upon himself and his offspring the terrible fate that Sophocles documents in the Theban trilogy. Note here that the incest is simply a contingent and unfortunate consequence of the graver crime of patricide; it is not the cause of the pollution or anything of particular concern to the oracle and hence of the gods (fate). But it is certainly dealt with; and when Oedipus puts out his eyes it is to hide this from himself, not the memory of the patricide. Why then does Sophocles not deal with the "crime of Laius" in the same brutal way that he deals with the incest?

One must assume that he was aware of the legends; they were the

source of his plots as much as Holinshed or Plutarch or Saxo Gram-
maticus were sources for Shakespeare. But Shakespeare edited the
legends too, to suit the taste of his time. One can only assume that
Sophocles was responding to a real change of values regarding sodomy
in Greece. This is something that even the "devaluation of patriliny"
theory has missed: one of the worst offenses against patriliny is a refusal
to continue the line. Thus, patrilineal societies, while often recognizing
sodomy for ritual or initiatory purposes, frown on it as a "lifestyle"—
it strikes at the root of patrilineal succession and the need for sons.
(We need not remind ourselves of the terrible fate of the Sodomites
in the Old Testament—an archetypical patrilineal-patriarchal society,
but we might remember that Cadmus was a Semite—or, rather, a
mythologized memory of a Semitic colonization.) True, it can, as it
eventually was in Greece (and certainly in Thebes), be incorporated
into an overall sexual lifestyle that insists equally on procreation. That
is, it is still frowned upon as an exclusive practice, but is allowed as
"recreational sex" so long as the procreative functions are fulfilled. It
can, as it was in fifth-century Athens, even come to be elevated to an
aesthetically superior way of sex, once patrilineal succession has given
way to partible inheritance and a balance between pleasure with boys
and procreation with wives ensured. Thus Sophocles would probably
not have wanted to make a central theme of his drama the abhorrence
of sodomy that went with the archaic patrilineal principle.

The consequence was that a gap was left in the story. The fate of
Oedipus was made contingent—a matter of unfortunate coincidence,
rather than divinely cruel necessity. The truth is that Oedipus, as an
instrument of divine justice, had to kill his father, and in doing so take
upon himself, with Christlike innocence, the sin and its consequences.
This is underscored in the last act of the trilogy, when, near his death
at Colonus, he is indeed transformed into a divine figure who is taken
into the underworld by the gods, and who brings, if not salvation (a
much later concept), at least divine benefits on those who succored
and believed in him (i.e., the Athenians under Theseus). But it is not
really intelligible unless we know what sin he was atoning for in the
first place. The terrible sacrifice of Oedipus redeemed the Greeks for
their sin against natural procreation; and as in later Christian—although
Greek-derived—theology, although they continued to sin, they continued to be redeemed. Was this hidden message perceived by the
Athenian audience who watched the electrifying ending of the Oedipus
saga at Colonus? We can never know for sure. But if it were so, would
it not make a more convincing and astounding theory of the camshaft
operation than "undervaluation of kinship" and the like? At the very

least, whatever the sin of Laius, the preeminence of the patricide as the polluting element does something to reinforce the "patrilineal ideology" argument, which is, after all, what we are promoting here.

As a "bridge passage" (to use the jazz idiom) to the next stage of the argument, let us return to the Furies at the end of the trial of Orestes. They are not pleased. Not a bit. They complain bitterly to Athena of being slighted and threaten pretty terrible retribution on the Athenians. But the wise Athena is equal to the challenge. She offers them a place of honor as a kind of supernatural police force in Athens. From then on they will not just be the avengers of murdered kin, but will be the guardians of the peace of the *polis*. Here is how Kitto (1951) beautifully describes the denouement:

> So, to Aeschylus, the mature polis becomes the means by which the Law is satisfied without producing chaos, since public justice supersedes private vengeance; and the claims of authority are reconciled with the instincts of humanity. The trilogy ends with an impressive piece of pageantry. The awful Furies exchange their black robes for red ones, no longer Furies, but "Kindly Ones" (Eumenedes); no longer enemies of Zeus, but his willing and honored agents, defenders of his now perfected social order against intestine violence. Before the eyes of the Athenian citizens assembled in the theater just under the Acropolis— and indeed guided by citizen-marshals—they pass out of the theater to their new home on the other side of the Acropolis. (77)

"Public justice supersedes private vengeance." Indeed it does, but here again our individualism creeps in. For what is superseded is not so much "private vengeance" as the automatic divine retribution meted out to the slayers of kin. In the clever action of Athena, the state takes over from supernatural sanction the right to settle disputes about slain kin. The purpose of the Furies is diluted to one of general protection of the state rather than specifically the avenging of murdered kin. In the future, juries will decide these things; bodies of citizens chosen by lot will determine what crimes against kinship deserve retribution. And the retribution will come from the state or its agents, and for its purposes. If "private" in Kitto's quote is read to mean "cosa nostra," then it is acceptable; that is, not vengeance as a matter for the individual, but vengeance as a matter for kin groups, or their divine surrogates. The taming of the Furies is a brilliant metaphor for the taming of kinship itself. Antigone and Orestes will, in future, have to deal with Creon's secretaries. The Furies now sit behind desks in government offices. You know they do; you have seen them.

My mention of "cosa nostra" was not just for effect. I promised to get from the Virgin (Antigone) to the Godfather (Don Corleone) and this I cannot do except sketchily, for it would involve a rewriting of Western history and I am not equipped to do that. All I can do is make a few suggestions and hints that future rewriters might want to take into account. And my first suggestion concerns the endlessly fascinating Don—in some ways the most interesting Don since Quixote; a Don for our times, as it were. He too is tilting at windmills; he is tilting at Creon's secretaries, in fact. He too is asserting anachronistic values in a hopeless battle against contemporary alienation. He even has a kind of gentleness that Mario Puzo portrays very lovingly and that Marlon Brando charmingly interpreted. Yes, he had people killed—but they by and large deserved it; and let us not forget that Quixote was a would-be knight, quite ready to slay his enemies if they had been real enemies. Both our Dons were warriors; it is just that we approve the warriordom of Quixote—because we know it was harmless and well intentioned—while we disapprove that of Corleone (or do we?). But in any case, let me recall for you a key moment in *The Godfather* where the old Don is being told of the deeds of valor performed in the war (World War II) by his eldest son, Michael. He is told of the citations for bravery, the purple hearts, the medals of honor, the courage over and above the call of duty, etc. He listens patiently, shakes his head, and says: "He does these things for strangers." As one who has lived for twenty years in New Jersey, and who has been if not on intimate, at least fairly close, terms with members of several "families," I can vouch that Puzo's book is essentially documentary, not fiction. Most of the better stories he admits to getting from his grandmother, and they were for real.

The Mediterranean cultures held onto their kinship values long after they had been at least officially abandoned in the north. They took them wherever they went and melded them with those of the locals. When I was in Colombia a few years ago, I was being taken 'round the estate of a friend whom we can, adding to our list of Dons, correctly call Don Mario (since that was what his tenants, servants, and employees called him). His majordomo, riding a mule with iron-clad (conquistador) stirrups (to protect against cacti) and carrying a huge machete and rifle—looking in fact like a latter-day Quixote—introduced to me all the retainers. He ran through the list of all possible relatives: brothers, nephews, cousins, wives of cousins, sons-in-law, husbands of nieces, brothers-in-law, brothers of husbands of nieces of brothers-in-law, and on and on. Finally I stopped him and asked, in my bad Spanish, "Juan, do you never employ anyone who is not related to you by blood or marriage?" "But of course not, señor," he replied without hesitation, "they would steal from Don Mario, and what could we do?" In Colombia, we could not call the authorities, that's for sure. When the state fails to protect, people look longingly at the certainty of kinship. I did not say that idly: I have seen it in operation. I have seen it in South and Central America, in Italy (particularly Sicily but not only there), in Ireland and in the Middle East, and even in Louisiana. Those who saw that remarkable film about corruption in the New Orleans police department *The Big Easy* will not forget the dramatic ending. The Cajun cop hero, converted by the beautiful assistant D.A. to the side of right, surrounded himself by only those fellow Cajun cops who were uncles and cousins as he took on the murderous drug dealers in the department in a fight to the finish. But these represent areas where the state has not thoroughly established its rule over kinship; where it cannot guarantee order and hence must relinquish its monopoly over violence to groups that can, even in a limited way. These are the last outposts, for where the modern state is strong and centralized it is the end process of that long struggle with the particularism of kinship that was my theme, and which led us back to the Greeks to see its beginnings.

Through the middle ages, the Church struggled to assert its temporal control of marriage and kinship, wresting this control from pagan-based custom. But as late as the nineteenth century, in many parts of Europe, this was still not totally in effect. The use of prohibited degrees, which were ever more widely extended, while partly a venal device to gain money from the sale of indulgences (as Luther complained) was also a way of forcing marriage outside the circle of kin. (The Napoleonic Code, later, reversed this trend by enforcing a modified form of partible inheritance. Napoleon, as First Consul, was unwilling to go the whole way with the Revolutionary insistence on totally partible inheritance to promote "equality." He saw the need for strong nuclear families and the keeping intact of small family fortunes to promote business. But the results in the Code were essentially a compromise: inheritance was still partible and most of what had been the privilege of the "family councils" was passed over to the state courts—see Fisher [1906].) By instituting celibacy the Church outlawed kinship from its own ranks (theoretically) and promoted a system of meritocracy, even if the term *nepotism* had to be invented later to cover the reproductive proclivities of various ecclesiastical dignitaries: kinship fights back (beautifully satirized by Browning in "The Bishop Orders His Tomb at St. Praxed's Church"). And of course, none of this prevented rich clerics from benefiting their relatives: "There is nothing," the Irish proverb has it, "as conceited as a Monsignor's niece." Nevertheless, the church, while promoting "the family," continued to carry on its own form of war against kinship. After the Merovongians, it persuaded the European

monarchies and nobility to accept at least legal monogamy, although
even here they fought back with, for example, the legitimization of
bastards. But the Church was on a winning ticket here since increasing
democratization always means a growing unpopularity with polygamy.
Polygamy creates mate shortage with a more than fair share of brides
going to the wealthy and powerful. Monogamy comes closer to ensuring
fair shares and is usually more popular with the people. The Church's
notion that marriage and kinship are incompatible with certain avo-
cations persisted in many areas until very recently: fellows of Oxford
and Cambridge colleges had to be celibate, and even the Royal Canadian
Mounted Police required seven-year's celibacy from recruits (see Balch
1985, for an excellent discussion of these issues).

What was happening throughout Europe, in varying degrees, was
the growth of a now triangular struggle. Volumes have been written
on the Rise of Individualism, as we have seen, and kinship has been
seen as the enemy of the individual as much as of the state. But very
little has been written on the struggle of kinship with both these
institutions. For the state, despite its persecution of the individual from
time to time, is much happier with individuals as units than with kinship
groups for the simple reason that they are easier to control. If it wants
to reduce kinship to the nuclear family (or less), then it wants to reduce
its legal units to the individual voter of the eighteenth-century formula:
the creature of the social contract, who rises yet again in the pages of
Rawls's (1971) mammoth tome—kinless, sexless, ageless, and devoid
of anything but a sense of personal survival. (Which leads rather amaz-
ingly to fair shares for all and a liberal democratic welfare state. One
can take the social contract wherever one wants, it seems.) I think the
real paradox here is that the state, at least in the bourgeois democracies,
does not so much oppose individuals as promote them. It will, naturally,
from time to time, persecute and repress certain individuals; it always
has. But it prefers the individual contractors precisely for this reason:
they are a lot easier to persecute and control than large and powerful
kin groups. Thus it comes easily to the nation-state to promote the
values of individualism while remaining totally suspicious of the claims
of kinship. The law, recently, recognized the rights of a viable fetus as
a "person" who could sue at about the same time as the Supreme
Court contemptuously turned down the rights of polygamists. On this
score at least, state and individual can been seen in league against
kinship. One of the few books to deal with this as an issue is, as one
would expect, not by a social scientist, but by a talented amateur, Alex
Shoumatoff (1985, see especially ch. 6, 7, and 8).

The state, often using the celibate and meritocratic church as its agent, weighed in later than the church in the struggle, since it took longer to became effective and more centralized. The Tudors in England led the way in the taming of the noble houses (Henry VII was perhaps the first great "modern" king in this respect at least) and the setting up of a secular meritocracy of government: the beginning of the civil service, recruited from the ambitious bourgeoisie, themselves wedded to the small nuclear family, and decidedly anti-aristocratic. The Bourbons followed suit in France, and the height of royal power under the Sun King saw the abject surrender of the nobles to the demands of a court-centered charade brilliantly planned by Louis XIV to just that effect. Peter the Great, later but in the same vein, tamed the Boyars and pushed the state to the forefront, bringing in foreigners and Jews if necessary, to forge an administration loyal to him rather than to its kin-based "houses." Areas in which the state could interfere with the family and override the "patria potestas" gradually increased with the growth of state power, although many anachronisms lingered. The taxing of large fortunes has proceeded to the point where the accumulation of wealth in powerful kinship groups is virtually impossible. The imposition of primogeniture, mentioned earlier, allowed single heirs to accumulate fortunes while sloughing off siblings and their descendants; the later taxing of these fortunes reduced even the remnants of wealthy kin groups if not to genteel poverty at least to genteel political impotence. The Nixon government's attack on the large "foundations" was only one blow struck against private fortunes that could act as rival centers of power and influence. But it was not only the rich and powerful who were so reduced. The "policing of families" (to use the title of an interesting book on the subject—Donzelot, 1979) continued unabated until "family law" and public administration took over most of the functions of the family. Some critics have even seen the Reagan administration's indifference to the fate of the "family farm" and the "family business" as a latter-day example of the state's hostility to kinship in favor of agrobusiness and big business generally. The family farms almost always had an "extended" look with at least two related adult males and their families involved in production. The latest developments in "birth technologies" and the demand for their regulation is taking the state into the very act of procreation itself: not only the familial organisms but their genes are now matters for legislative control.

Socialist governments have been even less hospitable to kinship, for obvious reasons, and while Communist experiments with the abolition of the family have not survived, very few functions are left to it. Yet even here, nepotism, however restricted, is evidently a plague of society.

Kinship may be dead, but it won't lie down. I don't know enough about their history, but it is obvious that in China and Japan similar struggles between kinship and the state went on. In China the final solution has been to institute the nuclear family reduced to one child per couple, thus saying good-bye to the clans and to polygamy. In Japan, more interestingly, the integration of kinship values into managerial practice which has been so incredibly successful tells its own story. "If you can't lick 'em join 'em" seems to have been the Japanese response, and while the actual forms of traditional kinship diminish, its spirit lives in their form of industrial organization that baffles our imaginations so used are we to the linkage of industry and the "individual" contracting laborer and entrepreneur.

In the United States, where the hereditary principle was abolished with such ceremony two hundred years ago, the Kennedy "clan" continues to exercise its fascination. Bobby may well have been the best lawyer in the country, but few people believe that this was the basis of his selection as attorney general; and whether Teddy would be a ranking senator without his family connections is, to say the least, an open question. The best way to get to the top, as some wag put it, is to start at the top. A fine kinship principle, but not one that in theory should operate in a democracy where all individuals are created equal. But then we know that they are not created equal. Apart from anything else, they each have a unique body of kin surrounding them, and that makes them different from each other. Hobbes was wrong: the state of nature was not, and the state of culture only struggles to be, a war of all against all. This is another blatant statement of individualist prejudice. The original social contract was not between individuals but between genes. There was never a war of all against all; it was always a war of some against others, and the some and the others, until the advent of the state, were always kin. Once the state emerged, the battle shifted and continues now between kinship and the state itself. And the final social contract will not be signed until the conditions dreamed of in most utopias are realized and the genes neutralized once and for all (Kummar 1987). It won't be in our lifetimes, or the lifetimes of our kin.

As an epitaph let me return to the notion that kinship is alive in legend. The immense popularity of Frank Herbert's *Dune* novels is not solely to do with ecology as many commentators would have us think. Central to the ongoing complicated plot are the machinations of the Bene Gesserit, a strange order of far-from-celibate nuns whose purpose over the eons is to control breeding and bloodlines, among other reasons to produce a messiah (although this backfires, but then he was an Atreidiesg—they should have known what they were messing with). While this is a kind of eugenics program, it is in private hands (the order belongs to no government) and nobility of blood plays a central role in the dynastic quarrels that make up most of the plot. Kinship and descent are central here, as they are in the conception of the monstrous Bene Tleilax, who combine a strangely one-sided (very few females) breeding system in which sperm is periodically "distributed," with a gruesome cloning mechanism, the secret of which is their power in the universe. They are all related, and, it turns out, most appropriately, all secret Muslims—of a suitably modified kind—bent on jihad against the infidels, i.e., the rest of the universe. The whole *Dune* series, in effect, could be looked at as a myth about the intermeshing of kinship and society.

And then there is the inimitable Kurt Vonnegut. He puts it in a nutshell in his novel suitably called *Slapstick*. The President of the United States at some indistinct time in the future when the earth has been degravitated by miniaturized Chinese as one of his first acts of office decides to restore kinship to its proper place by instituting an almost Chinese system of proper names. His campaign slogan is "Lonesome no more" and he assigns by computer ten thousand middle names based on a combination of objects and numbers. Everyone with the same middle name belongs to that "family" and has familial obligations to the others. Family clubs rapidly spring up, and people take to the whole scheme with great seriousness. Wars become harder to fight— the country has broken up into warring chiefdoms—because family members don't like to kill each other and they are scattered through the bellicose factions. "I realized that nations could never acknowledge their own wars as tragedies" says Vonnegut, "but that families not only could but had to" (214). Police forces are not needed because a rule springs up that if a family member commits a crime then whoever knows about it calls ten other family members and they settle it. The most moving and astonishing part of the book describes a "family meeting" of the Daffodils in Indianapolis (the president is a Daffodil from that city—Wilbur Daffodil-11 Swain). The family becomes a little parliament, governed strictly by Robert's Rules of Order, which settles matters among its members in a charmingly pragmatic fashion. And, yes, he deals with the issue of "relatives" possibly not liking each other. To end my point that kinship is alive and well in legend (and that these mythmakers may be the more acute sociologists of our time) let me quote from the president's comments on the essay he and his sister wrote as children when they first conceived the idea of the families.

I found it absorbing. It said there was nothing new about artificial extended families in America. Physicians felt themselves related to other physicians, lawyers to lawyers, writers to writers, athletes to athletes, politicians to politicians, and so on. Eliza and I said that these were bad sorts of extended families, however. They excluded children and old people and housewives, and losers of every description. Also, their interests were so specialized as to seem nearly insane to outsiders. "An ideal extended family," Eliza and I had written, "should give proportional representation to all Americans according to their numbers. The creation of ten thousand such families, say, would give rise to ten thousand parliaments, so to speak, which would discuss sincerely and expertly what only a few hypocrites now discuss, which is the welfare of all mankind. (1976:156–57)

I won't quote more, although there is much that is quotable and directly related to our theme, since I don't want to spoil the pleasure of those who haven't read it. I am just helping to make my point that kinship is indeed "alive in legend," which is where we should look for true insights, surely not to the social scientists.

But to leave on an up note, in one of the most charming utopias of our own age—*Always Coming Home*—the daughter of a famous anthropologist, Ursula Kroeber Le Guin (1985), envisages a postholocaust future somewhere in northern California, where small and loosely allied villages, on the model of the Pueblos (particularly Zuni) her father loved and studied, manage, with primitive electricity, a dash of geomancy, horse-drawn railways, and controlled literacy, to live a pleasant and varied life allowing for the full range of human passions. And they are, of course, organized into exogamous matrilineal clans, themselves linked to occupational guilds. We should have expected nothing less from a close kinswoman of the great Kroeber. And she, along with many other observers, professional and lay, have noted a tendency to return to kinship after the hysterical tide of the narcissistic individualism of Tom Wolfe's "me-decade" has receded. Tiger (1978) even notes that the burgeoning of step-parenthood, seen as an attack on "family values" by the doomsayers, in fact creates large extended families where a child has double the number of parents and grandparents in each generation and a host of new cousins and half-siblings. Perhaps out of this side effect of the "breakdown of marriage" we may yet forge truly organic and truly kin-based social units. In years to come, another tragedy of *Antigone* may enthrall us with a sense of meaning as immediate to us as it was to fifth-century Athens—much as the tragedy of Mary-Beth Whitehead, in her heroic struggle with the supremacy of contract over motherhood has engaged us, on one or the other side of the battle, over the past years. Guess which side I was on (Fox 1988).

NOTES

The original version of this paper was delivered to a seminar at the University of Virginia. I would like to thank David Sapir and the other members of the Department of Anthropology for their lively and stimulating comments. For particular insights and criticisms I am deeply indebted to Paul Friedrich, Dell Hymes, Philip Bock, Peter Kibby, Lowell Edmunds, Robert Storey, Robert Fagles, and Felix Browder. Richard Handler called my attention to the quote from T. S. Eliot that I have used as an epigraph.

1. He actually seems to have made a habit of it as regards burial, since he denied proper burial to the fallen Argives, sparking heroic deeds of cadaver rescue by Theseus, King of Athens, who was later to give shelter to the wandering Oedipus—see Jebb (1902:201–2).

2. Three of the above I took from the notorious Cliffs Notes, which I had picked up in the bookstore to observe the received wisdom that was being transmitted to students—it was the "Antigone-as-individual" line, of course. But interestingly, the author, to illustrate the problems of translation, had included a few samples of attempts at the opening lines.

3. Several critics, including a smart graduate student at the University of Virginia, have insisted that I give the second and some subsequent lines so that this discussion of the first line may have a context. Here is the original with Jebb's translation:

> ἆρ᾽ οἶσθ᾽ ὅ τι Ζεὺς τῶν ἀπ᾽ Οἰδίπου κακῶν
> ὁποῖον οὐχὶ νῷν ἔτι ζώσαιν τελεῖ;
> οὐδὲν γὰρ οὔτ᾽ ἀλγεινὸν οὔτ᾽ ἄτης ἄτερ
> οὔτ᾽ αἰσχρὸν οὔτ᾽ ἄτιμόν ἐσθ᾽, ὁποῖον οὐ
> τῶν σῶν τε κἀμῶν οὐκ ὄπωπ᾽ ἐγὼ κακῶν.

"Knowest thou what ill there is, of all bequeathed by Oedipus, that Zeus fulfills not for us twain while we live? Nothing painful is there, nothing fraught with ruin, no shame, no dishonor, that I have not seen in thy woes and mine."

4. It is one of Steiner's great contributions to take us beyond the well-known passages from Hegel in the *Philosophy of Religion* into other sources of his opinions on Antigone and tragedy generally. Of other commentators, Kojève (1947) and Derrida (1974) seem to come close to a good understanding of the nature of the conflict—insofar as one can extract the sensible from the fanciful in the latter, and plough through the neo-Hegelian density of the former.

5. For the record, in answer to the old anthropological chestnut "is the family universal?" one can respond that two things are universal but not necessarily isomorphic: the household and the kinship roles indicated by the terms for primary kin.

6. Velikovsky (1960) adds to the complications the theory that Egyptian Thebes may well have been the source of the whole Oedipus legend, via the real story of Akhnaton, who married his mother and destroyed at least the memory of his father and brought about the destruction of his line. Sphinxes,

of course, were Egyptian, not Greek mythological creatures. There is also the burial of a princess alive in there somewhere, which could be the source of the whole Antigone episode.

Redneck Girl: From Experience to Performance

Bruce T. Grindal and William H. Shephard

The "redneck" proletarian culture of the American South presents interesting possibilities for a collaboration between anthropology and the dramatic/performing arts. This essay examines one such collaboration between Bruce Grindal, the ethnographer and author of the short story "Redneck Girl," and William Shephard, the dramatist and director of the stage performance of *Redneck Girl* that took place on the main stage theater at Washington State University in November 1986. To describe this collaboration, we have chosen to engage in a metadialogue in which we endeavor to recreate this collaboration as it unfolded over a period beginning with Grindal's initial encounter with "redneck girl" on a bus trip across north Florida in 1982 and his subsequent completion of a short story in March 1985; to Shephard's reaction to the story and his writing of a play; to Grindal's reaction to Shephard's draft and his collaboration; to Shephard's rewrite and eventual production and direction of *Redneck Girl;* and finally to our collective assessment of the performance's impact upon the audiences that had viewed it.

We say *metadialogue* because what we are writing in this article is a reflection after the fact. Both Grindal and Shephard have seen the performance and have discussed it with each other and others, and not only the performance but also separate videotape showings of the performance, one that took place at the 1987 meetings of the American Anthropological Association. Thus we are creating a dialogue from the vantage point of the present.

This essay, we feel, addresses many of the theoretical and personal issues that confront the collaboration between humanistic ethnography and dramatic performance. However, this is not a theoretical work. We cite bibliographic references only when they entered into our thinking at the time. Instead, we present our experiences, thoughts, reflections, and creations as a case study. We hope they will invite dialogue. If so, what we have to say will have accomplished its purpose.

The *la donnée* of Redneck Girl (Grindal)

In November 1982, I was returning to my home in Tallahassee on a Trailways bus from Sarasota, Florida. On the trip I met a young southern working-class woman whom I call "redneck girl." For two hours she talked to me about the hardships of her life and her longing for a better one. When the bus arrived in Tallahassee, I got off and she moved on west across the Sunbelt. I never saw her again. I never thought to ask her name.

Two days after my encounter with "redneck girl" I wrote a letter to my good friend, Alfred McClung Lee. In it I recorded my immediate recollections.

> Last Sunday I was coming back on a bus from Sarasota, Florida. On the last leg of the journey, a girl got on at Lake City. It was getting dark and with the exception of the dim floor lights and occasional reading lights, the bus was dark. There were only about five people on the bus: a crusty old Cajun with a handlebar mustache lying at the back of the bus by the toilet, and three young rednecks in dirty flannel shirts. The bus was headed for Tallahassee, Mobile, New Orleans, and Houston. Most were sleeping or in solitude, for the bus was quiet.
>
> The girl, who sat two rows in front of me was fidgeting in her seat, looking at her reflection in the window glass. She then got up, reached for a large handbag in the over-head rack, and pulled out a black-and-white zebra patterned pull-over. She put it on, spending a long time standing, looking at her reflection, adjusting her collar, fidgeting with her hair, and murmuring, "Oh Shit," from time to time. Then she turned to me and asked, "What time is it?"
>
> So began an interesting conversation in which she told me the story of her life. Her parents divorced when she was 16, whereupon she "split" her home in Pascaguola, Mississippi. According to her, she has been a bartender, hotel clerk, waitress, and a singer in a rock band. She was a cute woman of about 24. She was a little fat, she told me, because she had lately been drinking too much champagne and Seagrams. She has been on her own for eight years; street-wise, yet naive. As she said, she wants to be somebody—something like an airline stewardess or gymnast—something she can do for the rest of her life. She also wants love and babies. She was now going to see her grandparents in Mobile—then to see her mother and stepfather in New Orleans. The first time in seven years.
>
> Then she started talking about childhood friends she had had and how they had gotten killed. Both killed by "colored people," to use

her words. One girl was shot by a "colored man" in a Laundromat in Pascagoula; another friend, a boy, and his wife were shot dead when two "colored men" pulled their car over on the I-10 Interstate.

I recall saying, "Mississippi must be a violent place." "Hell, man," she said, "It's not even civilized. If you come to Pascaguola don't stop. Just drive on through to New Orleans and Houston."

This encounter impressed me for reasons I'm still not sure that I understand. The memory of our conversation remained in my mind, constantly churning up creative and fictional possibilities. Two years after the encounter I wrote a short story about the incident.

Henry James (1948) once stated that any piece of fictional writing must begin with a single given idea or *la donnée*. This "given idea" may be cerebral or philosophical or it may be a fleeting sensuous moment of experience. Most often it is a combination of the two. Above all, the *la donnée* is irreducible. It stands alone and demands to be accepted on its own terms. It defies any further description, analysis, interpretation, or explanation. This single, precious, unique kernel of experience lies at the heart of any piece of fictional writing. For James it is the cause of the creative process itself. Thus other ideas, experiences, and mental images of the writer come to adhere to the givenness of this single experience and over time become transformed into a piece of fictional writing.

To me, the *la donnée* of redneck girl was contained in this letter and was fixed at that single magical moment when, after having described the gruesome deaths of her friends in Mississippi, she threw her head back in defiance and said, "Hell man, it's not even civilized. If you come to Pascagoula, don't stop. Just drive through to New Orleans and Houston." As she spoke the curls of her blonde hair carelessly flew aside, reflected in the window by the yellow overhead lamp. And all the while the bus, like an island in nowhere, was rolling down an anonymous American highway into the opaque night.

This moment stuck in my mind. A kind of thought piece that, the more I reflected upon it, the more it gave sense and form to the life of redneck girl. What was it like to travel from city to city along the east coast of Florida, playing juke joints with flamepots in spandex pants? What was it like to share a motel room with the boys in the band? How did redneck girl keep her virtue and dignity, which she did? And what about her family, her mother whom she couldn't stand and her father whom she referred to as a "dark man" and about whom she did not wish to talk? What experiences in her past life accounted for her turning to the highway and staying away from either parent for eight years? Indeed, what did I really recall from our two-hour conversation? What was it that I imagined? What was it that I wished I had asked but didn't? What had my mind created?

There then emerged in my mind the possibility of a fictional story, a human drama about the restless proletarian culture of the American South. It was to be a young woman's story about a hard life and the heroic defiance of will necessary to live it. It was also to be a story about the ghosts of a frightened heart and the frail hope of personal salvation.

From that time and for over a year, the story "Redneck Girl" took on a life of its own. My experience as an ethnographer of southern culture, and particularly my deeply felt personal experiences, came to adhere to the *la donnée* of "Redneck Girl" in intuitively unpredictable ways. To deconstruct the story and recount this process as it occurred at the time would be a lengthy task. One part of the story's text, however, illustrates this intuitive junction between the ethnographer's personal experiences and the artistic creation, and I would like to offer it as an example.

In the first part of the story, redneck girl describes her life on the road as a singer in a country band. In Jacksonville, Florida, she lives in a beachfront motel with the boys in the band; plays in honkytonk bars to sailors and hookers; attends all-night house parties with "young rednecks, queers, punks, reggae musicians, and other off-the-wall types"; and is part of the Jacksonville beach scene with its pickup trucks, beer drinking, and young women in bikinis and suntan oil. During this time a good friend of hers, Gloria, is gang raped by a group of young men and is later left on the steps of her motel room. That night, redneck girl stays awake with her friend, drying away her tears and putting "Noxema on her bruises." In the early morning she leaves the motel room and takes a walk on the deserted beach. She is weary with life and feels a strong loathing for her world—for its restlessness, lust, and violence. This loathing moves her to sublime poetic sentiment and in turn to a recollection about her past life as a child in Mississippi and to a deep reflection upon the mystery of her dreams and her confrontation with death.

"Do you like poetry, professor?"

"Yes," I replied.

"Well, that morning I get up and leave Gloria sleeping there. I put on my clothes and take a walk on the beach. It's early morning, but the sun's hot. There's nobody. Just a lot of beer cans, and burger wrappers, and all kinds of junk flattened in the sand from all the cars driving on the beach. So I'm walking and I see this fish in the sand.

Must have been run over by a thousand cars. Looked just like the bottom of an old shoe. I kicked it over in the sand. Flat as the ace of spades. So I get to feeling poetic. 'Shit—look at you, you dumb shit— one time you swam in the sea, you were young, and fresh, and wet— you smelled clean—now you don't even smell anymore—you dumb shit.' "

She continued gazing out the window, murmuring softly to herself. Slowly she reclined back into her seat. Through the crack in the seat I could see strands of her blonde hair and the vague reflection of her face in the window. Her voice was distant and barely audible.

"Back in Mississippi there used to be this fat boy. Go everywhere with his mother. Just trailed behind her in his flip-flops, sweatshirt and big fat boy pants. He was so fat and ugly, that people no longer paid mind to laugh at him. They always used to go for dinner at the Sizzlin' Steak down on U.S. 90. The boy, he'd get big plates of food. You know, baked potato with lots of sour cream and butter, and one of those cream pies, the kind they put cool whip on. The mother, she'd always take a salad and cup of coffee, and just sit there and watch him eat. He'd always get up for another piece of pie and she'd just sit there and smoke another cigarette and drink her coffee and watch him eat. I used to have dreams about that boy. I would see him lying in the gutter of some street. Sometimes he'd be by the side of the highway and I'd think he was a big furry animal crawling along sniffin' at the ground. Other times, he'd be in an alley by the side of some bar. He'd be crawling and sniffin' at the walls like some lost dog."

"What ever happened to him?" I asked.

"You know," she paused. "You know, he got himself killed. Run over by a car. Just like that." She laughed softly and was quiet.

That passage was inspired by two experiences in my own life. Once, during my wilder bachelor days, I took a road trip to Jacksonville, Florida, with two male friends. There, we stayed at a beachfront motel and spent two days and nights living a life of decadence, chasing women and carousing through the all-night beachfront bars. Having awakened depressed from such a night, having taken a walk on the beach in the early morning, and having seen a flattened fish in the sand, I recalled having felt a sublime poetic sentiment for life. Some years later, my wife and I were driving from New Orleans when we stopped for dinner at a "Sizzlin' Steak" on U.S. 90 in Pascagoula, Mississippi. There we saw a fat boy dining with his mother. The humor and pathos of that scene, as spoken in the words of redneck girl, also conveyed the poetic sense of the sublime.

Thus, my professional and personal experiences, and particularly my deep-felt sentiments for life, adhered to redneck girl and came alive in her words. She assumed a life of her own. I, the ethnographer, the writer, the confessor, could only tag along beside her and take down in my notebook the words that she said.

In the spring of 1985, I finished the first draft of "Redneck Girl" and sent a copy to my good friend William Shephard, who was then teaching in the Department of Dramatic Arts at the University of California at Davis. In my letter I expressed some questions about the story. I wasn't sure, for example, what I had created. Was it a short story, a novella, a play, or a piece of ethnographic narrative? I also questioned my role as an ethnographer and as a storyteller. Who was I to divulge such a personal and intimate account of an individual's life?

Suggestion of Dramatic Form (Shephard)

After reading a rough draft of Bruce's short story, "Redneck Girl," in March 1985, I immediately felt that it had strong potential as a dramatic performance. I had been captivated by the narrative of the central character, retracing her steps through the light and shadows of her past experience. Moreover, I sensed that the bus journey on which she felt compelled to reveal herself to a complete stranger was, in fact, secondary to a much deeper psychic journey in which she sought to penetrate the core of her recurring anxiety. It seemed to me that redneck girl's story demanded dramatic realization to bring the dreamy incon-sistency of her earthy observations, her troubled fantasies, and her nightmares into conscious perspective. I wanted to undertake this per-ilous journey with her, and there was no way other than bringing redneck girl to life in the active medium of the stage.

The arrival of Bruce's story was nothing out of the ordinary; we had been exchanging scholarly papers and bits of creative writing for some time. More important, we are close friends. I might even say that there is a type of kinship between us, a bond of sympathy based on a shared perception of the forces that deeply affect our lives. I read the story on the same afternoon it arrived in the mail and immediately telephoned Bruce in Tallahassee, proposing that we collaborate on making it into a play. Although we had a common interest in ethno-graphic fiction, I had never received a story from him that offered such an opportunity to bridge the discipline of our respective fields. There was more than narrative in the central character's tale; there was an active anamnesis (Jung 1969:189–90) going on—a deliberate reliving of past events that were leading redneck girl to an important discovery about her life. Bruce's descriptions of the humming monotony of the bus ride, the flickering of spectral visions on the rain-washed windows, and the heavy remembrances of southern swamps and palmetto scrubs seemed to cry out for an artist's rendering—but what sort of artist? At first glance, the story seemed well-suited to film, in which the visual dynamics of flashbacks, instantaneous change of locale, and the montage of dream states could be accomplished by technical means. Upon closer inspection of the text, however, I realized that the power of the piece was in its language, and language is one of the primary mediums of the theater.

Somehow Bruce had captured the vocal patterns and inflections of redneck girl with an amazing sense of detail. True to his background as an ethnographer, he had successfully absorbed the character of her experience and recreated it in his story. A number of questions nagged me. Redneck girl was an actual person Bruce encountered on a bus between Lake City, Florida, and Tallahassee. Was it ethical to transpose someone's life experience into dramatic form without their expressed consent? I felt that the presence of the anthropologist was essential to the development of the woman's story, but could I create a character based on Bruce himself? In short, what did artistic intention owe to life experience if the two happened to come into conflict? Bruce was excited about the prospect of making the story into a play, and I was eager to begin. At the same time, I was uneasy about the project. Bruce and I had never collaborated on an artistic project before. What if he hated what I did to his story? I knew that this experience had been intensely personal for him, and though I was profoundly stimulated by his story I realized that I probably saw things in it he might not have originally intended. Such speculations were fruitless before the play was written, but I was anxious that our friendship should remain unaffected in any case.

As I sat down to write the first draft of the play, I pondered the significance of the bus trip as a medium for the rest of the story. It seemed integrally related to the woman's confession—for such it was, an intimate portrait of herself to a stranger whom she never expected to see again. A bus is a unique form of transportation that encourages such revelations under the proper circumstances. A long bus ride is definitely more tedious than any other form of mass transit. There is no respite from the cramped space one is forced to occupy, and there is little comfort upon arrival at one's destination. The fatigue of a long bus trip is cumulative, and at night, under the harsh eye of the overhead reading light, conversations may easily be affected by the droning of the wheels and the confinement of the surroundings. At such moments passengers are like prisoners, confined to their seats for a specific period of time, and their exchanges may reveal a deeper level of communication than under ordinary circumstances. The presence of the bus was essential to the story, but I had difficulty imagining how it could be accomplished on stage. In the story, characters and events in redneck girl's life should seem to emerge from the bus and return to it.

Redneck girl's description of the people who inhabited her world was rich and varied. The descriptions of her mother; the spaced-out chick, Gloria; her beautiful high school friend, Rita; her father and his swamp woman; the owner of the cocktail lounge; Low-Down Sam—all were dramatically fascinating, but where would they all come from in a stage production? They were obviously fragments of a much larger picture—pieces of redneck girl herself, her private phantoms that emerged with gathering intensity. To solve the problem, I referred to the structure of Bruce's story, characters and events emerging from the bus and returning to it. I decided that, in addition to redneck girl and the anthropologist, there would be other passengers on the bus who would leave their seats to become characters in the woman's story from time to time. But they would always return to their anonymity as bus passengers.

The next major problem in the play was properly arranging the sequence of events. The play would begin on the bus and would end with its arrival in Tallahassee, but the structure of what took place in between was crucial. Bruce's story was divided into three principal segments which I will call "Leaving Home," "Painful Reflections," and "Finding the Self." These blocks of actions were separated by two intervals on the bus during which the action remained suspended in the monotony of the ride—reflective pauses enabling the anthropologist (and the reader or audience) to assimilate the texture of the young woman's story. If there was, to borrow from Conrad (1971), a "heart of darkness" in both redneck girl's narrative and her inner journey, it occurred during the middle segment, "Painful Reflections," where she encountered her father and the Cajun woman he lived with back in the swamp. There was hoodoo, madness, violence, and brutality in that incident; yet this particular recollection seemed to have a liberating effect on the central character. This scene would be a definite turning point in the action of the play. In Bruce's story, redneck girl's recollection of the incident was extremely vivid, but there was something important missing from her description—a traumatic experience she was trying to forget. I felt a strong compulsion to complete the action of this scene in the playscript, to dramatize the traumatic experience in hopes of discovering its significance to the rest of the story.

In our phone conversation at the time Bruce suggested that redneck girl had been raped by her father during that visit in the swamp;

however, the truth remained obscure. In redneck girl's own words: "Look, professor, there are some things I don't say to nobody. They hurt too much. You say these things, you'll just cry and fall apart. And they'll be nobody there to put you together again." In dramatic terms, the scene in the swamp revolved around the mysterious character of the dark woman, the "haint" who lived with the father. I wasn't sure why I was convinced of the dark woman's importance to the story as a whole; nevertheless, I proceeded with my creative hunch and wrote the scene.

In addition to completely fictional characters like the "haint," it was also difficult to deal with the character of the anthropologist. I recognized Bruce immediately in his story; I could picture him so vividly, vacillating between professional curiosity and unabashed fascination. As a result, my portrait of him was admittedly an affectionate one—perhaps too encumbered by my personal bias for the anthropologist to become a character in his own right. There were other problems as well. Too many of the characters in redneck girl's story seemed forced and artificial, even clichéd. Still, I continued writing, hoping for some breakthrough that would give me a key to the dramatic structure of the whole.

When I finished the first draft of the play, I wasn't happy with it, yet it did represent a dramatic structure of sorts. I also knew that it couldn't develop completely as a play without the presence of live actors, working with the language and their respective roles. Nevertheless, I sent the script off to Bruce in early June 1985 and eagerly anticipated his reply.

Who Is the Professor?
The Struggle for Collaboration
(Grindal)

In early June, I received a letter from Bill along with the first draft of the play. Needless to say, I was excited and I read it immediately. Particularly, it was exciting to see my story come alive in the eyes and words of another. The story had ceased to be wholly mine.

Bill had grasped the dramatic sense of the story. The conversation between redneck girl and the professor was divided into three parts, or episodes. In the first, redneck girl tells of her leaving home at the age of sixteen to escape from a possessive mother and an enigmatic and threatening father. She tells of her life on the road as a singer in a country band and the restlessness and tough cruelty of that life. In the second episode, she relates painful memories about her past life as a girl in Mississippi: the brutal death of her best friend and her dreaded confrontation with her father in the swamp. In the final episode, events of her life force redneck girl to confront her past and present life. Her decision to return home was her attempt at personal salvation, her finding of the self.

In my own writing, I had sensed this dramatic structure by creating breaks in the conversation. During these pauses, the professor would reflect upon the atmosphere of the bus and the moods they created. For the most part these reflections were left as parenthetical notations to be developed later. In Bill's dramatization, the pauses in the conversation became changes of scene, and my introspective reflections were developed more fully in the character of the professor.

I was particularly impressed by how Bill had taken redneck girl's story and through the use of flashback had recreated on stage four of its episodes: the gang rape of her friend, Gloria, in Jacksonville, Florida; redneck girl's meeting with her childhood friend in Mississippi; redneck girl's dreaded encounter with her father and his woman in a bayou swamp in Louisiana; and finally, in the only scene of the second act, her fateful meeting with her father's black friend, "Low-Down Sam," while working as a cocktail hostess in Jacksonville. These were the same episodes I would have chosen. When I realized this, I knew intuitively that Bill and I were on the path of collaboration.

What Bill had done was to take what was essentially redneck girl's monologue, as the "professor" saw her, and make her into a new character: redneck girl as the audience would see her, as she came alive in relation to the other characters in the play. While I liked what Bill had done, there were disparities in our respective approaches to the story. As a writer and self-reflecting ethnographer, I sought to stress subtlety, understatement, quietude, pause, and reflection. Bill, on the other hand, emphasized directness, action, and overstatement. In some scenes, the characters seemed stereotyped and overacted. For example, in one scene of the first draft, a young redneck, Bubba, says, "Big ol' rattler, killed his fuckin' ass." This line, like those in several other scenes, seemed to me crude and overstated. I didn't want to question Bill's style, because I knew that this language was characteristic of the life redneck girl knew. Yet, by overstatement, the very subtleties I wished to convey in redneck girl's conversations with the professor were lost.

In the staging of the play, Bill envisioned the passengers on the bus leaving their seats and entering into the scenes as characters in redneck girl's story. Redneck girl likewise would leave her seat and, while continuing to converse with the professor, would enter the scenes as the person she was at that time. While I regarded this idea as ingenious, I had difficulty visualizing how the logistics could be accomplished. Further, there were problems with the transitions between the scenes. In Bill's first draft, each scene ended with the bus stopping in a town along the way and the passengers exiting. I felt that this device broke the "spell" of the story, which required the sustained isolation of the bus.

My main problem with Bill's play, however, had to do with the character of the professor. When I wrote the story, I had wished to minimize my presence. Thus the character of the professor was necessary merely as someone to whom redneck girl could tell her story. Beyond this, I had not consciously reflected upon the role I had created for myself. Bill, on the other hand, felt the need—and rightly so—to develop the professor as a character in the action. For the most part I resisted his interpretation of the professor whom I saw portrayed as a bumbling, apologetic character given to excessive sentimentality. Particularly, I resisted Bill's idea of having the professor reveal intimate details about his personal life—details which, in fact, were about my own personal life. In one scene, Bill had redneck girl and the professor touch each other briefly. No, I said to myself, this is not as it should be. The distance must be maintained. Redneck girl was not to be a story with a happy ending. The professor does not offer redneck girl the sage advice of his experience. Everything is not all right. There is still the horror and dislocation of redneck girl's reality and the professor's estrangement from that world.

Who then was the professor? Indeed, who was I? Was I the person I really was at that time? Bruce Grindal, the professor and family man, who talked with a young woman for two hours on a bus, recalled some of what she said, and then never saw her again. Or was I the ethnographer? Bruce Grindal, "moonlighting" on a personal experience, interested, as a humanistic anthropologist, in a life history about the proletariat culture of the American South and one young woman's struggle for meaning in that world. Or was I the writer? The person who took liberties with the actual events and, for reasons of both personal and artistic choice, joined them together into a story that had characters, dialogue, plot, climax, and resolution. Or was I the character in the story that I wrote? The professor, the middle-aged family man, who in the eyes of redneck girl was a person to be respected, a nonthreatening male with whom she could confide her life's story. Or was I the character in the play Bill Shephard had written? The man, the character in a complex drama, a person whom I could see only through a distorted mirror.

These questions were the cause of profound reflection, and I wasn't sure then, as now, how to answer them. Why was the man interested in redneck girl? Why did he ask the questions that he did? Was he a voyeur? Did he want to get her into a motel room? No, he had a wife and children waiting for him at home, which is not to say that at another time in his life he might not have entertained the thought. Instead his attitude was one of infatuation. The professor was captivated, charmed by her. He wished to draw out her story—to take it to the depths of her soul, and in a more subtle and unspoken way, to the depths of his own soul. At first the professor, by virtue of his age and social position, is the senior, the dominant person. He directs the conversation and at times tries to be clever and glib. However, as redneck girl's story unfolds, he is reduced to humility; he can but only witness the passion and pathos of her life. Increasingly, the professor realizes the vast schism that separates his world of hearth, home, and respectability from the deep, dark, restless world of redneck girl. In the end they part strangers without ever having touched hands.

In sum, the character of the professor, while minimal in terms of the lines in the play, was very important. In a most fundamental sense, he stood at the center of the action and caused it to come into being. Had the professor been a voyeur, a dirty old man, or had he been smug and self-important in his respectability, the story of redneck girl would not have happened, the dramatic action would not have unfolded. There had to be a subtle chemistry in the professor's relationship to redneck girl. At the time, I had trouble articulating this concern. I could see also that Bill was having a similar problem.

On 17 June, I communicated these thoughts to Bill as best I could articulate them at the time.

Solving the Dramatic Dilemma (Shephard)

Within a few weeks of sending Bruce the first draft of the play, his comments came back in a letter that revealed both concern and encouragement. Bruce's criticisms of the first draft were basically sound and far less extreme than I had expected. There was essentially no disagreement in our perceptions of the story's significance; there was only a difference in our styles of expression. Bruce's style tended to be more literary—relying upon narrative, allusion, and metaphor—while mine tended to be more dramatic—relying upon the development of action through dialogue. Nevertheless, I agreed with him that some of the story's unique character had been weakened by the addition of some superfluous scenes; so I immediately began a second draft of the script. However, I continued to be frustrated by the technical problems associated with the bus. I tried various other stage devices, such as the play taking place in the waiting room of a bus stop, but I wasn't satisfied with the results. I came up against a creative block that seemed insurmountable at the time; therefore, I decided to put the project aside for a while.

I didn't return to the play until August 1986 at which time I began teaching in the Theater Program of Washington State University in Pullman. I was asked to direct a show for the fall season. When I suggested a world premiere of *Redneck Girl* for the WSU main stage, I was delighted and somewhat surprised that my proposal had been accepted. Not only was I given adequate financial and technical support for the project, but Richard Slabaugh, the faculty scenic designer I was working with, came up with some innovative ideas for handling the problem of the bus. Soon, I was on the phone with Bruce, telling him that our script would be performed and that I would keep him posted on developments during the rehearsal process. The next problem I faced was finding actors who could undertake the difficult task of recreating the cultural context of the deep South. Fortunately, I was able to assemble a promising cast that included a mixture of relatively experienced student performers and some who had never acted before.

I began rehearsals by cautioning the actors against adopting superficial mannerisms of southern speech and behavior without a thorough understanding of the cultural context of the play. Consequently, we spent a good deal of time in our early rehearsals examining the script line by line. Ultimately, the role of translator was my responsibility since my mother's family came from southwest Georgia and I had begun learning cultural signifiers of the rural South at an early age. In addition, I had taught in the rural environment of north central Florida for three years. My family background and personal experiences had given me a strong sense of the play's cultural weave, and I proceeded to deconstruct its significance for the actors. Next, we developed a series of improvisations centered on the cramped monotony of the bus while listening to selections of popular country music that captured various moods of the story: Piney woods and sandy clay . . . dirt roads jutting into darkness . . . all night jukes, dog fights, and drunkenness . . . violence and tenderness . . . restless spirits in search of love and redemption. However, there were parts of the play, such as the scene in the swamp, that we couldn't approach without adequate preparation. The young actors were initially unsure of themselves and each other, and the play contained scenes and language that were highly provocative. However, through the repetition of psychophysical exercises designed to forge a link between physical action and the actors' imagination, we were able to develop a good ensemble capable of responding to each another with confidence.

Ideally, the rehearsal of a play should be a process of discovery for everyone involved; that is, the true creative dimension of a performance should emerge with the fusion of the individual talents. From the first rehearsals, I was inclined to be optimistic. The contributions of the stage designer, Richard Slabaugh, and the costume designer, Debbie Shephard, gave me the freedom of exploring a variety of options with the actors. Dick's design of the bus that moved on and off stage and came apart in sections was an ingenious solution to staging problems inherent in the script. As the structure of the bus was altered to accommodate transitions in redneck girl's story, the audience was aware of both the locale suggested by the narrative and the presence of the anthropologist, still sitting in a part of the bus that had moved upstage. He not only heard the story but witnessed it as well. Debbie's understated costume designs provided both thematic continuity and character versatility in a variety of moods. And my conversations with Bruce during the rehearsal period were particularly illuminating: the problem I first had with the character of the anthropologist was solved. I was no longer trying to depict Bruce in the role; the man on the bus became a hybrid character, containing elements of both our personalities. In addition, he became less important as a separate entity in the play and more of a respondent. Bruce felt, and I agreed, that the anthropologist should remain neutral, playing the part of a foil or active witness to redneck girl's story—encouraging her to tell it without imposing his own wishes and desires on the process. I also agreed with Bruce that the end of the play needed to remain ambiguous, forgoing the appearance of a happy ending in favor of optimistic uncertainty. In this way, redneck girl's future remained an open question, leaving the audience to ponder the outcome of her story.

Throughout the rehearsal process the play underwent a series of transformations: from script to rehearsal to performance. Even though I had coauthored the playscript, I had to rediscover the play's structure of action in my role as the director. In other words, intimate acquaintance with the text was not enough to create a performance; I had to go back to square one and find a connecting thread of action in redneck girl's experience. The first part of the play, "Leaving Home," seemed to be concerned with those parts of redneck girl's past experience that shaped her perception of the world around her—her conceptual model of the way things were. The disturbing influence of her mother, the charm and dangers of the young sailors, Gloria's naive vulnerability, the ironic poem about the fish in the sand, and the dark vision of the fat boy, crawling along the side of the road like a lost animal, created a vortex of reflection that led redneck girl deeper and deeper into the heart of her unconscious conflict.

The middle of the play, "Painful Reflections," involved a descent into redneck girl's inner world, where she confronted the powerful shadows of her nightmares. During the rehearsal process, it became apparent that redneck girl was using the anthropologist in the role of a counselor or therapist with whom she could face her deepest fears. Her stories about the violent death of her high school friend, the brutal assault of the girl in the laundromat, and the despair she experienced performing in the sleazy bar in Ft. Lauderdale all created a sense of dissociation that led redneck girl deep into the heart of her childhood fears: dreams and visions of dark people who wanted her blood. By going into the swamp to find her father, she consciously sought to integrate a missing part of her life, a part that had been banished or set aside when she was very young. It was there that she came face to face with, in Jungian terms (1969:8–9), her own shadow—the dark, negative side of her own personality, embodied in the character of the "haint." Moreover, there seemed to be a relationship between redneck girl's vampire nightmare about her high school friend and the dark woman in the swamp; both represented negative aspects of the central character's psyche. Therefore, the staging attempted to capture the dreamlike inconsistency of her associations rather than an objective rendering of past events.

The last section of the play, "Finding the Self," returned to redneck girl's worldly reality, the fundamental life choices she was forced to make. After days and nights on the alcoholic treadmill of the Jacksonville bar, numbing her troubled existence with Seven and Sevens while entertaining male customers in the perennial twilight of the cocktail lounge, redneck girl comes to the brink of mental and spiritual collapse. Her defenses exhausted by the endless rounds of watered-down booze, stale cigarette smoke, and sleazy pick ups—redneck girl is ready to meet the enigmatic figure of Low-Down Sam. As we rehearsed this part of the play, the question of whether or not redneck girl had actually killed her father, as Low-Down Sam asserted, was powerfully suggestive—not so much with regard to the circumstances of her father's death, but in the confrontation between the old black man and the young woman. Low-Down Sam reflected the true face of redneck girl's sensuality, her earthy sensitivity, a part of herself that she was continually denying: her interracial family background. As a child and a young adult, the dark faces in her dreams terrified redneck girl by their incessant demands for recognition; the so-called "colored men" in her stories, the dark men responsible for violence and death when no other suspects could be found, were the specters of her unconscious conflict. She comes face to face with her denial in one traumatic moment—learning of her father's death and being confronted with Sam's devastating question, "Why you kill yo' Daddy, girl? You know yuh Daddy just a crazy country boy; never knew how to live in white folks world."

The bus trip is almost over. Redneck girl is sitting at a small table that was part of the Jacksonville bar moments ago, but is now a table in the Tallahassee bus stop. Throughout the play the anthropologist has listened to her story from his seat on the bus as if there were multiple levels of reality coexisting in the same cramped space of the bus interior. Perhaps the listeners have traveled even farther than the storyteller since theirs was a journey into the unknown, into sympathetic realms of their own beings they weren't conscious of. But how were these realms activated; what makes this particular story so captivating? The answer, in practical stage terms, is found in the character of the young woman and in the poetic resonance of her story. Redneck girl is sensuous, gutsy, and, at the same time, vulnerable. We find something in her that is close to ourselves—that life force, that will not only to survive but to triumph. Her observations are varied and complex, ranging from awkwardly articulated poetry to penetrating statements about life. And regardless of how she expresses herself, her words often have that unmistakable ring of truth.

After the play opened on 6 November 1986, the ethical question of using details from someone's life as the basis for a play was answered by the performance. Redneck girl's story had undergone what Robert Jones once referred to as the theater's ability to transform life into art through the mysterious "sea change" of the stage (1941:25). The play was no longer one person's story; it had become the story of everyone who had contributed to its creation. The original incident was like a magnet that attracted layer upon layer of details and associations from a variety of people, giving it resonance beyond its actual significance. I'm happy to say that I succeeded in accompanying redneck girl on part of her journey, and along the way I came to regard her with affection and admiration. The trip was not only worthwhile but inspiring.

Reflections on Audience Response (Shephard)

In retrospect, it's often difficult to measure audience response to a play in other than general terms, particularly when the subject matter is specialized in terms of cultural context. Admittedly, the responsibility of conveying the imaginative world of the play falls on the shoulders of both the playwright and director; however, we were attempting to go farther by capturing the cultural significance of redneck girl's story.

Immediately following the opening night performance of *Redneck Girl* at Washington State University's Jones Theater on 6 November 1986, a discussion took place in which the audience members were able to ask questions of the actors, Bruce, and myself concerning the genesis and creative evolution of the play's subject matter. The evening had certainly been charged with expectation on our parts. To begin with, a sizable portion of questions ranged from differences between the play and Bruce's original story to occult practices in the deep South. To my surprise, there seemed to be little concern over the ethical question of using details from someone's life story without their expressed consent. Most of the questions centered on the collaborative process between Bruce and myself and how the actors felt playing their particular roles. Essentially, Bruce and I recapitulated details of our collaboration and added salient reflections on the relative ease with which it had taken place. For their part, the actors seemed to have become involved with the lives of their characters despite the fact that most of them had little knowledge of the South.

Those in the audience who had firsthand experience of life in the deep South expressed sympathy with the portrayal of the characters and particularly with the notion of hoodoo or superstition as a distinguishing characteristic of southern culture. In contrast, the northwestern segment of the audience found the belief in "haints" and supernatural forces in the swamp a bit hard to swallow. As one reviewer commented: "It's when the play departs from the truth and enters the realm of conjecture that it becomes weakest. When the redneck girl goes back to visit her daddy who is now living in a bayou with a Cajun witch, she isn't the same girl we've grown to like. And we certainly don't believe that this self-sufficient, strapping gal is going to let herself be raped by a decrepit old man because his witchy wife had danced around in the swamp wearing a black negligee" (Reynolds 1986).

One the other hand, another reviewer experienced the same scene in a significantly different way: "However . . . the play is very theatrical. A standout is the scene where the redneck girl confronts her father, played by T. K. Trompler, and his voodoo conjuring mistress, dynamically played by Rita Weikal. . . . The scene, which takes place in an eery swamp, blends appropriate scenery with evocative lighting, sound, and surprise special effects to create a very strong effect" (Goldthorpe 1986:3).

It should be noted that both reviewers were women. Initially, I had been very curious to see how such a play—written and staged by men yet expressing a young woman's point of view—would be received by women in the audience. There didn't seem to be any argument on that score. Largely due to Bruce's sympathy for redneck girl and his skill as an ethnographer, the play faithfully depicted the young woman's personal conflicts without distorting the dramatic action through male bias. Generally speaking, the audience responded both collectively and as individuals. Some felt that the enigmatic ending of the play was appropriate to the action while others wished for a happier or even a romantic conclusion to the play. Nonetheless, the audience became involved in redneck girl's story enough to care about what eventually became of her.

The Search for Authenticity (Grindal)

I attended the first three performances of *Redneck Girl* at Washington State University in Pullman, Washington. Admittedly, my response at the time was more emotional than critical. On opening night, while sitting in the audience waiting for the play to begin, Bill's wife, Debbie, had to hold my hand to calm my nervous excitement. I was so over-whelmed by the beating of my heart that I could hardly breathe.

What impressed me most about the performance was the ease with which Bill and I had worked together. *Redneck Girl* had become a seamless creation, beginning as a factual event, transformed into a story, then a play, and finally into a dramatic performance with actors, sets, costumes, and lighting. We were like two brothers. In fact, after the play, when Bill and I were together on the stage discussing the play with the audience, one woman remarked that we looked like brothers. Indeed, she said, how could two men see so intimately into the life of a woman?

While I have many impressions of the performance, one aspect totally surprised me. That is, the play had funny parts—laugh lines. Indeed, the *la donnée* of *Redneck Girl,* which I had conceived in all seriousness, was greeted by laughter.

> Woman: God knows everybody's crazy. I could tell you stories that would make your hair stand on end, pro-fessor. Once knew this girl back home—strange girl. She had big brown cow eyes and a little, squeaky voice like a mouse. Always talkin' to herself like she was really talkin' to somebody else? Well, one morning the police found her in a Laundromat in Pascagoula. Somebody'd raped her and beat her up.

Then thrown her into one of those "Big Boy" dryers and turned it on hot.

Man (Pause): Mississippi must be a violent place.

Woman: (Laughs—a tough, worldly laugh) Hell, man, if you ever come through Pascagoula, don't stop. Just keep drivin' on to Gulfport or New Orleans.

Whereas I, the writer, had conveyed the moral weight, ambiguity, and heaviness of the story, Bill had lightened the story; he had given to it drama and movement. I was not sure then as now that I really understood the laughter evoked by the *la donnée* of *Redneck Girl*.

In the spring of 1986, I showed the videotape of the stage performance in Tallahassee, Florida. Bill had earlier sent me the videotape of a subsequent rehearsal which had been staged particularly for the purpose of producing a videotape. The tape had been done as Bill described, with a tilting camera tied together with duct tape. While Bill knew to focus on the scenes and dialogue, the recording was not professional. The colors bled, the focus was often inaccurate, and above all, there was 120-cycle static that frequently interrupted the dialogue, often at crucially dramatic parts that required silence and subtlety. I say this because, as was obvious to those who viewed it, the videotape *was not* the performance.

The videotape was shown at the Center for Professional Development in Tallahassee. There were five television monitors in the auditorium and about one hundred people were in attendance. Unlike the stage performance at Washington State University where nobody knew me personally, the people whom I invited were my colleagues, friends, and students. Thus they were people who could compare the character of the professor with what they knew about me personally. Also, they were people who lived in the panhandle of north Florida and who in varying ways knew the life of the South.

After the showing, I received many comments, most of which were flattering. The comments of three individuals, however, stood out in my mind.

1. There was Evelyn, my travel agent. She is a middle-aged, attractive, bleached blond. She grew up as a redneck girl in Lake City, Florida, and knew the life. She gave me a kiss on the cheek.

2. There was Rhonda, a very intelligent and soft-spoken graduate student. She grew up in a middle-class Methodist preacher family in Alabama. Her comments: "I liked the play, but you know, MoBILE is pronounced MObile." She paused. "So redneck girl ran away from

home because her mother made her put on Porcelana Fade Cream. That's deep shit." She smiled.

3. There was Gloria, an older student, a "returned woman." She had grown up in south Georgia and was currently working and enrolled in the university. Five years earlier, her husband had been knifed and killed, which left her a widow with three small children. After the showing, I felt a need to apologize to her for using the name of Gloria in the play, and portraying the character as a hippie airhead. "No problem," she said. "I know the Gloria you are talking about. I liked the play, really. It has guts."

These comments, while they did not constitute professional criticism, were nonetheless very important to me. That the performance had "guts," that it conveyed the "deep shit" of life spoke to the heart of the story. These women knew redneck girl and could identify with her and with the characters and situations in her life. Their understanding of redneck girl's story, and my unspoken understanding of their understanding, constituted in my own mind an intersubjective verification of the performance's authenticity.

In November 1987, the videotape was again shown at the meetings of the American Anthropological Association in Chicago. The showing took place in a hotel conference room as an "organized session," part of a general program format that normally consisted of the reading of scholarly papers and the presentation of research findings. Bill Shephard and I both presented short papers; the remaining two hours of the session were devoted to the videotape presentation and general discussion. There were about thirty people in attendance.

Somehow the video presentation seemed out of place. I recalled feeling a certain uneasiness when reading my paper. Such a scholarly exercise seemed inappropriate to the showing of what to me was a deep personal experience. Had people come to listen to and to criticize a scholarly work or had they come to witness a stage performance? I could sense a similar uneasiness among the anthropologists who attended the video showing. Afterwards in discussion, Greg Reck expressed his own uneasiness at seeing a fellow anthropologist and also a friend portrayed as a character in a dramatic performance. Should the anthropologist, who normally observes and writes about others, now become an object to be observed by others?

This uneasiness was compounded by the performance of the actor who played the part of the anthropologist. The actor was only eighteen years old and theatrically inexperienced. His attempt at portraying a man over twice his age often came off as pompous and somewhat ridiculous. As Miles Richardson (pers. comm.) commented, "The anthropologist in the play, not Bruce Grindal, whom I admire and respect, but the anthropologist in the play was an embarrassment to us all. When he announced to the girl that he was an anthropologist, he claimed an authority that he never obtained."

Thus, many in the audience were curious about me personally. How did my personality as an ethnographer compare with that of the actor in the performance? The discussion that followed dwelt primarily with the character of the ethnographer and how the ethnographer's interpersonal style affects the outcome of his or her work. Dan Rose (pers. comm.) aptly observed my style was one of "sophisticated naiveté." Unlike Clifford Geertz, whose style engages his informant in intellectual argument, Rose and others saw my style as both more personal and more self-effacing. I had little concern for intellectual outcome; rather I wished to penetrate life experience for its own sake and to expose its deeply shared emotional truths.

A final (but major) criticism of the performance was raised by Miles Richardson. He objected strongly to the primitively magical portrayal of the Cajun woman in the swamp scene. As an anthropologist, but also as a southerner from east Texas, the scene struck a "raw nerve." "At the time, I thought, 'That's my culture you're fucking with, buddy.' I suspected that the Cajuns of Louisiana—different from the 'Cajuns' of Alabama—would accuse the authors of using Hollywood more than ethnography in the portrayal of the 'steamy' scene along the bayou. 'Goddamn it,' I thought again, 'they ought to at least get it right' (pers. comm.).

Perhaps it would have been ethnographically more accurate to have referred to the woman as Creole instead of Cajun. However, given redneck girl's background and particularly the biracial Alabama Cajun background of her father, the term *Cajun,* as redneck girl used it, probably had a wider frame of reference. Also redneck girl's memory of the scene in the swamp was a dream fantasy. It crossed the boundary between ethnographic fact and the imagination—and not only redneck girl's imagination, but also my literary imagination and Bill Shephard's theatrical imagination.

Conclusion (Grindal and Shephard)

Thus we come to a dilemma. What is our obligation to the truth, if indeed we can really know the truth? What part does the literary imagination and artistic choice have in the telling of the truth? And finally, should the truth really be told, if its telling touches the "raw nerves" of a culture, revealing secrets that others would wish not to be exposed?

Richardson's criticism raises a central issue involved in the tension between ethnographic reporting and artistic choice—the vulnerable and indeterminate nature of truth. Thus we wish to conclude by saying that "redneck girl" had no conclusion. She exists in the creative imagination and thus continues to live. Her story, hopefully, will be retold.

When Questions Are Answers:
The Message of Anthropology according to the People of Ambae

William L. Rodman

An Introduction

This is what I think happened, my reconstruction of an event that occurred over thirty years ago on a remote island in the South Pacific. What follows is a fiction, but it's as true a fiction as I can write on the basis of my own experience on the island and the information available to me. Minor details in my account might be incorrect but what is important is that today people on the island believe that the meeting between the anthropologist and the teenager took place, and that from that meeting they discovered the message of anthropology to the native peoples of the world. What I found, many years after the event, is that their interpretation of the message of anthropology had played a critical role in changing their way of life.

In the late 1950s, an anthropologist spent a few days as the guest of an Australian couple who maintained a trade store on the weather coast of Aoba, a northern island in the New Hebrides archipelago. The anthropologist had just completed ten months of fieldwork on the neighboring island of Pentecost; he was on his way home—Aoba was just a stopover, a place to wait for a boat that would take him to a place to wait for a plane back to North America.

At some point during the anthropologist's brief stay on the island, a young man named Andrew Namala walked down to the coast from his inland village.[1] He was a quiet young man, the brother of a school-teacher but the son of a chief. He was close to his father, a man who had killed many pigs and gained high rank in the graded society (*hungwe*) before Church of Christ missionaries in the 1940s convinced their followers on the island to give up all customary activities. Andrew's father remained a traditional chief, for not even a missionary can strip a man of his rank in the graded society, but he was a nonpracticing chief, a chief in cultural exile who had become a proper Christian in the Church of Christ.

The day that Andrew walked down to the coast, the wife of the trader was tending store. She was a big, friendly woman, fluent in the local Pidgin English—Bislama—and knowledgeable about the personal lives of almost everyone who visited her store. She knew Andrew, and she knew his father, too. One thing she knew about Andrew's father was that the old chief was one of the few men in the Church of Christ skilled in the art of sand drawing.

Figure 1. Sand drawing entitled "The War-Club of the Spirits" (Rungwe Bulana Tamate), drawn by "Andrew Namala," Ambae Island, Vanuatu

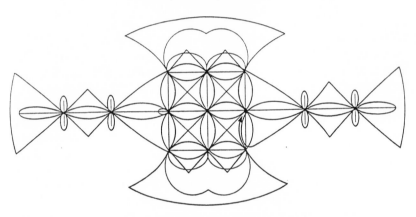

Sand drawings have an irresistible appeal for ethnographers. Copies of the drawings can be found in the works of Codrington (1969[1891]), Rivers (1968[1914]), Deacon (1934), Layard (1942), Harrisson (1937), and almost every other ethnographer with an interest in material culture who has worked in the northern New Hebrides.[2] (See figure 1.) It's not hard to explain why the drawings have attracted so much attention. They excite the basic ethnographic impulse to record and preserve. The artist's medium is fine sand or dirt as soft as talcum powder; if the artist is skillful, he creates a thing of beauty that cannot last beyond a single afternoon. Sand drawings are symbolically charged filigree that the wind blows away, myths in pictures that the tide wipes clean. The trader's wife knew that the anthropologist had collected some sand drawings on Pentecost, so she introduced him to Andrew, the son of a local expert.

The anthropologist and the teenager went outside the trade store to talk. It was hot in the store, and there were shade trees just outside—a wild mango, a rose apple, and some others. Moreover, there was a breeze off the sea.

At first, the anthropologist's questions concerned sand drawings and then, when that subject ran dry, he asked the young man about a range of other topics—magic, supernatural power, subsistence techniques, the experiences of local people in World War II, and recent changes in patterns of nutrition, all topics on which he had collected information during his recent fieldwork. In a casual way, he seems to have been seeking information concerning Aoba that he could compare with data he gathered on Pentecost. Yet it's hard to consider the encounter an "interview." It wasn't planned; it lacked formality; from the anthropologist's point of view, it may even have lacked a sense of occasion. It was a way to pass the time before dinner, a pleasant way to decompress from fieldwork.

The anthropologist left Aoba a few days later. During the decades that were to follow, he never published anything that derived from his talk with the teenager. It's unlikely the conversation changed his life in any significant way.

To Andrew, however, the encounter *was* a meaningful event. It puzzled him. Who was the outsider? Why was he interested in the local way of life? What did his questions *mean?* In 1982, Andrew spoke to me of the interview as if it happened yesterday. As I listened, I found that most of the anthropologist's questions have an air of plausibility. I recognized them as legitimate questions for an ethnographer to ask, as questions I might ask someone in an unfamiliar locale.

Andrew's life was changed as a result of his encounter with the outsider and so, at least indirectly, was the way of life of the people with whom he lived. They included the 343 members of the Church of Christ in the Longana district of the island, now called Ambae, in the new Pacific nation that changed its name from "New Hebrides" to "Vanuatu" at the time of Independence in 1980 (see figure 2). Andrew discovered an implicit pattern in the questions the anthropologist asked, and once the hidden meaning of the questions was revealed to him, the meeting took on new and deeper significance. Andrew's memory of his encounter with the anthropologist became instrumental knowledge, *used* knowledge, a key ideological justification for a profound change in the practice of a peoples' social affairs.

What follows here is primarily an account of how members of the Church of Christ on the island where I conduct fieldwork discovered the true meaning of anthropology and what that knowledge did to

Figure 2. Maps of Vanuatu (New Hebrides) and Ambae (Aoba)
showing locations of events discussed in the text

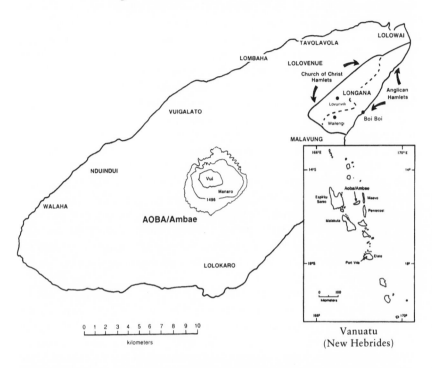

their lives. They shared their interpretation of the meaning of anthropology with me for a reason—because they wanted to teach me a
lesson. So this is my story too, my explanation of how and why a
group of chiefs on Ambae decided that the time had come to teach
me the message of anthropology.

Pretext

In 1982, early in my third term of fieldwork in the district of Longana
on Ambae, a young man brought me a message from a friend who
lives in a hill village some distance away from the hamlet where I stay
on the island. The message was in Bislama and was handwritten in
pencil on part of a page torn from a school exercise book: "Come see
me Friday afternoon," the note said, and it was signed "Nicodemus."
I turned the scrap of paper over and scrawled "Friday's fine. See you
then," and gave it back to the messenger. I didn't add, but I felt, that
wild boars couldn't keep me away.

Nicodemus Wai (as anyone in Longana will tell you—and the phrase never varies) is "different from other men." One way in which he differs is that he talks differently: sometimes, even in private conversation, he sounds like he learned how to talk by listening to Churchill's speeches on shortwave radio. He seems to think in rhetoric; his mind pumps metaphors as naturally as water issues from a spring; his stories have all the shadings of vivid dreams. But Nicodemus isn't just a dreamer. He expresses himself in action as well as words. In the late 1960s, he became an early supporter of Jimmy Stevens, a.k.a. President Moses, the charismatic descendant of a Tongan princess and a Scottish seaman who founded a political movement with millenarian overtones called "Na Griamel."[3] Na Griamel began on the island of Espiritu Santo, thirty miles across the sea from Aoba/Ambae. Partly through Nicodemus's efforts, the entire population of the Church of Christ of the district of Longana on Aoba became supporters of the movement. Then, in the mid-1970s, Nicodemus became the voice of Radio Vanafo, Jimmy Stevens's illegal radio station, located deep in the Santo bush. In those days, Nicodemus sometimes referred to himself as "a revolutionary pussycat," "pussycat" being a reference not to his disposition but to his ability to slip away from trouble unseen.

I had last seen Nicodemus in 1979. A year later, the Anglo-French Condominium of the New Hebrides became the independent Republic of Vanuatu. Achieving independence wasn't easy for the nationalists who opposed British and French rule: two months before the date set for independence, Jimmy Stevens led a rebellion against the central government. When Vanuatu became a new nation, Na Griamel was firmly in control of Espiritu Santo (known locally simply as "Santo"), the largest island in the archipelago. Jimmy Stevens renamed Santo "Vermarana" and declared the island independent of the rest of the country. Since I had last seen Nicodemus, troops from Papua New Guinea had smashed Na Griamel's radio transmitter, the Santo Rebellion had failed, and Jimmy Stevens had been tried, sentenced to prison, escaped, and attempted unsuccessfully to make a run for New Caledonia in a glass-bottomed boat he stole from a guided tour company in the capital, Port Vila.

Nicodemus and I lived in villages only a few miles apart, but we seldom met because my hosts and his kin were political enemies who also belonged to rival religions. Longana runs about eight kilometers along a coastal track, which ends at a dry riverbed that marks one boundary of the district. There, the road turns and begins to rise abruptly for one-and-a-half kilometers into the foothills of the interior of the island. Two groups live in the district. The coastal population are Anglicans, followers of tradition, and supporters of the majority political party and the central government. They are the people with whom I have worked since my first fieldwork on the island in 1969. The 549 Anglicans live in scattered hamlets separate from those of the 343 members of the Church of Christ, all of whom live in the hills and most of whom at the time of independence were among the most loyal supporters of Jimmy Stevens and Na Griamel. Like most of the people with whom I was in daily contact, I seldom ventured into the Church of Christ area, and never without an invitation.

I heard from my Anglican adoptive kinsmen that Nicodemus had been implicated in the theft of a large quantity of medical supplies from the Santo hospital during the Rebellion. I heard he had surrendered to police, been pardoned, found God, and started his own church, which lacked a name, the idea being that labels such as "Anglican" and "Church of Christ" only serve to create conflict and obscure the essential unity of Christians everywhere. I heard all these things as rumors and I badly wanted to see him: the "revolutionary pussycat" was leading one of the most interesting lives of anyone I knew.

On Friday, when I crested the hill that led into Nicodemus's village, I saw him walking toward me, a big, broken-toothed smile on his face. I also saw something else, a sight to which I ascribed no particular significance at the time: Nicodemus's brother, Andrew Namala, sitting in front of the village's men's house in the company of a number of older men. Andrew was carving a *rungwe*, a traditional fighting-club that men of rank now use as a walking stick. He saw me, grinned, and waved. I waved back. He then returned to whittling and conversation with the other men.

I expected Nicodemus to take me to his house, a place where we would not be disturbed. Instead, he directed me to a small house with walls of split and woven bamboo that stood on the edge of a clearing, about a hundred feet away from the men's house. He explained to me that it was a house the village had built for visitors; inside, it was cool and clean, a good place to talk.

Nicodemus and I seated ourselves on benches and faced each other across a bare table. We chatted about our families as I set up my tape recorder. I tested the microphone and then I asked him: "Have you been back to Jimmy Stevens's headquarters on Santo since the Rebellion?"

"Yes, just once," he replied in a thoughtful voice. "It used to be a pretty place, but it's not anymore." His tone was that of a man evoking memories within himself, trying to see the scene as it was. "The soldiers ruined everything, the peoples' way of life, the gardens, everything. All that's left there now is a French school." He paused and then took a deep breath. "The reason I went back there is that an old friend of mine had died. . . ." And at that instant the storyteller in Nicodemus took over. He told me about the end of the Rebellion, about the dawn raid on Jimmy Stevens's headquarters, about murders reported as accidents, about the secret involvement of Americans belonging to the Phoenix Foundation in the Rebellion. I found out why he had been accused of the theft of the medical supplies and why he was never charged with the crime. He told me the story of his surrender to the government troops and why they let him go. He seemed to me much older than the last time I had seen him, and he told me how tired he was of being a "diver in deep waters"; now, he said, he had "come to the surface for air." His only wish was to lead a quiet life, as a husband, as a father to his five children, and as pastor to his flock in the Church-With-No-Name.

The packed earth beneath my bare feet became cooler, and the shadows within the house deepened. We had been talking for about three hours when a boy scurried into the house, climbed into Nicodemus's lap, and whispered in his ear. Nicodemus nodded and lowered the boy to the ground. He slapped his hands on the table with an air of finality: the spell was broken, the interview over. He rose in a way that indicated he expected me to do the same. "Bill," he said, "the chiefs are waiting for you. Your kava is ready."

Kava (*Piper mythysticum*) is a drug about which I feel profound ambivalence. It is a bitter brew that everyone on Ambae admits tastes awful: one of its several origin myths attributes its taste to the fact that it first grew from the decaying vagina of a murdered woman. That myth makes sense of why, today, Ambaen men hawk and spit after every shell. It's also a powerful enough drug to alter perception in fundamental ways. Once I drank a shell so strong that everything I saw for the next 20 minutes flickered, just like an old-time movie. Most often, however, one or two draughts of kava merely numbs the tongue, eases the mind, and generates companionship and goodwill among the drinkers. For a male fieldworker, accepting a host's invitation of kava is a social necessity; it's better to accept and throw up than to refuse, however smilingly.

The men's house was filled. Every man of rank in the Church of Christ area was there. Andrew Namala greeted me at the doorway, and then I went from man to man, shaking hands in greeting, my body bent slightly from the waist in a position of respect. In the center of the clubhouse, there were five split coconut shells filled with kava. The chief of highest rank in the men's house told me which shell of kava

I was to drink. He glanced around the men's house. "Thaddeus, you come drink with us," he said. "You too, Sam . . . and you, Andrew." He then took a twig and passed down the line of shells, dipping the stick in the kava, raising it to his mouth and tasting it, and then moving on to the next shell. I'd seen this done before, though not often, and until I learned better I'd always assumed that the chief was testing the kava for poison, symbolically if not actually. In fact, the trajectory of the twig is from the chief's mouth to each cup, not the reverse: the ritual is done so that guests will absorb some knowledge from their host.

I drank my kava, stepped outside the men's house, spat, made other terrible sounds, then came back inside, passed around a pack of Camels, and settled against a bamboo wall. It was strong stuff, and I began to feel the hum and glow of the kava working on me. I smoked a cigarette, pleasantly stoned, listening, watching as other men drank their shells of kava.

When everyone in the men's house had downed a shell of kava, the quality of sound in the room changed, became softer, quieter, and someone began to tell a story. It was a few minutes before I realized that I was listening to something more than idle men's house conversation. With some difficulty, I switched on my tape recorder. Andrew squatted a few feet away, still working on his club in the semidarkness. There was a moment of silence as one story ended, then he began to speak.

Text

"There was a man who came here shortly after World War II ended." (He confers with others in the men's house about the visitor's name. Someone suggests "Mr. Allen," but Andrew shakes his head and continues.) "We don't remember his name but he came here to find out about our sand drawings and about the messages we leave for each other on the ground. Before he came here, he visited the island of Pentecost, and then he arrived at Boi Boi, the landing down on the coast. He stayed in the house of the trader who lived there—Mr. Mueller.

At that time, I was a young man, maybe seventeen or eighteen. Sometimes, I would walk down to the coast to visit the Muellers' trade store. One day, as I approached the store, Mrs. Mueller saw me coming, and she yelled to me:

'Hey! Isn't your father the chief who knows about sand drawings?'

'Yes,' I said, 'and so do I.'

'Aww, you're just a kid; you don't know any sand drawings.'

'Oh yes I do,' I said ... Now I remember! Mr. Jones! Mr. Jones was his name. Mrs. Mueller introduced me to him.'

'Do you know any sand drawings?' he asked me.

'A few,' I replied.

We went outside the store and sat down. Mr. Jones opened his book and showed me a drawing.

'Do you know this one?' he asked. 'It's from Pentecost.'

'Yes,' I said, 'I know it.'

'What is it called?'

I told him.

He showed me another drawing. 'What's this one?'

'It's called fresh coconuts,' I said.

Altogether, Mr. Jones asked me if I knew four different drawings. I knew each one.

'Enough,' he said, 'I want to ask you some questions. In the past, did some men around here know how to make thunder?'

'Yes,' I said. 'They did.'

'What about now?'

'No longer.'

'O.K.,' he said, 'let me ask you about something else: in the past, did some men around here know how to make earthquakes?'

'Yes,' I said. 'They did.'

'What about now?'

'No longer.'

'What about cyclones? Did men know how to make them?'

'Yes.'

'Now?'

'No.'

'Why do such men no longer exist?' he asked me.

Well, I didn't really know, so I just told him the first thing that came to mind. I said: 'What happened was that the missionaries arrived. They showed us the Bible and told us to leave our heathen ways. They told us to burn or throw away our magical substances and to forget about them.'

Then Mr. Jones asked me: 'Did you go to Santo during the war?'

'No,' I told him. 'I was too young. When the men of my village returned from Santo, they told us: "It's over: the war has ended." '

'How do you think America managed to win the war?' he asked.

'I don't know,' I said.

'Do you drink tea?' asked Mr. Jones.

'Yes.'

'When you drink tea, do you eat anything?'

'Yes. Sometimes cabin biscuits, sometimes bread.'

'Do you like the taste of tea, biscuits, and bread?'

'Yes.'

'Fine,' said Mr. Jones. 'Do you eat rice?'

'Yes.'

'When you eat rice, do you eat any other food at the same time?'

'Sometimes meat, sometimes tinned fish.'

'Do you like the taste of rice, meat, and tinned fish?'

'Yes.'

'All right,' said Mr. Jones, 'I have another question: do you know how to make a garden?'

'Yes.'

'Then tell me how you do it. What do you do when you want to clear land?'

I showed him how I held my bush-knife and how I used the knife to clear land.

It was then that I realized that he was teaching me a lesson, a lesson about the value of traditional culture [*kastom*].

'Look,' he said, 'rain drives sunlight away. Night replaces day. Think again about the reason why the Americans won the war. Have you figured it out? I'll tell you. It's because the soldiers carried the Bible with them. The Bible provides White men with their *kastom*. Why have you people lost *your kastom*?'

My word! Then I understood.

I shared with Mr. Jones my knowledge of sand drawings and I showed him the signs we write on the ground, the four main ones, the one that tells your friends to wait for you, the one that says: 'I'm tired of waiting—I've gone in this direction.' But I knew that there were many other signs I didn't know, that nobody knew any more.

Before Mr. Jones departed from the island, he told me he would put the signs I had shown him into a book he would write after he returned to America. 'I'll put the signs in a book,' he said, 'and then it won't matter if I die or if you die. Even when we both are dead, the signs will remain in the book for our children to see.'

You know, Bill, I think the kinds of things I've been talking about— sand drawings, signs, that sort of thing—are the real *kastom* of Longana. Lots of people who don't know much about *kastom* just talk about pigs. Pigs, pigs, pigs. But pigs aren't the backbone of *kastom*. Pigs are just a kind of money."

Context

Even at the time, bone-tired, the kava still working on my brain, I had the feeling that Andrew was trying to tell me something of importance to him, something much more than merely an anecdote about his encounter with a White man many years ago. When he finished the story, he lapsed into silence and returned to chip, chip, chipping away at his fighting-club. The light in the men's house was dim and fallow, the golden last light of late afternoon. Andrew worked on his club, his shoulders hunched, his face a dark and pensive mask. The time did not seem right to ask him questions. Soon, men seated in the shadows of the men's house returned to quiet conversation and then later we all went to another hill village where a mortuary feast was in progress. My "father"—old Mathias Tari—was there. We drank a shell of kava together, my second, his first, and waited for the bundles of food to come out of the earth oven. When we received our food, we set off down the hill toward home, the old man leading, me following behind, slipping, sliding, but somehow never quite falling.

Days passed, then weeks, and eventually I transcribed the tape of my interview with Nicodemus. There, on the end of the last tape in the Nicodemus series, was Andrew Namala telling his story. This time, listening to him, I began to notice details—the way in which he knitted the segments of the narrative together, the progressions in the encounter between the anthropologist and the teenager, the apparent revelation at the climax of the story: "My word! Then I understood." But *what* had he understood? Why, then, did he share his knowledge willingly, even joyously, with the outsider? What was the lesson about *kastom* that he thought the anthropologist had taught him?

From these questions came others. I reflected on the occasion, and I began to wonder about the context in which Andrew told me his story. The recounting of the tale had been truly a performance, and Andrew had played to a packed (men's) house: why had so many chiefs gathered in his village on a work day, a Friday in the cool season? Then, too, there was the puzzle of why he had told me the story. Why in public? What was the significance of the last bit, the part he directed at me as if underlining the story's message: things like sand drawings are the backbone of *kastom* of Longana, pigs are not. Now *there's* an unorthodox view! When men speak of *kastom* in Longana, they mean pig-killing, rank-taking, the graded society (*hungwe*): I'd heard men use *kastom* as a synonym for "pig-killing" hundreds of times.[4] Andrew himself had been an important catalyst in the recent revival of pig-killing in the Church of Christ area in Longana. In 1979, I'd seen him take the second-highest rank, killing tusked boars in the midst of a thunderstorm, a man radiant with energy, in complete control of his body, his every movement clean and precise; Andrew's was the best of the many rank-takings I'd seen. That was then, three years ago, but now he was taking the line that "lots of people who don't know much about *kastom* just talk about pigs." Hell, everybody in Longana who engages in *kastom* talks about pigs. So what was he trying to tell me?

Some mysteries, if you dream on them enough and have enough context, reveal themselves. It took me a while, but eventually I understood. The key to understanding Andrew's interpretation of his talk with the anthropologist (and also the key to the way in which he told me the story) is *qaltavalu*, literally "hidden talk," a form of communication based on a system of implicit meanings. People sometimes *qaltavalu* in everyday life; for example, a man may ask a woman for a plate of rice and not have food in mind at all. More commonly, it occurs as a rhetorical device in speeches: rival chiefs use *qaltavalu* against each other to devastating effect. "Hidden talk" is the process; shame is the product. *Qaltavalu* says to a rival: "Look, I am speaking about you in public, and *you* understand my meaning, even if everyone else does not. Shall I make my meaning explicit, or will you change your way of acting?" Or, perhaps, ". . . provide me with the support I need?" The threat of public exposure often is sanction (or blackmail) enough in a society in which men dread public humiliation.

Qaltavalu has a third use: it's one of the most important customary techniques of instruction. Teachers on Ambae seldom state the obvious. Instead, they teach by parable, by indirection raised to the level of a fine art. They figure that students are most apt to remember a lesson if they have to work to figure out what the lesson is.[5]

Andrew's encounter with the anthropologist made little sense to the hill people in terms of their prior dealings with Europeans. By the 1950s, Longanans in the Church of Christ area had had limited experience with White people: in fact, most peoples' knowledge of Whites resulted exclusively from their contacts with the Australian trader and his wife (who were the only resident Whites in the district), missionaries, and very, *very* rarely, a government official. Longanan followers of the Church of Christ had heard missionaries preach against *kastom* as a mark of moral backwardness, as beliefs to be uprooted, substances to be destroyed, and behaviors to be transformed. In contrast to missionaries, traders and the occasional district agent didn't seem to regard *kastom* as immoral, but they didn't take local traditions very seriously either: to them, *kastom* is play, a harmless set of activities that waste time and money.

In contrast to missionaries, traders, and district agents, the anthropologist clearly was interested in *kastom*. Andrew, the son of a chief, chose to interpret his meeting with the outsider in terms of a category of Ambaen culture, *qaltavalu*. What was the hidden meaning of the encounter? What was the anthropologist (cast in the role of "teacher") *really* saying? Viewed within the framework of ordinary conversation, the questions communicate little information. What, after all, does winning a war have to do with the taste of tea? But as *qaltavalu*—aiiyahhh!—patterns begin to emerge, and implicit links between the questions appear. Andrew puzzled over the meaning of the questions until they provided him with an answer to the problem of the anomalous White man.

He opens his narrative with the incident involving the trader's wife. He depicts her as *assuming* that members of the younger generation no longer know their own traditions. Andrew proves her wrong when he correctly identifies the Pentecost sand drawings. By so doing, he demonstrates to the anthropologist his interest in *kastom* and qualifies himself as a worthy recipient of the anthropologist's message.

The next section of the narrative consists of a set of questions that have in common the theme of lost power. The storyteller has the anthropologist establish an implicit relationship between lost power and the loss of tradition. The "teacher" is drawing his "student's" attention to the fact that, in the past, men possessed great supernatural powers: no one today knows how to make thunder, earthquakes, and cyclones. Then, abruptly, the anthropologist asks: "Why do such men no longer exist?" and Andrew, free-associating, is forced to confront the fact that missionaries were responsible for the loss of the knowledge and magical substances that had been the source of customary power.

The conversation appears to change course when the anthropologist asks Andrew: "Did you go to Santo during the war?" In fact, in his questions about World War II, Mr. Jones reveals his true intent, but not in an obvious way. "How do you think America managed to win the war?" is another question probing the theme of power. It's an extension of his previous questions, but Andrew doesn't catch the drift of his "teacher's" line of reasoning: "I don't know," he replies.

So Mr. Jones tries another tack: "Do you drink tea?" he asks. All the next set of questions concern diet. In a broader sense, however, the questions elicit information about change and the presence of foreign elements in Longana; Andrew is made to come face to face with his alienation from tradition. He is forced to admit he not only eats White people's food; he *likes* it.

All is not lost, however. Mr. Jones is a good teacher, a master of *qaltavalu,* so he nudges his student with yet another question: "Do you know how to make a garden?" This most straightforward of questions, reconsidered as *qaltavalu,* is transformed into something like: "Do you remember the most fundamental traditional skill of all— how to make a living from the earth?" Andrew responds affirmatively. This allows the "teacher" to lead him in the direction of a reconsideration of his essential values. He asks Andrew to demonstrate the skills that bind him to the land. Andrew does so, and at last he understands that Mr. Jones is using customary means to make a point about *kastom.* But what *is* the point? Andrew still is not sure, so Mr. Jones steps out of character and makes his message explicit: in effect, he tells the young man that Americans are strong because their *kastom,* which can be found in the Bible, is powerful; Americans remain strong because they remain true to the traditional values associated with their own way of life. Missionaries deprived the islanders of indigenous *kastoms* and, as a result, people lost much of their power.

So what was the anthropologist's hidden message? What was the true meaning of the encounter and the questions he asked? The answer in the questions isn't hard to discover. The anthropologist made Andrew work toward an understanding that *kastom is* important: it is the way to power; those who lose their *kastoms* are powerless. By the end of the narrative, Andrew has discovered the "true" message of anthropology: anthropologists are an equal and opposing force in the world to certain kinds of missionaries. They are a counter to anti-*kastom* Christianity and those missionaries who urge people to abandon their traditional ways. The aim of anthropology is to teach all peoples to value their traditional ways.

The anthropologist's message to Andrew became Andrew's message to his people. At first, no one listened. For 15 years, he lived as an outsider in his own society, a man with a passionate concern for *kastom* in a Christian community that believed (with equal fervor) that *kastom* is anti-Christian. He learned from his father and then, when his father died and there was no one else in the Church of Christ who could teach him *kastom,* he sought out chiefs in the Anglican sector of the district. It took courage to go to those chiefs. At that time, Anglicans and members of the Church of Christ regarded each other with mutual suspicion and hostility. He went to the chiefs and he learned from them. Gradually, he became a master of tradition.

Then the times changed. In the 1970s, with the waning of colonialism, *kastom* became a symbol of national identity in the New Hebrides, a rallying cry of the pro-independence movement (Tonkinson 1982). The Anglicans in Longana all joined the Vanuaku Pati, which promoted *kastom* in the interests of national unity. Everyone in the Church of Christ joined Na Griamel, which claimed that the majority political party "pays only lip service to . . . customs, while Nagriamel made the respect for them a basic part of its party's philosophy" (Stevens, quoted in Plant 1977:44). Not only politicians rode the pro-*kastom* bandwagon; missionaries with an eye to the future did too. Church of Christ missionaries now maintained a cautious silence on matters of *kastom:* in the hill country of Longana, no one mistook the church's new attitude as one of approval or even tolerance; some men, however — and Andrew was one of them — thought that the church would no longer interfere in customary activities such as pig-killing and kava drinking. In this time of uncertainty, when men were still trying to interpret their changed circumstances, Andrew used the story of his meeting with the anthropologist as an ideological resource. He found a willing audience for its message. Men now were willing to listen to the idea that *kastom* is a path to power, nationally, locally, and personally. After a hiatus of 40 years, members of the Church of Christ in Longana began to take rank again, and Andrew was one of the first. He started on the lowest level of the graded society (as was proper) and, within seven years, he had climbed to the second-highest rank.

I went to four pig-killings in the Church of Christ area in the late 1970s, when I spent 12 months in Longana. I went, but without much enthusiasm. I went mainly because people expected me to go, because if I stayed home it would have been an insult to the rank-taker and his sponsor. I had seen close to forty ranks taken in the Anglican area and I had written a Ph.D. dissertation on the topic. I had been there, done that, knew the moves, and wanted to get on to something else. What really interested me at the time was the fact that colonial authorities had withdrawn from participation in local legal affairs. People in Longana were beginning to codify their own laws and develop their own courts: that was what I wanted to study, not rank-taking.[6] I stayed in the Anglican area of Longana, and I visited the Church of Christ mainly to see friends, like Nicodemus Wai, and to attend the occasional rank-taking.

When I next visited Longana, in 1982, I found that the pace of rank-taking in the Church of Christ had accelerated. Suddenly, *everybody* in the hills seemed to be killing pigs — grandfathers, church leaders, teenagers wearing Sony Walkman headsets. Pig-killing had become a fad, a craze, a way to wow your neighbors. Abuses were common: some men were skipping ranks, others were holding ceremonies with little or no preparation in the complex rituals. The first Church of Christ rank-taking I saw in 1982 was awful: the kid taking the rank clearly didn't know what he was doing, his resources were minimal, and the pigs died hard, screaming like babies. Andrew was one of the teenager's sponsors, a secondary sponsor without much say, and there was little he could do to improve the situation. At one point, he raced by the grassy hill where I was sitting and he yelled over his shoulder: "*Hemia i kastom ya, be i kastom olbaot!*" The phrase doesn't translate easily, but it means something like: "I guess this is *kastom* but it's sure a mess!" It wasn't long after that ceremony that Nicodemus invited me to his village.

There's no doubt in my mind that Nicodemus's invitation was a pretext, a way to get me to the village without arousing my suspicions, and that Andrew told me the story of his encounter as a *qaltavalu*. In fact, the *qaltavalu* was multileveled and complex.

In a sense, Andrew was trying to teach me the same lesson that the anthropologist had taught him. He had seen me mainly in two contexts: at rank-takings and in his brother's company. As far as he could tell, I was interested in pigs and in certain kinds of radical change. Somehow, I had lost the grand vision of anthropology: obviously, I needed re-routing. He was saying to me: *kastom* is the true interest of anthropology; there is much *kastom* you do not know; don't listen to people who equate pigs with *kastom*; pigs are business, *kastom* is art, and art endures.

He was shaming me, in a sense, but he was also flattering me, trusting my local knowledge; a novice wouldn't catch the *qaltavalu*. Writing this essay, it occurs to me that I wasn't the only target of his *qaltavalu* that afternoon. Quite possibly, he had a larger purpose, an aim rather more important than teaching an anthropologist the meaning of anthropology. *Qaltavalu* is a subtle system of meaning, and Andrew was a master of the form, and quite capable of sending a message to two audiences at once. I think now that I was Andrew's pretext for aiming a *qaltavalu* at the other men in the men's house. They—not me—were his monster, his creation made of parts of the old culture, slugging back kava as if there had never been years of abstinence, killing pigs with a passion for prestige but without skill, without grace, with no respect. They needed to slow down, to relearn the lesson that *kastom* is various and subtle, a matter of the mind as well as public display. They too needed to relearn the hidden message of anthropology that Mr. Jones taught so many years ago.

Conclusions

I returned to Ambae in 1985, just in time to attend Andrew Namala's mortuary feast. He died suddenly, of uncertain causes, precisely one hundred days before I returned to the island. Some people—perhaps most—attributed his death to sorcery. Indeed, there were men with knowledge of magical spells who had a good motive to try to kill him. Andrew was ambitious, much admired, much envied, and a master of *qaltavalu*. If *qaltavalu* poses the question, then sometimes men in danger of public humiliation find an answer in sorcery.[7]

At the mortuary feast, Andrew's widow asked me to photograph his ceremonial regalia, which she laid out over his grave. There was the bustle in which I saw him kill pigs, the armbands he'd earned, the thick belt he'd made himself lined with cowrie shells, and also a traditional fighting-club, the one he'd been carving that afternoon in the clubhouse when he told me the *qaltavalu*. I stood there with my camera, and I was aware of his widow behind me, weeping softly and saying her dead husband's name over and over. Then I took the shot and moved back to where the men were drinking kava.

That ends my narrative, and you may have realized that I, too, have been engaging in *qaltavalu,* but my point is not what some may think, that we have lost our vision and should return to our roots and study "tradition." That was Andrew's *qaltavalu* to me, not my *qaltavalu* to you. My *qaltavalu* concerns our hidden talk to each other, in writing, in narratives buried in the text of our ethnographies. This essay presents a narrative explanation, "an account of the linkages among events as a process one seeks to explain" (Roth 1988:1). Embedded in the narrative is an allegory about several kinds of interpretive quest. The anthropologist I call "Mr. Jones" was "as much the question as the questioner" (Parker 1985:65). So was I, and so are all fieldworkers: the people we study study us, even in moments when we do not seek to study them. We are not just observers observed; we are interpreters interpreted. To figure out what the devil they think they are up to requires us to try to figure out what they think *we* are up to—our motivation, purposes, and (sometimes) the moral message we bring with us. This is an Other side to reflexivity, one crucial to understanding the dialogics of encounters in field research, and one that anthropologists have only begun to explore.[8]

NOTES

Reproduced by permission of the American Anthropological Association from *American Anthropologist* 93:2, June 1991. Not for further reproduction. I owe a great debt of gratitude to "Andrew Namala," who tried his best to teach me the meaning of anthropology. I would not have understood the lesson he was trying to teach me without the help of my ni-Vanuatu father, Mathias Tariundu, who taught me how to recognize and interpret *qaltavalu*. I also thank Margaret Rodman, Jean-Marc Philibert, Jane Philibert, Andrew Lyons, Harriet Lyons, Laird Christie, and students in my graduate seminar on interpretive anthropology at McMaster University, especially Hillary Rodrigues, for helpful comments on earlier drafts of this essay. I am much obliged to members of the Anthropology Club of Wilfred Laurier University for inviting me to present an earlier version of this essay as a talk. Finally, I wish to acknowledge the support and assistance of the Social Science and Humanities Research Council of Canada, which funded much of the research on which this essay is based and to whom I am deeply grateful.

1. All names in this essay are pseudonyms. However, all statements of the pseudonymous Ambeans (including Andrew Namala's story in the section entitled "Text") are translated versions of comments I tape-recorded in Bislama.

2. The man I call "Andrew Namala" drew the sand drawing represented in figure 1. The name of the sand drawing is "The War-Club of the Spirits" (*Rungwe Bulana Tamate*). As much of a sand drawing as possible is drawn in one continuous line. I use the masculine pronoun in my description of the drawings because, on Ambae, the person who works the sand drawings is always male.

3. John Beasant's (1984) *The Santo Rebellion: An Imperial Reckoning* provides a detailed account of the career of Jimmy Stevens, Na Griamel, the Rebellion, and its aftermath. Other useful sources of information are Hours (1976), Jupp and Sawer (1979), MacClancy (1980), and Plant (1977).

4. A complete discussion of the important role that graded society (*hungwe*) plays in politics, economics, and kinship on Ambae can be found in Rodman (1973) and in Blackwood (1981). Additional, more abbreviated, accounts of the rank association can be found in Rodman (1977, 1982, 1985).

5. Parallels to the Ambean notion of *qaltavalu* can be found elsewhere in Oceania and in other parts of the world. Strathern (1975:185), for example, discusses the "veiled speech" (*ik ek*) that Melpa of Highland New Guinea use in a number of contexts, including children's games, love songs, public argument and debate, and formal oratory. The Melpa also have a concept of "hidden truth" similar to that of Ambae (Strathern 1989:301). Unlike Ambae, however, Melpa figurative speech apparently is not used in education as a formal means for the transmission of knowledge. Outside Oceania, "hidden talk" as a pedagogical device sometimes occurs in places where a person's knowledge is supposed to grow in small increments, as among the Saramaka of Surinam, where old men teach their younger kinsmen in a style marked by ellipsis, concealment, and partial disclosure (Price 1983).

6. I discuss the results of my research in Rodman (1985).

7. Sorcery is part of *kastom*; it's the dark twin of benevolent magic, the magic that brings gentle rains and cures the ill and makes the pigs grow tusks as round as ridgepoles and as big as a big-man's palm. You can't have the one without the possibility of the other.

8. Despite the growing interest in reflexive and dialogical perspectives in anthropology, anthropologists have devoted little attention to the Other's view of anthropology and the anthropological Self. Some notable exceptions to the general lack of the consideration of the topic include Jean-Paul Dumont (1978), Dwyer (1977, 1982), Feld (1987), Page (1988), Ruby (1982), and Stoller (1987). Despite the efforts of such scholars, it still can reasonably be said that "rarely have we heard much of how the anthropologist was perceived by the people he or she studied, or of the impact that participating in anthropological research may have had on their lives" (Hoskins 1985:147). In a similar vein, Renato Rosaldo (1988:83) points out that "anthropologists often talk about seeing things from the native point of view. . . . Yet we have given little thought to how members of other cultures conceive the translation of cultures."

Ethnography as a Form of Life: The Written Word and the Work of the World

Dan Rose

One can readily imagine that the corpus of anthropological work, with some minor exceptions, will in some future, more clear-sighted time, be perceived as little more than a reflection of the attitudes and the intellectual play of an imperial civilization. And the record will reveal, I think, that anthropologists had only the most abstract interest in the cultures they studied.

— Stanley Diamond, 1980

It should be clear then that much of the talk about reform and change from the point of view of white South Africa in general is premised not on what the whites of South Africa may have to unlearn, but on what black people, those "prospective citizens of the Republic," need to be speedily introduced to so that they can become "responsible" citizens of the future, so that they can become Westerners in black skins. In a nutshell, the entire ideology of reform is based on the "humanization" of the oppressed according to the specifications of South African capital, which, itself, is governed according to the specifications of the international corporate world.

The practical aspects of this modern form of colonial "pacification" imply the implementation of modern principles of business management.

— Njabulo Ndebele, 1987

For certainly the development of social anthropology in England is linked to the spread of our colonial empire and its administrative, missionary and commercial needs.

— E. E. Evans-Pritchard, 1969

In the fall of 1969 I began to conduct ethnographic inquiry as a graduate student of anthropology. Until the fall of 1971 I did ethnographic fieldwork without revealing my identity as an anthropologist. The idea behind the lack of revelation was simple: become as intimately involved in the everyday life of people as possible, unencumbered by an academic identity.

The United States cities of the late 1960s were still addressing the emotional issues raised by the confrontations between African-American people and the police, from the burning of neighborhoods in one of the most dramatic forms of social protest in American history. Anthropology departments at that time were politically polarized. In some departments the hostility between students and faculty centered on such issues as Vietnam, but, most immediately, faculty were criticized for the lack of relevance anthropology had shown to the peoples it had studied in a postcolonial era of Western economic hegemony. Criticism was also leveled at anthropology for its failure to engage socially, politically, and intellectually the issues facing the country—civil rights and citizenship, our own complex streams of cultures and the problems of identity and domination in the so-called melting pot.

I chose my doctoral dissertation fieldwork site partly in response to the student critique of those times, in an effort to make of anthropological training critical relevance to the country. In South Philadelphia, where I decided to become employed in an African-American man's auto repair shop, I took up residence next door, lived on the street in the summer, and did pickup work, finally free-lancing like an underemployed handyman, like others who lived in the area. At night I transcribed fieldnotes sometimes too drunk to focus well, or worked on them the next morning, more sober, less close to what had gone on the day before.

Because I did not disclose my identity and take up residence officially as an anthropologist present only to study the people, what occurred was a collapse of the distance between my neighbors and myself. I had no identity, no role to hide behind except what I could pick up locally. Like several of my men friends there I became an urban adventurer wandering through the city at night creating minor adventures that ended sometimes early in the mornings with me drunk and worn out. At first I worked twelve-hour days in the repair shop and was exhausted by the sheer madness of trying to repair autos with poor tools, low-level skills, and the frustrated motivations of an ethnographic fieldworker.

The fact that I did not explicitly say I was conducting anthropological fieldwork led rapidly to a disintegration of my assumptions about what information I could gather. The worst worry was that I could not gather data, as we called it, about the people that conformed to what anthropologists usually acquire. I could not use the tools in which I was trained: no interviews, no census, no key informants, no interrogating people about their assumptions, no eliciting dreams, no eliciting performances such as woofing, sounding, or playing the dozens.

I feared that what was occurring was a complete lack of matchup between what I had read in graduate school and the entries in my fieldnotes. At the time I could think of no greater anxiety.

Over the years I felt that the logic of inquiry that I had learned from a graduate education of reading, seminars, and talking had been detonated by the field experience. Ethnography as knowledge about our own culture or about others opened up for me as a *radically fractured* way of life. My assumptions derived from reading ethnographies could not be played out in the field given the covertness, lack of explicitness, and lack of sacred status claimed by ethnographers for their inquisitive role.

The logic of inquiry, extremely simplified, can be evoked by a figure of boxes and arrows.

Figure 1. The Logic of Inquiry

Each box represents an ethnographer's activity, and the arrow, a line, not so much of causality as of logical progression. First, one becomes socialized in graduate school to one's profession, to the conduct of ethnography. The whole aim of this socialization is to duplicate at one level the achievements of the discipline, and, at another level, contribute uniquely to the growth and development of knowledge. Second, one conducts inquiry along the lines one has read. I simplify of course, but it is as if doing ethnography is to construct a text from the experiences with others, but experiences carefully controlled by the profession. In a strong sense all experiences were normatively laid out in advance by peers, professors, monographs, articles, and books. In addition, one carefully grooms a persona, an identity that conforms to the expectations but becomes the persona necessary to engage in certain experiences, to craft the expected texts. Our texts are forms of how we know. If inquiry does not conform to texts one has read, the terrible reality, at least the fear, is that one's experiences will not be relevant for the texts one will write.

Third, the success in crafting a text has everything to do with a career since, with a few exceptions, careers are text-dependent. We write to be recognized and promoted, but we write also to confirm that identity we acquired in graduate socialization. One assumes the culture of anthropology in graduate school. Central to the culture and the identity that goes with it are the field experiences for the text. Life chances within a career are closely associated as a result of publishing books in genres that resemble, or at least address in a conforming way, the literature cited in the ones that preceded them. Important for my argument is that written words and careers take place within an academy crosscut by disciplines—and both the academy and disciplines are corporations, the context of ethnographic texts.

For me ethnography as a way of life was radically broken open by the way I lived through fieldwork. As a result I wonder about the form of life that ethnographers have cultivated since Malinowski. I join my voice with those who in growing numbers question the assumptions and practices of anthropology (Clifford 1983; Clifford and Marcus 1986; Jean-Paul Dumont 1986; Marcus and Cushman 1982; Marcus and Fischer 1986). When Clifford Geertz was awarded the National Book Critics Circle Award for Criticism in 1988 (Geertz 1988), a larger social legitimacy was offered regarding the anthropologists' concerns with culture and interpretation, inquiry and text, documentation and criticism. If Geertz raised the literary and interpretive possibilities within the anthropological endeavor, then Marcus and Cushman in 1982 focused on what a number of authors had been attempting in writing ethnography, to experiment until they had broken with the old categories and inaugurated a new narrative responsiveness to changing world cultural relations. Much of my recent work has benefitted from the experimental moment but is not derived from it. This essay was written after the difficult final drafting of *Black American Street Life* (1987) and in a linked relation with "Reversal" (1991a), an article that seeks to answer some of the questions raised here. Both "Ethnography as a Form of Life" and "Reversal" have commonalities with an article entitled "Transformations of Disciplines through Their Texts" (1986), which amplifies points made on the socialization of anthropologists through their reading and its effect on ethnographic practice. In *Patterns of American Culture* (1989), the pervasiveness of the corporation within the culture of Anglo-American capitalism is framed more broadly. The two books and three essays form a multiple set of inquiries that demand one another and offer a working out of the problematic of conducting ethnography in the United States within the social forms that contain our lives and obscure to ourselves what we may indeed be doing. By such questioning I do not mean to engage in some self-indulgent re-flexivity, but in querying the construction of our largely taken-for-granted way of life that is dependent on the texts and the cultural contexts of academic anthropology.

It seems that when young anthropologists leave graduate school for the field there are thousands of possibilities that wait for them: the people will be hostile, as the Nuer quite justifiably were to Evans-Pritchard, or the people one lives among may delight in telling stories for the anthropologist's publicly announced book. On the other hand, despite the ever-different empirical realities of field stays, there has been a dominant mode of authentication for anthropological work: the ethnographic monograph or book. The genre has been stable for quite some time, and its history, largely obfuscated, has existed longer than the academic discipline. To deal with the luxuriant diversity of human cultural life, anthropologists tended to standardize within a way of life, within the quotidian of the academy, with carefully conceived and highly monitored genres, the deeper identity of the writing and the experiences-for-the-writing. If the writing was not monolithic and was itself diverse, the diversity was carefully controlled, its boundaries visible to both readers and authors. The canon through this century has accumulated until we have between eight and ten thousand scientific anthropological books about other cultures (not counting dissertations, travel accounts, anthologies, etc.), recognizable as such in anthropology libraries, a corpus that has as much as anything else defined a discipline, a way of knowing, a way of experiencing, indeed, a way of life.

It is as if we know by our texts.

It is as if fieldwork is an extension of our anthropological, academic, everyday life, a deformation of the outer skin of our Western culture that never breaks. The skin does not rupture. In the field we are still academics, safe behind the membrane, we keep the same hours, do the same sorts of things, or do different things temporarily in order to advance our life chances back home. In brief, in the field we work. In the office we work. We work and we write.

1

What relationships should ethnographers take up with peoples of other cultures? Can we not move beyond abstract relations with them?

These questions have been made more pressing by the concern with experimentation in the ethnographic text. The experimentation can be superficial unless the way of life on which ethnography is based is subjected to greater risks, thereby made more truly experimental. The text, of itself, cannot adequately break new ground. Ethnographers' lives, like the works they have written, have been standardized since Malinowski. A summer in the field, a year in the field, two years in the field, subsequent summers in the field, and an occasional semester.

The hard questions facing ethnographers include, is the one- or two-year field stay adequate to the demands of real cultural knowledge? Is any historically, textually ritualized formula for cultural knowledge adequate to its contemporary demands?

2

We do not have an adequate understanding of our own culture of ethnographic inquiry—I mean an understanding beyond the confessional, self-observing pieces written in resistance to the hyperscience of sixties' cognitive anthropology. We do not understand ourselves as living within a culture of anthropologists, a subculture within university life. We do not talk about that in profoundly self-critical ways. I would like to comment on the formation of ethnography as a form of life, as a culture for conducting inquiry into culture.

3

The ethnographers' interests narrow when there is exaggerated and exclusive concern with their own texts. One could examine only field-notes, finally only field anecdotes, etc., working into smaller and smaller subsets of prose. At the same time, anthropologists' horizons have expanded outward toward cultural theory. It is the sacred activity of fieldwork that needs rethinking toward new forms of involvement. The idea of fieldwork needs not only critique but reformulation based on new relationships that we can take up across boundaries. New relationships across cultural lines imply profound changes in the culture of ethnographers (Hannerz 1987; Rose 1990).

4

There is strong evidence that what we read affects directly what we perceive in the field. We know by our texts; we ask native women questions concerning our anxieties as feminists, we examine subincision ceremonies as exaggeration of our concern with our penises. How do we break the narrowed cycle of conformity? How do we truly seek out and establish new modes of contact across cultures, through our lives, breaking with the received information in the books we have written, breaking our academic everyday life and the conventions of the academy?

5

Ethnographers, like machinists, roofers, executives, and middle managers in corporate life, spend many of their waking hours laboring. The diffuseness of the tasks, such as committee work, talking with students, preparing to teach, faculty meetings, conducting research in the library, interviewing, or writing a paper to be read at the annual meetings, does not lessen its claim on our time or our thought. A number of academics stress that they think always about their work and that the hours in their office is no indicator of their intellectual labors. We read and write, prepare and lecture inside legally incorporated bodies, institutions, legal-rational organizations.

6

By *ethnography as a form of life,* I borrow a phrase from Wittgenstein. By it I mean that there are formal frameworks to our lives that contain them, such as corporations, of which we are all members. By *corporation* I mean the legally chartered public, private, and not-for-profit institutions that are the scaffolding—or form—of life in America. The corporations, as they have evolved, are, as Weber first realized, cultural formations as well as legal-rational ones. The corporations that make up Japan differ culturally in their history and very foundations from Anglo-American ones; and the Anglo-American corporations are not at all identical with French, German, or Spanish companies.

7

Ethnography, rather than retaining for itself some privileged place in Western thought, might well be examined as just one among a number of apertures that the West, mainly Anglo-American anthropology, has opened on other cultures. Rather than a hierarchy of methods of inquiry across cultures, we might democratically juxtapose ethnography with cultural journalism or ship captains' logs to see what conventions underlie observation and the making of texts consumed by the larger society, although I don't propose to do just that.

8

To think about ethnographic texts and contexts, I want to examine some works from the late sixteenth and early seventeenth century, then read some documents from the first half of the nineteenth century. In Foucault's *Archaeology of Knowledge and the Discourse on Language* (1972) we are taught to look for discontinuities, strata that give way suddenly to a subsequent occupation, disruptions in the record, and new discursive formations that displace older ones.

Despite the finding of breaks and fissures in the record around new formations, say, the abrupt disappearance of expedition anthropology and the establishment of academic anthropology at the turn of the twentieth century, continuities do remain, hidden from sight, often denied or obscured in the effort to legitimize the new order. I propose to read the continuities of concern in the following texts in order to claim that our interests and our institutional order, texts and contexts, have formed a tradition, albeit a constantly reobscured one that informs the present way of life of ethnographers. The texts I consult include Shakespeare's *The Merchant of Venice* and *The Tempest*. Two documents appeared between the performances of *The Merchant of Venice* (1596) and *The Tempest* (1613). The first document, which appeared in 1598, was the English translation of a book written in Dutch, *The Voyage of John Huygen van Linschoten to the East Indies,* and the second, not a published book at all, was the letters and charters of the subscribers to the London Company of Merchants to the East Indies (1599 and after). The other readings include the *Report of the 1841 Meeting of the British Association for the Advancement of Science.*

9

Shakespeare's east-west geography stretched from the Bermudas to Greece, and those fictional terrains contrast interestingly with the economic and institutional developments through the last years of Elizabeth's reign. These fictional spaces were isomorphic with the rise both of capitalism and anthropology on the edges of the Atlantic and Indian and Pacific oceans. His vision of the spatial extent of the economy was revealed in *The Merchant of Venice,* which depicted commercial transactions between friends and individuals known to one another. Just before he wrote the play, the English maritime economy had been frustrated in the Mediterranean, and, in competition with the Dutch, Portuguese, and Spanish, had begun to look to India and to the New

World. The new route to India was not through the Mediterranean and then overland, but around the Cape of Good Hope.

On stage Shakespeare's Bassanio asked to borrow interest-free money from a rich merchant friend, Antonio, the merchant of Venice, so that he, Bassanio, might successfully court Portia, herself heiress to a great fortune. Bassanio would, if he married Portia, be able to amply reward Antonio's favor. Antonio, in keeping with a typical practice in the late sixteenth century, had his liquid capital tied up in ships that were even then sailing toward port. As a result he felt forced to turn to Shylock for a loan with interest to grant his good friend Bassanio the necessary funds for courtship. In the person of Shylock, however, Shakespeare accurately perceived a worldwide trading network, far larger than the geographical setting of his plays. In his negotiations for lending the money, Shylock, wise to the investments and vulnerabilities of Antonio's trade, tells Bassanio, "My meaning, in saying he is a good man, is to have you understand me, that he is sufficient. Yet his means are in supposition: he hath an argosy bound to Tripolis, another to the Indies; I understand, moreover, upon the Rialto, he hath a third at Mexico, a fourth for England, and other ventures he hath, squandered abroad."

The point here is that each loan was requested and granted by individuals who represented themselves, or, perhaps, in the case of Shylock or Antonio, family firms, but not corporations. It is worth emphasizing that from Mexico and the West to the Indies and the East, Shylock documented the space of early capitalism. In London, at this same time, there had been experimentation with the newer and non–kin-based joint stock companies, where merchants would raise capital among themselves for joint ventures, usually for long-distance trade both East and West, and this trade was the source, Braudel shows, of the rise of capitalism (1986:ch. 5). Shakespeare could represent the economic flows between individuals, for individuals certainly lend themselves better to dramatic treatment than do institutions. But the then-current economic formations, indeed the rise of capitalism, lay in large part in firms that were based on neither friendship per se, nor kinship. I will develop this point more fully below.

Moving westward in Shakespeare's fictive space, *The Tempest,* located at the western geographical extreme, was a work that, although a romance, closely resembled what we now think of as science fantasy and scarcely alluded to money at all. The Duke of Milan, we learn, had been betrayed by his brother and deposed. Not killed, however, he and his three-year-old daughter were set adrift at sea and mercifully provided provisions. The desert island on which Prospero, the deposed duke, finally landed was inhabited by an ugly monster, Caliban, who was, in the fantasy of the time, enslaved by magic and forced to do royal Prospero's bidding.

The New World, already dimly apperceived, perhaps, with the twin terms of savagery and slavery, was not portrayed by Shakespeare as the landscape of economic opportunity but of romance and of controlled irrationality and civilized judgment. The Europeans on the island were, through luck and magic, able to return, with wrongs righted between them, back to Europe, Caliban—and even magic itself—left behind. Contrary to Shakespeare's vision of the New World, if that indeed is what it was, the northern littoral of North America was about to be colonized by England by means of a series of privately held companies, corporations designed to make fortunes for the investors. The English colonies were nearly all established and managed by private concerns. Shakespeare had no way of foreseeing the developments, but I want to stress that the economy was moving from the Mediterranean to the world in new ways, particularly in corporate institutional formations and not in family firms.

Shakespeare's dramaturgical geography, classical, Gothic, and fantasied savage, then, simultaneously dramatized and contrasted with events in London that were pushing the North European movement of the economy away from the Mediterranean toward the western Atlantic and toward the longer, more arduous, and more remunerative voyages to the East Indies.

◇　◇　◇

Shakespeare's career spanned the last years of Queen Elizabeth's reign and into King James's; *The Tempest* was performed in 1613 on the occasion of the marriage of King James's own daughter, Elizabeth. No doubt many in the court had read Richard Hakluyt's *The Principall Navigations, Voiages and Discoveries of the English Nation,* first published in 1589 and enlarged and reissued between 1598 and 1600. Important as these works were for playgoers and business dealers, other books written at the time proved catalytic to the imagination of London merchants and to the making of new forms for raising and deploying capital.

Literary theorists remain marvelously silent on texts that tell us, or that we can tease into telling us, what to do. Fiction, on which literary theory practices most, does not in any direct sense point to the world and say, "You can do this." Fiction, except for the foolhardy, is not normative, its functions and felicities lie elsewhere. Other, nonfictional kinds of literature do construct sets of directions for operating significantly in the world. They are, in a sense, prescriptive. For example, much of the writing in the *Wall Street Journal* serves normatively for the investor. Travel accounts of the sixteenth century are another textual source where localities were transformed into consideration through writing such that those localities could be revisited, the second time for profitable trade. Description in the travel accounts had a declarative function and placed peoples, animals, localities, and goods in plain sight of the mercantile—the early capitalist—imagination (Buisine 1981:264).

The adventurers, the merchants of Genoa, Amsterdam, or London, read several types of texts before they risked launching their ships with trade goods. In a sense, this is much the way ethnography is conducted—we read to guide the flow and type of field experiences, they in their time read to know where and what to trade.

In the years 1595 and 1596, two volumes were published that created a stir in Amsterdam, indeed they were texts that launched ships, and in 1598, the English translations accomplished the same reaction in London. The books were John Huygen van Linschoten's *Itinerario*, a graphic account of his travels from Spain to India with the newly appointed Portuguese Archbishop of Goa. In form the book has interesting resonances with Malinowski's *Argonauts of the Western Pacific* (1961). Linschoten's introduction was a personal narrative, the "I was there" story-preface that tells of his childhood in Haarlem. The first sentence reveals that texts he read preceded the documents he wrote, so that he was prepared beforehand to formulate his experiences as a voyager. "Beeing young, [and living idlelye] in my native Countrie, sometimes applying my selfe to the reading of Histories, and straunge adventures, wherein I tooke no small delight, I found my minde so much addicted to see and travaille into strange Countries, thereby to seeke some adventure, that in the end to satisfie my selfe, I determined, and was fully resolved, for a time to leave my Native Countrie" (1970).

Malinowski wrote within the frame of science while Linschoten employed the genre of *straunge adventures*. Linschoten did leave after reading and sailed for Spain where two of his brothers were living. One of them, a ship's purser, found a passage for him with the newly appointed Archbishop of Goa, and in 1583 when he was twenty, he sailed to the Indies. In 1592 after nine years away he returned to Utrecht and with the help of the physician, Bernard ten Broecke, wrote his *Itinerario* which, under Linschoten's patent, was published three years later, together with pieces of other travel accounts and technical textual commentary written in by the doctor. The documentation was so powerful that the Dutch dispatched ships to India with Linschoten's volumes in the captain's cabin, and the merchants later formed the Dutch East India Company.

The account, which is not a gentlemanly travel account per se, is rather a complex documentary of tradable goods, ports, comments on the Portuguese amounting to intelligence reports, and observations of peoples and customs. There is a good bit of observation on the people inhabiting Goa, and in chapter 33, for example, "of the heathens, Indians and other strangers dwelling in Goa," he noted the range of peoples there, funerary practices, dietary differences, beliefs, wedding ceremonies, witchcraft, but above all, with a very fine eye to material culture, sometimes described where goods could be found *by street*.

If one classified all he noted and described, it would encompass and exceed, perhaps, the *Notes and Queries on Anthropology* (Royal Anthropological Institute 1951), at the same time one could find resonances between his observations of place and those of a good ethnographer. I want to stress the continuities here of adventurers' and merchants' texts with ethnographic writing within the larger frame of a historic and continuing aperture by West Europeans on peoples of other cultures.

◇   ◇   ◇

The effect in London of the translation of Linschoten's book was immediate. A number of well-to-do merchants agreed to form a joint stock company to lobby the Queen's Privy Council for a patent to trade in the East Indies.[1] On 31 December 1600, a charter was granted to the London Company of Merchants to the East Indies, also known as the East India Company, with a monopoly for fifteen years when it would expire and come up for renewal.

Thomas Smith, a leading London merchant who already had experience and some successes and frustrations with merchant companies, was appointed by Queen Elizabeth to be the first governor of the East India Company, but in the future, the company was to elect their own governor from among their board of directors.[2] The charter, which was a legal document drawn up in Elizabethan prose (which reads like the legal documents of today) by the Privy Council,[3] established what became a board of directors and granted a monopoly of trade for Asia, Africa, and America with the caveat that the merchants would not trade with Christian princes in amity with the queen. Those out of favor with the queen, such as the Portuguese, were fair game for privateering, itself an activity legitimated through crown charters, and all ships at that time were well-armed for that purpose. The merchants' patent or charter permitted them exemption from import duties on the first four voyages, and there were limits on the transactions in silver, the monetary metal of preference in India and the Spice Islands.

What I want to emphasize here is the power of writing that directs action, a kind of rhetoric that lets readers imagine what they can indeed do, its very immediate precedence over action, and the ways in which genres perpetuate themselves through successive generations of writers. The captain's journal, for example, was persuasive enough to warrant an ironclad rule in the East India Company: "Every captain, master, master's mate, and purser should keep a journal which was to be handed in at the end of the voyage. That such accounts were put to practical use in later voyages helps explain the fact that not more of them survived" (Strachan and Penrose 1971:13). I also want to point out that the Linschoten account was catalytic to the formation of a private corporation within a public corporation, the East India Company within the legal entity of the English Crown.

The corporation was at that time a subject of change and experimentation and at those early phases of capitalism had not yet coalesced into the modern corporation we associate with midnineteenth-century capitalism to the present (Chandler 1977).

◇   ◇   ◇

In Shakespeare's *Merchant of Venice* we do not find an elaborate look into the interior of a business because commercial transactions were sublimated by the playwright to the interpersonal. With the rise of the English East India Company we can witness more than face-to-face intrigues. In the corporation there was both internal differentiation and external relationships. The corporation was dependent on an outside or higher authority for its own authority and legitimacy. Although the queen as regency of a corporate body, the state, was believed, by herself and her subjects, to depend upon the dispensation of God, the state later acquired legitimate authority from the will of the people, which was documented in a constitution for its supreme legitimacy. With the corporation one finds a legal license from the higher to the lower power, spelled out in writing, a document that charters the organization.

Inside the company there were officers duly appointed and elected who had to be legally and financially responsible and who were themselves governed by a board of directors. Power was slightly diffused in this way. The officers of the company had great powers in the Elizabethan company. The crown transferred civil authorization over matters of justice to the incorporated merchants. In commissioning the first voyage of the newly formed East India Company, Queen Elizabeth sent an epistolary legal document to James Lancaster, captain of the departing fleet of ships. She wrote: "& eury pson and psons ymployed vsed or shipped or weh shall be ymployed vsed or shipped in this voiadge in the said ffower shipps, or any of them, to giue all due obedience & respect vnto you, during the said voiadge, & to beare themselues one towardes another in all good order. . . . Wee doe hereby authorize you, to Chastice Correct & ponish all offenders, and transgressors in that behalfe according to the quallitie of their offence" (Birdwood and Foster 1893:3–4). This was a standard letter to captains of ships that indicates that the state franchised its voyagers with a legal privilege. Similar rules were written into the charter of the East India Company. The corporation had the power to make civil decisions over the men in their employ. Indeed the powers were far reaching: "being so assembled . . . to make, ordain, and constitute such, and so many reasonable laws, constitutions, orders and ordinances, for the good government of the same company" (1893:163–88). Later the East India company was granted the right to prosecute criminal offenses, and its power continued to broaden as it began to rule the Indian subcontinent. It is as if some powers of the state were transmitted and internalized inside the corporation, as if they had been legally standardized within an extended but corporately internalized civil polity.

The overall goal or mission of the authorized company was made explicit. The explicitness continues up to the present as an integral part of a corporate charter or constitution.

The corporation, even in Elizabeth's day, required massive amounts of information from outside itself in order to operate. There are numerous examples in addition to Linschoten's of valuable information making its way into the knowledge of the directors of a company. In an anonymous book arguing for free trade and the abolition of the East India Company's monopoly, a historical note revealed the dependence of Queen Elizabeth's first ambassador to India, Sir Thomas Rowe, on the court of the Great Mogul. Sir Thomas learned, and it would not be difficult to imagine that he applied some diligence to it, which articles Europeans made that were most adapted for the India market: "knives of all sorts; toys of the figures of beasts; rich velvets and satins . . . wines of Alicant . . . fine light armour . . . large looking glasses . . . French tweezer-cases; table books; perfumed gloves . . . dogs of various natures . . . and, in general any thing curious for workmanship, not at present known in India" (Anonymous 1807). The items seem exotic even today, but the point is that propitious acquisition of information made for the success not only of countries at that time but for the companies licensed by them.

We can identify here, I think, a corporate principle, a way of forming social institutions that while vastly changed have at the same time retained their overall recognizability as having continuity within Anglo-American culture. The corporate principle came increasingly in western north Europe, and in the United States of America later, to supplant the family and kinship as the fundamental motif for social organization. By *corporate principle* I mean a group of people who agree to form an organization legitimized by a higher authority but separate from it, for agreed-upon purposes. The corporate principle, an incorporating principle, pulls the membership together by a text, its charter, a duly elected set of officers, some general membership, a budget, and some range of activities that members wish to pursue so as to alter some existing state of affairs. This bare-bones definition has been permuted in as many ways, probably, as there are corporations, but it was this evolving form of association that underlay capitalism and modernity as we know it. Frederic Maitland, the noted political theorist, observed, "For, when all is said, there seems to be a genus of which State and Corporation are species" (1958:ix). When we look to the primitive world, anthropologists have told us that we can understand its organization through principles of kinship. If we look, on the same grounds, at the modern West, we find it organized as sets of nested corporations, and in the United States they are grouped into public, private, and not-for-profit sectors. Indeed, under King James, in the first year of his reign, it was proposed in the Privy Council that the New World be colonized as a public corporation by the crown (a model followed by Spain). "The view did not prevail," as Griffiths explains, "and the matter was left to private enterprise licensed but not financed or organized by the state" (1974:141).

When we link together text and context we join Linschoten with the Dutch East India Company and to the London Company of Merchants. Writing, inscription, books, knowledge were housed in gigantic corporate entities. Writing flows into, through and within, and to the outside of companies. Flows of information are stimulated and highly managed. The companies are built, have been built of paper, legal, informational, on the social, material, and cultural worlds of importance to the companies.

A final coda on the English East India Company. The corporation was chartered entirely within the private sector as was the Hudson's Bay Company and the Falkland's Company, but like the somewhat similar English corporations that colonized America's northeastern seaboard, the East India Company began with its expanded civil charter to rule, to take over the function of the modern nation. In India, Brian Gardner wrote, the East India Company became a leviathan. "A government which, through might of arms, was the most powerful in Asia; a government, the revenue of which was greater than that of Britain; a government which ruled over more people than the present government of the United States; a government owned by businessmen, the shares of which were daily bought and sold. As Macaulay said, 'It's strange, very strange' " (1971:11).

There was enormous criticism of what the East India Company became on the part of Indian intellectuals and within England, notably by Adam Smith and Karl Marx. Finally, changing conditions brought it down. More powerful than the great dynastic families that preceded it, the London Company of Merchants, transformed into the East India Company, existed from 1600 through 1813, when its monopoly was ended by Parliament. It then staggered on without its monopoly for twenty more years until it finally ceased operations.

◇   ◇   ◇

I want to weave corporation and text together because in reality they cannot be sorted from one another. Ethnography as cultural practice will be foregrounded as a form of life within a social form, the corporation. The ethnographic book is a form of knowing and a more or less stable genre, but one that at the same time always changes. I begin in the past and move forward. In 1841 in the report of the British Association for the Advancement of Science (BAAS), there was a committee report of the Natural History Section that had ties with the past that would affect the course of ethnographic inquiry over the next 150 years. Two years earlier a Dr. Prichard had read the paper "On the Extinction of Some Varieties of the Human Race." He pointed out that science would suffer an irretrievable loss if a large portion of humanity counted by tribes were permitted to die out, uninvestigated. In response to his paper a committee was appointed to prepare a questionnaire called "Travellers and Others" to carry with them on their journeys.

The appointed committee, reviewing other efforts at ethnographic inquiry, cited the *savans* of the Ethnographical Society of Paris who had printed a set of questions earlier; the committee found the French queries useful and freely appropriated them where relevant. The citation to the French contribution was, perhaps, not grudging, but like the competition between the English and Dutch merchants two hundred years before, a real rivalry. This time the struggle was in the realm of science and was just as deeply felt. The committee wrote: "Britain, in her extensive colonial possessions and commerce, and in the number and intelligence of her naval officers, possesses unrivalled facilities for the elucidation of the whole subject; and it would be a stain on her character, as well as a loss to humanity, were she to allow herself to be left behind by other nations in this inquiry" (British Association for the Advancement of Science 1841:332). The rhetoric was that of science—and one could almost sense a sacred quality to the word when it was used—but contained within a nationalist framework. Science was understood then, as it is today, as an instrument of a nation competing against other nations.

Although the queries of the committee were a far cry from Linschoten's observations, they may be seen as a continuing development and refinement, with borrowings from other sources, of an observational opening by the West on non-Western peoples. In 1841 the social formation that internalized the necessity for information was not a merchant company but what was to become after 1862 a not-for-profit corporation (by virtue of the English Parliament's Companies Act of 1862) devoted to the advancement of science, the BAAS, in this case, by the branch of natural history, an arm of investigation that included human natives, native vegetation, and native animals. Humans under the aegis of nineteenth-century science were naturalized like flora and fauna, and their grid of specification was, like zoological phenomena, to be classified by race and language.

The imprimatur of the medical profession may well be seen on the form the queries took. The physical, which was coterminous with racial, came first. In the entire document there were ten major headings and eighty-nine numbered queries. One of the headings was a query without a number, so there were actually ninety general questions with unnumbered subquestions.

Within the queries such concerns remained as had been expressed during the Elizabethan voyages, colonization, and commercial relations. To be sure, newer interests were reflected, such as the hiring of laborers and the conduct of censuses. It is as if the categories of the queries were a fusion of science and the preoccupations of a corporate colonial power to whom textual knowledge was critical to its competitive edge and future successes. There was no precursor in the questions to a theory of culture that emerged in the modern period. The questions have a kind of uninspired pragmatic quality to them. The greatest curiosity, if we can judge by the length of the passages, was apparently

Table 1. Queries of the BAAS

Headings	Numbered Questions
Physical Characteristics	12
Language	4
Individual and Family Life	33
Buildings and Monuments	3
Works of Art	2
Domestic Animals	1 (not numbered)
Government and Laws	13
Geographic Statistics	7
Social Relations	2
Religion, Superstitions, etc.	13
Total	90

aroused by physical differences and family life, two concerns a physician might well find most important on a day-to-day basis.

As the nineteenth century progressed, the queries of the natural history section of the BAAS gave way to *Notes and Queries on Anthropology,* a document first published in 1874 and revised and reissued in 1892, 1899, 1912, 1929, and 1951, the sixth edition. Even as late as 1951, one can find textual affinities between the 1841 queries and the 1951 *Notes* although between the two publication dates the academic discipline of social anthropology became highly developed. The publication of the 1951 *Notes and Queries on Anthropology* (Royal Anthropological Institute 1951), revised by a committee set up by Section H of the BAAS, was organized as follows. I reassemble and juxtapose the 1841 queries next to those from the *Notes.*

The earlier queries had a category for domestic animals while concern with animals was distributed in *Notes and Queries* into the "Social Anthropology" and "Material Culture" sections. In the 1841 queries, the economy was absent as a numbered set of questions but still surfaced under such headings as "Works of Art." After asking for the particulars in artworks, the committee wrote: "Such particulars will not only throw light on the character and origin of the people, but will, directly or indirectly, influence the commercial relations which may be profitably entered into when commerce alone is looked into" (British Association for the Advancement of Science 1841:337).

Throughout the 1841 queries there is a subtext of corporate capitalist interests manifest in references to colonization, commerce, men who bear arms, and labor force potential. In the *Notes and Queries* of 1951, by contrast, a phenomenal preoccupation with social organization be-

Table 2. *Notes and Queries* Compared with 1841 Queries

Notes and Queries on Anthropology 1951	Queries Respecting the Human Race 1841
Part 1 Physical Anthropology	Physical Characters
Part 2 Social Anthropology	
Introduction	
Methods	Geographical Statistics
Social Structure	Social Relations
Social Life of the Individual	Individual and Family Life
Political Organization	Government and Law
Economics	
Ritual and Belief	Religion, Superstition, etc.
Knowledge and Tradition	
Language	Language
Part 3 Material Culture	Buildings and Monuments
	Works of Art

came apparent from the spatial orders of the household, settlement, and region to the kinship, economic, and political formations. The two texts are very different indeed and I do not mean to attempt to reduce the disciplinary complexities of the 1951 *Notes and Queries* to the brief travelers carried with them 110 years earlier. At the same time, the reader can find those deeper continuities that characterize cultural persistence at the most fundamental level, for example, the desire by corporate managers for systematic—even strategic—social knowledge written down.

◇   ◇   ◇

On 31 October 1914 Bronislaw Malinowski wrote in his diary (1967:30) that he tried to synthesize his fieldwork results by reviewing the fourth edition (1912) of *Notes and Queries on Anthropology.* Later in *Argonauts* he urged on others that same sort of manipulation of fieldnotes while in the field, and in his own practices we can see the domination of the experience of the text. Text precedes experience, gives it shape; consciousness is continually informed by the literary material one has read. In Malinowski's diary entry we have the same relationship of precedence of text before field experience that we find in Linschoten's readings of *straunge adventures* prior to having his own adventures and then writing them up.

At the same time in Malinowski there is ample evidence that he carried with him his European context, which is nothing less than well-socialized behavior to corporate settings. A constant thematic in the diaries is the effort to work, to make science, to sublimate pleasure, even leisure reading, to the intellectual labors at hand. Not only was text overlaid on daily life, gathering it up, regrouping it as written documentation, but the institutional behavior of an academic was clearly visible in the work load, the hours spent recording and participating for the sake of science itself.

By *context* I mean the tacit corporate context, the formation of the self around disciplined work and labor within an institution. Life in the organization entails being managed by others, the internalized management of oneself, the attitudes that one has unconsciously acquired toward the expectations of how one ought to comport oneself in the large firm, such as a university or profession. One of the best documented work loads of an ethnographer in the field, a corporate work site recreated in the field, is in Harold Conklin's brief log of a day, 18 July 1953. While he offers in a note the caveat that no day is typical he represents one almost as if it were the log in a highly controlled military mission: "0600 I am awakened by the excited shouting of six Parina children who have found a neighbor's goat giving birth . . ." to the close of the day: "2345 I spread out my mat. . . . But first, "Nonga," Balyan, and I, discuss indirect manners of speech in Hanunoo." The account was written originally as part of a report to the Social Sciences Research Council concerning his grant from them. The implied gigantism of a busy day as an ethnographer can be readily understood in this bureaucratic context where he had to justify the ways of ethnographers to man, even if it could not be believed to be an ordinary day (Conklin 1964:119–25).

I know of at least one anthropologist who believed that report of a July day to be no work of fiction but the ordinary energetic, and to him admirable, form of life Conklin led. From 0830 to 1200, three and a half hours, Conklin wrote fieldnotes and checked details of the previous evening with two eyewitnesses. The amount of work implied by the text, "A Day in Parina," portrayed a staggering quantity of ethnographic labor. It was almost like an academic's busiest day at the office.

Jeremy Boissevain worked just as hard apparently, sometimes he was able to squeeze in a short nap, but he was not only able to arise at six as Conklin had done, but go from fifteen to forty-five minutes longer, till twelve or twelve-thirty A.M. (Boissevain 1970:74–77). Most ethnographers do not log their day for us as Conklin and Boissevain did. Evans-Pritchard (1940) writes eloquently of the Nuer's opposition to his efforts to study them, but gives no graphic detail of an ordinary day spent with them.

◇ ◇ ◇

I want to pursue the work habits of ethnographers who take their corporate settings with them in mind and in practice to the more remote geographies. For the most part anthropologists do not spend much time reporting on details concerning their everyday lives. We are given hints of what people do in the field. There is diversity, of course, and a great deal of continuity over time.

In 1943 William Foote Whyte, while studying Italian-American men, got up at nine in the morning, went to a restaurant for breakfast, and used the remainder of the morning to type his fieldnotes of events from the evening before. He then ate lunch in a restaurant and set out for the street corner. He was back in the Martini household where he boarded for dinner with them, then back to the street corner for the evening. Apparently he went to bed around midnight (1955:297). In 1966, Hortense Powdermaker discussed her day, and we catch a valuable glimpse of the dominion of writing in the course of an ethnographer's day: "Malinowski had also told us to note down everything we saw and heard, since in the beginning it is not possible to know what may or may not be significant. I faithfully tried to carry out this injunction" (1966:61).

In 1963 (published in a second edition in 1972) Gerald Berreman wrote that he and his interpreter spent the first three months of his field stay keeping house and "attempting to establish rapport" under difficult circumstances (1972:xxiii). While one gains an impression from Powdermaker of the ethnographer with pencil in hand, one feels with Berreman the maddening frustration of not being able to work. In 1971, Gerardo Reichel-Dolmatoff published in English an account of Amazonian cosmology based on work with a key informant, Antonio Guzman. "The investigator and the informant met during a six-month period for one to three hours daily in an office where, surrounded by books, maps, and photographs, our conversations developed without interruption or distraction by others" (1971:xviii). In 1973, Robert Levy reported that he used psychological check sheets with informants, and we clearly see a text designed in advance that structures what both the anthropologist and the people from whom he elicits must do (1973:xx-xxi). In 1974, Carol Stack also issued schedules, but, she explained, she and some of the people she lived with "together . . .

worked out questions on various topics to ask the families studied" (1974:xvii–xviii).

In 1979, John Miller Chernoff revealed not so much the way a work day progressed, though he does convey that through much of the book, but how to enter other ways of life and participate at some level pretty much like one's subjects: "To arrive at the point where one sees the life of another culture as an alternative is to reach a fundamental notion of the humanistic perspective, and to accept the reality of one's actions to the people who live there is to understand that one has become part of their history" (1979:9, 19–21). In 1979, a collection of papers on long-term fieldwork was published. The long duration of field engagement did not of itself alter the relations of anthropologists to those studied or the texts that served as models for the experiences and for writing them up (Foster et al. 1979:134, 169–71). In 1982, Steven Feld recorded the variation of his days in the field, interviewing, transcribing, taking musical recordings (1982:13). In 1983, Marjorie Shostak could, as had always been done by anthropologists, report on work with her major informants and her agenda for asking questions and directing conversations (1983:intro.).

In 1981, Anthony Seeger published a valuable portrait of a person who faced the agony of attempting to move by means of documentation an unincorporated way of life into a corporate one (1981). I review briefly what he recounted in order to further the point that we carry our corporate cultures with us in highly formal ways when we do ethnography. I distrust those who admit to "letting the data" tell them what to do and think, since what they learned to let the data do represents only a marginal difference from structuring it as self-consciously as one can. Both the follow-your-nose and the rational, preplanned field styles rely upon a socialization to the same canonical features.

We can envision Anthony and his wife Judy Seeger in their effort to impose a way of life on the Suya of Brazil's Matto Grosso or finding accommodation between their way of life and the Suya's or as the Suya making an effort to accommodate the Seegers with their own best effort or as the Suya simultaneously resisting and aiding the Seegers. Whether we want to examine the cultural relation in terms of power (imposition), or epistemology (mutual accommodation), or language (discourse, discursive relations) in which each constructed the other, we still have incommensurable forms of life interpenetrating with linguistic, authoritative, and epistemological conflicts and contradictions.

Rather than reduce my review of the Seegers' involvement in Suya

life to a single factor, I prefer to examine it as forms of life in juxtaposition, as the uncertain double ground of inquiry.

Through Anthony Seeger's characterization of the field stay, we can
observe the frustration of the corporate objective, its work ethic, and
its self-defined rationalities. His rationalities, for example, were clearly
evidenced when he wrote, "I terminated my fieldwork not because I
believed I knew everything but because I thought I knew enough about
those areas that interested me" (1981:16). It was systematic questioning,
he explained, and careful listening that provided him with the information for his book. That systematic questioning was checked, he
mentions, directly against the *Notes and Queries on Anthropology*.

Seeger's construction on the contact of ethnographer's culture with
Suya culture was that of frustration, the perceived continuing failure
to achieve what a rationalized field method and doctoral dissertation
proposal promised in advance of what he would find. During the first
few months he reflected a common feeling among ethnographers: "I
felt as though I was accomplishing nothing" (7). He had to hunt and
fish to support Judy and himself, he had to get up early and treat
peoples' illness, forage, tend a garden eventually, and his "informants"
were either, he worried, hungry and hunting and fishing or full and
sleeping. He did not unearth immediately the ritual information for
which he was searching because it was the wrong season for ritual
performance, it turned out in one case. And in another, it was because
people would not talk about it.

There was a raw contact zone between cultures: an academic had
resentfully to hunt and fish; he had to learn the language without an
instructor or times set aside for it by the Suya; the Seegers had to
purvey gifts and medicine; they were recipients of stories and songs;
the role, as he expressed it, of eavesdropper, gadfly, dependent, and
manipulator of conversations became onerous. His dependency was
overwhelming and he wrote that he was operating as a Suya twelve-
year-old when he left.

While the bureaucratic norm of corporate academic life dominated
his work expectations, it was the text he was planning to construct,
the dissertation, that dominated much of that effort. "I always carried
a small notebook with me and wrote down everything of interest. On
long days of fishing I would think about what I had learned and write
down questions to be asked. I would arrange questions into lists on
a given topic. Equipped with these general lists I would look for any
person who could answer one of the various groups of questions" (14).
Through a haze of frustration, fishing for example, while wishing to
hear a story or ask a question, Seeger complained in a way wholly

familiar to ethnographers. Although they lived in a large household of thirty-five people with whom they could sing for fifteen hours at a time, and Judy could tell Anthony what the women were saying, the field experience was one of conflicting rationalities, physical sickness, and resistance to the Suya way of life even while trying to capture *a priori* chosen features of it.

The institutionally situated rationalities, I am indicating, themselves lead to severe frustrations and, as well, to arbitrary involvement. Knowledge gathering and what is accumulated is itself highly arbitrary to fit into documentation recognized by peers as important within the traditional framework of the incorporated discipline. Seeger wrote that he chose to give himself five years to accomplish his work with the Suya and then turn to other societies and intellectual concerns. "This book," as he phrased it, "is an important step in that process" (13).

◇ ◇ ◇

I find it remarkable that in the relentless and what appears to be the rather humorless efforts of the Seegers there was not some critical reflexivity, some questioning of the entire ethnographic enterprise. There was none and it is remarkable for that. The other ethnographers mentioned did not question the historically constituted relationships between cultures that ethnographic practice requires of its members. Indeed the ethnographic inquiry has been sacrosanct and left almost wholly uncriticized in its institutional standardization; it is the text that has received critical attention, not relationships across cultural boundaries. The level of internal criticism has tended to be, for example, conservatively made of models of particular cultures that are found wanting when applied to cultures geographically remote. We need to move beyond that kind of conservative, internal critique to ask the more fundamental questions directly of our observational practices.

Due to severe depopulation, the cultural life of the Suya had been set irreversibly on a new course. Seeger lamented: "The material I was unable to obtain on social organization and defunct ceremonies was just what I had hoped to get from the Suya groups reported on the Arinos River in 1970" (1981:16). Why did he not begin to break with his carefully cultivated graduate student expectations and try to examine how people manage the contact directly or indirectly with an encroaching national and world civilization of which the Seegers were a part? Or, more to the point I am making, ask in a way that might affect ethnographers' practices; what am I doing here? I do not mean to reduce this larger question to a personal level. I am really not asking the Seegers this question at all, but anthropologists.

The logic of inquiry, illustrated at the beginning of this essay, showed that first we read, then experience the world in the light of that reading, then publish the results of our reading and experiencing, in our case within the culture of American corporate life, the university, and profession. The question arises as to whether or not we can break the logic by taking up new relations within other cultures such that we begin to draft new forms of texts and explore new modes of experience. Maitland was critical of the corporations that England exported and with which it colonized. He went so far as to suggest that the English were not well-equipped to think about the challenges posed by Ireland, commonwealths, and corporations that had evolved since the sixteenth century under the crown. The development of empire was neither anticipated by theory nor guided by traditional thought concerning the relations between state and corporate bodies. I am urging that within the larger scheme of things, of the West that continuously demands information on the rest of the world, that we consider the openings, such as ethnography, through which information flows. The boundary across which the information is gathered is a corporate one, and it keeps its edges rather sharply defined. Is it not possible to define the corporate boundary in new ways, to rethink relationships between ourselves and others? This is an issue that demands the attention of anthropologists to be sure. But other branches of learning and practice need also to rethink and anticipate what sorts of openings are desired between cultural orders and with what forms of relationships we might engage them. What new cultural formations and identities may arise?

10

We are witnessing a momentous reconfiguration of the cultural sciences and I want to address briefly, and in somewhat condensed manifesto-like manner, the new textual formation. It is ultimately, however, the interior, co-evolving relations between texts and lives that is of moment, but, in this section, the emphasis will be suggestive of method and point toward radical directions for future authorship and what this implies for our lives in the departmentalized university.

Over this last twenty years there has been a sea change in ethnographic practices that has attended the rise of a number of cultural shifts, and responding to these, in 1982 George Marcus named the revolution of the writing of ethnography *the experimental moment* and focused on ethnographies as texts, i.e., on the rhetorical construction of ethnographic writing and reading and what about it was changing. That transformation of experimentation and concern with writing is now in its first phase complete; we have a growing number of narrative ethnographies, and those written since 1985 include John Dorst's *The Written Suburb* (1989), Michael Jackson's *Barawa* (1986), Kirin Narayan's *Storytellers, Saints, and Scoundrels* (1989), Robin Ridington's *Trail to Heaven* (1988), Dan Rose's *Black American Street Life* (1987) and *Patterns of American Culture* (1989), John Stewart's *Drinkers, Drummers, and Decent Folk* (1989), Paul Stoller's and Cheryl Olkes's *In Sorcery's Shadow* (1987), and Stoller's *Fusion of the Worlds* (1989).

In each of these volumes there is a longer or shorter temporal unfolding in the narrative; the author is an integral part of the action.

Borrowing from Bakhtin's theoretical observations (1981), one can observe that the novel has invaded the scientific monograph and transformed it, not through the use of fiction particularly, but through the descriptive setting of the scene, the narration of the local peoples' own stories, the use of dialogue, the privileging of the objects of inquiry along with the subject or author who writes, and the notation by the author of emotions, subjective reactions, and involvement in ongoing activities.

Bakhtin shows that the novel includes a multilayered consciousness, radical temporal coordinates, and maximal contact with the present. These features are becoming more readily used in the narrative ethnography. The future of ethnography lies in a more sophisticated and self-conscious relationship with the novel, that is, with the possibilities of social inquiry that the novel, itself an experimental form, has opened to us.

One of the great achievements of the twentieth century is Hermann Broch's trilogy, *The Sleepwalkers* (1964), published in Vienna in 1932. It is a multigenre or polyphonic novel dominated by a single theme, that of the loss of cultural values. The theme is manifest at two levels: in the lives of the characters who live between its covers and in the multiple genres used by Broch to convey narrative, poetically induced feeling, and idea.

The Sleepwalkers begins with and contains a kind of nineteenth-century realist narrative, but subverts itself halfway through by using such genre elements as the reflective and critical philosophical essay, lyrical poem, legal contract, stream-of-consciousness poetic, and an excerpted newspaper article.

I would argue that the future of ethnography, whether in sociology, anthropology, psychology, critical legal studies, planning, or folklore, will be a polyphonic, heteroglossic multigenre construction and will include:

1. the author's voice and own emotional reactions;

2. critical, theoretical, humanist, mini-essays that take up and advance the particular literature or subliterature of the human sciences and particular disciplines; perhaps an ethnography will develop one or two ideas that provide coherence to the entire book;

3. the conversations, voices, attitudes, visual genres, gestures, reactions, and concerns of daily life of the people with whom the author participates, observes, lives with will take form as a narrative and discourse in the text; *there will be a story line;*

4. a poetic will also join the prose;

5. pictures, photos, drawings will take up a new, more interior relation to the text, not to illustrate it, but to document in their own way what words do in their own way;

6. the junctures between analytic, fictive, poetic, narrative, and critical genres will be clearly marked in the text but will cohabit the same volume.

Multigenre fiction and poetry has been present in America throughout the Modernist period in such experimental forms as Williams Carlos Williams's *Paterson*. Milan Kundera discusses the European version of polyphonic novels in his book of essays *The Art of the Novel* (1988). In the essays there are discussions that point back to his and other novels, and we can find fictional prototypes that we modify for our own future anthropological and sociological genres.

In his reading of Broch's *The Sleepwalkers*, Kundera shows the directions in which the novel—and we generalize to the social sciences—is moving: "The unachieved in [Broch's] work can show us the need for (1) a new art of *radical divestment* (which can encompass the complexity of existence in the modern world without losing architectonic clarity); (2) a new art of *novelistic counterpoint* (which can blend philosophy, narrative, and dream into one music); (3) a new art of the *specifically novelistic essay* (which does not claim to bear an apodictic message but remains hypothetical, playful, or ironic)" (1988:65).

Bakhtin has argued that genres are complex representations of and forms for the way we experience the world. As compelling as the realist epistemology is to social scientists, Derrida subverts the whole notion of genre by showing that neither in their interior or at their boundaries are these insubstantial creatures firmly themselves; they elude classification at the very moment the critic begins to order them (Derrida 1981). Nevertheless, through our received genres—the analytical book, the scholarly article, the essay, the evocative narrative ethnography—we attempt to gain a critical grasp on the most problematic phenomena of our time—our lives in the rapidly growing embrace of the cultures of capitalism.

Our texts will become a more sophisticated, multiple, heterophonic site of a struggle, just as are our lives in society.

One of the implications of the multigenre ethnography will be a transformation in reading, in graduate education, and in the subsequent conduct of inquiry:

1. what we will read in graduate student socialization will include
   a. the scholarly classics of the field and the current issues identified and debated in the scholarly books and journals;
   b. relevant fictional literature, popular culture, television, movies, popular music, etc.;
   c. critical theory, whether in gender studies, film criticism, literary theory, philosophy, or adjacent cultural sciences;

2. out of this multigenre mix a new sort of encultured student will be formed who will conceptualize fieldwork differently than now. *Above all, graduate students' inquiry might well have to acquire a narrative sort of quality, that is, students will seek to place themselves in unfolding situations, to live through complex ongoing events—the stuff of stories—* rather than looking among them for the meanings of gestures, the presentations of selves, class relations, the meaning of rituals, or other abstract, analytical category phenomena on which we have historically relied. Jackson, elaborating on his radical empiricism, helps make this point:

> Many of my most valued insights into Kuranko social life have followed from comparable cultivation and imitation of practical skills: Hoeing on a farm, dancing (as one body), lighting a kerosene lantern properly, weaving a mat, consulting a diviner. To break the habit of using a linear communicational model for understanding bodily praxis, it is necessary to adopt a methodological strategy of joining in without ulterior motive and literally putting oneself in the place of other persons: inhabiting their world. Participation thus becomes an end in itself rather than a means of gathering closely observed data which will subject to interpretation elsewhere *after the event;* (1989:135)

3. from a complex, across-the-human-sciences-sort-of-reading, from leading lives of narrative inquiry, new multigenre textual constructions will appear. These will be montages of events and analyses connected to ideas or events with digressive analytical and critical essays dominated by an authorial voice—either of the writer or of the subjects studied by the writer.

There are to some, disturbing, to others, exhilarating, implications in a heterophonic ethnography: multiple-genre writing (Ulmer 1989) is part of a massive reconfiguration of the human sciences and the once-secured disciplinary order of the university. We can already witness:

1. the dissolution of boundaries between literature, sociology, anthropology, critical theory, philosophy, cinematography, computer science, and so on;

2. an ultimate transparency and probable liquidation of that series of sacred centers—those bodies of received and once firmly purchased ideas—that now constitute, somewhat precariously, each of the academic disciplines in the human sciences.

In the last section I want to break entirely with the descriptive, analytical, critical writing pursued in the first ten parts. Instead, I turn to one of those quintessential Modernist genres, the manifesto, that may again serve to stimulate thought and action. For me the idea in the manifesto represents the playing out of the career trajectory begun as a doctoral student with covert inquiry that turned into an effort to break out of the confines of corporate institutionalization. After this manifesto I suppose that it would be possible to rationalize and formulate method, but at present I urge the anarchic.

After the Death of Ethnography

These words contain a virus that can infect you.

It enters through the eyes.

If you continue to read, you may be irreversibly affected and may never be able to think about the practice of ethnography the same way again.

From this sentence on, read at your own peril.

After the death of ethnography as we know it, the new ethnographer becomes an amoral opportunist and enters the lives of people whenever and wherever it fits with one's madness or desire.

To become, as a new ethnographer, profoundly involved in people's lives, one must go native and disappear in order to act only as a covert operator.

This leads to an irreversible immorality,

the unethical,

to madness,

the estranged,

the hopelessly difficult,

coldness and heat,

extreme psychic distress,

advancing schizophrenia,

a sense of boundless adventure,
indeterminacy,
lack of certitude,
desire for fiction,
endless anxiety,
intellectual excitement.
voyeurism,
lying,
smuggled motives,
rich eros,
despair alternating unpredictably with euphoria (controlled only by human-processed substances),
incessant breaking of unspoken contracts,
a kind of freedom,
and a lack of fixed coordinates.

NONE OF THE ITEMS ON THE LIST WERE CENTRAL TO THE MALINOWSKIAN AGENDA

Above all the ethnographer becomes an agent provocateur.

Covertness is absolutely necessitated by the evil inherent in "gathering data, information, or 'the truth' " about one another anyway when indeed all of life teeters on the edge of the abyss of mystery and all knowledge conceals itself.

In leaving behind the descriptive-analytical and the hermeneutic-critical practices as a substitute for ethnography as ethnography, one enters the world beyond the prison of the text. It begins beyond writing, outside the book, anterior to author-ity with the (re-)configuration of one's life, with disguised observation from slightly mistaken assumptions, sidelong glances, and is manipulative, imperious, hopelessly ambitious and derives its energy from the perverse.

We accept readily the worst side effects of the positivist agenda and push through them as through a crumbling doorway to the other side.

There is no turning back.

Above all the new ethnographers resolve in advance and renew their resolve from day to day so as to greedily suffer the consequences of their mutable choices, decisions, opportunisms, bald calculations, unethicalness, despair, desperation, and guilt in order to freely and with abandon engage and contend.

Risk your life,
your rank,
your future,
your marriage,
your children's health,
your literature review,
your footnotes,
your reading habits,
your paycheck,
your choice of geographic location.

Your effects on those you live among: They will become extremely angry
or may bless you with admiration for your audacity or eventual wisdom,
or, they may do neither;

they can avoid you,
excoriate you,
venerate you,
embrace you,
denounce you,
ignore you,
lie to you,
poison you,
ruin your career and damage your most intimate relationships,
spitefully and cynically use you,
deploy you for their own selfish ends to serve their maddest pretensions
     or neurotic interests,
swamp you,
reduce you,
fondle you,
provide false knowledge,
laugh at you,
ridicule you,
jest about you and say all manner of evils about you behind your back,
test you,
reward you,
shower money and favors on you,
make you stay late and miss your flight, or defer to you.
They may seek to bond with you forever and ever,
employ you,
treat you pornographically as objects for uncontained lust,
viciously gossip and slander you,
use rumor and scapegoating,
iconization,
canonization,
or veneration to deal with you.

We now realize we can escape the sanctimonious ethics of positivism and embrace out of control the politics of misframing, mistaken identities, mixed identities, contaminated personas, subverted claims; we are now energized by the fear of discovery and deeply uncertain or unclear as to the identities of our children.

Go native. The people of the entire planet are merely a variant of your own identity as a human—or something very close to that.

The early academic ethnographers feared that to act unethically, within the narrowed confines of a scientific truth and falsity, was to undermine what was believed to be the replicable findings of a comparative science of human culture and society. If you as ethnographer acted unethically, so the argument went, the next investigators in the field who were there to "verify" or "falsify" the truth of your assertions would be unwelcome because the people so betrayed would distrust and resist all scientists, perhaps all science. The agenda of replication of true findings and assertions would be permanently undermined. The house that science built would collapse and our knowledge of humanity would perish with it. With the total discreditation and deliquescence of positivist inquiry, we no longer need to fear the repressed moral implications of *fact, truth, veracity, validation,* and the scientific accumulation of knowledge.

Fact gathering was always profoundly and immorally intrusive, cruelly invasive and insensitive to the most sacred social rituals, based on bad faith observation and an alienated data acquisition that forced the observer into inevitable unethical acts and situations *but with the immediate denial of all that.* Now we are forced to wade through the detritus of positivist denial and embrace what it savagely repressed. Positive science when realized in ethnographic practice created false relationships based largely on the premeditated refusal or congenital inability to sustain interhuman contact beyond instrumental interpersonal manipulations "for science."

At the very instant of death of an old ethnography we witness the birth of its feral child who grows up improperly socialized, without parental-canonical-guidance, who vows within itself to repudiate the pa-maternity.

> It flows into the sensibility. Abandoning Occidental usages of speech, it turns words into incantations. It extends the voice. It utilizes the vibrations and qualities of the voice. It wildly tramples rhythms underfoot. It pile-drives sounds. It seeks to exalt, to benumb, to charm, to arrest the sensibility. It liberates a new lyricism of gesture which, by its precipitation or its amplitude in the air, ends by surpassing the lyricism of words. It ultimately breaks away from the intellectual subjugation of language, by conveying the sense of a new and deeper intellectuality

which hides itself beneath the gestures and signs, raised to a dignity of particular exorcisms. (Artaud 1938:91)

NOTES

1. Obviously in the telling I have simplified the history of the East India Company unconscionably; John Bruce, not mentioning Linschoten, gave a number of reasons why the "John Company," as it came to be known in London, emerged when it did: the overland route beyond the Mediterranean had become too dangerous, Drake had returned in 1580 from a circumnavigation of the earth by way of the Cape of Good Hope showing the parvenu English that such a course could be navigated by them, Cavendish had duplicated Drake's feat six years later, and the merchants who wanted to incorporate as the London Company of Merchants had provided the Privy Council with a memorial (read "intelligence report") on where the Portuguese settlements were and where the English might trade. Three ships were sent out with terrible losses but one returned with impressive cargo captured from a Portuguese ship. "Whether it was from the information collected from these detached voyages to the East Indies, from the example of the associations . . . as having received the protection of the Crown, or from the Dutch . . . it is impossible to decide" (Bruce 1810:110).

2. Merchants comprised over 85 percent of the representation of the East India Company at its inception. The gentry who were active in trade indulged on the whole more in colonization and exploration schemes (Rabb 1967).

3. "The Council, therefore, did act in a corporate fashion and there is justification for saying that its promulgations influenced the history of Elizabethan England" (Ponko 1968:7).

The Postmodernist Turn in Anthropology: Cautions from a Feminist Perspective

Frances E. Mascia-Lees, Patricia Sharpe, and Colleen Ballerino Cohen

At this profoundly self-reflexive moment in anthropology—a moment of questioning traditional modes of representation in the discipline—practitioners seeking to write a genuinely new ethnography[1] would do better to use feminist theory as a model than to draw on postmodern trends in epistemology and literary criticism with which they have thus far claimed allegiance. Unlike postmodernism, feminist theory is an intellectual system that *knows* its politics, a politics directed toward securing recognition that the feminine is as crucial an element of the human as the masculine and thus a politics skeptical and critical of traditional "universal truths" concerning human behavior. Similarly, anthropology is grounded in a politics: it aims to secure a recognition that the non-Western is as crucial an element of the human as the Western and thus is skeptical and critical of Western claims to knowledge and understanding.

Anthropologists influenced by postmodernism have recognized the need to claim a politics in order to appeal to an anthropological audience. This is evident even in the titles of the two most influential explications of this reflexive moment: *Anthropology as Cultural Critique: An Experimental Moment in the Human Sciences* (Marcus and Fischer 1986) and *Writing Culture: The Poetics and Politics of Ethnography* (Clifford and Marcus 1986). Indeed, the popularity of these books may be due as much to their appeal to anthropologists' traditional moral imperative—that we must question and expand Western definitions of the human—as to the current concern with modes of expression. Postmodern in their attention to texture and form as well as in their emphasis on language, text, and the nature of representation, these two works seek to connect this focus with the politics inherent in the anthropological enterprise. George Marcus and Michael Fischer's *An-*

thropology as Cultural Critique, for example, starts off with a restatement of anthropology's traditional goals: to salvage "distinct cultural forms of life from the processes of global Westernization" and to serve "as a form of cultural critique of ourselves" (1986:1). In keeping with postmodernism's emphasis on style, the authors claim that it is through new types of experimental ethnographic writing that anthropology can best expose the global systems of power relations that are embedded in traditional representations of other societies.

Underlying the new ethnography are questions concerning anthropology's role in the maintenance of Western hegemony: how have anthropological writings constructed or perpetuated myths about the non-Western Other? How have these constructed images served the interest of the West? Even when critiquing colonialism and questioning Western representations of other societies, anthropology cannot avoid proposing alternative constructions. This has led to the recognition that ethnography is "always caught up with the invention, not the representation, of cultures" (Clifford 1986a:2; see Wagner 1981 for an elaboration of this idea). And, as James Clifford suggests, the resultant undermining of the truth claims of Western representations of the Other has been reinforced by important theorizing about the limits of representation itself in diverse fields (1986a:10).

Postmodernist anthropologists, with their focus on classic ethnographies as texts, wish to call attention to the constructed nature of cultural accounts. They also wish to explore new forms of writing that will reflect the newly problematized relationship between writer, reader, and subject matter in anthropology (Marilyn Strathern 1987b:269; Clifford 1986b:117) in an age when the native informant may read and contest the ethnographer's characterizations, indeed may well have heard of Jacques Derrida and have a copy of the latest Banana Republic catalogue (Stoller 1988). Postmodernist anthropologists claim that the aim of experimentation with such forms as intertextuality, dialogue, and self-referentiality is to demystify the anthropologist's unitary authority and thus to include, and structure the relationships among, the "many voices clamoring for expression" (Clifford 1986a:15) in the ethnographic situation. However, these new ways of structuring are more subtle and enigmatic than traditional modes of anthropological writing: they may serve to make the new ethnographies more obscure and thus difficult for anyone but highly trained specialists to dispute.

The essays in James Clifford and George Marcus's *Writing Culture: The Poetics and Politics of Ethnography* are concerned with the explication of the relation between the ethnographic field situation and the style of the ethnographic text. In his introduction to the book, for example, Clifford explains the effects of the new ethnographers' use of dialogue: "It locates cultural interpretations in many sorts of reciprocal contexts, and it obliges writers to find diverse ways of rendering negotiated realities as multisubjective, power-laden, and incongruent. In this view, 'culture' is always relational, an inscription of communicative processes that exist, historically, *between* subjects in relation to power" (1986a:15).

Thus, Clifford argues that new ethnographers, those anthropologists who do not just theorize about textual production but who write cultural accounts, employ experimental writing techniques in an attempt to expose the power relations embedded in any ethnographic work and to produce a text that is less encumbered with Western assumptions and categories than traditional ethnographies have been. Michelle Rosaldo, for example, has attempted to make the initial cultural unintelligibility of the voice of an Ilongot headhunter persuasive not so much through argumentation or explication as through repetition (1980). In *Nisa: The Life and Words of a !Kung Woman* (1981), Marjorie Shostak juxtaposes the voice of the Other with the voice of the ethnographer to offer the reader the possibility of confronting the difference between two distinct modes of understanding. In *Moroccan Dialogues* (1982), Kevin Dwyer experiments with a dialogic mode of representation to emphasize that the ethnographic text is a collaborative endeavor between himself and a Moroccan farmer. Other experimental works have concentrated on exposing how the observation as well as the interpretation of another culture are affected by a researcher's cultural identity and mode of expression. In *Princes of Naranja: An Essay in Anthrohistorical Method* (1986), for example, Paul Friedrich gives an extensive discussion of his own personal history, showing how his childhood farm experiences predisposed him to a study of agrarian life and how an almost unbelievable series of physical mishaps led him to reorganize his entire book. He also shows how this reordering and his choice of stylistic devices, such as texturing and "historical holography," help convey a sense of Naranjan life as complex.

However, what appear to be new and exciting insights to these postmodernist anthropologists—that culture is composed of seriously contested codes of meaning, that language and politics are inseparable, and that constructing the Other entails relations of domination (Clifford 1986a:2)—are insights that have received repeated and rich exploration in feminist theory for the past forty years. Discussion of the female as Other was the starting point of contemporary feminist theory. As early as 1949, Simone de Beauvoir's *The Second Sex* argued that it was by constructing the woman as Other that men in Western culture have constituted themselves as subject. An early goal of this wave of feminism was to recover women's experience and thereby find ways that we as women could constitute ourselves—claim ourselves—as subjects. This feminist theory does have similarities with traditional anthropology. Both are concerned with the relationship of the dominant and the Other and with the need to expand and question definitions of the human. However, even forty years ago a crucial difference existed between anthropological and feminist inquiries. While anthropology questioned the status of the participant-observer, it spoke from the position of the dominant and thus for the Other. Feminists speak from the position of the Other.

This is not to oversimplify. It was not possible for feminists to speak directly as Other. Women in consciousness-raising groups were not simply giving voice to already formulated but not yet articulated women's perspectives; they were creatively constructing them. In telling stories about their experiences they were giving them new meanings, meanings other than those granted by patriarchy, which sees women only as seductresses or wives, as good or bad mothers. Similarly, feminist scholars sought to construct new theoretical interpretations of women. Yet, even when attempting to speak for women, and as women, feminist scholars wrote within a patriarchal discourse that does not accord subject status to the feminine. In this way feminists exposed the contradictions in a supposedly neutral and objective discourse that always proceeds from a gendered being and thereby questioned the adequacy of academic discourse. Thus, feminist theory, even in the 1970s, was concerned not simply with understanding women's experience of otherness but also with the inscription of women as Other in language and discourse. This was particularly evident in feminist literary criticism, which moved from the cataloguing of stereotypes (see especially Ellmann 1968 and Pratt 1982) to the study of female authorship as resistance and reinscription (see especially Gilbert and Gubar 1980; Showalter 1977; and Moers 1976). French feminists, notably Hélène Cixous and Luce Irigaray, playfully exploited language's metaphoric and polysemic capacities to give voice to feminist reinterpretations of dominant myths about women (Cixous 1983; Irigaray 1981).

A fundamental goal of the new ethnography is similar: to apprehend and inscribe Others in such a way as not to deny or diffuse their claims to subjecthood. As Marcus and Fischer put it, the new ethnography seeks to allow "the adequate representation of other voices or points of view across cultural boundaries" (1986:2). Informed by the notion of culture as a collective and historically contingent construct, the new ethnography claims to be acutely sensitive to cultural differences and, within cultures, to the multiplicity of individual experience.

However, despite these similarities, when anthropologists look to a theory on which to ground the new ethnography, they turn to post-modernism, dismissing feminist theory as having little to teach that anthropology has not already known. For example, Marcus and Fischer claim, "The debate over gender differences stimulated by femin-ism . . . often [falls] into the same rhetorical strategies that once were used for playing off the dissatisfactions of civilized society against the virtues of the primitive" (1986:135). By focusing exclusively on those feminists who valorize "essential" female characteristics, such as moth-erhood and peaceableness, Marcus and Fischer construe feminism as little more than the expression of women's dissatisfactions with a sinister patriarchy. Thus, their ignorance of the full spectrum of feminist theory may partly explain their dismissal of it.

Similarly, Clifford justifies the exclusion of feminist anthropologists from *Writing Culture: The Poetics and Politics of Ethnography* with a questionable characterization of the feminist enterprise in anthropol-ogy: "Feminist ethnography has focused either on setting the record straight about women or revising anthropological categories. . . . It has not produced either unconventional forms of writing or a developed reflection on ethnographic textuality as such" (1986a:20-21). Clifford nonetheless uses Marjorie Shostak's *Nisa: The Life and Words of a !Kung Woman* as a primary example in his essay "On Ethnographic Allegory" in the same volume. In this essay he calls Shostak's work at once "feminist" and "original in its polyvocality," "manifestly the prod-uct of a collaboration with the other," and reflexive of "a troubled, inventive moment in the history of cross-cultural representation" (1986b:104–9). He therefore reveals not only that he clearly knows of at least one feminist ethnography that has employed "unconventional forms of writing" but also that he prefers to write *about* feminists rather than inviting them to write for themselves.

This contradiction makes sense in the context of Clifford's essay on ethnographic allegory. In it he seeks to demonstrate that the new ethnography is like traditional anthropological writings about the Other in that both use allegory. He argues that all ethnography is inevitably allegorical since it at once presents us with a representation of a different reality and continuously refers to another pattern of ideas to make that difference comprehensible. It is odd that Clifford uses a feminist ethnography as his only example of how new ethnography is allegorical, since, in view of his statement about feminist ethnography's lack of experimentation in his introduction, he himself should suspect that

Shostak's work is not representative of the new ethnography. Such a contradiction seems to betray Clifford's tendency to equate women with forces of cultural conservatism. In dismissing the novelty of feminist work in anthropology, Clifford seeks to validate *Writing Culture* as truly innovative: "The essays in this volume occupy a new space opened up by the disintegration of 'Man' as *telos* for a whole discipline" (1986a:4). Like European explorers "discovering" the "New World," Clifford and his colleagues perceive a new and uninhabited space where, in fact, feminists have long been at work.

How can we understand this dismissal of feminism in favor of postmodernism, the dismissal of political engagement in favor of a view that "beholds the world blankly, with a knowingness that dissolves feeling and commitment into irony" (Gitlin 1988:35)? Anthropologists should be uncomfortable with an aesthetic view of the world as a global shopping center and suspicious of an ideology that sustains the global economic system (see Jameson 1983). Of course, there are many postmodernisms (Tress 1988), just as there are many feminisms, and within both movements definitions are contested. While there is also considerable overlap (see Flax 1987 and Craig Owens 1983; Fraser and Nicholson 1988 was very helpful to us on this point), postmodernism is unlike feminism in its relationship to the ferment of the 1960s. While contemporary feminism is an on-going political movement with roots in the sixties, "Postmodernism is above all post-1960's; its keynote is cultural helplessness. It is post–Viet Nam, post–New Left, post-hippie, post-Watergate. History was ruptured, passions have been expended, belief has become difficult. . . . The 1960's exploded our belief in progress. . . . Old verities crumbled, but new ones have not settled in. Self-regarding irony and blankness are a way of staving off anxieties, rages, terrors, and hungers that have been kicked up but cannot find resolution" (Gitlin 1988:36). The sense of helplessness that postmodernism expresses is broader, however, than the disillusionment of the sixties' leftists; it is an experience of tremendous loss of mastery in traditionally dominant groups. In the postmodern period, theorists "stave off" their anxiety by questioning the basis of the truths that they are losing the privilege to define.

The political scientist Nancy Hartsock (1987) has made a similar observation; she finds it curious that the postmodern claim that verbal constructs do not correspond in a direct way to reality has arisen precisely when women and non-Western peoples have begun to speak for themselves and, indeed, to speak about global systems of power differentials. In fact, Hartsock suggests that the postmodern view that truth and knowledge are contingent and multiple may be seen to act as a truth claim itself, a claim that undermines the ontological status of the subject at the very time when women and non-Western peoples have begun to claim themselves as subject. In a similar vein, Sarah Lennox (1987) has asserted that the postmodern despair associated with the recognition that truth is never entirely knowable is merely an inversion of Western arrogance. When Western white males—who have traditionally controlled the production of knowledge—can no longer define the truth, she argues, their response is to conclude that there is not a truth to be discovered. Similarly, Sandra Harding claims that "historically, relativism appears as an intellectual possibility, and as a 'problem,' only for dominating groups at the point where the hegemony (the universality) of their views is being challenged. [Relativism] is fundamentally a sexist response that attempts to preserve the legitimacy of androcentric claims in the face of contrary evidence" (1987:10). Perhaps most compelling for the new ethnography is the question Andreas Huyssen asks in "Mapping the Postmodern": "Isn't the death of the subject/author position tied by mere reversal to the very ideology that invariably glorifies the artist as genius . . . doesn't post-structuralism where it simply denies the subject altogether jettison the chance of challenging the ideology of the subject (as male, white and middle-class) by developing alternative notions of subjectivity?" (1984:44).

These analyses clearly raise questions about the experience of Western white males and how it is reflected in postmodern thought. To the extent that this dominant group has in recent years experienced a decentering as world politics and economic realities shift global power relations, postmodern theorizing can be understood as socially constructed itself, as a metaphor for the sense of members of the dominant group that the ground has begun to shift under their feet. And this social construction, according to Hartsock, Lennox, Harding, and Huyssen, is one that may potentially work to preserve the privileged position of Western white males. If so, then the new ethnography, in its reliance on postmodernism, may run the risk of participating in an ideology blind to its own politics. More than that, it may help to preserve the dominant colonial and neocolonial relations from which anthropology, and especially the new ethnography, has been trying to extricate itself.

But to phrase this argument exclusively in these terms is to obscure the fact that the significant power relations for many of these new postmodernist anthropologists are not global but parochial, those that are played out in the halls of anthropology departments, those that are embedded in the patriarchal social order of the academy in which male *and* female scholars maneuver for status, tenure, and power. In an article in *Current Anthropology,* P. Steven Sangren argues that although postmodernist anthropologists call for a questioning of *textually* constituted authority, their efforts are actually a play for *socially* constituted authority and power (Sangren 1988:411). He thus suggests that it is first and foremost academic politics that condition the production and reproduction of ethnographic texts. Moreover, according to him, "Whatever 'authority' is created in a text has its most direct social effect not in the world of political and economic domination of the Third World by colonial and neocolonial powers, but rather in the academic institutions in which such authors participate" (1988:412).

While postmodernist anthropologists such as Clifford, Marcus, and Fischer may choose to think they are transforming global power relations as well as the discipline of anthropology itself, they may also be establishing first claim in the new academic territory on which this decade's battles for intellectual supremacy and jobs will be waged.[2] The exclusion of feminist voices in Clifford's and Marcus's influential volume and Clifford's defensive, convoluted, and contradictory explanation for it are strategies that preserve male supremacy in the academy. Clifford seems well aware of this when we read in the same introductory pages in which he presents his defense of excluding feminist writers his statement that "all constructed truths are made possible by powerful 'lies' of exclusion and rhetoric" (1986a:7).

The lie of excluding feminism has characterized most postmodernist writing by males, not simply that in anthropology. One notable exception, Craig Owens's "The Discourse of Others: Feminists and Postmodernism" (1983), demonstrates the richness of insight into cultural phenomena that the conjunction of feminist and postmodern perspectives offers. For anthropologists, his analysis of the message humans transmit to possible extraterrestrials, the space age Other, is particularly telling. Of the schematic image of a nude man and woman, the former's right arm raised in greeting, which was emblazoned on the Pioneer spacecraft, Owens observes, "Like all representations of sexual difference that our culture produces, this is an image not simply of anatomical difference but of the values assigned to it" (61). A small difference in morphology is marked or underscored by the erect right arm, signal that speech is the privilege of the male. Owens notes that deconstruction of this privilege by male postmodernists is rare: "If one of the most salient aspects of our postmodern culture is the presence of an insistent feminist voice . . . theories of postmodernism have tended either to neglect or to repress that voice. The absence of discussions of sexual difference in writings about postmodernism, as well as the fact that few women have engaged in the modernism/postmodernism debate, suggest that postmodernism may be another masculine invention engineered to exclude women" (1983:61).

While "engineered," with its suggestion of conscious agency, may grant academic males too much sinister awareness, Owens's observation of the evidence is accurate: "Men appear unwilling to address the issues placed on the critical agenda by women unless those issues have been first neut(e)ralized" (62). This suggests their fear of entering into a discourse where the Other has privilege. Intellectual cross-dressing, like its physical counterpart, is less disruptive of traditional orders of privilege when performed by women than by men.[3] Fearing loss of authority and masculinity, male critics have preferred to look on feminism as a limited and peripheral enterprise, not as one challenging them to rethink their own positions in terms of gender.[4] "Although sympathetic male critics respect feminism (an old theme: respect for women)," Owens acknowledges that "they have in general declined to enter into the dialogue in which their female colleagues have been trying to engage them" (62).[5]

The case of Paul Rabinow is illustrative. His is the one article in *Writing Culture* that appears to deal seriously with feminism. However, he concludes that feminism is not an intellectual position he personally can hold. Seeing himself as "excluded from direct participation in the feminist dialogue" (1986:258), he constructs an alternative "ethical" position for anthropologists: critical cosmopolitanism. "This is an oppositional position," he argues, "one suspicious of sovereign powers, universal truths . . . but also wary of the tendency to essentialize difference" (258). Ironically, however, Rabinow not only universalizes, stating "we are all cosmopolitans" (258), but also essentializes difference when he excludes himself from the feminist dialogue solely because he is male. Seeing himself as unable to participate in feminist and Third World discourses, he identifies with the Greek Sophists, "cosmopolitan insider's outsiders of a particular historical and cultural world" (258). In thus constructing himself as just one more Other among the rest, Rabinow risks the danger he ascribes to critics such as James Clifford: "obliterating meaningful difference" (257), obliterating and obscuring some of the privileges and power granted to him by race, nationality, and gender.[6] He describes his decision to study elite French male colonial officials as proceeding from this oppositional ethical stance: "By 'studying up' I find myself in a more comfortable position than I would be were I 'giving voice' on behalf of dominated or marginal groups" (259). An exclusive focus on the elite, eschewing the dominated or marginal, is a dangerous, if comfortable, correction. Feminists have taught us the danger of analyses that focus exclusively on men: they have traditionally rendered gender differences irrelevant and reinforced the Western male as the norm. Rabinow's earlier *Reflections on Fieldwork in Morocco* relied exclusively on male informants, presenting women only marginally and as objects of his sexual desire, communicating through "the unambiguity of gesture" (1977:67). Ironically, he claims his new work will broaden "considerations of power and representation" which were "too localized in my earlier work on Morocco" (1986:258), yet he focuses even more explicitly on men. This can be defended only if Rabinow struggles with his earlier insensitivity to gender issues and, in this study of elite powerful males, undertakes that part of the feminist project particularly suited to male practitioners: deconstructing the patriarchy.[7]

Feminists' call for self-reflexivity in men is related to postmodernist anthropology's goal of self-critique; when anthropologists include themselves as characters in ethnographic texts instead of posing as objective controlling narrators, they expose their biases. This coincides with the goals of postmodernism as characterized by Jane Flax: "Postmodern discourses are all deconstructive in that they seek to distance us from and make us skeptical about beliefs concerning truth, knowledge, power, the self, and language that are often taken for granted within and serve as legitimation for contemporary Western culture" (1987:624). Yet interest in these questions in postmodernism is abstract and philosophical, paradoxically grounded in a search for a more accurate vision of truth. Feminist theory shares similar concerns to these postmodern ideas, as Flax notes, but feminist theory differs from postmodernism in that it acknowledges its grounding in politics.

The one theorist who has grappled with the problems that arise with merging feminism and anthropology is Marilyn Strathern, who notes that "anthropology has interests parallel to feminist scholarship," which would lead us to expect "radical anthropology to draw on its feminist counterpart" (1987a:276–77). She notes, however, that feminism has affected only the choice of subjects of study in social anthropology, not its scholarly practices: "Where social anthropological categories of analysis have changed, it has been in response to internal criticism that has little to do with feminist theory" (281). Strathern seeks to explain why anthropology has failed to respond to feminism as a profound challenge by showing how the two endeavors are parallel yet mock each other. Feminism mocks experimental anthropology's search for an ethnography that is a "collaborative production . . . a metaphor for an ideal ethical situation in which neither voice is submerged by the Other" (290), while anthropology mocks feminists' pretensions to separate themselves from Western "cultural suppositions about the nature of personhood and of relationships shared equally by the [male] Other" (291).

Strathern thus suggests that there can be no true merging of feminism and the new ethnography, but this contention is based on a problematic formulation. Even the brief quotations above indicate Strathern's disturbing use of the term *Other* to refer to " 'patriarchy,' the institutions and persons who represent male domination, often simply concretized as 'men' " (288). This, she believes, is the Other of feminism, the Other that feminists must remain in opposition to for "the construction of the feminist self" (288). This feminist need to remain distinct from a wrongheaded male Other is at odds, she argues, with the new ethnography's desire to get close to and know the Other. But in this latter usage of the word *Other,* she refers to the traditional anthropological subject of study, non-Western peoples. In her awkward parallel usage, Strathern seems to ignore differential power relations, failing to acknowledge that one term in each pair is historically marked by privilege. She does not see that women are to men as natives are to anthropologists. And, thus, even if as feminists we remain in opposition to men to construct ourselves, it does not mean that we must fear getting to know the non-Western Other. We may, however, be cautious in our desire to do so. Feminists can teach new ethnographers that their ideal of collaboration "is a delusion, overlooking the crucial dimension of different social interests," Strathern suggests, wrongly attributing this insight to the oppositional position feminists strike in relation to the patriarchal Other (290). Our suspicion of the new ethnographers' desire for collaboration with the Other stems not from any such refusal to enter into dialogue with that Other but from our history and understanding of being appropriated and literally spoken for by the dominant and from our consequent sympathetic identification with the subjects of anthropological study in this regard.

This leads to the questioning, voiced recently by Judith Stacey (1988), of whether any ethnography of the Other can be compatible with feminist politics. Stacey argues that despite the appearance of compatibility between feminist researchers seeking an "egalitarian research process characterized by authenticity, reciprocity, and intersubjectivity between the researcher and her 'subjects' " and the face-to-face and personalized encounter of the ethnographic field experience, major contradictions exist. First, the highly personalized relationship between ethnographer and research subject, which masks actual differences in power, knowledge, and structural mobility, "places research subjects at grave risk of manipulation and betrayal by the ethnographer" (23). Additionally, she points to the contradiction between the desire for collaboration on the final research product and the fact that "the research product is ultimately that of the researcher, however modified or influenced by informants" (22–23). Stacey's response to these contradictions is to despair of a fully feminist ethnography. "There can be ethnographies that are partially feminist, accounts of culture enhanced by the application of feminist perspectives," she argues, and there can be "feminist research that is rigorously self-aware and therefore humble about the partiality of its ethnographic vision and its capacity to represent self and other" (26). But how are these goals to be realized? And has feminism nothing more to teach the new ethnography?

We have suggested that an important aspect of feminist scholarship is its relationship to a politics. Marilyn Strathern notes that within feminist writing, "play with context [similar to that used by the new ethnographers] is creative because of the expressed continuity of purpose between feminists as scholars and feminists as activists" (1987b:268). Feminism teaches us to take up a particularly moral and sensitive attitude toward relationships by emphasizing the importance of community building to the feminist project, and it also demands scrutiny of our motivations for research. In their current experimentation, anthropologists need a renewed sensitivity to "the question of relationships involved in communication" (269). They need to learn the lessons of feminism and consider for whom they write.

Throughout her discussion of postmodernist anthropology, Strathern displays suspicions, like those other feminists have, of its claims to use free play and jumble, to present many voices in flattened, nonhierarchical, plural texts, to employ "heteroglossia (a utopia of plural endeavor that gives all collaborators the status of authors)" (267). Irony, she argues, rather than jumble is the postmodern mode, and "irony involves not a scrambling but a deliberate juxtaposition of contexts, pastiche perhaps but not jumble" (266).

Strathern contrasts this illusion of free play in postmodernist anthropology with feminist writing: "Much feminist discourse is constructed in a plural way. Arguments are juxtaposed, many voices solicited. . . . There are no central texts, no definitive techniques" (268). Unlike postmodern writing, however, which masks its structuring oppositions under a myth of jumble, feminist scholarship has "a special set of social interests. Feminists argue with one another in their many voices because they also know themselves as an interest group" (268). Thus, although feminism may originally have discovered itself by becoming conscious of oppression, more recently feminists have focused on relations among women and the project of conceiving difference without binary opposition. Feminist politics provide an explicit structure that frames our research questions and moderates the interactions in which we engage with other women. Where there is no such explicit political structure, the danger of veiled agendas is great.

Anthropologists could benefit from an understanding of this feminist dialogue. Just as early feminist theory of the Other is grounded in women's actual subordination to men, so more recent trends in feminist theorizing about difference are grounded in actual differences among women. For example, the recent focus in mainstream feminist theory upon the diversity of women's experiences bears relation to the postmodern deconstruction of the subject but stems from a very different source: the political confrontation between white feminists and women of color (see Lugones and Spelman 1983 for a compelling representation of this dialogue). In response to accusations by women of color that the women's movement has been in actuality a white, middle-class women's movement, Western white feminists, together with women of color, have had to reconsider theories of *the* woman and replace them with theories of multiplicity. In a similar vein, the need for building self-criticism into feminist theory has been expressed with the recognition that what once appeared to be theoretically appropriate mandates for change may have very different results for different populations of women. For example, some scholars claim that antirape activism has served to reinforce racial stereotypes—the rapist as black male—that pro-choice legislation has provided a rationale for forced sterilization and abortions among the poor and women of color, and that feminist-backed no-fault divorce legislation has contributed to the feminization of poverty. The new ethnography draws on postmodernist epistemology to accomplish its political ends, but much feminism derives its theory from a practice based on the material conditions of all women's lives.

Both postmodernist anthropology and feminism assume a self-consciously reflexive stance toward their subjects, but there are significant differences between them. For, as Sandra Harding has suggested, at the moment that feminist scholars begin to address themselves to women's experiences, their inquiry necessarily becomes concerned with questions of power and political struggle and their research goals become defined by that struggle. This is because "the questions an oppressed group wants answered are rarely requests for so-called pure truth. Instead, they are questions about how to change its conditions; how its world is shaped by forces beyond it; how to win over, defeat or neutralize those forces arrayed against its emancipation, growth or development; and so forth" (1987:8). The feminist researcher is led to design projects that, according to Harding, women want and need.

Indeed, in this sense, feminist research is more closely aligned with applied anthropology, whose practitioners also often derive their questions from and apply their methods to the solution of problems defined by the people being studied, than with new ethnographers.[8] Applied anthropologists frequently function as "power brokers," translating between the subordinate, disenfranchised group and the dominant class or power. To understand the difference in approach between the new ethnographer and the applied anthropologist, it is useful to look at Clifford's essay "Identity in Mashpee" (1988).

The Mashpee are a group of Native Americans who in 1976 sued in federal court for possession of a large tract of land in Mashpee, Massachusetts. The case revolved around claims of cultural identity: if the individuals bringing suit could prove an uninterrupted historical identity as a tribe, then their claim for compensation would be upheld. In his article, Clifford makes use of trial transcripts, transcripts of interviews with witnesses for the defense, and snippets of information from the documents used in the case to reconstruct Mashpee history. As a new ethnographer, Clifford analyzes these as commentaries on "the ways in which historical stories are told" and on "the alternative cultural models that have been applied to human groups" (289). Such readings as this can and do elucidate who speaks for cultural authenticity and how collective identity and difference are represented. Indeed, for the new ethnographer, the Mashpee trial emerges as a sort of natural laboratory in which multiple voices contributing to a collectively constituted cultural reality can be heard. It illustrates how the postmodernist emphasis on dialogue helps anthropologists to study native populations as they change and interact in response to the dominant culture rather than simply as representatives of a pure and dying past. However, Mascia-Lees, as someone who has worked with and for the Mashpee in their federal recognition appeal, would argue that it is highly doubtful whether Clifford's insights provide the Mashpee with explanations of social phenomena that they either "want or need."

We must question whether the appearance of multiple voices in Clifford's text can act to counter the hegemonic forces that continue to deny the Mashpee access to their tribal lands. Who is the intended audience for this analysis: the Mashpee or other scholars in institutions under Western control? And whose interests does it serve? Following Harding's claim that feminist research seeks to use women's experiences "as the test of adequacy of the problems, concepts, hypotheses, research design, collection, and interpretation of data" (1987:11), we might even go so far as to ask whether Clifford's representation uses the Mashpee's experience as a test of the adequacy of his research. Clifford sees himself as rejecting the Western privileging of visualism in favor of a paradigm of the interplay of voices. Yet perhaps dialogue, even the proliferating Bakhtinian dialogic processes Clifford favors, is saturated with Western assumptions. We need to ask whose experience of the world this focus on dialogue reflects: that of the ethnographer who yearns to speak with and know the Other or that of Native Americans, many of whom have frequently refused dialogue with the anthropologist, whom they see as yet one more representative of the oppressive culture and for some of whom dialogue may be an alien mode.

This yearning to know the Other can be traced to the romanticism so frequently associated with anthropologists' scholarly pursuits. Traditionally, this romantic component has been linked to the heroic quests, by the single anthropologist, for "his soul"[9] through confrontation with the exotic Other (see Sontag 1966; Geertz 1988). This particular avenue for self-exploration has been closed recently by the resistance of Third World peoples to serving in therapeutic roles for Westerners as well as by the sense on the part of anthropologists that twentieth-century "natives" may themselves be in need of therapy, "neutered, like the rest of us, by the dark forces of the world system" (Tyler 1986:128).

Yet the romantic tradition in anthropology is being sustained by the postmodernist mandate for self-reflection. For in turning inward, making himself, his motives, and his experience the thing to be confronted, the postmodernist anthropologist locates the Other in himself. It is as if, finding the "exotic" closed off to him, the anthropologist constructs himself as the exotic.[10] This is clearly the case, for example, in *Princes of Naranja* (1986). Here Paul Friedrich's characterization of the salient features of his own life history connects in the reader's mind with images of the Tarascan princes who have appeared on earlier pages: home-bred fatalism, peer rivalry, and personal experiences with death and danger. Since Friedrich's self-reflection was written some thirty years after his initial fieldwork experience in Naranja, it seems likely, although Friedrich does not suggest it, that this inscription of his own childhood history may have been as much affected by his Naranja experience as vice versa. Ironically, Friedrich's book, which opens up the possibility of demystifying the Other, reveals that this process may lead to a mystification of the Self. In this light, it is hardly surprising that Clifford's work is so popular. Clifford, the historian, has turned ethnographers into the natives to be understood and ethnography into virgin territory to be explored.

This current focus on self-reflexivity in postmodernist anthropology is expressed not only in works that make the ethnographer into a

character in the ethnographic text but also in analyses of earlier ethnographic writing (see, for example, Geertz 1988; Clifford 1988; Marilyn
Strathern 1987b). Of this process Marilyn Strathern comments,

> Retrospectively to ask about the persuasive fictions of earlier epochs is
> to ask about how others (Frazer, Malinowski, and the rest) handled
> our moral problems of literary construction. In answering the question,
> we create historic shifts between past writers in terms persuasive to our
> own ears, thereby participating in a postmodern history, reading back
> into books the strategies of fictionalisation. To construct past works as
> quasi-intentional literary games is the new ethnocentrism. There is no
> evidence, after all, that "we" have stopped attributing our problems to
> "others." (1987b:269)

Furthermore, much of this historical analysis deals with colonialism,
affording the contemporary anthropologist a field of study in which it
is possible to hold a critical and ethical view. Paradoxically, however,
it simultaneously replays a time in which Western white males were of
supreme importance in the lives of the Other just at this moment when
the anthropologist fears his irrelevance.

Such paradoxes, which emerge from the joining of postmodernism
with anthropology, pose the most difficult questions for practitioners
of the new ethnography at present: once one articulates an epistemology
of free play in which there is no inevitable relationship between signifier
and signified, how is it possible to write an ethnography that has
descriptive force? Once one has no metanarratives into which the
experience of difference can be translated, how is it possible to write
any ethnography? Here, too, lessons from feminism may be helpful;
since current feminist theory lives constantly with the paradoxical
nature of its own endeavor, it offers postmodernism models for dealing
with contradiction. As Nancy Cott suggests, feminism is paradoxical
in that it "aims for individual freedoms by mobilizing sex solidarity.
It acknowledges diversity among women while positing that women
recognize their unity. It requires gender consciousness for its basis, yet
calls for the elimination of prescribed gender roles" (as quoted in Frye
1987:2). Postmodern thought has helped feminists to argue that wom-
en's inferior status is a product of cultural and historical constructions
and to resist essentialist truth claims, but the danger for feminists is
that "in deconstructing categories of meaning, we deconstruct not only
patriarchal definitions of 'womanhood' and 'truth' but also the very
categories of our own analysis—'women' and 'feminism' and 'oppression' " (Cott, as quoted in Frye 1987:2).

That feminist theory, with its recent emphasis on the diversity of
women's experience, has not succumbed entirely to the seduction of

postmodernism and the dangers inherent in a complete decentering of the historical and material is due in part to feminist theory's concern with women as the central category of analysis and with feminism's political goal of changing the power relationships that underlie women's oppression. Feminists will not relinquish the claim to understanding women's gendered experience in the hierarchical world in which we continue to live (Frye 1987).

This situatedness affords feminists a ground for reclaiming objectivity for our enterprise while at the same time recognizing the partiality of truth claims. Recent works by feminist critics of science have challenged traditional definitions of objectivity as disinterestedness and have reappropriated the term for the situated truth that feminism seeks. This argument is well stated by Mary Hawkesworth: "In the absence of claims of universal validity, feminist accounts derive their justificatory force from their capacity to illuminate existing social relations, to demonstrate the deficiencies of alternative interpretations, to debunk opposing views. Precisely because feminists move beyond texts to confront the world, they can provide concrete reasons in specific contexts for the superiority of their accounts. . . . At their best, feminist analyses engage both the critical intellect and the world; they surpass androcentric accounts because in their systematicity more is examined and less is assumed" (1989:557).

Truth can only emerge in particular circumstances; we must be wary of generalizations. Such a politics demands and enables feminists to examine for whom we write. Marilyn Strathern is one anthropologist who has found this lesson of value: "In describing Melanesian marriage ceremonies, I must bear my Melanesian readers in mind. That in turn makes problematic the previously established distinction between writer and subject: I must know on whose behalf and to what end I write" (1987b:269).

Hidden power relations constitute problems not only for women or feminist scholarship but also for men and for the dominant discourse whose claims to objectivity are marred by distortions and mystification. The very fictional forms that postmodern epistemology suggests are the ideal vehicles for uncovering these power relations actually may tempt the new ethnographer to write without deciding who the audience is. The new ethnography must embed its theory in a grounded politics, rather than turning to a currently popular aesthetic without interrogating the way in which that thinking is potentially subversive of anthropology's own political agenda.

It is true that postmodernism, with its emphasis on the decentering of the Cartesian subject, can be invigorating to those traditionally excluded from discourse. Jane Flax has stressed this liberating potential, arguing that postmodern experimentation encourages us "to tolerate and interpret ambivalence, ambiguity, and multiplicity" (1987:643). Similarly, the historian Joan Scott (1987) has recently argued that the postmodern rejection of the notion that humanity can be embodied in any universal figure or norm to which the Other is compared acts to decenter the Western white male. In Craig Owens's words: "The postmodern work attempts to upset the reassuring stability of [the] mastering position [of the] subject of representation as absolutely centered, unitary, masculine" (1983:58). Indeed this seems to be the political motivation underlying the new ethnography, but actual postmodern writing may not serve these political ends. Rather, it may erase difference, implying that all stories are really about one experience: the decentering and fragmentation that is the current experience of Western white males.

Moreover, even if we grant that postmodernism's potential lies in its capacity to decenter experience, a number of questions still arise. Can we think of difference without putting it against a norm? Can we recognize difference, but not in terms of hierarchy (Scott 1987)? Perhaps more to the point in terms of the new ethnography, what are the implications of polyvocality? If the postmodernist emphasis on multivocality leads to a denial of the continued existence of a hierarchy of discourse, the material and historical links between cultures can be ignored, with all voices becoming equal, each telling only an individualized story. Then the history of the colonial, for example, can be read as independent of that of the colonizer. Such readings ignore or obscure exploitation and power differentials and, therefore, offer no ground to fight oppression and effect change. Moreover, in light of the diversity of the experience that the new ethnography wishes to foreground, anthropologists need to consider what provisions will have to be made for interdiscursive unintelligibility or misinterpretation. The traditional ethnographer's translation of other cultures into the discourse of Western social science has long been recognized to be problematic. A text that subtly orchestrates the translation of that experience in the mind of each reader, an interpreter who may be able to draw only on common-sense categories saturated with the assumptions of the Western tradition, is certainly no less so. However brilliant the deconstruction of the text of culture, however eloquent the oral history of the informant, the Other may still be reconstituted in the language of the dominant discourse if there is not an analysis that "regards every discourse as a result of a practice of production which is at once material, discursive, and complex" (Henriques et al. 1984:106). Without a politically reflexive grounding, the Other can be reconstituted too easily as an exotic in danger of being disempowered by that exoticism.

Furthermore, the new ethnography's shift from a scientific to a more literary discourse may constitute a masking and empowering of Western bias, rather than a diffusing of it. When the new ethnography borrows from literary narrative in an effort to rid itself of a unitary, totalizing narrative voice, it turns understandably, if ironically, to modern fiction for its models. The disappearance of the omniscient controlling narrative voice that comments on the lives of all characters and knows their inner secrets is crucial to the modernist transformation of fiction evident in the works of writers such as Joseph Conrad, Henry James, Virginia Woolf, James Joyce, Gertrude Stein, and William Faulkner, a transformation that coincided with the breakdown of colonialism. As critics have pointed out, such authors who experiment with point of view, presenting a seeming jumble of perspectives and subjectivities in a variety of voices, may well be writing no more open texts than classic works in which all action is mediated by a unitary narrative voice (see Barthes 1974; Booth 1961). The literary techniques of fragmentation, metaphor, thematic and verbal echo, repetition, and juxtaposition, which the new ethnography borrows, are all devices through which an author manipulates understanding and response. They function to structure the reader's experience of the apparently discontinuous, illogical, and fragmentary text. Through them, and by refusing to speak his or her views and intentions directly, the author achieves a more complete mastery (Felman 1977:203–7). Anthropologists seeking to write new ethnography and borrowing this range of devices from literature may unknowingly, in the process, pick up literary emphasis on form and the aesthetic of wholeness, both of which constitute traps for the ethnographer. These aesthetic criteria invite the manipulation of narrative devices in polyvocal works, whose apparent cacophony mirrors the diversity and multiplicity of individual and cultural perspectives, to resolve subtly all elements into a coherent and pleasing whole. These narrative devices potentially structure and control as surely as does the narrator of classic works, whether literary, historical, or ethnographic.[11]

These cautions can, of course, be viewed as excessively formalist, as failing to see the new ethnography as more than stylistic innovation. Stephen Tyler, in his incantatory, wildly enthusiastic—if self-contradictory—celebration of new ethnography, labels such a view a "modernist perversion" (1986:129). To him the new ethnographic writing is evocative rather than representational; like ritual or poetry "it makes available through absence what can be conceived but not represented" (123). Indeed, readers wishing to experience the self-congratulatory ideology underlying the new ethnography, unqualified by subtlety or academic caution, should read Tyler's unproblematized claims: that postmodernist ethnography emphasizes "the cooperative and collaborative nature of the fieldwork situation" and "the mutual dialogical production of discourse" (126); that in privileging discourse over text it is concerned "not . . . to make a better representation, but . . . to avoid representation" (128); that it is "the meditative vehicle for a transcendence of time and place" (129). Tyler says that "ethnographic discourse is not part of a project whose aim is to create universal knowledge" (131) but rather the "consumed fragment" of an understanding that is only experienced in the text, the text which is evocative and participatory, bringing the joint work of ethnographer and his native partners together with the hermeneutic process of the reader (129–30).

However, Jonathan Friedman coming at this from a Marxist perspective and Judith Stacey from a feminist one are highly skeptical of the claim that postmodernist revision of ethnographic practice is significantly more than a matter of style. Friedman calls for a dialogue that is intertextual, not merely intratextual, since "it is clearly the case that the single dialogic text may express the attempt to recapture and thus neutralize, once more, the relation between us and them by assuming that the anthropologist can represent the other's voice" (1988:427). Stacey argues that "acknowledging partiality and taking responsibility for authorial construction" are not enough: "The postmodern strategy is an inadequate response to the ethical issues endemic to ethnographic process and product" (1988:26). The new ethnography threatens to subsume the Other either in a manipulative, totalizing form whose politics is masked or in the historically contingent discourse of each reader's response. In their borrowing of techniques from fiction, new ethnographers do not claim to write purely imaginative works. They continue to make some truth claims: their use of dialogue is presented as reflecting their experience in the field and the fragmentation of their texts is presented as mirroring their postmodern condition. As Tyler puts it, "We confirm in our ethnographies our consciousness of the fragmentary nature of the postmodern world, for nothing so well defines *our world* as the absence of a synthesizing allegory" (1986:132, emphasis added).

This is not necessarily true for non-Western males or for all women. The supposed absence of all metanarratives—the experience of helplessness and fragmentation—is the new synthesizing allegory that is being projected onto white women and Third World peoples who have only recently been partially empowered. To the extent that the new ethnography's political strength lies in a social criticism based on the "sophisticated reflection by the anthropologist about herself and her own society that describing an alien culture engenders," as Marcus and Fischer have suggested (1986:4), it is disheartening as anthropology. It has lost its claim to describe the Other and yet seems devoid of the capacity to empower anyone but the writer and the reader for whom it serves as academic collateral or therapy. Anthropology is potentially reduced to an identity ritual for the anthropologist. If the new ethnography is that, then it must be seen as a facet of postmodernism's ultimate defense of the privilege of the traditional subject, even as paradoxically it deconstructs subject status.

While postmodern thinking has indeed invigorated many academic disciplines, anthropology must reconsider the costs of embracing it. Those anthropologists sensitive to the power relations in the ethnographic enterprise who wish to discover ways of confronting them ethically would do better to turn to feminist theory and practice than to postmodernism. Ultimately, the postmodern focus on style and form, regardless of its sophistication, directs our attention away from the fact that ethnography is more than "writing it up." From women's position as Other in a patriarchal culture and from feminists' dialogue and confrontation with diverse groups of women, we have learned to be suspicious of all attempts by members of a dominant group to speak for the oppressed, no matter how eloquently or experimentally. Politically sensitive anthropologists should not be satisfied with exposing power relations in the ethnographic text, if that is indeed what the new ethnography accomplishes, but rather should work to overcome these relations. By turning to postmodernism, they may instead be (unwittingly or not) reinforcing such power relations and preserving their status as anthropologists, as authoritative speakers. Anthropologists may be better able to overcome these power relations by framing research questions according to the desires of the oppressed group, by choosing to do work that Others want and need, by being clear for whom they are writing, and by adopting a feminist political framework that is suspicious of relationships with Others that do not include a close and honest scrutiny of the motivations for research.

Within Western culture, women's position has been paradoxical. Like a Third World person who has been educated at Oxbridge, feminist scholars speak at once as the socially constituted Other and within the dominant discourse, never able to place ourselves wholly or uncritically in either position. Similarly, although ethnographers are speakers of the dominant discourse, they know the experience of otherness, albeit a self-inflicted and temporally limited one, from their time in the field.

They may be able to draw on their experiences as outsiders in that situation to help them clarify their political and personal goals and to set their research agendas. While it is complex and uncomfortable to speak from a position that is neither inside nor outside, it is this position that necessitates that we merge our scholarship with a clear politics to work against the forces of oppression.

NOTES

Reprinted with permission from *Signs: The Journal of Women in Culture and Society* 15 (Autumn 1989). © 1989 by the University of Chicago. We wish to thank Mary Margaret Kellogg for her generous support of the Women's Studies Program at Simon's Rock College of Bard and its Faculty Development Fund. Support from that fund and from Vassar College made it possible for us to present an earlier version of this paper at the Eighty-sixth Annual Meeting of the American Anthropological Association in Chicago, Illinois. We also wish to thank Francis C. Lees for keeping us warm and well fed while we worked, Nancy Hartsock for her inspiration and helpful suggestions, and Alissa Rupp and William Maurer for their assistance.

1. The term *new ethnography* is commonly used to refer to cultural accounts that are reflexive in a sense seldom seen in traditional ethnographic writing. This reflexivity can take the form of identification of the fieldworker as an actor in the ethnographic situation, as in Paul Rabinow's *Reflections on Fieldwork in Morocco* (1977), Barbara Myerhoff's *Number Our Days* (1978), Paul Friedrich's *The Princes of Naranja: An Essay in Anthrohistorical Method* (1986), Marianne Alverson's *Under African Sun* (1987), J. Favret-Saada's *Deadly Words: Witchcraft in the Bocage* (1980), and Manda Cesara's *Reflections of a Woman Anthropologist: No Hiding Places* (1982); it can present a commentary on cultural difference through the highlighting of intersubjective interactions, as in Marjorie Shostak's *Nisa: The Life and Words of a !Kung Woman*(1983), Kevin Dwyer's *Moroccan Dialogues* (1982), and Vincent Crapanzano's *Tuhami: Portrait of a Moroccan* (1980); it can experiment with traditional ethnographic rhetorical forms, as in Edward Schieffelin's *The Sorrow of the Lonely and the Burning of the Dancers* (1976) and Michelle Rosaldo's *Knowledge and Passion: Ilongot Notions of Self and Social Life* (1980); or it can offer a close scrutiny of global systems of domination through the examination of symbolic manifestations in the lives of individuals, as in Michael Taussig's *The Devil and Commodity Fetishism in South America* (1980), June Nash's *We Eat the Mines and the Mines Eat Us: Dependency and Exploitation in Bolivian Tin Mines* (1979), and Gananath Obeyesekere's *Medusa's Hair: An Essay on Personal Symbols and Religious Experience* (1981). In addition, there is a recent movement to read traditional ethnographic texts, such as Bronislaw Malinowski's *Argonauts of the Western Pacific* (1961) and E. E. Evans-Pritchard's *The Nuer* (1940), for their narrative structure or rhetorical style as well as to claim early texts once presented as "mere fiction,"

such as Elenore Smith Bowen's (pseudonym for Laura Bohannan) *Return to Laughter: An Anthropological Novel* (1954) and Gregory Bateson's *Naven: A Survey of the Problems Suggested by a Composite Picture of a Culture of a New Guinea Tribe Drawn from Three Points of View* (1936), as precursors to the "new ethnography." This list is not exhaustive or particularly selective; many of these ethnographies employ several reflexive strategies. There is only limited consensus among people talking about the new ethnography on which works are exemplars of the trend.

2. In their reply to Sangren, Michael Fischer and George Marcus (written with Stephen Tyler) call Sangren's concern an "*obsession* with academic power and status" (1988:426, emphasis added).

3. Craig Owens notes that writing for women requires intellectual cross-dressing: "In order to speak, to represent herself, a woman assumes a masculine position; perhaps that is why femininity is frequently associated with masquerade, with false representation, with simulation and seduction" (1983:59). See also Mary Russo's "Female Grotesques: Carnival and Theory" (1986:213–29). For a broad discussion of the advantages of cross-dressing for women, see Susan Gubar's "Blessings in Disguise: Cross-dressing as Re-dressing for Female Modernists" (1981:477–508). A suspicious look at some male responses to feminist literary criticism in terms of current interest in male cross-dressing, as evidenced by the film *Tootsie*, is Elaine Showalter's "Critical Cross-dressing: Male Feminists and the Woman of the Year" (1983:130-49). Male anxiety about the implications of doing feminist criticism was voiced by Dominick LaCapra in a discussion of his paper "Death in Venice: An Allegory of Reading" at a conference at the Woodrow Wilson Institute entitled Interpreting the Humanities (1986). When asked about gender issues in Mann's story, he replied: "I can't do transvestite criticism like Jonathan Culler," a reference to the chapter "Reading as a Woman" in Culler's *On Deconstruction: Theory and Criticism after Structuralism* (1982:43–64). Freud's similar fear of identification with the feminine is discussed in Charles Bernheimer and Claire Kahane's edited volume *In Dora's Case: Freud-Hysteria-Feminism* (1985).

4. Evelyn Fox Keller has described the recurrent mistranslation of gender and science as women and science, showing how gender questions are considered to be of concern only to women, in "Feminist Perspectives on Science Studies" (1988).

5. This observation, of course, is well known to feminists who have been consistently frustrated by the marginalization of feminist insights (see, for example, Miller 1986).

6. Deborah Gordon (1988) has noted that not only is the critical cosmopolitan "not clearly marked by any 'local' concerns such as gender, race, nationality, etc.," but that "the Greek sophists who are Rabinow's fictive figure for this position were European men."

7. Lois Banner argued that this is the appropriate task for males who are sympathetic to feminism in her response to Peter Gabriel Filene's plenary address "History and Men's History and What's the Difference" at the Con-

ference on the New Gender Scholarship: Women's and Men's Studies, at the University of Southern California, February 1987.

8. Applied anthropologists, like feminist scholars, also frequently participate in collaborative research projects, helping to undermine the traditional, and largely unjustified and false, notion of research and scholarship as the heroic quest by the lone scholar for "truth." Sandra Harding (1986) has recently made the point that this notion often obscures the contributions made by women to the scientific enterprise since what they do, especially in the laboratory, can be dismissed as domestic work in the service of the male scientist.

9. We have chosen to retain the masculine pronoun here and in subsequent parts of the text when referring to individuals steeped in traditional anthropological ideas and practices. As feminist anthropologists have shown, even though anthropology has traditionally included women as researchers, the field has been plagued with androcentric assumptions. See Sally Slocum's "Woman the Gatherer: Male Bias in Anthropology" (1975) for one of the earliest works to expose this bias.

10. On the use of the generic he, see note 9 above. Here we wish to highlight that postmodern ethnographers, like their traditional forebears, speak from the male/dominant position and have seen self-reflection, collaboration, and textual experimentation as "new" only when it has been practiced by men.

11. This has been acknowledged by Clifford in *The Predicament of Culture* (1988) as well as by Geertz in *Works and Lives* (1988) and has been well described by Bruce Kapferer in his review of both books in "The Anthropologist as Hero: Three Exponents of Post-modernist Anthropology." According to Kapferer, "Present attempts to give voice-edited texts of tape recorded interviews, for example—can be made into the vehicle for the ethnographer's own views. The ethnographer hides behind the mask of the other. This could be more insidious than in the less self-conscious ethnography of yore. It can be another mode by which the other is appropriated and controlled" (1988:98).

Tribal Fire and Scribal Ice

Ivan Brady

They who make a practice of comparing human actions are never so perplexed as when they try to piece them together and place them in the same light, for they commonly contradict one another so strangely that it seems impossible they should have come out of the same shop.

—Michel de Montaigne, 1580

Our discourse remains caught between the fire of fieldwork (speaking, being, procreating, describing, kama) and the ice of ethnology (writing, ordering, asceticism, comparing, tapas).

—James A. Boon, 1982

Anthropology's intellectual history suggests that anthropologists are not often given to thinking about thinking in a way that is simultaneously self-conscious and critical. Rarer still is an anthropology that engages the thick philosophies of hermeneutics, structuralism, and literary criticism under the same cover. With the notable exception of recent work by Clifford Geertz, Paul Rabinow, James Clifford, and a few others, anthropology of this rich philosophical sort has been distinctly European, at best piecemeal, and even then more commonly located in departments of literature, religion, and philosophy than in departments claiming anthropology by name.[1] James A. Boon's *Other Tribes, Other Scribes: Symbolic Anthropology in the Comparative Study of Cultures, Histories, Religions, and Texts* (1982) has one foot placed self-consciously in this continental genre and the other placed critically in more parochial anthropology. His interdisciplinary strengths pull the reader through a vast comparative field of little cultural equations and a smaller number of much larger principles concerning the nature and history of ethnographic thinking since the Enlightenment.[2] And his style is as rare as his project: although the text is overcompressed in places, in part because of the huge subject matter, and therefore difficult to read at times, the overall result is an unusually literate and erudite statement about issues central to anthropology's postmodern refiguration of itself as an art and a science.

Having made some preliminary remarks about this project elsewhere,[3] my main purposes here are: (1) to evaluate Boon's arguments about uniformitarian thinking in anthropology; (2) to locate some of the irony, contradiction, and paradox that he has discovered and developed in that framework—in part under cover of the "moiety" value in anthropological debates; and (3) to identify what is structural and hermeneutic in his approach—itself a contradictory combination and a pattern of some consequence for understanding the postmodern predicament of ethnological theory (especially "interpretive" theory) in contemporary anthropology. For context, I shall start by briefly discussing some of the wide interdisciplinary field Boon's project alternately supports and subverts.

The Boat Floweth Over

The hermeneutic idea that all authors, readers, and observers are culturally "situated" works against much of the philosophical framework for being objective in anthropological research and writing. It is also an idea that is central to Boon's beginnings.[4] But it is not the usual stance for text and theory construction in anthropology. The usual stance is one of detached objectivity—a view of the world that has roots in the Enlightenment's search for reductive order in all things, including the ever-unfolding world of other cultures and one that by and large represents the touchstone of "anthropological science" as opposed to, say, "anthropological poetry" or some other more subjectively loaded form of cross-cultural discovery and reporting.[5] It is important for understanding Boon's position to note that conventional structuralism is much more closely aligned with the former than with the latter. Like much of what goes under the heading of "semiotics" and, in a different context, the established run of behaviorism in the social sciences, conventional structuralism is fundamentally positivistic in method and philosophy. The softer approaches of "interpretive" social science incline toward the poetic and can be smuggled under the umbrella of modern hermeneutics. But the history of hermeneutic thought also has a positivistic cant, and the role of self-conscious interpretation in hermeneutic exercises has always been a matter of contention.[6] Being consciously situated as a cultural observer in this context creates a certain amount of theoretical chaos. The outlook from anthropology is equally clouded.

Knowingly costumed by the culture of the maker or not, and much in the spirit of Montaigne's lament, ethnology ordinarily leads its pursuers through an intellectual landscape that is contentious and plural in its arguments about ways to study human beings. The camp banners are truly diverse. One extreme, what might be called (mindless) behaviorism/materialism, for example, shelters the work of many anthropologists and appears to operate on experientially secure ("real") ground. But its failure to examine the organism's "black box" produces a lopsided assessment of biocultural anatomy and the human condition. Material stomachs are presumed to determine behavior by emptying straight into the cultural brain. No feedback of any consequence (or at least none worth savoring) is said to occur. No matter what they think (or think they think), cultures ultimately dance only to tunes played cryptically by deep genes and feeding machines.[7] Or so the story goes. The opposite camp has its own slogans and falls into a different kind of trap: (timeless and disembodied) cerebralism says we are what we think.[8] Stomachs are interesting but irrelevant to the symbolic construction of life. The neighborhood that envelops this camp is less extreme and represents the primary opposition to (mindless) materialism: culture is knowledge—a structured and structuring system of symbols and meanings that is prerequisite to the study of human beings in any other aspect. But there is much disagreement over the degree to which culture in this form has its own organizing momentum and can be isolated from the historical and material circumstances in which it is realized.

The continental banners are philosophically pretty and apply to anthropological thinking in a variety of ways, but they also mark imperfect camps: (Husserlian) phenomenology gives a great beginning and then dies on the vine of immaculate perception; (post-Diltheyan) hermeneutics realistically denies the textual and intellectual freedom claimed by both detached authorship and readership and then spirals into perpetual suspicion as textual meanings peel off only to reveal other more mystifying meanings; (Marx's) Marxism uncovers and insists on recognizing the fleshy hand-to-mind processes and tainting ideology of bourgeois culture for artifact production of any kind, including theoretical texts, but is never quite sure at what point (if ever) the theory sets the knower free from its own context, its own cultural and historical situations; (overdrawn) structuralism formalizes the intellectual bones of the problem in potentially interesting ways but (contrary to much of its rhetoric) kills the historical action of original performance altogether.[9]

No one really knows what to do with the intellectual mix these various interests present in relation to one another. So, caught in the crossfire without secure paradigms, power claims privilege more often than the noble vice versa: the theory with the biggest congregation, the sharpest wit, the most intimidating costumes, and the puffiest castles arbitrarily claims Essence and Truth. Similarly, the need for analytic closure sometimes overshadows the essential contestability of ethnographic results; *ceteris paribus* gets lost in footnotes, exceptions are left on the cutting room floor, and some thinkers begin to etch their insecure results in stone, only to become fair game for ambitious skeptics with hammers.[10]

Certainly not all of the enterprise is so dreary, so wanting in secure outcome. But intellectual progress in the study of humanity has been fitful, changing notoriously with the times. It seems fair to assert that, despite Montaigne's learned complaint more than four hundred years ago and some progress along the way, nothing agreeable is easily developed—or lasts very long—in the analytic wonderland we call anthropology. That is both its economy and its history. Simply lamenting this pattern for its apparent lack of permanence or unity, however, does little to resolve the problem. It may in fact obscure important points about the structural integration of diversity and the historicity of Truth. Perhaps that is the normal cost of things not easily seen wherever observers in the service of "objectivity" remove themselves from the analytic equations they use to scrutinize Others. It is at least something positivism insists on wherever it obtains, even (or especially) in the transcendental designs of structuralist thinking. Mediating this problem from the vantage point of a culturally and (though he does not emphasize it) materially situated observer who calculates the relativity and historicity of all knowledge, Boon gives us structural hermeneutics—with a difference.

Structural Hermeneutics—with a Difference

Other Tribes is an ambitious project in symbolic anthropology. It is aimed creatively at the study of meaning in anthropological accounts, and that is necessarily a problem of hermeneutics and history. Boon makes it more obviously structural as well. Just as he once turned structuralism (in relation to symbolism) on itself as subject and method (Boon 1972), here he turns hermeneutic and structuralist method on ethnology and its texts, which, with a few tricks, is another way of turning ethnology on itself. This turn of platform raises a special variety of interpretive problems (see Dreyfus and Rabinow 1982:xv-xxiii; Feld 1982; Seung 1982).

Faced with seemingly unsolvable difficulties in the search for truth and order in surface structure—in the sometimes dizzying symbolic and semantic complexities of texts, totems, and everyday practices, among other possibilities—scholars have forever looked deeper for that elusive "reality beyond appearance," for transcendental qualities in the things and patterns of our lives. In hermeneutics (since Heidegger), the search for such truth has taken a couple of important forms of special interest to anthropology. One is what Ricoeur calls the "hermeneutics of suspicion," where the "deep" meaning in texts is thought to be purposefully hidden and is in some ways recoverable through interpretation, but never absolutely. Interpretations are necessarily a cover and stimulus for other interpretations, and so forth. Another form, which Dreyfus and Rabinow call the hermeneutics of "everyday life," rests in part on the extension of the concept of text as a written cultural artifact to cultural practices of any kind.[11] In this form of hermeneutic inquiry unintentionally hidden meanings are not only recoverable but ought to be recognizable to the participants once pointed out to them (see Dreyfus and Rabinow 1982:xviii–xix; cf. Certeau 1984); it is also presumed that the wider system of symbols and meanings in which such particulars obtain can in some coherent way be rendered (and "read") ethnographically (see Geertz 1973, 1983).

In structuralism (since Saussure) the most conspicuous searches for order have been for the "grammars" (the logical patterns and rules) of cognitive structuring in language (Chomsky), in human maturation (Piaget), in cultural practices such as totemism and myth (Lévi-Strauss), and in literary theory and stylistics (Barthes, Todorov, etc.—see Howard 1982:xiv). By seeking similar patterns of meaning as the product of shared systems of signification as they obtain in anthropological texts, Boon makes his already hermeneutic project both semiotic and structural. And that opens the door to a sometimes hotly contested variety of possible contradictions in method, theory, and interpretive results. In the broad disciplinary sense of methods applied to the same subject matter, Ruwet's (1963:567–68) summary of the limitations of each perspective is pithy and to the point: "structural analysis necessarily implies an abstraction, and thus in a sense an impoverishment; while hermeneutic interpretation, lacking distance in regards to its object, is incapable of achieving a general theory, of discerning in its object, a transformation of other objects belonging to the same ensemble" (Boon's translation, 1972:120). In a more personal sense, the reality for an anthropologist caught between the cracks, Feld (1982:15) says, is that "in one instance the [observer] is thought of as decoder and translator and in the other as experiencer and interpreter."

None of this deters Boon. Quite to the contrary, he exploits the

tensions and self-contradictions of structural and hermeneutic alignments as well as their relationships to a host of other related philosophical, anthropological, and linguistic problems. The challenge of
playing in this heavily mined field, Feld (1982:15) suggests, is "to integrate the study of how symbols are logically connected with the study
of how they are formulated and performed in cultural experience."
Boon agrees, but he also resists any movement toward naive syntheses
in the process. Synthetic compromises are not sought as solutions.
They, too, are terms in wider cultural and symbolic equations and must
be understood in that capacity, in *their* mutually constructive relations
of opposition, parallelism, and negation. Nothing is innocent, everything potentially "signifies," even the tools we use to study cross-cultural
thought (1982:152). Boon thus asks for consciousness of what we are
thinking *with* as well as what we are thinking *about*, and that has
special complications of its own as a principle of analysis.[12]

We are in this context being "structural" when we look for the
grammar or underlying organizational logic of meaningful human behavior in language or other cultural forms; we are being "hermeneutic"
when we look for meaning in actions, or the products of action,
themselves. But it is equally important to recognize that in some respects
no synthesis (naive or otherwise) is needed. Neither stance completely
excludes the other. They are interdependent perspectives. In fact, structural theory and hermeneutic thought not only agree in a number of
ways (Hoy 1978:144; see also Boon 1982:138), the latter presupposes
much of the development of the former: "There can be no structural
analysis . . . without a hermeneutically enlightened comprehension of
the transfer of meaning (without 'metaphor,' without [translation]),
without this indirect meaning—attribution, which constitutes the semantic field, from which one then distils structural homologies" (Ricoeur, as quoted in Bleicher 1980:226; see also Maxwell 1984:264–
66). Working in the other direction, structural analysis can provide
some distancing from the object of analysis that does not necessarily
destroy all of its extant properties (Bleicher 1980:227). It can provide,
in other words, a platform for generalizing about culture in a way that
does not totally impoverish what one might discover and defend hermeneutically from the same sources. Structural understanding is also
essential to the "re-aquisition of meaning," to any "re-thinking" or
"re-claiming" of existing texts and ideas in cultural analysis (Bleicher
1980:227; see also Barthes 1973:58; Abel 1980:44), and this argument,
in turn, may be "extrapolated to cover all understanding of texts in
which both 'sense' and 'event' are joined in mutually enhancing harmony" (Bleicher 1980:227). If we include the engaged harmony (ho-

mology) of disagreement and mutually constructive doubt—the "moiety" value of perpetually joined and mutually constructive opposition—the self-conscious pursuit of "sense" and "event" in ethnographic thought might be put forth as the best measure of Boon's entire project, as its *raison d' être*.

These conflicts also set structural thinking against the role of the historical in culture. But that liability is often exaggerated in the literature (cf. Seung 1982:20; Eagleton 1983:104ff.). Boon (1984:811) argues that "no serious structuralism has ever sought to ignore or to purge historical evidence (historical consciousness is another matter)." One can also argue (via Lévi-Strauss and Boon) that ethnology and history are "disciplinary moieties in mutual need of each other" and that "through famous formulations of *langue/parole* and synchrony/ diachrony, structuralists have converted the subject matter of both history and ethnology to transforming variations rather than linear, purposive development" (Boon 1984:811). Hermeneutics, for its part, offers even less escape from the historical. It takes the history "of" and "in" texts as its paradigm case. Indeed, "the methodological questions raised in hermeneutics . . . probe into the very possibility of thinking historically" (Hoy 1978:7; see also Crapanzano 1977:69; Bleicher 1980:16ff.). But Boon writes that hermeneutic interpretation in anthropology

> involves more than History (whether defined religiously or philosophically) pulling itself away from its own would-be presence and interpreters striving to obliterate the distance between the self and the lost. Anthropology offers an enriched field of multiple languages and plural cultures. Again, a hermeneutics appropriate to plural cultures and histories brushes alongside negative dialectics whose nemesis is standardized (Enlightened) uniformity and whose circles or spirals of interpretation (versus explanation) are nothing if not bumpy. Any anthropological hermeneutics becomes—like anthropology's social theory—a hermeneutics with a difference. (1982:234)

To Boon this is also structuralism with a difference—in fact a "hermeneutic-cum-structuralist cross-cultural reading of structuralism" with a difference (see Boon 1982:152; Bleicher 1980:222ff.). And the order is not accidental. Structural thinking can be thought of roughly as the genealogy function for what is hermeneutic in interpretation. It is discovered (or invented) approximately as an analytic and transformative addition to what is already known (or believed to be known), and it is used strategically in interpretations of the universe of cultural discourse much as one might use a genealogical grid (cf. Polanyi and Prosch 1975:177–78). Hermeneutic and structural processes in this sense both figure fundamentally in the ordinary logic and semantic processes of human understanding. But hermeneutic problems embody the "chicken and egg" dilemma of meaning that is prerequisite to the acquisition of other meaning. So structures brought to mind in analysis would seem to be carved cognitively and culturally out of something resembling a hermeneutic nexus.

These are special issues of cultural transformation and semiotic convertibility and are important to Boon for those reasons. But he avoids the narrow-minded hermeticisms that have traditionally characterized efforts to isolate them.[13] He finds structures and their transformations in the coda of underlying rules as they get played out in the complexities of everyday performance, as might be expected. He also finds them in the theories invented to account for their playing out—more of the problem of what we are thinking *with* as well as what we are thinking *about*. He carries this metaphase through studies of some easily discovered and some other more cleverly concealed orders of cultural existence (Ours and Theirs) and ends up arguing that theories of cultures, like cultures themselves, are caught up in a multidimensional cultural and historical field of binary oppositions, parallelisms, and redundancies that gravitate toward dissolution and "nothingness" in the long run. Dialectical transformations in the relationships and interaction of interpretations and their objects over time give these systems both change and stability.[14] Overall this field represents to Boon the stuff of "cultural semiotics," which, he insists, to be successful analytically must also be managed with a difference: it "must include a view of itself," and that view "must be reflexive" (1982:235).

Said simply, hermeneutics is to everyone the study of meaning in texts. Semiotics is to Boon the *comparative* study of meaning in texts or any other cultural form and in this capacity functions as the clearinghouse term for his project (1982:115–16). It mediates between hermeneutics and structuralism for him, but the connection is uneven. Resembling the structuralism/hermeneutics relation, but for different reasons, sometimes the opposite reasons, semiology and structuralism are in fact inseparable, for "in studying signs one must investigate the system of relations that enables meaning to be produced and, reciprocally, one can only determine what are the pertinent relations among items by considering them as signs" (Culler 1975:4). Through such linkages Boon pits meaning against meaning, text against text, and self-consciously turns his semiology on itself; he tracks and criticizes the formalism-structuralism of anthropology, linguistics, literary theory, and related interests as it might apply to itself in those contexts and to ethnology. His theoretical base is thus, like Lévi-Strauss's, plainly Saussurean in arguing that the value of signs in language and culture is established through mutual opposition and negation. It also resembles Lévi-Strauss's work in other ways. By putting anthropology somewhat in the place of myth in Lévi-Strauss's analysis, Boon isolates and analyzes its underpinnings as a "code" of perception, information, and explanation about the nature of the world and our place in it. But he does not rest there and nowhere does he argue for simple models of signification (cf. Culler 1975:15; Seung 1982:8ff.).

Because the relationship between the knower and the known is constructive, the context of signification and communication is critical for understanding and interpreting texts or anything else. The context Boon has in mind is the field of contrasting symbolic relations itself as nested further in "psychological, demographic, and environmental conditions" (1982:121). Cultural meaning is in this case asserted to be, paradoxically, "both context-laden and context-convertible." That is a fact assured by the functions of symbols as key devices in cultural systems: "Thanks to symbols, cultural meanings are rich, deep, multivocal, many layered, highly wrought, and shared but also rarifiable, subject to abstraction, exportable, often communicated." The meanings are in this sense "not substantively shared but rather *exchanged*" (121). Reaching deeper in this same pattern of symbolic variability, Boon suggests that the paradox of experience given by symbols is carried by the equation: "same stimulus (presumably), variable responses (culturally)" (121). The patterns of systems of symbols and meanings are thus not fixed as monoliths anywhere. As already noted, they change dialectically over time.

So Boon is not necesssarily being antisystem by theoretically opening up to influence from the world of action what was hermetic to Saussure (or Chomsky or Lévi-Strauss). He is just enlarging the scope of systemic analysis (albeit in a way that runs a high risk of analytic chaos). He sees the network of symbols and social practices as systems in a cultural field that both signify and communicate and are articulated in many ways. He reaches beyond unrealistically introverted models of *langue* as a closed system of signs whose meanings are derived only in relation to another. He sees a hierarchy of relations for every sign—a multi-tiered context of contrasts that far exceeds simple binary oppositions in determining what signs are in relation to what they are not, and, in its dialectics, might in fact be generalizable to whole cultural systems. In this he follows Ricoeur and others by considering the meaning-contexts and meaning-constituents of both structure and event. By not being blind to the historicity of forms, he is able to follow the hermeneutic thrust of Nietzsche, Marx, Freud, and others in puzzling over the power and intentions of our "historical interlocutors," as Levine (1985:145) refers to them. And, while agreeing that "a sense of discovering and de-constructing may give us a fleeting sense of latency and hiddenness," Boon joins Foucault and Derrida in resisting much of the "lure of commentary that claims to convert surface to depth" (Levine 1985:145), at least insofar as such conversions are said to reveal monolithic structures (cf. Boon 1982:137).

Insofar as Boon is concerned both with order in symbolic life and with giving meaningfully enriching interpretations to the cultural and historical circumstances that render the symbols themselves meaningful—especially in the production of ethnographic thought and in "meta-interpretations" of it—the yield on this level is properly called "structural hermeneutics." But several versions of this are possible (see Howard 1982:xiv; Margolin 1978; Ricoeur 1979). In Boon's writing the result closely resembles "interpretive analytics," what Dreyfus and Rabinow (1982:183) have called Foucault's method for studying "human seriousness and meaning." Interpretive analytics does not rely on privileged access of the interpreter to "deep meaning, a unified subject, [or] signification rooted in nature" (183). It avoids many of the pitfalls of parochial structuralism and the hermeneutics of suspicion while drawing distinct advantages from both. Foucault accordingly resisted the label of structuralism right up to the time of his death. His willingness to explore new avenues of discovery and the diversity of topics that flowed bountifully from his almost unstumpable curiosity make him less conspicuously a structuralist than Boon (see Dreyfus and Rabinow 1982; Lemert and Gillan 1982; Rabinow 1984). Strictly interpreted, however, the label is also too confining for Boon.

Any such argument should also consider the work of the literary critic Roland Barthes, and Boon does so in several parts of his book. Barthes is often called a "structuralist," but, like Foucault, he generally resisted the term for all its unwanted baggage. Forming opposition to Lévi-Strauss on several levels, the works of Barthes and Foucault give analytic and ontological privilege to *parole* over *langue*—to the historical action of discourse and performance over the synchronic structure of language—but, like Boon, not exclusively. Foucault's epistémè guides behavior but is not a conscious model, so there is some special appeal to Lévi-Straussian structuralism—and to Boon—in it. Barthes, on the other hand, recognized in his popular *Mythologies* (and elsewhere) that one is "dealing with two different types of manifestation: form has a literal and immediate presence and it is extended" (1972:121). And he moved clearly in opposition to both the hermeneutics of suspicion and to Lévi-Strauss on the subject of myth: "However paradoxical it may seem, *myth hides nothing*: its function is to distort, not to make disappear. There is no latency of the concept in relation to the form: there is no need of an unconscious in order to explain myth" (121). This is to Sontag (1982:xvii) the recycling of an "aesthete's" principal thesis: "surface is as telling as depth."¹⁵ Moreover, in the extreme, "the aesthete position not only regards the notions of depth, of hiddenness, as a mystification, a lie, but opposes the very idea of antithesis"; and "to speak of depth and surfaces is already to misrepresent the aesthetic view of the world—to reiterate a duality, like that of form and content, it precisely denies" (Sontag 1982:xxviii; see also Scholes 1974; Harland 1987).

Boon would agree with the argument that surface can be as telling as depth in cultural analysis, but for almost the opposite reasons. One is that they say different things: "context and performance, just like everything else, must be coded at the *langue* level (the level of the conditionally possible) if they are to be transmitted to the next generation, or to outsiders, including linguists or anthropologists" (1982:136–37). But the delivery of such structures as performance is a transformation of meaning and levels. He would also insist on recognizing the existence of the apposition itself as a cultural construct and on exploring the historical, semantic, and theoretical *relation* between the two terms in anthropology and its texts (116). He concludes that "we cannot accede to a final semiotics by ever elaborating models of communication events. Rather, playing Saussure and Peirce off against each other returns us to that fundamental paradox of context-laden (Peirce) *plus* context-convertible (Saussure) that underlies semiotic meaning" (137). The argument that cultural meanings are in this way "both deep and exportable" thus opens some important questions about pointing culture theory "away from generative transformational linguistic models towards dialectics, or metacommentary, or whatever we call that cultural capacity for systems of meaning (language included) to keep one step removed from themselves" (137).¹⁶

Maneuvering in this mix as it occurs in the world of anthropological texts—where, to Boon, as I have already said, "everything threatens to signify" (152)—he sees a hologram of interconnections. The terrain he maps is filled with the deep cultural tracks and complex artifacts of anthropological writers and readers. He isolates and analyzes systems of systems and relations of relations (including those of form and content, product and process, syntax and semantics) as they are nested in an equally complex range of historical and theoretical contexts. He seeks the comparative discovery of order in somewhat unexpected encounters of otherwise familiar language, thought, and objects (see especially pp. 152–53, 213–17, 236–37) in the arts and sciences of several disciplines. If one were to chart these oppositions in proper structuralist style the resulting map would be dizzying and unnecesarily destructive of cultural context. Fortunately, Boon connects the parts, even (on every other breath) as he raises new ones in a raveling complexity. Said structurally, we learn that Durkheim : Weber :: Jajmani : Dumont :: hierarchy : low status :: class : totemism :: music, and so on. Much to read, much to consider. And although a coherent reading comes through with patience, one can argue securely from this viewpoint that structural problems are unrealistically overdrawn when they are locked away from performance. They are necessarily part of a larger set of cultural and material circumstances. They need not be reduced to pure logics through decoding and translation or in other ways rendered impervious to experience. Such reductions are useful for certain purposes. But, besides being mostly unnecessary, they introduce a host of empirical distortions to cultural studies that can neither be identified nor corrected easily, at least not without refined reconstructions of context—the data for which are generally not reported and remain undiscoverable by readers from afar.

Anthropology Is Genre-laden

Boon's concern with the fact that anthropology anchors itself and its study of the diversity of human meaning "in the field" and that it expresses itself through writing makes *Other Tribes* an especially timely project.[17] He knows what some other anthropologists have begun to take quite seriously: ethnographic experience is gained primarily through fieldwork; interpretations of it, however, are conveyed primarily through inscription in books, "at a symbolic remove from whatever immediacy or presence ethnography presumes to recall" (1982:20; see also Crapanzano 1977; Marcus 1980; Porter 1984; Marcus and Fischer 1986; Clifford and Marcus 1986; Clifford 1988; Geertz 1988). Elaborating this point, Boon (1982:20) says: "the literary analogy acknowledges that living cultures in anthropology are inherently written, inscribed; how else could we 'know' them? What anthropologist, furthermore, would deny that writing—literature, ethnographic detail, ethnological generalization—is constrained by conventions that at their fullest extent we call cultures?"[18] Fieldwork itself and the act of its inscription are thus circumstances that necessarily soak the anthropological effort with cultural conventions, only some of which are recoverable in analysis and not all of which are easily identified in cross-cultural encounters.

By interpreting more than just the "cultural logics" that ethnographers have put forth in their texts, by clinging to the metaphors they use to describe the Others of their experience (cf. Dening 1980:44, 86–87; Brady 1982a; Foster 1982), and by reaching beyond structures of significance to include their social import and history, Boon brings his project full circle, for the wider nesting of meaning and action is the context for ferreting out the structural relations of interest to the project in the first place.[19] Each text encountered in the net of this hermeneutic spiral is conventionalized discourse transformed to writing and therefore bound to particular culture content and culturally defined space and time that cannot be read perfectly, either in its own right or straightforwardly as exemplar of the cultural systems in which it is found. That holds even with knowledge of the cultural rules and material circumstances that underwrite the text's construction: readers are active agents, creative in their appropriations (see Culler 1975; Eco 1979; Eagleton 1983). Beyond that, since productions of cultural constructs (as texts or any other form, including myth) contain within themselves the possibilities of "re-productive" change in enactment, that is, the seeds of their own dialectical transformations (see Sahlins 1981, 1985), interpretations must allow for considerable distortion of their forms and historical contexts in the long run.

There are various other author, reader, and observer puzzles that intrude on the meanings of cultural expressions in ways that range from simple to unfathomable (see Hirsch 1976; Bauman 1978; Hoy 1978; Rabinow and Sullivan 1979; Bleicher 1980; Howard 1982; Bernstein 1983). But the argument that authors and readers are culturally situated has a special place in this milieu. The conventional stance for launching a text, for example, is to deny (or disregard) the premise that text and maker are intersubjectively and inextricably bound to each other by cultural context and history. Stitched and trimmed, the text emerges—monsterlike—as an independent artifact of mind. But the economy of politics in such arrangements hides theory makers (ethnographers and their interpreters) behind a false dichotomy of thinkers and thoughts, thereby creating only an illusion of relatively unsituated and unmotivated argument. A quandary follows: denying the fiction of disinterested detachment reveals a distortion of empirical reality and increases the argument's contestability; keeping it supports a claim to "science" in text production and gives individual projects greater focus through the shortcut of *ceteris paribus* but cannot guarantee a higher or more satisfying intellectual yield for the effort. Boon requires that this discrepancy somehow be accounted for in endeavors to "inscribe" Others—a matter to which I shall return in a moment.

Boon also makes the case that ethnography is necessarily exaggerated in its cultural appropriations, thereby compounding further the "perfect vision" issue of objective readers, writers, and observers, irrespective of their analytic persuasions. But he suggests that such exaggeration ("ethnographic hyperbole") can be turned on its head and used to advantage in the development of self-conscious science. The exaggeration of cultures, in other words, is exploitable as semiotic method. Done conscientiously, it allows for a special recognition and interpretation of the differences we perceive from Own to Other. It points to the fact that Truth in ethnographic accounts is less discovered than invented, that ethnographic Others are always in part exaggerated creatures of our own surmise. And it thereby presents an opportunity to "better appreciate how conceptualizations of the exotic and the domestic—even their most basic institutions—are inextricably intertwined" (1982:154).[20]

Noting that no ethnography can escape these issues legitimately, Boon faces them directly. He challenges the variously projected and inscribed meanings of written anthropological texts in relation to their unwritten cultural connections. He is concerned to reveal both the logical and epistemological arrangement of the meaningful parts and the meaningful parts of the logical arrangements of these texts over time. He seeks the discovery of meaning and cultural instructions for interpretation in ethnological analysis and the symbolic forms it contains. The idea is to do so in a way that enlarges our interpretations of Others reflexively—that improves understanding of Ourselves in relation to these same Others and the things we write about them. Together, these interests push the project into "intertextual" space (shades of Barthes and Bakhtin) that: (1) links texts to other texts as layers of culture and history; (2) counterposes them as statements about the cultures that produce them and the cultures they purport to represent; and, as a matter of some analytic frustration, (3) fosters perpetual interpretation by giving up no final reading (no "last text") and granting absolute privilege to no particular language of discourse or analysis. It follows that, no matter how structural its bones or hermeneutic its wrappings, this analytic space is not properly exhausted by any conventional "ism." Therein lies a struggle between what are in the upshot of Boon's thesis, and in the long run of debate in anthropology, philosophies of art and science.

Should Anthropology Fight or Marry?

Boon's enlarged structuralism is ever-mindful of the values and tensions of juxtaposing art and science, and it plays them out in practical ways under the headings of language and culture. In fact, generalizing from its particulars for a moment, *Other Tribes* begs a question that has always divided anthropology as the most scientific of the humanities and the most humanistic of the sciences: in an analytic world over-poetized to some and overscientized to others, can there be any agreeable Truth? The answers are hermeneutic and epistemological (not to mention insecure). The overriding problems are structural, historical, cultural, and diverse in their ramifications. More important, drawn through the structural logics of Boon's project, the question itself shows all the earmarks of a *bricoleur's* dream: a *relation* of contradiction between two elements of apparently great consequence and scope in the modern world—art and science.

Lifted carefully from the dizzying complexities of action and everyday life, a large-minded structuralist can see the opposition: art and science are set off like Saussurean moieties in a marked opposition of signs and interests. Not knowing whether to fight or marry in the long run, the proponents of each camp resist a permanent solution because the relationship in its opposition is everything worth fighting/marrying for: a perpetual source of identity. Each special interest emerges as an entity in contrast with the other—in differential or positional meaning in relation to each other—and in relation to a larger system of cultural differences.[21] By fighting *and* marrying in some strained combination (among other possibilities), the contradictions of identity and interest are maintained. Art and science in this sense, one might say, "need each other to set themselves in mutually constructive doubt" (Boon 1984:809). This is an alignment of some unexpected consequence, if anthropology's frequent calls for integrating its art(s) and science(s) can be taken seriously.[22] Contrary to uniformitarian wisdom and the would-be "lumpers" of conflicting interests, however, the only real danger from this structuralist's perspective is the ironic (and vaguely oxymoronic) one that, through some powerful elevation, science and art in anthropology *will be* collapsed into categorical homogeneity and singularity of purpose—perhaps only to be resuscitated into a system of oppositions on other levels of contrast as "science-art" versus "religion-truth," or something, but collapsed, nonetheless, at a cost to the original alignments of people, resources, and the cultural categories assigned to both.

A long stare into this anthropological mirror puts new light on some old contests and raises important questions: with such productive tensions institutionalized, valued as life-giving in their opposition as mutually determining differences and conventionally reproduced over time, how could there be any uniform solution to the kind of conflict we find between art and science in anthropology?[23] Or, for that matter, between Marxism, mindless materialism, structuralism, or any other combination of "isms"? What is the reality of practice claimed by one to the exclusion of the other? Half a moiety? Why seek a transformation to homogeneous interests and categories in the first place? Whose truth? Whose camp? How do we decide? Where do we go from here? As *bricoleur,* Boon has a map and a plan—even if the trail is tough to follow.

Artful-Science: The Bricoleuring of Symbolic Forms

It should be obvious by now that Boon's response to the challenge of this enormous and complex subject matter is eclectic. His project is structural, hermeneutic, and more. It is informed by contemporary hermeneutics and, with varying degrees of acceptability, by French structuralism. It is also informed by literary and intellectual history, linguistics, the sociology of religion, comparative mythology, and his own energetic fieldwork. And it is integrated most of all, as I have said, by a sense of semiotics as the comparative study of meaning in texts. The result, however, is not parochially any of these things, even as it manifests some of all of them. It is a constructive unearthing of the study of meaning—structuralism tempered by history, constrained by literary criticism, and so on, but otherwise unleashed as comparative method.

One tightly argued effect of this effort is to show that, in the hands of an expert *bricoleur*/critic (the "anthropologist of symbolic forms"), structuralism is not only not dead (cf. Rabinow and Sullivan 1979:11; Kurzweil 1980; Clarke 1981; Pace 1983), it thrives in the marrow of our greatest perplexities wherever humans study other humans, that is, culturally in the roots of ethnological thinking, analytically in the hermeneutics of cultural texts, and perhaps even more fundamentally in the systems of symbols and meanings that define for us the nature of the world and our place in it. That in itself admits various kinds of scientific possibilities to what otherwise might remain a singularly uncomparative playground for the interpretation of anthropological texts. But none of these possibilities are easily realized by conventional social science. Truth is not "given" freely in any experience. It must be ferreted out of the fabric of culture and interpreted—comparatively: "Indeed, without comparative analytic frameworks, every culture, whatever its 'genius', remains impenetrable."[24] "Such are," Boon adds rhetorically, "the dilemmas of the anthropologist of symbolic forms" (1982:ix).

Much like Foucault, most hermeneuticists since Heidegger, and especially Rorty (1979) with his pragmatic criticism of philosophic discourse and its pretentions, Boon seeks to unmask various forms of anthropological discourse that pretend to have uniformitarian Truth and privileged vision (the impossibilities of "mirror of nature minds") under control. Insisting on our situatedness is another way of denying an Archimedean vantage point beyond culture and time that positivism, in its extreme, must control to rise above (or dive beneath?) the subjectivities it so often decries as irrelevant to analysis or expungeable through proper method. But this is not an argument to abandon the enterprise. None of this is to say that empirical generalizations are somehow to be ruled out just because our inquiry is symbolically loaded, culturally situated, and necessarily imperfect in its results.[25] It is only an argument to explore anthropology critically and strengthen it where possible. As Boon says, invoking a simple but consequential relativism not ordinarily applied to the "knowers" of anthropological science:

> Knowledge of other cultures and eras depends on the cultures and eras doing the knowing. This fact should not obstruct but inform comparative anthropology throughout history. Because these limits cannot be transcended, they must be incorporated in our theories—and what better place to acknowledge them than in the history of cultures that imperfectly understand each other? The same limits might also give pause to message senders of all eras, including our own, by allowing us to recognize ourselves as not-inevitable. It is the mysteriously durable Enlightenment dream of direct, uniform knowledge communicated easily—independent of cultures, eras (or galaxies)—that certain schools of anthropological interpretation salutarily doubt. (1982:45)

Epistemic genres and endless texts pose inescapable problems for us as anthropological fieldworkers and writers, to be sure. But it is important to note that no controversy easily (or ordinarily) addressed by arch-positivists is acquitted by that knowledge. The effect is more the opposite. Saddled with a bundle of uncloseable art and roped in by so much that is hermeneutic, Boon knows that many of the people who claim a purer form of ethnographic science will object: "if anthropology is as genre-laden as literature, what becomes of the issues of falsifiability and accuracy?" One possible answer: the standardization of such things as "functionalist fieldwork and monograph writing into 'normal' anthropological science does not mean that the standards [are] natural or objective; it means, rather, that they [are] consensual: disciplinary 'social facts' " (1982:20). "Like cultures and languages themselves," the issues of science in anthropological research are "complexly conventionalized" (20). Theory production (including its constitutional problems of argument form and evidence rules) is thus situated and relative, not naked and free. It is enfranchised culturally as "text."

This insistence on boundedness, diversity, and relativity does not mean, of course, as some wild-eyed relativist might claim, that all points of view are equally valuable.[26] Rather, the argument is simply that: (1) cultures are various and so are our vantage points for studying them; (2) since what flows between anthropology and its object is inherently contestable by being culturally and conventionally loaded, a defensible stance should at minimum be able to: (a) specify a coherent motivation for engaging in anthropological observation in the first place; (b) justify its Truth claims in full view of the reciprocal semantic and empirical flow from observer to observed; and, (c) speak satisfactorily to the larger job being done intellectually and philosophically by the project as a whole. Naive positivism and related exclusionary dogma cannot survive as satisfactory argument under this scrutiny.[27] Montaigne's lament was also loaded against this diversity of thought and object; it was looking for (but predated to some extent) the narrow uniformitarianism that Boon criticizes. And Boon may have exaggerated the degree to which this uniformitarian outlook actually dominates Western thought today, including anthropology. But he understands fully that his text lies within another text, that his theories must also apply to himself (and to us) as maker and "Being-in-the-World," and that is not by any stretch Enlightenment naïveté.[28]

Semiotics and Paradox—Again

By adding expert insight on semiotic structuralism to a cogent sense of theory as text and culture history as dialectical situation, Boon also adds great potential for obfuscation.[29] Indeed, a major liability of semiotics in general is the impenetrable semiospeak that often accompanies it. Mixing hermeneutic and structuralist thought in any formal analytic capacity is asking much of the reader in the first place. Mediating that mix formally through a screen of semiotics, as Boon does, runs a higher risk of being misunderstood. The incompatibilities can be overwhelming, as Eagleton (1983:198) says in a comparable context: "However generously liberal-minded we aim to be, trying to combine structuralism, phenomenology and psychoanalysis is more likely to lead to a nervous breakdown than to a brilliant literary career [cf. Ricoeur 1983]. Those critics who parade their pluralism are usually able to do so because the different methods they have in mind are not all that different in the end . . . [and] some of these 'methods' are hardly methods at all." But Boon has a better frame than most: semiotics is field; structuralism is method; hermeneutics is inevitable. He is also sensitive to the phlegm of semiospeak.

Since none of these things emerge freely or unambiguously in analysis, given that "cultures interpenetrate symbolically, as they are constituted," and knowing that the problem must be comparative in its framework, Boon asks in his preface: "How can I inscribe the power of symbol systems to establish cultures that appear intellectually consistent, emotionally compelling, and convincing even as they change? How can I demonstrate that the difference between any two human languages, and cultures, is as intriguing as the possibility that chimpanzees, for example, might have language? ... How can I use the somber-sounding analytic distinctions like arbitrary/motivated, conventional/constitutive, models of/for, without reducing cultures to numbing jargon?" (1982:ix). He manages to get through that danger admirably but not without difficulty. The fact that his own thesis signifies self-consciously in a cultural field and is itself open to historical change complicates matters. Fortunately, it does not also conceal overstated conclusions: "The book's fluid discussion of fieldwork values, historical hermeneutics, comparative typologies, contemporary semiotics, and exotic societies and texts remains suggestive at best." His goal is "to provide convincing examples of the interrelationship of these concerns" (xi).

In that connection, in keeping with the post-structuralist, deconstructionist trends of modern philosophy and avant-garde social science (via Jacques Derrida, Adorno's negative dialectics, etc.), and very un-Enlightenment-like, Boon argues that approaches to the study of culture by semioticians and linguists have managed to render change intelligible by renouncing beliefs that "a purposive direction underlies the history of language" and culture and that semiotic approaches in general give greater favor to views of "systematic diversity, enriched translations, and comparative interpretations" (x). Part 2 of *Other Tribes* is especially critical of "Enlightenment theories of society and diversity that," through their simple "formulas and grammarlike abstraction," manage to "avoid recognizing the interplay of ideal/actual/negative in social orders, both their own and others" (52). Boon opposes "to such views arguments that the apparently simplest and the most exotic societies are, like all systems of signs and symbols, self-contradictory" (52).

The case for the success of this semiology (indeed, for the book as a whole) depends to a large extent on a complicated deconstructive logic and reflexivity. At one point (46), for example, Boon argues that "by cutting both Patagonians and the Enlightenment down to comparative size, we may (Enlightenment-like?) outgrow superstitions of uniform, unadulterated objectivity across cultures." The layered dialectics of such thinking are likely to drive less structural readers into frustration.[30] The Enlightenment's analytic baggage is both used and hoisted on its own petard in a manner that is self-confirming and denying and never exactly a tautology—just a complicated dialectical progression of levels of evidence, oppositions, and interpretations that teases irony to its limits. Like cultures, moieties, languages, written texts, discursive arguments, "artful-science," and symbolic constructions in general, such statements admit themselves as cultural constructs into the realm of the contingent. The fact that they incline "toward an implicit negativity"—perhaps toward their "opposites," more completely their "undoing," or simply "what they are not" (see especially chapters 3–4)—means that perfect knowledge has no chance in this environment; paradox does.[31] Boon writes:

> The extent to which Enlightenment expectations persist in anthropology is apparent from high hopes (1) that our thus-far inferior science shall soon achieve paradigm breakthrough into genuine experimental falsifiability, firm correlations, prediction, and sound application; and (2) that anthropology and history will one day merge into regnant objectivity—and its moral equivalent "tolerance"—in human affairs. Well-meaning visionaries go so far as to anticipate, through anthropology, emancipation into "empathetic and comparative appreciation of human solidarity in cultural difference": "the comparative understanding of others contributes to self-awareness; self-understanding, in turn, allows for self-reflection and (*partial*) self-emancipation; the emancipatory interest, finally, makes the understanding of others possible" (Scholte 1973:448, emphasis added). Although I share Scholte's will toward empathy and understanding, I underscore that parenthetical "partial" gratefully. Cultures in communication—like moieties—properly leave a little mutual mystery to each other: chiaroscuro . . . [and] Paradoxes by their nature must be entered into, scrupulously, not solved. (1982:46)

Conclusions: Scribal Ice Has a Flammable Thaw

In the split of philosophical and theoretical camps, Boon has scientific and poetic stakes everywhere. Given a choice between competing ideas, he captures both in categorical opposition and then explores the possible semantic and historical space encumbered by their relationship to each other. Never innocent as a procedure, this jockeying of terms drags whole philosophies into juxtaposition as part of the baggage. The resulting load is heavy and represents one of the main obstacles to short-term interpretations of Boon's work. It yields no easy closure in a conventional sense. But that is a measure of the author's intention; the lack of easy or conventionally satisfying analytic closure is only a liability in conventional terms—in the parochial quest for uniformitarian Truth.[32] Moving beyond narrow conventional solutions to anthropological problems, Boon sets a course for metatheory and problem identification on a grand scale. He would have us see our paradoxes and our follies more clearly as they distribute in opposition and as they dissolve into new relations with other terms and other times. That is Truth enough for the moment. By treating the field of anthropology itself as a cultural system that is comparable to what we expect to find in exotic societies—complete with chiefs, ancestors, genealogies, and rules for successful cloning of the received wisdom over the years— Boon would have us get to know our own anthropological totems and moieties better, and in so doing bring our consciousness of Self, Other, and In Between to better grip, especially as these things are transformed into writing. He would have us map the territory of ethnology, ethnography, history, and crossovers in theory without (on Korzybski's good advice) confusing the map with the territory.

Those are tall orders in a discipline that all too often competes for monotonic truth: "Epistemologies and methodologies can be variable, plural, reflexive-like texts, like cultures. Indeed, they must be" (Boon 1982:152). Closure of any kind in this arena requires precious justification, and even then the most fervent participants cannot escape the fact that analytic satisfaction is (like Alka Seltzer) built to fall apart in the long run: "any synthesis, even this one, will be finally rejected" (27). The problem is knowing how to interpret these arrangements of symbolic parts systematically, without denying their possible social realities or foreclosing prematurely on discoveries of their cultural depth, categorical horizons, or potential for dialectical change. The options are legion, but, of course, not of equal practical or intellectual value.

Looking beyond the dilutions of synthetic compromise in the study of Others and keeping with his special valuation of categorical exaggeration, Boon's "trope" surfaces ultimately as a self-conscious semiotic view of cultures that, like Hindu mythology, subscribes to "an exhaustion of extremes" (235). Inspired by O'Flaherty's (1973:82) declaration that "Hinduism has no use for Middle Paths; this is a religion of fire and ice," Boon carries the analogy to ethnology and the history of its practice: "The fire/ice-like golden extremes of anthropology are, I suggest, the tribal and the scribal" (1982:235). But even this simple lumping buries significant differences and obscures powerful processes of cultural appropriation and expression through the making of texts.

Put abstractly, the fiery tribal extreme has two senses, each anchored in a certain history: (1) an ethnological sense of aboriginal tribal cosmology that defines "the limits of humankind quite narrowly" and "organizes its system of differences as mutual necessities"; and (2) a holy scriptural sense of biblical tribal cosmology that desires "to propagate a universalistic ethic" and "organizes its system of differences as mutual exclusions, at least until the Apocalypse" (1982:236). And how do they figure in the icy scribal extreme? In our monster-making textualities? Our appropriation of deed by word? Our transformative and often self-congratulatory inscription of the Other, the Un-Self, the Unfamiliar, and the Lost? Boon argues that

> some scholars suspect that the "scribal" dimension of history and the centralizing tendencies facilitated by writing doom the first kind of cosmology [ethnological/aboriginal] to the fate of the second [holy/biblical], eventuating in a spiceless "monoculture" of our doleful globe (Lévi-Strauss 1955, 1973). Thus small-scale reciprocal clans are eventually converted into exclusivistic sects, or stratified castes, or exploitative classes. Whether or not this view is adequate, anthropology's boldest hope has been a *victimless interpretation,* a deprivileged inscription extended to all cultures, not just ones chosen by God, or emergent through History, or emboldened by military might or economic advantage; above all not just ones centralized, homogenized, rationalized. In the extreme, anthropological writing transposes, at times even rivals, the rituals, forms, and institutions and messages of those who do not write: nonliterates. Or anthropology converts to writing aspects of literate cultures ignored or denied by their own institutional writing. Typically and paradoxically, anthropology writes the unwritten (the oral, the ritual, the total); or it rewrites the written (history, literature, ceremony) in light of values accentuated by the otherwise unwritten (myth, action, ritual). The discourse of cultures produces texts of the tribal/scribal, like two moieties dancing coolly and culturally in each other's flame. (236; cf. Crapanzano 1977:72)

Alert to the prospect "that all such differences [and *their* contraries] must be begged," Boon notes his effort to bridge the tribal and the scribal, "from the antecedents of Frazer's prose of rites to the implications in Geertz's rites of prose," and to do so "without cooling the fire or melting the ice" (1982:236). But that analytic suspension of moment cannot remain in actuality. Caught between the "fire of fieldwork" and the "ice of ethnology"—between eras and epistemes, "just as it is caught between cultures" (45)—the "history of writing cultures becomes a shifting collage of contraries threatening (promising) to become unglued" (237). So, in the spirit of sustained ambiguity in analysis, mutually determining negation and differences in language and

culture, the historicity of Truth in science, and our inevitable situatedness as "Beings-in-the-World," he asks: "What, then, is the rejoinder
of cross-cultural interpretation—goaded by fieldwork, resulting in writing—to the specter of uniformitarianism? Their/our answer lies not
in a language but in a translation; not in a culture or an era but
dialectically in between. Insofar as all passing forms of enchant-
ment . . . leave traces in ethnological discourse, the paradox of their
fate, and that of the discourse itself, intensifies" (237). On that mark
(and given a little shove), the present text provokes new discourse even
as its fire and ice trope dissolves instructively into an old paradox, one
befitting the impermanence of anthropology's wonderland, Boon's "exhaustion of extremes" as a mode of discovery, and the everlasting
sustenance of perpetual interpretation: stretched far enough into dissolution, even ice burns; the elemental constituents of water are flam-
mable. . . .

NOTES

My thanks to James Boon, Stephen Saraydar, Paul Rabinow, George Marcus,
and Stephen William Foster for their comments on an earlier draft of this
essay. Remaining weaknesses are mine; some of the strengths came from
elsewhere.

1. Besides these three, I have in mind here especially the work of Paul
Ricoeur—in particular his *Hermeneutics and the Human Sciences* (1981) and
his essay "On Interpretation" (1983). For a recent evaluation of Ricoeur's
thought, see Phelps (1983). For a broad sampling of scholars whose work in
self-conscious cultural analysis represents directly (or offers vital connections
to, e.g., Barthes to Marx, Becker to Freud, etc.) the intellectual justification
for anthropology's existence today, see also the major works of Gregory
Bateson, Ernest Becker, David Bidney, Michel de Certeau, Vincent Crapan-
zano, Roy D'Andrade, Greg Dening, Jean-Paul Dumont, Johannes Fabian,
Jeanne Favret-Saada, James Fernandez, Gilbert Herdt, George Marcus, Robert
Murphy, Wendy Doniger O'Flaherty, James Peacock, Lola Romanucci-Ross,
Michelle Rosaldo, Renato Rosaldo, Marshall Sahlins, Bob Scholte, Bradd
Shore, Richard Shweder, Milton Singer, Susan Sontag, Dan Sperber, Herbert
Spiegelberg, Dennis Tedlock, Stephen A. Tyler, Roy Wagner, Annette Weiner,
Hayden White, and Boon; from a more epistemological standpoint, see the
various anthropological writings of Peter Berger, Richard Bernstein, Mary
Douglas, Hubert Dreyfus, Paul Feyerabend, Martin Hollis, I. C. Jarvie, Thomas
Kuhn, Steven Lukes, Richard Rorty, and Peter Winch. This list is by no means
complete. Some other anthropologists do things differently, and sometimes
with great success. But few of them write about their work with a productive
justification of "self" in the process. Of Boon's work, *Other Tribes* comes
closest to this criterion (cf. Boon 1972, 1977).

2. Formerly professor of anthropology, comparative literature, and Southeast Asian studies at Cornell University, Boon is now professor of anthropology at Princeton University.

3. See Brady (1986a) for a brief review of *Other Tribes*.

4. And basic to Marxist thinking as well. "Situatedness" in this or any context must not be seen exclusively as a property of the individual. It is a cultural problem and therefore social, political, and economic in its manifestations—see Bloch (1983). See also Polanyi and Prosch (1975) on the intellectual and political responsibilities that follow from this knowledge; Eagleton (1983:124) on the question of whose interests are being served and the problems of institutional change linked to structural analyses; Zipes (1979) on the "Disneyfication" of American culture as an example of material nesting and cultural change in relation to what can otherwise be isolated as "literary" matters; Marcus and Fischer (1986) on the problem of anthropological writing and political economy; Geertz (1988) and Clifford (1988) on the cultural situations and authorial investments of several specific anthropologists.

5. For recent examples of poetic literature in anthropology, see Prattis (1985) and Brady (1991).

6. The struggle for an objective and detached "science of interpretation" is especially apparent in hermeneutic thought before Martin Heidegger and his student, Hans-Georg Gadamer, elevated the conversation about "situatedness" and hermeneutic philosophy from the study of texts per se to the study of meaning and understanding in the act of being human—for the actors as well as for those who would observe the actors systematically. For the best of the early effort see the various writings of Wilhelm Dilthey; for a more contemporary examination of the problem of positivism and uniformitarian thinking in hermeneutics, compare Hirsch (1976) and Hoy (1978).

7. This narrow version of what is human and what can be studied from that list resurfaced recently in a critical context (with commentary) in *Current Anthropology*. See Westen (1984) and Harris's (1984) remarkable response. Tuzin's (1984) scholarly piece in the same issue is especially interesting by comparison. His materialism is anything but mindless and can be cited as a refined example of what Harris's theoretical program can never achieve because of its gross reductionisms. See also Sahlins (1976).

8. The theoretical crossover here contains a fascinating conceit that is widely shared and seldom challenged: as a privileged "scientific" observer— more or less "culture-free"—*I* am able to say that *other* people are what *we* think, whether *they* know it or not. It is difficult to get around this judgment without abandoning ethnographic inquiry altogether.

9. In the strict Saussurean sense of privileging synchrony (*langue*) over diachrony (*parole*), Lévi-Strauss is vulnerable to this last criticism. But the criticism is generally overdrawn. Much of Lévi-Strauss's original argument about the place of history in structural studies was simply to caution against a strict historical interpretation of myth, not to deny the necessity of historical contextualization, etc. Sahlins (1981:6) reasons that "it is possible that the sacrifices apparently attending structural analysis—history, event, action, the

world—are not truly required." His *Islands of History* (1985) includes a detailed and mature elaboration of this argument (see also Sahlins 1976:3ff., 1981; cf. Fabian 1983:137–41).

10. Anthropologists are also keen on developing theories of the human condition—as my slightly cynical allusions here suggest—at the expense of method, to say nothing of epistemological justification for both. For a recent discussion of these problems, see Rubinstein and Pinxten (1984); Ulin (1984); Wuthnow et al. (1984); Ward and Werner (1984); and O'Meara (1989). Cf. Hoy (1978:32) in a criticism of Hirsch's (1976) positivistic hermeneutics and the separation of philosophical hermeneutics from its actual practice: "At the level of philosophical hermeneutics . . . while the question of different kinds of evidence is important, the general concern is more with *beliefs about* the nature of interpretation than with various techniques of actual interpretation" (see also Scholte 1984).

11. Taken generically, the idea of text as a cultural construct is easily (but problematically) extended to cultural artifacts of other kinds—indeed, to whole cultural systems of ordered symbols and meanings (see Geertz 1973). Boon does not hesitate to do so, particularly in his Balinese fieldwork. His project moves in this way into the broad area of a general science of semiology that Saussure (1959:16) envisioned but thought for sure would bring chaos if mixed analytically with an interpretation of the facts of performance per se. Boon also draws on Geertz's extension of the idea of text "beyond written material and even beyond verbal" to include social events on the order of Balinese cockfights (Geertz 1973:10, 448–49; see also Geertz 1983:31), and, indeed, to the idea of all culture as an "ensemble of texts" which the anthropologist strains to read "hermeneutically" (Geertz 1973:452; cf. Rice 1980:233–34). Edward Said argues in this same vein that "for the structuralists the whole world is contained within a gigantic set of quotation marks. *Everything,* therefore, is a text—or using the same argument, *nothing* is a text" (as quoted in Boon 1982:234). By upgrading this semiotically to *"nothingnesses are texts"* (1982:234), Boon reverberates both Derrida's and Heidegger's sense of negativity in language, thought, and action, not to mention the void of Nirvana (cf. Seung 1982:277). Lévi-Strauss (1985:118) offers an even broader and more fundamental (though not necessarily agreeable) view on extensions of the notion of text. Cf. Ricoeur (1979); Fernandez (1985); and O'Meara (1989).

12. Self-consciousness is a serious issue in anthropology today, especially as more "experimental" ethnographies continue to appear on the horizon in opposition to the more conventionally "self-less" forms (see Brady 1985, 1986b for reviews of some recent examples; Rose 1989 for the real thing; compare Dening's [1980, 1988] narrative with the standard fare in anthropology). Keeping this kind of visibility/invisibility problem in mind, and shifting informatively through the levels of reader, writer, and observer, Boon's text is that of a self-conscious observer who is not always obtrusively self-present. More important, and perhaps more exemplary of his thesis, Boon's self-consciousness is really "self-system" consciousness—an attempt to put

his own culture in both a hermeneutic and a semiotic context and to play that off in structural oppositions (and related symbolic transformations) against the world of anthropology as it is constituted analytically and as it relates both analytically and historically to Others. The analytic goal is *not* to deliver the text itself. It is instead supposed to be the informed unlocking of meanings in transformations, in contrast, in the system of symbols and meanings that defines for us the nature of the world and our place in it—in *relation* to other such cultural patterns as they either sit already or can be dragged analytically into a semiotic equation. Boon keeps Lévi-Strauss's spirit of reflexiveness intact in this respect: if such a thesis "has any unity, that unity will appear only behind or beyond the text and, in the best hypothesis, will become a reality in the mind of the reader" (Lévi-Strauss 1969:6). See Boon's discussion (1982:ch. 5, 6, 7).

13. Contrary to claims by many of Lévi-Strauss's critics (particularly by "non-anthropologists") that "he is erecting a peculiarly pessimistic, impoverishing, and mechanized view of what men do," Boon (1972:12) says we should remember something often acknowledged by Lévi-Strauss himself: he "would not have the first thing to say unless men were out there myth making, painting, marrying, exchanging goods—unless men were making exchanges among themselves and between themselves and features of their experience, unless they were stating themselves and those features all *in terms of* one another—i.e., unless they were creating 'texts' " (cf. Rabinow and Sullivan 1979:10-13).

14. The danger in perpetual transformations of symbolic structures is nihilism—complete indeterminacy. Boon shares but does not restrict himself to: (1) Kenneth Burke's fondness of interpretation for the sake of interpretation—shades of Nietzsche—but he was more suspicious about the *power* of interpretation; and (2) Lévi-Strauss's sense of perpetual coding and decoding from one cultural realm to another and across cultural boundaries without firm closure on any of it (cf. Roe 1982; Rabinow and Sullivan 1979:12; Rabinow 1983; Harland 1987).

15. Similarly, culture to Geertz is not reducible to universal structures of mind (or anything else); it is resolutely particular, specific, and circumstantial. It is accessible as surface structure, as symbolic order, and, although "public" and available for all to take in some measure, it is nonetheless analytically anchored in a more particular (but equally public and accessible) concept of the symbol (cf. Rabinow 1983). But, as Rice (1980:48) says, Geertz is inconsistent here: in some cases he sees cultures as at best "indirectly accessible" to the ethnographer, "leading to a view of anthropology as severely limited in the kinds of conclusions it may justifiably draw"; in others he sees cultures "as empirically accessible, leading to a view of anthropology as a science whose conclusions are, or at least will eventually be, reliable" (cf. Geertz 1973:9, 16, 24, 25, 27). Boon opts plainly for the first, despite his flirtation with the second through some aspects of structuralism (cf. Lévi-Strauss 1966:58; 1985:103-4). Cf. Schneider (1976, 1980) on meaning and cultural depth and the nature of "epitomizing symbols."

16. These are just a few of the reasons why Boon's inspiration and methods owe less to the modified structuralism of Barthes and Foucault than to the theoretical stretch he has mined from Saussure to Peirce, from Lévi-Strauss to Geertz—not to mention the many different ways Max Weber and the two standard products of the New Criticism, ambiguity and irony (see Seung 1982:271), show up in his work. The list is long; the creative mix is Boon's alone.

17. Cf. Porter's (1984) penetrating criticism of Derek Freeman's (1983) book on Samoa and Margaret Mead (see also Brady 1983, 1986b), which Porter treats productively as a text, subject to literary criticism, etc. He (1984:19) says: "As far as representation is concerned [as an issue in modern literary theory], it has gone largely unrecognized, at least in the United States, that ethnographic works which are field studies of specific cultures are governed by conventional literary modes of representation just as much as realist novels or the travel journals of non-anthropologists. As a result of the influence of modern literary theory, the claims once made for realist representation in fiction have been radically revised. But there is not too much evidence of such critical scrutiny among professional anthropologists." That is changing today. See Ricoeur (1979, 1984); Marcus and Cushman (1982); Marcus and Fischer (1986); Clifford and Marcus (1986); Harland (1987); Clifford (1988); Geertz (1988); Brady (1991).

18. Consistent with these tensions between doing and writing ethnography, Boon starts Part 1 of *Other Tribes* ("Initiations") with "reflections on fieldwork and the kinds of writings it is expected to produce." Part 2 ("Systematics Notwithstanding") attends "to several prominent bodies of comparative social theory"—to some of the great interpreters of societies encountered in and out of "the field," including Mauss, Marx, Durkheim, Weber, Hocart, Lowie, Peirce, Saussure, Lévi-Strauss, Geertz, and others—which Boon rereads "with an eye toward tribal and traditional civilizations in an effort to interconnect them" (x). Part 3 ("Essays in Exotic Texts") combines "comparative social theory and mythology, structural analysis, and interpretive theories of texts and contexts, both ethnographic and historical" into "a discourse of cultures" (x). Here Boon "converts the dialectical systems and assorted semiotics of Part II to more flowing, plural 'textualities'; yet the same problems and principles obtain" (151). The exemplars in this section center on a splendid (and extended) discussion of kings and Others inscribed by Samuel Purchas in 1625 and a detailed analysis of Balinese incest that embodies much of the character and most of the problems of Boon's project.

19. Cf. Lévi-Strauss (1985:103), addressing a problem about which he has often been misunderstood—the problem of empirical access to underlying structure.

20. See also Needham (1985:179–80). Boon (1982:46) says: "Experience across cultures, like communication across languages, is neither unique nor universal. Its advantage lies rather in the sense of exaggeration it ensures. Every culture appears, vis-a-vis every other, exaggerated (just like every language), hence the exhilaration of the imperfectible effort we call translation.

I propose, then, that ethnographic writing about other cultures consists, like cultures themselves, in an exaggeration of differences. We start with the exaggerations (the languages, the cultures), and only certain kinds of theories—each itself an unwitting exaggeration—and attempt to compromise the mutual exaggerations into cozy universals. Standard anthropological genres—"objective" description (reportage), taxonomic labels (by-lines), realistic monographs (naturalism)—overlook their own symbolic nature and hyperbolism. As a counterbalance, this book champions instances of cross-cultural discourse that acknowledge the hyperbolic nature of perceived cultures and their comparison. This discourse of cultures confesses its own exaggeration and seeks to control and assess it by becoming interpretive, at times even literary, while remaining both systematic and dialectical."

21. "Through inscription, all cultures may stand as moieties, each to another the vis-a-vis. Toward this end anthropologists write. . . . Anthropology thus generates books of cultures by fieldworkers who become figures of and for the always-stylized, sometimes sluggish exchange of remotest meanings" (Boon 1982:26).

22. Cf. Shankman's recent contribution (1984) to the long line of such remarks in anthropology about the mutual exclusiveness (and competition) between art and science in anthropology. He recognizes that anthropology has both art and science embedded in its history and constitution, and profitably so. But he does not explain the mutually constructive opposition of this pairing or others like it. He does say that where "humanism" has put "science" on the run for its shortcomings, "it need not be this way. There is room for humanistic and scientific approaches, understanding *and* explanation, and the study of meaning *and* behavior, but only if anthropologists are sufficiently informed to recognize the strength, limitations, and differences of their approaches" (1984:692; cf. Berreman 1968; O'Meara 1989; Brady 1991). See also Wagner (1981:158; 1986) for an argument contrary to Boon's plan of "exhausting extremes" to better reveal cultural constitutions in analysis, but to much the same end and without advocating naive synthesism.

23. Geertz and others "abandon Enlightenment hopes that there will yet be found some uniformitarian common denominator behind cultural variation, some decultured foothold that affords readier access to different cultural systems than comparative scholars could have if they were beginning afresh each time" (Boon 1982:25; see also Polanyi 1962; Polanyi and Prosch 1975:63–64 for comparable arguments).

24. Cross-cultural interpretation is only "given" naively in experience—it must in fact "be *made* to happen, using symbolic conventions derived from sources outside the conditions of fieldwork proper" (Boon 1982:8–9).

25. Boon (1982:47) writes: "The two stock assumptions—anthropology is inferior science, and its mission is objective tolerance—are intertwined. Those who bemoan anthropology's scientific shortcomings underestimate its characteristic accomplishments: discovering subtlety, pattern, dialectics, and innuendo in human matters that, viewed by agencies of analysis outside anthropology, appear merely misguided, laughable, or simply transparent. An-

thropology forestalls any culture's sense of its own inevitability. Culturally all peoples are capable of comparing each other with relative disinterest, but politically there is rarely the opportunity and almost never the prescription to do so. Professional anthropology safeguards convictions—often contrary to the *amour propre* of nation states—that cultures can and ought to encounter."

26. See Hoy (1978:69) on the problem of "contextualism" versus "radical relativism"; also Hollis and Lukes (1982); Lukes (1982:298ff.).

27. Having begged a dual issue here—one appropriately of extremes—let me clarify it: arch-positivists know the rules of inquiry and apply them with strict (if not religious) dogmatism to the realities they confront. Naive positivists know little of the rules; they just take reality for granted as it presents itself to them and strive to be "objective" in their reports (see Brady 1982b). Most anthropology is done under the latter rubric. See also the related commentary by Barbara Frankel in Ward and Werner (1984:93).

28. Note that Geertz implicitly gave a big concession to arch-positivists and naive realists when he dubbed his own very popular efforts (1973, 1983) in contradistinction as "interpretive." Of course, the whole enterprise is interpretive. Furthermore, "interpretive" anthropology—as part of the post-structuralist, deconstructionist movement in contemporary philosophy and social science—contrary to some confusions in anthropology's literature—is not necessarily: (1) anti-empirical—how can any discipline operate without an empirical ground? (2) anti-objective (see Rorty 1979:361–63; Spiegelberg 1975:72–73); or, (3) anti-science (cf. Jennings 1983; Shankman 1984). But responsible social science of this kind does reject (as unnecessarily incomplete, among other problems) dogmatic empiric-*ism* that forecloses on the study of meaning in favor of an exclusive focus on behavior (cf. O'Meara 1989; Brady 1991).

29. Geertz (1983:120) resists any such mix if it does not "move beyond the consideration of signs as means of communication, codes to be deciphered, to a consideration of them as modes of thought, idiom to be interpreted" (cf. Geertz 1983; Rabinow and Sullivan 1979:3, 1987).

30. Cf. the defensible anthropological conclusions, contrary to popular Western views and those held by many "sister" disciplines, that: "the experience of tribal and traditional populations reveals that kinship and marriage are a metainstitution and myth and ritual a metaclassification: an institution of institutions and a classification of classifications" (Boon 1982:229; see also Foster 1981).

31. Cf. Barthes (1977:157–58): "The Text is that which goes to the limit of the rules of enunciation (rationality, readability, etc.). . . . The Text tries to place itself very exactly *behind* the limit of the *doxa* (is not general opinion—constitutive of our democratic societies and powerfully aided by mass communications—defined by its limits, the energy with which it excludes, its *censorship?*). Taking the word literally, it may be said that the Text is always *paradoxical.*"

32. Sperber (1983) echoes the common criticism of structuralism in his

caustic review of *Other Tribes,* that structuralism can be very systematic without necessarily entailing attempts to explain things causally (cf. Eagleton 1983; Abrahams 1984; Harland 1987). It offers the view, in other words, that "an element may be explained by its place in a network of relations rather than in a chain of cause and effect" (Culler 1975:255). Certainly Boon has followed suit and to that degree is vulnerable to the criticism. But he has also argued that the arrangements (and therefore the "meaning-contexts") of the symbolic parts he has culled from ethnology change dialectically and are thus matters of processual "consequence." That works against the endurance of monotonic truth in the long run but not completely against the idea of cause and effect as Sperber has envisioned it (cf. Boon 1982:114, 116).

References Cited

Abel, Elizabeth
1980 "Redefining the Sister Arts: Baudelaire's Response to the Art of Delacroix." In *The Language of Images.* ed. W. J. T. Mitchell. Chicago: University of Chicago Press, pp. 37–58.

Abrahams, Roger D.
1984 Review of *Other Tribes, Other Scribes,* by James A. Boon. *Journal of American Folklore* 97(386): 487–89.
1983 *The Man-of-Words in the West Indies: Performance and the Emergence of Creole Culture.* Baltimore: Johns Hopkins University Press.

Alverson, Marianne
1987 *Under African Sun.* Chicago: University of Chicago Press.

American Missionary Society
1899 *Patik dohot Uhum ni Halak Batak.* Singapore: American Mission Press.

Anonymous
1807 *Free Trade to the East Indies.* London: C. Chapple.

Artaud, Antonin
1938 *The Theater and Its Double.* trans. M. C. Richards. New York: Grove Press.

Atkinson, Jane M.
1984 "Religions in Dialogue: The Construction of an Indonesian Minority Religion." *American Ethnologist* 10(4):684–96.

Babcock, Barbara A.
1986 "Modeled Selves: Helen Cordero's 'Little People.' " In *The Anthropology of Experience.* ed. Victor W. Turner and Edward M. Bruner. Urbana: University of Illinois Press.

Bakhtin, M. M.
1981 *The Dialogic Imagination.* ed. Michael Holquist, trans. Caryl Emerson and Michael Holquist. Austin: University of Texas Press.

Balch, Stephen H.
1985 "The Neutered Civil Servant: Eunuchs, Celibates, Abductees, and the Maintenance of Organizational Loyalty." *Journal of Social and Biological Structures* 8:313–28.

Banner, Lois

1987 "Plenary Address." Presented at the Conference on the New Gender Scholarship: Women's and Men's Studies. University of Southern California.

Barthes, Roland

1977 *Image, Music, Text.* trans. Stephen Heath. New York: Hill and Wang.

1974 *S/Z.* trans. Richard Miller. New York: Hill and Wang.

1973 "The Structuralist Activity." In *European Literary Theory and Practice.* ed. Vernon W. Gras. New York: Dell.

1972 *Mythologies.* trans. Annette Lavers. New York: Hill and Wang.

Bateson, Gregory

1936 *Naven: A Survey of the Problems Suggested by a Composite Picture of a Culture of a New Guinea Tribe Drawn from Three Points of View.* Stanford: Stanford University Press.

Bauman, Zygmunt

1978 *Hermeneutics and Social Science.* New York: Columbia University Press.

Beasant, John

1984 *The Santo Rebellion: An Imperial Reckoning.* Honolulu: University of Hawaii Press.

Becker, A. L.

1979 "Text-building, Epistemology, and Aesthetics in Javanese Shadow Theater." In *The Imagination of Reality.* ed. A. L. Becker and A. Yengoyan. Norwood, N.J.: Ablex, pp. 211–43.

Benveniste, E.

1969 *Le vocabulaire des institutions indo-européenes.* 2 vols. Paris: Minuit.

Bernal, M.

1987 *Black Athena: The Afroasiatic Roots of Classical Civilization.* Vol. 1: *The Fabrication of Ancient Greece, 1785–1985.* New Brunswick, N.J.: Rutgers University Press.

Bernheimer, Charles, and Claire Kahane (eds.)

1985 *In Dora's Case: Freud—Hysteria—Feminism.* New York: Columbia University Press.

Bernstein, Richard J.

1983 *Beyond Objectivism and Relativism: Science, Hermeneutics, and Praxis.* Philadelphia: University of Pennsylvania Press.

Berreman, Gerald D.

1972 [1963] *Hindus of the Himalayas.* Berkeley: University of California Press.

1968 "Ethnography: Method and Product." In *Introduction to Cultural Anthropology.* ed. James A. Clifton. New York: Houghton Mifflin, pp. 337–73.

Berry, James

1984 *News for Babylon.* London: Chatto and Winders.

Birdwood, Sir George, and William Foster (eds.)

1893 *The Register of Letters &c. of the Governour and Company of Merchants of London Trading into the East Indies 1600–1619.* London: Bernard Quaritch.

Blackwood, Peter

1981 "Rank, Exchange, and Leadership in Four Vanuatu Societies." In *Vanuatu: Politics, Economics, and Ritual in Island Melanesia.* ed. Michael Allen. London: Academic Press, pp. 35–84.

Bleicher, Josef

1980 *Contemporary Hermeneutics: Hermeneutics as Method, Philosophy, and Critique.* Boston: Routledge and Kegan Paul.

Bloch, Maurice

1983 *Marxism and Anthropology.* Oxford: Clarendon.

Bock, Philip

1979 "Oedipus Once More." *American Anthropologist* 81(4):905–6.

Boissevain, Jeremy

1970 "Fieldwork in Malta." In *Being an Anthropologist.* ed. George S. Spindler. New York: Holt, Rinehart, and Winston, pp. 58–84.

Boon, James A.

1984 "Structuralism Routinized, Structuralism Fractured." *American Ethnologist* 11(4):807–12.

1982 *Other Tribes, Other Scribes: Symbolic Anthropology in the Comparative Study of Cultures, Histories, Religions, and Texts.* New York: Cambridge University Press.

1977 *The Anthropological Romance of Bali, 1597–1972: Dynamic Perspectives in Marriage and Culture.* Cambridge: Cambridge University Press.

1972 *From Symbolism to Structuralism: Lévi-Strauss in a Literary Tradition.* New York: Harper and Row.

Booth, Wayne

1961 *The Rhetoric of Fiction.* Chicago: University of Chicago Press.

Bowen, Elenore Smith

1954 *Return to Laughter: An Anthropological Novel.* New York: Harper and Row.

Bradley, A. C.

1909 "Hegel's Theory of Tragedy." In *Oxford Lectures on Poetry.* London: Macmillan.

Brady, Ivan

1991 (ed.) *Anthropological Poetics.* Savage, Md.: Rowman and Littlefield.

1986a Review of *Other Tribes, Other Scribes,* by James A. Boon. *American Anthropologist* 88(1):240–41.

1986b Review of *Mead's Other Manus: Phenomenology of the Encounter,* by Lola Romanucci-Ross. *American Anthropologist* 88(4):995–96.

1985 Review of *Tuvalu: A History,* by Simati Faaniu, Vinaka Ielemia, Taulo Isaka, et al. *Pacific History Bibliography and Comment,* 1985, pp. 52–54. Canberra: Journal of Pacific History.

1983 (ed.) "Speaking in the Name of the Real: Freeman and Mead on Samoa." Special section, *American Anthropologist* 85(4):908–47.

1982a "*Les îles Marquises:* Ethnography from Another Beachhead." *American Ethnologist* 9(1):185–90.

1982b "The Myth-Eating Man." *American Anthropologist* 84(3):595–611.

Braudel, Fernand

1986 *The Wheels of Commerce.* New York: Harper and Row.

British Association for the Advancement of Science

1841 *Report of the 1841 Meeting of the British Association for the Advancement of Science.* London: John Murray.

Broch, Hermann

1964 [1932] *The Sleepwalkers.* trans. Willa Muir and Edwin Muir. New York: Grosset and Dunlap.

Brown, Lloyd

1984 *West Indian Pottery.* 2d ed. London: Heinemann.

Bruce, John

1810 *Annals of the Honourable East India Company from Their Establishment by the Charter of Queen Elizabeth, 1600, to the Union of the London and English East-India Companies 1707–8.* London: Cox, Son, and Baylis.

Bruner, Edward M.

1993 "Epilogue: Creative Persona and the Problem of Authenticity." In *Creativity in Anthropology.* ed. Smadar Lavie, Kirin Narayan, and Renato Rosaldo. Ithaca: Cornell University Press.

1990 "The Scientists vs. the Humanists." *Anthropology Newsletter.* Feb., p. 28.

1986a "Experience and Its Expressions." In *The Anthropology of Experience.* ed. Victor W. Turner and Edward M. Bruner. Urbana: University of Illinois Press.

1986b "Ethnography as Narrative." In *The Anthropology of Experience.* ed. Victor W. Turner and Edward M. Bruner. Urbana: University of Illinois Press.

1984a (ed.) *Text, Play, and Story: The Construction and Reconstruction of Self and Society.* 1983 Proceedings of the American Ethnological Society. Washington, D.C.: American Anthropological Association. Reprint, 1988. Chicago: Waveland Press.

1984b "Introduction: The Opening Up of Anthropology." In *Text, Play, and Story.* ed. Edward M. Bruner. 1983 Proceedings of the American Ethnological Society. Washington, D.C.: American Anthropological Association. Reprint, 1988. Chicago: Waveland.

n.d. "Between Tourism and Ethnography." Unpublished ms.

Buckley, Thomas

1987 "Dialogue and Shared Authority: Informants as Critics." *Central Issues in Anthropology* 7(1):13–23.

Buisine, Alain

1981 "The First Eye." *Yale French Studies* 61:261–75.

Burnett, Paula
1986 *Caribbean Verse in English.* Harmondsworth, England: Penguin.

Campbell, L.
1896 *Sophocles.* London: J. Murray.

Carle, Rainer (ed.)
1987 *Cultures and Societies of North Sumatra.* Veröffentlichungen des Seminars der Indonesische und Südseesprachen der Universität Hamburg, Band 19. Berlin: Dietrich Reimer Verlag.

Carroll, Michael
1978 "Lévi-Strauss on the Oedipus Myth: A Reconsideration." *American Anthropologist* 80(4):805–14.

Certeau, Michel de
1984 *The Practice of Everyday Life.* Berkeley: University of California Press.

Cesara, Manda
1982 *Reflections of a Woman Anthropologist: No Hiding Places.* New York: Academic Press.

Chandler, Alfred D., Jr.
1977 *The Visible Hand: The Managerial Revolution in American Business.* Cambridge: Harvard University Press.

Chernoff, John Miller
1979 *African Rhythms and African Sensibility.* Chicago: University of Chicago Press.

Cixous, Hélène
1983 "The Laugh of the Medusa." In *The Signs Reader: Women, Gender, and Scholarship.* ed. Elizabeth Abel and Emily K. Abel. Chicago: University of Chicago Press, pp. 279–97.

Clarke, Simon
1981 *The Foundations of Structuralism: A Critique of Lévi-Strauss and the Structuralist Movement.* Totowa, N.J.: Barnes and Noble.

Clifford, James
1988 *The Predicament of Culture: Twentieth-Century Ethnography, Literature, and Art.* Cambridge: Harvard University Press.

1986a "Introduction." In *Writing Culture: The Poetics and Politics of Ethnography.* ed. James Clifford and George E. Marcus. Berkeley: University of California Press, pp. 1–26.

1986b "On Ethnographic Allegory." In *Writing Culture: The Poetics and Politics of Ethnography.* ed. James Clifford and George E. Marcus. Berkeley: University of California Press, pp. 98–121.

1983 "On Ethnographic Authority." *Representations* 1:118–46.

Clifford, James, and George E. Marcus (eds.)
1986 *Writing Culture: The Poetics and Politics of Ethnography.* Berkeley: University of California Press.

Codrington, R. H.
1969 [1891] *The Melansians: Studies in Their Anthropology and Folklore.* Oxford: Oxford University Press.

Conklin, Harold
1964 "A Day in Parina." In *In the Company of Man*. ed. Joseph B. Casagrande. New York: Harper, pp. 119–225.

Conrad, Joseph
1971 *Heart of Darkness*. New York: W. W. Norton.

Crapanzano, Vincent
1980 *Tuhami: Portrait of a Moroccan*. Chicago: University of Chicago Press.
1977 "On the Writing of Ethnography." *Dialectical Anthropology* 2(1):69–73.

Culler, Jonathan
1982 *On Deconstruction: Theory and Criticism after Structuralism*. Ithaca, N.Y.: Cornell University Press.
1975 *Structuralist Poetics: Structuralism, Linguistics, and the Study of Literature*. Ithaca, N.Y.: Cornell University Press.

Dalimunte, Abd. Rachman, and Sondak Pohan
1986 *Adat daerah Tapanuli Selatan, surat tumbaga holing*. Padangsidimpuan: privately published.

Darnton, Robert
1985 *The Great Cat Massacre and Other Episodes in French Cultural History*. New York: Vintage.

Deacon, Bernard
1934 *Malekula: A Vanishing People in the New Hebrides*. London: G. Routledge and Sons.

de Beauvoir, Simone
1949 [1953] *The Second Sex*. French ed. 1949. Reprint, 1953. New York: Alfred A. Knopf.

Deloria, Vine
1969 *Custer Died for Your Sins*. Norman: University of Oklahoma Press.

Dening, Greg
1988 *History's Anthropology: The Death of William Gooch*. ASAO Special Publications, no. 2. Washington, D.C.: University Press of America.
1980 *Islands and Beaches: Discourse on a Silent Land: Marquesas 1774–1880*. Honolulu: University Press of Hawaii.

Departemen Pendidikan dan Kebudayaan
1983–84 *Ungkapan tradisional yang berkaitan dengan sila-sila dalam panca sila*. Jakarta.

Derrida, Jacques
1981 "The Law of Genre." In On Narrative. ed. W. J. T. Mitchell. Chicago: University of Chicago Press, pp. 51–77.
1974 *Glas*. Paris: Gallimard.

Diamond, Stanley
1980 "Anthropological Traditions: The Participants Observed." In *Anthropology: Ancestors and Heirs*. ed. Stanley Diamond. The Hague: Mouton.

Dodds, E. R.
1951 *The Greeks and the Irrational*. Berkeley: University of California Press.

Donzelot, J.
1979 *The Policing of Families.* New York: Pantheon.
Dorst, John D.
1989 *The Written Suburb: An American Site, an Ethnographic Dilemma.*
Philadelphia: University of Pennsylvania Press.
Dreyfus, Hubert L., and Paul Rabinow
1982 *Michel Foucault: Beyond Structuralism and Hermeneutics.* 2d ed. Chicago: University of Chicago Press.
Dumont, Jean-Paul
1986 "Prologue to Ethnography or Prolegomena to Anthropography." *Ethos* 14:352–63.
1978 *The Headman and I: Ambiguity and Ambivalence in the Fieldworking Experience.* Austin: University of Texas Press
Dumont, Louis
1986 *Essays on Individualism: Modern Ideology in Anthropological Perspective.* Chicago: University of Chicago Press.
1977 *From Mandelville to Marx.* Chicago: University of Chicago Press.
Dwyer, Kevin
1982 *Moroccan Dialogues.* Baltimore, Md.: Johns Hopkins University Press.
1977 "On the Dialogic of Fieldwork." *Dialectical Anthropology* 2:143–51.
Eagleton, Terry
1983 *Literary Theory: An Introduction.* Minneapolis: University of Minnesota Press.
Eco, Umberto
1979 *The Role of the Reader: Explorations in the Semiotics of Texts.* Bloomington: Indiana University Press.
Eliot, T. S.
1949 *Notes towards a Definition of Culture.* New York: Harcourt and Brace.
Ellmann, Mary
1968 *Thinking about Women.* New York: Harcourt, Brace, Jovanovich.
Evans-Pritchard, E. E.
1969 "Preface." In *The Observation of Savage Peoples.* trans. Joseph-Marie Degerando and F. C. T. Moore. Berkeley: University of California Press.
1940 *The Nuer.* Oxford: Oxford University Press.
Fabian, Johannes
1983 *Time and the Other: How Anthropology Makes Its Object.* New York: Columbia University Press.
Fagles, R. (trans.)
1984 [1982] *Sophocles: The Three Theban Plays.* Intro. and notes by B. Knox. New York: Penguin.
Favret-Saada, J.
1980 *Deadly Words: Witchcraft in the Bocage.* Cambridge: Cambridge University Press.
Feld, Steven
1987 "Dialogic Editing: Interpreting How Kaluli Read *Sound and Sentiment.*" *Cultural Anthropology* 2:191–215.

1982 *Sound and Sentiment: Birds, Weeping, Poetics, and Song in Kaluli Expression.* Philadelphia: University of Pennsylvania Press.

Felman, Shoshana
1977 "Turning the Screw of Interpretation." *Yale French Studies* 55–56:94–208.

Fernandez, James W.
1985 "Exploded Worlds—Text as a Metaphor for Ethnography (and Vice-Versa)." In *Anthropology after '84: State of the Art, State of Society, Part II.* ed. Stanley Diamond. Special issue of *Dialectical Anthropology* 10(1–2):15–26.

Filene, Peter Gabriel
1987 "History and Men's History and What's the Difference." Plenary Address given at the Conference on the New Gender Scholarship: Women's and Men's Studies. University of Southern California.

Finley, M. I.
1979 [1954] *The World of Odysseus.* 2d rev. ed. London: Penguin.

Fischer, Michael M. J., George E. Marcus, and Stephen A. Tyler
1988 "Comments." *Current Anthropology* 29(3):426–27.

Fisher, H. A. L.
1906 "The Codes." In *Cambridge Modern History.* Volume 9: *Napoleon.* ed. A. W. Ward, G. W. Prothero, Stanley Leathes. Cambridge: Cambridge University Press.

Fitts, Dudley, and Robert Fitzgerald
1949 *Oedipus Rex: An English Version.* New York: Harcourt and Brace.

Flax, Jane
1987 "Postmodernism and Gender Relations in Feminist Theory." *Signs* 12(4):621–43.

Fletcher, Alice C., and Francis La Flesche
1911 *The Omaha Tribe.* Twenty-seventh Annual Report of the Bureau of American Ethnology. Washington: Smithsonian Institution.

Foster, George, M. Thayer, M. Scudder, Elizabeth Colson, Robert V. Kemper (eds.)
1979 *Long-Term Field Research in Social Anthropology.* New York: Academic Press.

Foster, Stephen William
1982 "The Exotic as a Symbolic System." *Dialectical Anthropology* 7:21–30.
1981 "Interpretations of Interpretations." *Anthropology and Humanism Quarterly* 6(4):2–8.

Foucault, Michel
1972 *The Archaeology of Knowledge and the Discourse on Language.* New York: Harper.

Fox, Robin
1988 "In the Matter of Baby M.: Report from the Gruter Institute for Law and Behavioral Research." *Politics and the Life Sciences* 7(1):77–85.
1983 *Kinship and Marriage: An Anthropological Perspective.* Cambridge: Cambridge University Press.

Fraser, Nancy, and Linda Nicholson

1988 "Social Criticism without Philosophy: An Encounter between Feminism and Postmodernism." *Theory, Culture, and Society* 5:373-94.

Freeman, Derek

1983 *Margaret Mead and Samoa: The Making and Unmaking of an Anthropological Myth.* Cambridge: Harvard University Press.

Friedman, Jonathan

1988 "Comments." *Current Anthropology* 29(3):426-27.

Friedrich, Paul

1986 *The Princes of Naranja: An Essay in Anthrohistorical Method.* Austin: University of Texas Press.

1977 "Sanity and the Myth of Honor: The Problem of Achilles." *Ethos* 5:281-305.

1966 "Proto–Indo-European Kinship." *Ethnology* 5:1-36.

Frye, Joanne

1987 "The Politics of Reading: Feminism, the Novel, and the Coercions of 'Truth.' " Paper presented at the Midwest Modern Language Association Convention. Columbus, Ohio.

Gardner, Brian

1971 *The East India Company.* New York: McCall.

Geertz, Clifford

1988 *Works and Lives: The Anthropologist as Author.* Stanford: Stanford University Press.

1986 "Making Experience, Authoring Selves." In *The Anthropology of Experience.* ed. Victor W. Turner and Edward M. Bruner. Urbana: University of Illinois Press, pp. 373-80.

1983 *Local Knowledge: Further Essays on Interpretive Anthropology.* New York: Basic Books.

1973 *The Interpretation of Cultures.* New York: Basic Books.

Gellner, Ernest

1981 *Muslim Society.* Cambridge: Cambridge University Press.

Gilbert, Sandra, and Susan Gubar

1980 *The Madwoman in the Attic: The Woman Writer and the Nineteenth-Century Literary Imagination.* New Haven, Conn.: Yale University Press.

Gitlin, Todd

1988 "Hip-Deep in Post-modernism." *New York Times Book Review.* 6 Nov.

Gluckman, Max

1963 *Order and Rebellion in Tribal Africa.* London: Cohen and West.

Goldthrope, M.

1986 "Redneck Girl Is Worth Seeing, Despite Some Small Problems." *Daily News* (Pullman, Wash.). 10 Nov.

Goody, Jack

1986 *The Logic of Writing and the Organization of Society.* Cambridge: Cambridge University Press.

1977 *The Domestication of the Savage Mind.* Cambridge: Cambridge University Press.

1968 *Literacy in Traditional Societies.* Cambridge: Cambridge University Press.

Gottlieb, Alma

1992 *Under the Kapok Tree: Identity and Difference in Beng Thought.* Bloomington: Indiana University Press.

Gottlieb, Alma, and Philip Graham

1992 *A Parallel World.* New York: Crown.

Gordon, Deborah

1988 "Writing Culture, Writing Feminism: The Poetics and Politics of Experimental Ethnography." *Inscriptions* 3-4:7-24.

Graves, Robert

1960 *The Greek Myths.* Vol. 2. Harmondsworth, England: Penguin.

Griffiths, Sir Percival

1974 *A License to Trade: The History of English Chartered Companies.* London: Ernest Benn.

Grindal, Bruce

n.d. "Redneck Girl." Unpublished ms.

Grindal, Bruce, and William Shephard

1986 *Redneck Girl: A Play.*

Gubar, Susan

1981 "Blessings in Disguise: Cross-dressing as Re-dressing for Female Modernists." *Massachusetts Review* 22(3):477-508.

Gumperz, John

1976 "Language, Communication, and Public Negotiation." In *Anthropology and the Public Interest.* ed. P. R. Sanday. New York: Academic Press, pp. 273-92.

Hannerz, Ulf

1987 "Cosmopolitans and Locals in World Culture." Paper presented at the First International Conference on the Olympics and East/West and South/North Cultural Exchanges in the World System. Seoul.

Harahap, H. M. D.

1986 *Adat istiadat Tapanuli Selatan.* Jakarta: Grafindo Utama.

Harahap, T. Mr. Tagor

n.d. "Pastak Pago-Pago." Unpublished ms.

Harding, Sandra

1987 "Introduction: Is There a Feminist Method?" In *Feminism and Methodology.* ed. Sandra Harding. Bloomington: Indiana University Press, p. 1-14.

1986 *The Science Question in Feminism.* Ithaca, N.Y.: Cornell University Press.

Harland, Richard

1987 *Superstructuralism: The Philosophy of Structuralism and Post-structuralism.* New York: Methuen.

Harris, Marvin
1984 "Reply to Drew Westen's Cultural Materialism: Food for Thought or Bum Steer?" *Current Anthropology* 25(5):648–49.
Harrisson, Tom
1937 *Savage Civilization*. New York: Alfred A. Knopf.
Hartsock, Nancy
1987 "Rethinking Modernism." *Cultural Critique* 7:187–206.
Hasoendoetan, M. J. St.
1941 *Datoek toeongkoe adji malim leman*. Siantar: Sjarif, Soetan Martoewa Radja.
1940 *Nasotardago*. Sipirok: Stn. P. 1979. Reissued Proyek Penerbitan Buku Bacaan dan Sastra Indonesia dan Daerah, Departemen Pendidikan dan Kebudayaan, Jakarta.
[1930] *Parkalaan Tondoeng Hatiha dohot Hadatoean*. Sipirok, Sumatra: Stn. P.
1922 *Ranteomas oedoet ni Doea Sadjoli I*. Batavia: N. V. de Volharding Soetan Pangoerabaan.
Havelock, Eric
1978 *The Greek Concept of Justice*. Cambridge: Harvard University Press.
Hawkesworth, Mary E.
1989 "Knowers, Knowing, Known: Feminist Theory and Claims of Truth." *Signs* 14(3):533–77.
Henriques, J., W. Holloway, C. Urwin, C. Venn, and V. Walkerdine
1984 *Changing the Subject*. London: Methuen.
Hirsch, E. D., Jr.
1976 *The Aims of Interpretation*. Chicago: University of Chicago Press.
Hobsbawn, Eric, and Terence Ranger (eds.)
1983 *The Invention of Tradition*. Cambridge: Cambridge University Press.
Hollis, Martin, and Steven Lukes (eds.)
1982 *Rationality and Relativism*. Cambridge: MIT Press.
Hoskins, Janet
1987 "The Headhunter as Hero: Local Traditions and Their Reinterpretation in National History." *American Ethnologist* 14(4):605–22.
1985 "A Life History from Both Sides: The Changing Poetics of Personal Experience." *Journal of Anthropological Research* 41:147–69.
Hours, Bernard.
1976 "Leadership et Cargo Cult: L'irresistible ascension de J. T. P. S. Moïses." *Journal de la société des oceanistes* 32:207–32.
Howard, Roy J.
1982 *Three Faces of Hermeneutics: An Introduction to Current Theories of Understanding*. Berkeley: University of California Press.
Hoy, David Couzens
1978 *The Critical Circle: Literature, History, and Philosophical Hermeneutics*. Berkeley: University of California Press.
Huyssen, Andreas
1984 "Mapping the Postmodern." *New German Critique* 33(Fall 1984):5–52.

Irigaray, Luce
1981 "This Sex Which Is Not One." In *New French Feminisms*. ed. Elaine Marks and Isabelle de Courtivron. New York: Schocken Books, pp. 99–106.

Jackson, Michael
1989 *Paths toward a Clearing: Radical Empiricism and Ethnographic Inquiry.* Bloomington: University of Indiana Press.
1987 Review of *The Anthropology of Experience. Australia and New Zealand Journal of Sociology* (Nov.):436–37.
1986 *Barawa, and the Way Birds Fly in the Sky.* Washington, D.C.: Smithsonian Institution Press.

James, Henry
1948 *The Art of Fiction and Other Essays.* New York: Oxford University Press.

Jameson, Fredric
1983 "Postmodernism and Consumer Society." In *The Anti-Aesthetic: Essays on Postmodern Culture.* ed. Hal Foster. Port Townsend, Wash.: Bay Press, pp. 111–25.

Jebb, Sir Richard C.
1902 *The Antigone of Sophocles: With a Commentary.* ed. E. Shuckburgh. Cambridge: Cambridge University Press.
1900 *Sophocles: The Play and Fragments.* Cambridge: Cambridge University Press.

Jennings, Bruce
1983 "Interpretive Social Science and Policy Analysis." In *Ethics, the Social Sciences, and Policy Analysis.* ed. Daniel Callahan and Bruce Jennings. New York: Plenum, pp. 3–35.

Jones, Robert
1941 *The Dramatic Imagination.* New York: Theater Arts Books.

Jung, Carl
1969 *The Archetypes and the Collective Unconscious.* Princeton, N.J.: Princeton University Press.

Jupp, James, and Marian Sawer
1979 "New Hebrides 1978–79: Self Government by Whom and for Whom?" *Journal of Pacific History* 14:208–20.

Kapferer, Bruce
1988 "The Anthropologist as Hero: Three Exponents of Post-modernist Anthropology." *Critique of Anthropology* 8(2):77–104.

Keller, Evelyn Fox
1988 "Feminist Perspectives on Science Studies." *The Barnard Occasional Papers on Women's Issues* 3:10–36.

Kipp, Rita S., and Richard Kipp (eds.)
1983 *Beyond Samosir: Recent Studies of the Batak Peoples of Sumatra.* Ohio University Papers in International Studies, Southeast Asia Monograph Series no 62. Athens: Ohio University Press.

Kipp, Rita S., and Susan Rodgers (eds.)
1987 *Indonesian Religions in Trasition.* Tucson: University of Arizona Press.
Kitto, H. D. F.
1951 *The Greek.* Harmondsworth, England: Penguin.
Knox, B.
1984 "Introduction." In *Sophocles: The Three Theban Plays.* trans. R. Fagles. New York: Penguin.
Kojève, A.
1947 *Introduction a la lecture de Hegel.* Paris: Galilée.
Kondo, Dorinne K.
1990 *Crafting Selves: Power, Gender, and Discourses of Identity in a Japanese Workplace.* Chicago: University of Chicago Press.
Kummar, K.
1987 *Utopia and Anti-Utopia in Modern Times.* Oxford: Basil Blackwell.
Kundera, Milan
1988 *The Art of the Novel.* trans. Linda Asher. New York: Harper and Row.
Kurzweil, Edith
1980 *The Age of Structuralism: Lévi-Strauss to Foucault.* New York: Columbia University Press.
LaCapra, Cominick
1986 "Death in Venice: An Allegory of Reading." Paper presented at the Interpreting the Humanities Conference. Woodrow Wilson Institute.
Lane Fox, Robin
1973 *Alexander the Great.* London: Allen Lane.
Lavie, Smadar
1990 *The Poetics of Military Occupation: Mzeina Allegories of Bedouin Identity under Israeli and Egyptian Rule.* Berkeley: University of California Press.
Lavie, Smadar, Kirin Narayan, and Renato Rosaldo (eds).
1993 *Creativity in Anthropology.* Ithaca: Cornell University Press.
Layard, John
1942 *Stone Men of Malekula.* London: Chatto and Windus.
Le Guin, Ursula K.
1985 *Always Coming Home.* New York: Harper and Row.
Lemert, Charles C., and Garth Gillan
1982 *Michel Foucault: Social Theory as Transgression.* New York: Columbia University Press.
Lennox, Sarah
1987 "Anthropology and the Politics of Deconstruction." Paper presented at the Ninth Annual Conference of the National Women's Studies Association. Atlanta, Ga.
Le Page, R. B.
1969 "Dialect in West Indian Literature." *Journal of Commonwealth Literature* 7:1–7.

Le Page, R. B., and Andree Tabouret-Keller
1985 *Acts of Identity: Creole-based Approaches to Language and Ethnicity.* Cambridge: Cambridge University Press.

Levine, Stephen Z.
1985 "The Romance of Realism in Nineteenth Century Art." *Raritan* 4(3):133–45.

Levy, Robert I.
1973 *Tahitians: Mind and Experience in the Society Islands.* Chicago: University of Chicago Press.

Lévi-Strauss, Claude
1985 "Structuralism and Ecology." In *The View from Afar.* trans. Joachim Neugroschel and Phoebe Hoss. New York: Basic Books, pp. 101–19.
1973 *L'anthropologie structurale 2.* Paris: Plon.
1969 *The Raw and the Cooked: Introduction to a Science of Mythology.* Vol. 1. trans. John Weightman and Doreen Weightman. Chicago: University of Chicago Press.
1966 *The Savage Mind.* Chicago: University of Chicago Press.
1958 *Anthropologie structurale.* Paris: Librairie Plon.
1955 *Tristes Tropiques.* Paris: Plon.

Linschoten, John Huygen van
1970 [1598] *The Voyage of John Huygen van Linschoten to the East Indies.* 2 vols. The Hakluyt Society First Series nos. 70 and 71. New York: Burt Franklin.

Loebis, A. N.
1922 *Harondoek parmanoan.* Medan: Handel Mij Indische Drukkerij.

Lugones, Maria C., and Elizabeth Spelman
1983 "Have We Got a Theory for You! Feminist Theory, Cultural Imperialism, and the Demand for 'The Woman's Voice.' " *Women's Studies International Forum* 6(6):573–81.

Lukes, Steven
1982 "Relativism in Its Place." In *Rationality and Relativism.* ed. Martin Hollis and Steven Lukes. Cambridge: MIT Press, pp. 260–305.

MacClancy, Jeremy V.
1980 *To Kill a Bird with Two Stones: A Short History of Vanuatu.* Vila Cultural Centre Publications, no. 1. Port Vila.

McFarlane, A.
1978 *The Origins of English Individualism.* Oxford: Basil Blackwell.

McLennan, J. F.
1886 *Studies in Ancient History.* New York: Macmillan

Maitland, Frederic
1958 "Introduction." In *Political Theories of the Middle Age,* by Otto Gierke. Boston: Beacon.

Malinowski, Bronislaw
1967 *A Diary in the Strict Sense of the Term.* London: Routledge and Kegan Paul.
1961 *Argonauts of the Western Pacific.* New York: Dutton.

Marcus, George E.
1980 "Rhetoric and the Ethnographic Genre in Anthropological Research."
     Current Anthropology 21(4):507–10.
Marcus, George E., and James Clifford
1985 "The Making of Ethnographic Texts: A Preliminary Report." *Current
     Anthropology* 26(2):267–71.
Marcus, George E., and Dick Cushman
1982 "Ethnographies as Texts." In *Annual Review of Anthropology.* ed. Ber-
     nard J. Siegel, Alan R. Beals, and Stephen A. Tyler. Palo Alto: Annual
     Reviews, 11:25–69.
Marcus, George E., and Michael M. J. Fischer
1986 *Anthropology as Cultural Critique: An Experimantal Moment in the
     Human Sciences.* Chicago: University of Chicago Press.
Margolin, Uri
1978 "Conclusion: Literary Structuralism and Hermeneutics in Significant
     Convergence." In *Interpretation of Narrative.* ed. Mario J. Valdes and
     Owen J. Miller. Toronto: University of Toronto Press, pp. 177–85.
Mark, Joan
1988 *A Stranger in Her Native Land: Alice Fletcher and the American Indians.*
     Lincoln: University of Nebraska Press.
Marpaung, Bgd. Marakub
1969 *Jop ni roha pardomuan.* Padangsidimpuan: Pustaka Timur.
Marpaung, B. M., and B. R. Sohuturon
1962 *Pundjut-pundjutan.* Medan: Islamyah.
Maxwell, Nicholas
1984 *From Knowledge to Wisdom: A Revolution in the Aims and Methods
     of Science.* New York: Blackwell.
Mead, Margaret
1932 [1965] *The Changing Culture of an Indian Tribe.* Columbia University
     Press.
Miller, Nancy K.
1986 "Changing the Subject: Authorship, Writing, and the Reader." In *Feminist
     Studies: Critical Studies.* ed. Teresa de Lauretis. Bloomington: University
     of Indiana Press, pp. 102–20.
Moers, Ellen
1976 *Literary Women.* New York: Doubleday.
Montaigne, Michel de
[1580] 1956 "Of the Inconsistency of Our Actions." In *World Masterpieces.*
     ed. Maynard Mack. New York: Norton, Essays, bk. 2, ch. 1, pp. 936–
     42.
Moore, Gerald
1974 "Language of West Indian Poetry." *Bim* 57:69–76.
Morgan, Prys
1983 "From Death to a View: The Hunt for a Welsh Past in the Romantic
     Period." In *The Invention of Tradition.* ed. Eric Hobsbawm and Terence
     Ranger. Cambridge: Cambridge University Press, pp. 43–100.

Morris, D. R.
1965 *The Washing of the Spears: The Rise and Fall of the Zulu Nation.* New York: Simon and Schuster.

Morris, I.
1987 *Burial and Ancient Society: The Rise of the Greek State.* Cambridge: Cambridge University Press.

Morris, Mervyn
1985 "The Poetry of Mikey Smith." In *West Indian Literature and its Social Context.* ed. M. A. McWatt. Cave Hill, Barbados: University of the West Indies, pp. 48–54.

Murray, Oswyn
1986 "Life and Society in Classical Greece." In *The Oxford History of the Classical World.* ed. J. Boardman, J. Griffith, and O. Murray. Oxford: Oxford University Press.

Myerhoff, Barbara
1978 *Number Our Days.* New York: Simon and Schuster.

Narayan, Kirin
1989 *Storytellers, Saints, and Scoundrels.* Philadelphia: University of Pennsylvania Press.

Nash, June
1979 *We Eat the Mines and the Mines Eat Us: Dependency and Exploitation in Bolivian Tin Mines.* New York: Columbia University Press.

Ndebele, Njabulo S.
1987 "The English Language and Social Change in South Africa." *Tri-Quarterly* 69:217–35.

Needham, Rodney
1985 *Exemplars.* Berkeley: University of California Press.

O'Flaherty, Wendy Doniger
1973 *Asceticism and Eroticism in the Mythology of Siva.* New York: Oxford University Press.

O'Meara, J. Tim
1989 "Anthropology as Empirical Science." *American Anthropologist* 91(2):354–69.

Obeyesekere, Gananath
1981 *Medusa's Hair: An Essay on Personal Symbols and Religious Experience.* Berkeley: University of California Press.

Ong, Walter J.
1982 *Orality and Literacy: The Technologizing of the Word.* London: Methuen.

Ortner, Sherry B.
1984 "Theory in Anthropology since the Sixties." *Society for Comparative Study of Society and History* 26:126–66.

Owens, Craig
1983 "The Discourse of Others: Feminists and Postmodernism." In *The Anti-aesthetic: Essays on Postmodern Culture.* ed. H. Foster. Port Townsend, Wash.: Bay Press, pp. 57–82.

Owens, Joseph
1976 *Dread: The Rastafarians of Jamaica*. London: Heinemann.

Pace, David
1983 *Claude Lévi-Strauss: The Bearer of Ashes*. Boston: Routledge and Kegan Paul.

Page, Helen
1988 "Dialogic Principles of Interactive Learning in the Ethnographic Relationship." *Journal of Anthropological Research* 44:163–81.

Pane, H. Soetan Pane Paroehoem
1922 *Adat Batak II (dibagasan siriaon.)* Pematang Siantar: n.p.

Parker, Richard
1985 "From Symbolism to Interpretation: Reflections on the Work of Clifford Geertz." *Anthropology and Humanism Quarterly* 10:62–67.

Parsons, Talcott
1937 *The Structure of Social Action*. New York: McGraw Hill.

Partridge, Eric
1983 *Origins: A Short Etymological Dictionary of Modern English*. New York: Greenwich House.

Peacock, James L.
1984 "Religion and Life History: An Exploration in Cultural Psychology." In *Text, Play, and Story: The Construction and Reconstruction of Self and Society*. ed. Edward M. Bruner. Proceedings of the American Ethnological Society. Washington, D.C.: American Anthropological Association. Reprint, 1988. Chicago: Waveland, pp. 94–116.

Phelps, Louise Wetherbee (ed.)
1983 Ricoeur and Rhetoric. *Pre-Text: An Inter-Disciplinary Journal of Rhetoric* 4, nos. 3–4.

Plant, Chris (ed.)
1977 *New Hebrides: The Road to Independence*. Fiji: University of the South Pacific.

Plummer, John
1978 *Movement of Jah People*. Birmingham, England: Press Gang.

Polanyi, Michael
1962 *Personal Knowledge: Towards a Post-critical Philosophy*. Chicago: University of Chicago Press.

Polanyi, Michael, and Harry Prosch
1975 *Meaning*. Chicago: University of Chicago Press.

Pollard, Velma
1985 "Dread Talk—the Speech of the Rastafarians in Jamaica." In *Rastafari*. ed. R. Nettleford. Mona, Jamaica: University of the West Indies, pp. 32–41.

Ponko, Vincent, Jr.
1968 "The Privy Council and the Spirit of Elizabethan Economic Management, 1558–1603." *Transactions of the American Philosophical Society*, n.s. 58, part 4.

Porter, Dennis
1984 "Anthropological Tales: Unprofessional Thoughts on the Mead/Freeman Controversy." In *Notebooks in Cultural Analysis: An Annual Review.* ed. Norman F. Cantor and Nathalia King. Durham, N.C.: Duke University Press, pp. 15–37.

Powdermaker, Hortense
1966 *Stranger and Friend: The Way of an Anthropologist.* New York: W. W. Norton.

Pratt, Annis
1982 *Archetypal Patterns in Women's Fiction.* Bloomington: Indiana University Press.

Prattis, J. Iain (ed.)
1985 *Reflections: The Anthropological Muse.* Washington, D.C.: American Anthropological Association.

Price, Richard
1983 *First-Time: The Historical Vision of an Afro-American People.* Baltimore: Johns Hopkins University Press.

Puzo, Mario
1969 *The Godfather.* New York: Putnam.

Rabb, Theodore K.
1967 *Enterprise and Empire: Merchant and Gentry Investment in the Expansion of England, 1575–1630.* Cambridge: Harvard University Press.

Rabinow, Paul
1986 "Representations Are Social Facts: Modernity and Post-modernity in Anthropology." In *Writing Culture: The Poetics and Politics of Ethnography.* ed. James Clifford and George E. Marcus. Berkeley: University of California Press, pp. 234–61.
1984 (ed.) *The Foucault Reader.* New York: Pantheon.
1983 "Humanism as Nihilism." In *Social Science as Moral Inquiry.* ed. Norma Haan, Robert N. Bellah, Paul Rabinow, and William M. Sullivan. New York: Columbia University Press, pp. 52–75.
1977 *Reflections on Fieldwork in Morocco.* Berkeley: University of California Press.

Rabinow, Paul, and William A. Sullivan
1987 (eds.) *Interpretive Social Science: A Second Look.* Berkeley: University of California Press.
1979 "The Interpretive Turn: Emergence of an Approach." In *Interpretive Social Science: A Reader.* ed. Paul Rabinow and William A. Sullivan. Berkeley: University of California Press, pp. 1–21.

Rangkuti, Nursyafiah
1983 *Bahasa daerah Angkola dan Mandailing.* Medan: privately published.

Rawls, John
1971 *A Theory of Justice.* Cambridge: Harvard University Press.

Redfield, James
1975 *Nature and Culture in the Iliad: The Tragedy of Hector.* Chicago: University of Chicago Press.

Reichel-Dolmatoff, Gerardo
1971 *Amazonian Cosmos: The Sexual and Religious Symbolism of the Tukano Indians.* Chicago: University of Chicago Press.

Reynolds, D.
1986 "Redneck Girl Is Real, Yet Part of Writer's Creation." *Lewiston Morning Tribune,* 14 Nov.

Rice, Kenneth A.
1980 *Geertz and Culture.* Ann Arbor: University of Michigan Press.

Ricoeur, Paul
1984 *Time and Narrative.* trans. Kathleen McLaughlin and David Pellauer. Chicago: University of Chicago Press.
1983 "On Interpretation." In *Philosophy in France Today.* ed. Alan Montifiore. New York: Cambridge University Press, pp. 175–97.
1981 *Hermeneutics and the Human Sciences.* ed. and trans. John B. Thompson. New York: Cambridge University Press.
1979 "The Model of the Text: Meaningful Action Considered as a Text." In *Interpretive Social Science: A Reader.* ed. Paul Rabinow and William M. Sullivan. Berkeley: University of California Press, pp. 73–101.

Ridington, Robin
1988 *Trail to Heaven.* Iowa City: University of Iowa Press.

Ritter, E. A.
1957 *Shaka Zulu.* New York: Putnam.

Rivers, William H. R.
1968 [1914] *The History of Melansian Society.* 2 vols. The Netherlands: Oosterhout N. B., Anthropological Publications.

Roche, Paul
1958 *The Oedipus Plays of Sophocles.* New York: New American Library.

Rodgers, Susan
1991 "Imagining Tradition, Imagining Modernity: A Southern Batak Novel from the 1920's." 147 *Bijdragen tot de Land-, Tall, en Volkenkunde.*
1989 "Batak Heritage and the Indonesian State: Print Literacy and the Creation of an Ethnic Culture in Indonesia." Paper presented at the Midwest Meeting of the American Anthropological Association. Notre Dame University.
1988 "Me and Toba: A Childhood World in a Batak Memior." *Indonesia* 45:63–84.
1987 "City Newspapers and the Creation of a Batak Political Heritage." In *Cultures and Societies of North Sumatra.* ed. Rainer Carle. Veröffentlichungen des Seminars der Indonesische und Südseesprachen der Universität Hamburg, Band 19. Berlin: Dietrich Reimer Verlag, pp. 198–220.
1986 "Batak Tape Cassette Kinship: Constructing Kinship through the Indonesian National Mass Media." *American Ethnologist* 13(1):23–42.
1984 "Orality, Literacy, and Batak Concepts of Marriage Alliance." *Journal of Anthropological Research.* 40(3):433–50.
1983 "Political Oratory in a Modernizing Southern Batak Homeland." In

Beyond Samosir: Recent Studies of the Batak Peoples of Sumatra. ed. Rita S. Kipp and Richard Kipp. Ohio University Papers in International Studies, Southeast Asia Monograph Series no. 62. Athens: Ohio University Press, 21–52.

1981 "A Batak Literature of Modernization." *Indonesia* 31:137–61.

1979a "Advice to the Newlyweds: Sipirok Batak Wedding Speeches—Adat or Art?" In *Art, Ritual, and Society in Indonesia.* ed. Edward M. Bruner and Judith Becker. Ohio University Papers in International Studies, Southeast Asia Monograph Series no. 53. Athens: Ohio University Press, pp. 30–61.

1979b "A Modern Batak Horja: Innovation in Sipirok Adat Ceremonial." *Indonesia* 27:103–18.

1978 "Angkola Batak Kinship through its Oral Literature." Ph.D. diss., University of Chicago.

Rodman, William. L.

1985 " 'A Law unto Themselves': Legal Innovation in Ambae, Vanuatu." *American Ethnologist* 12(4):603–24.

1982 "Gaps, Bridges, and Levels of Law: Middlemen as Mediators in a Vanuatu Society." In *Middlemen and Brokers in Oceania.* ed. William Rodman and Dorothy Counts. ASAO Monograph no. 9. Ann Arbor: University of Michigan Press, pp. 69–95.

1977 "Big Men and Middlemen: The Politics of Law in Longana." *American Ethnologist* 4(3):525–37.

1973 "Men of Influence, Men of Rank: Leadership and the Graded Society on Aoba, New Hebrides." Ph.D. diss., University of Chicago.

Roe, Peter G.

1982 *The Cosmic Zygote: Cosmology in the Amazon Basin.* New Brunswick, N.J.: Rutgers University Press.

Rohlehr, Gordon

1972 "The Folk in Caribbean Literature." *Tapia* (17 Dec.):7–14.

Rorty, Richard

1979 *Philosophy and the Mirror of Nature.* Princeton, N.J.: Princeton University Press.

Rosaldo, Michelle

1980 *Knowledge and Passion: Ilongot Notions of Self and Social Life.* New York: Cambridge University Press.

Rosaldo, Renato

1989 *Culture and Truth: The Remaking of Social Analysis.* Boston: Beacon Press.

1988 "Ideology, Place, and People without Culture." *Cultural Anthropology* 3:77–87.

Rose, Dan

1991a "Reversal." In *Anthropological Poetics.* ed. Ivan Brady. Savage, Md.: Rowman and Littlefield.

1991b "In Search of Experience: The Anthropological Poetics of Stanley

Diamond." In *Anthropological Poetics.* ed. Ivan Brady. Savage, Md.: Rowman and Littlefield.

1990 *Living the Ethnographic Life.* Qualitative Research Methods vol. 23. Newbury Park, Calif.: Sage Publications.

1989 *Patterns of American Culture: Ethnography and Estrangement.* Philadelphia: University of Pennsylvania Press.

1987 *Black American Street Life.* Philadelphia: University of Pennsylvania Press.

1986 "Transformations of Disciplines through Their Texts." *Cultural Anthropology* 1:317–27.

Roth, Paul
1988 "Narrative Explanations: The Case of History." *History and Theory* 27:1–13.

Royal Anthropological Institute
1951 *Notes and Queries on Anthropology.* 6th ed. London: Routledge and Kegan Paul.

Rubinstein, Robert, and Rik Pinxten (eds.)
1984 *Epistemology and Process: Anthropological Views.* Ghent: Communication and Cognition Books.

Ruby, Jay (ed.)
1982 *A Crack in the Mirror: Reflexive Perspectives in Anthropology.* Philadelphia: University of Pennsylvania Press.

Russo, Mary
1986 "Female Grotesques: Carnival and Theory." In *Feminist Studies: Critical Studies.* ed. Teresa de Lauretis. Bloomington: Indiana University Press, pp. 213–29.

Ruwet, Nicolas
1963 *Linguistique et sciences de l'homme. Esprit* 322:564–78.

Sahlins, Marshall
1985 *Islands of History.* Chicago: University of Chicago Press.

1981 *Historical Metaphors and Mythical Realities: Structure in the Early History of the Sandwich Islands Kingdom.* ASAO Special Publications, no. 1. Ann Arbor: University of Michigan Press.

1976 *Culture and Practical Reason.* Chicago: University of Chicago Press.

Sangren, P. Steven
1988 "Rhetoric and the Authority of Ethnography." *Current Anthropology* 29(3):405–24.

Saussure, Ferdinand de
1959 *Course in General Linguistics.* ed. Charles Bally and Albert Sechedayes, with Albert Reidlinger. trans., with intro. and notes by Wade Baskin. New York: McGraw-Hill.

Schechner, Richard
1988 "Playing." *Play and Culture* 1(1):3–19.

Schieffelin, Edward
1976 *The Sorrow of the Lonely and the Burning of the Dancers.* New York: St. Martin's.

Schneider, David M.

1980 *American Kinship: A Cultural Account.* 2d ed. Chicago: University of Chicago Press.

1976 "Notes toward a Theory of Culture." In *Meaning in Anthropology.* ed. Keith H. Basso and Henry A. Selby. Albuquerque: University of New Mexico Press, pp. 197–220.

Scholes, Robert

1974 *Structuralism in Literature: An Introduction.* New Haven: Yale University Press.

Scholte, Bob

1984 "Reason and Culture: The Universal and the Particular Revisited." *American Anthropologist* 86(4):960–65.

1973 "Toward a Reflexive and Critical Anthropology." In *Reinventing Anthropology.* ed. Dell Hymes. New York: Random House, pp. 430–57.

Scollon, Ron, and Suzanne B. K. Scollon

1981 *Narrative, Literacy, and Face in Interethnic Communication.* Norwood, N.J.: Ablex.

Scott, Joan

1987 "History and the Problem of (Sexual) Difference." Lecture presented at Simon's Rock of Bard College, Great Barrington, Mass.

Seeger, Anthony

1981 *Nature and Society in Brazil.* Cambridge: Harvard University Press.

Seung, T. K.

1982 *Structuralism and Hermeneutics.* New York: Columbia University Press.

Shankman, Paul

1984 "On Semiotics and Science: Reply to Renner and Scholte." *Current Anthropology* 25(5):691–92.

Shostak, Marjorie

1983 *Nisa: The Life and Words of a !Kung Woman.* New York: Vintage.

Shoumatoff, Alex

1985 *The Mountain of Names: A History of the Human Family.* New York: Simon and Schuster.

Showalter, Elaine

1983 "Critical Cross-dressing: Male Feminists and the Woman of the Year." *Raritan* 3(2):130–49.

1977 *A Literature of Their Own: British Women Novelists from Bronte to Lessing.* Princeton, N.J.: Princeton University Press.

Siagian, T. P.

1966 "A Bibliography of the Batak Peoples." *Indonesia,* no. 1, pp. 161–84.

Siahaan, B. glr. Mangaradja Asal

1938 *Patik dohot oehoem ni sinoerathon djala pinatoere.* Lagoeboti: Zendings Drukkerij.

1937 *Tamba-tamba ni Umpama ni Halak Batak.* Tarutung: Silindung Drukkerij.

Simpson, George Eaton
1970 *Religious Cults of the Caribbean.* Rio Piedras, P.R.: Institute of Caribbean Studies.

Siregar Baumi, G., gelar Sutan Tinggibarani Perkasa Alam
1986 *Pabagas boru.* Padangsidimpuan: privately published.
1984a *Seni budaya tradisional daerah Tapanuli Selatan suku Batak Angkola-Padanglawas-Mandailing dan Pesisir.* Padangsidimpuan: privately published.
1984b *Surat tumbaga holing, adat Batak Angkola-Sipirok-Padangbolak-Barumun-Mandailing-Batang Natal-Natal.* Padangsidimpuan: privately published.
1980a *Methode baru pelajaran membaca dan menulis huruf-huruf Batak Tapanuli selatan. Aksara Batak Tapanuli Selatan.* Padangsidimpuan: privately published.
1980b *Horja godang mangupa di na haroan boru, horas tondi madingin sayur matua bulung.* Padangsidimpuan: privately published.
1978 *Mangampar ruji/mangkobar boru (musyawarah perhitungan mas kawin menurut adat Tapanuli Selatan.)* Tapanuli Selatan: privately published.

Siregar, Mr. Palti-Radja
1958 *Hukum warisan adat Batak, Angkola/Sipirok Mandailing dan Padanglawas.* N.p..

Slocum, Sally
1975 "Woman the Gatherer: Male Bias in Anthropology." In *Toward an Anthropology of Women.* ed. R. Rapp. New York: Monthly Review Press, pp. 36–50.

Smith, David M.
1986 "The Anthropology of Literacy Acquisition." In *The Acquisition of Literacy: Ethnographic Perspectives.* ed. B. Schieffelin and P. Gilmore. Norwood N.J.: Ablex, pp. 261–75.

Smyth, W. S.
1926 *Aeschylus: Vol. II.* Loeb Classical Library.

Soetan Martoewa Radja
1919 *Doea sadjoli.* Batavia: Landsdrukkerij.

Soetan Pangoerabaan
[1930] *Adat.* Sipirok: Stn P.

Sontag, Susan
1982 (ed.) *A Barthes Reader.* New York: Hill and Wang.
1966 "The Anthropologist as Hero." In *Against Interpretation.* ed. Susan Sontag. New York: Farrar, Straus, Giroux.

Sperber, Dan
1983 "Dialectical Drifting." *Times Literary Supplement,* 4 Nov.

Spiegelberg, Herbert
1975 *Doing Phenomenology: Essays on and in Phenomenology.* The Hague: Martinus Nijhoff.

Stacey, Judith
1988 "Can There Be a Feminist Ethnography?" *Women's Studies International Forum* 11(1):21–27.
Stack, Carol B.
1974 *All Our Kin.* New York: Harper and Row.
Steiner, George
1984 *Antigones.* Oxford: Clarendon.
Stewart, John O.
1989 *Drinkers, Drummers, and Decent Folk.* Albany: State University of New York Press.
Stoller, Paul
1989 *The Fusion of Worlds.* Chicago: University of Chicago Press.
1988 "A Dialogue on Anthropology between a Songhay and an Inquirer." Paper presented at the Eighty-seventh Annual Meeting of the American Anthropological Association. Phoenix, Ariz.
1987 "Son of Rouch: Portrait of a Young Ethnographer by the Songhay." *Anthropological Quarterly* 60:114–23.
Stoller, Paul, and Cheryl Olkes
1987 *In Sorcery's Shadow.* Chicago: University of Chicago Press.
Storr, F.
1912 *Sophocles: Vol. I.* Loeb Classical Library.
Strachan, Michael, and Boies Penrose
1971 *The East India Company Journals of Captain William Keeling and Master Thomas Bonner, 1615–1617.* Minneapolis: University of Minnesota Press.
Strathern, Andrew
1989 "Melpa Dream Interpretation and the Concept of Hidden Truth." *Ethnology* 28:301–15.
1975 "Veiled Speech in Mount Hagan." In *Political Language and Oratory in Traditional Society.* ed. Maurice Bloch. London: Academic Press, pp. 185–203.
Strathern, Marilyn
1987a "An Awkward Relationship: The Case of Feminism and Anthropology." *Signs* 12(2):276–92.
1987b "Out of Context: The Persuasive Fictions of Anthropology." *Current Anthropology* 28(3):251–70.
Sutan Tinggibarani Perkasa Alam, Dra. Rukiah Siregar, and Paruhuman Harahap
1977 *Burangir na hombang: Buku pelajaran adat [Tapanuli Selatan] siulaon sepanjang adat dipersembahkan untuk masyarakat dan naposo/naulibulung.* Padangsidimpuan: privately published.
Sutan Tinggibarani Perkasa Alam, Dra. Rukiah Siregar, and Drs. Bahasan Siregar Bgd. Mulia
1981 *Bona-bona ni partuturan cara-cara bertutur sopan santun dalam hubungan kefamilian menurut adat Tapanuli Selatan.* Padangsidimpuan: privately published.

Taussig, Michael
1980 *The Devil and Commodity Fetishism in South America*. Chapel Hill: University of North Carolina Press.

Tedlock, Barbara
1991 "From Participant Observation to the Observation of Participation: The Emergence of Narrative Ethnography." *Journal of Anthropological Research* 47(1):69–94.

Tiger, Lionel
1978 "Omnigamy: Towards a New Kinship System." *Psychology Today*, July.

Tonkinson, Robert
1982 "National Identity and the Problem of Kastom in Vanuatu."In *Reinventing Traditional Culture: The Politics of Kastom in Island Melanesia*. ed. Roger Keesing and R. Tonkinson. Special issue of *Mankind* 13:306–16.

Tönnies, F.
1887 *Gemeinschaft und Gesellschaft*. Leipzig: Fues Verlag.

Tress, Daryl McGowan
1988 "Comment on Flax's 'Postmodernism and Gender Relations in Feminist Theory.' " *Signs* 14(1):196–200.

Turner, Edith
1989 "From Shamans to Healers: The Survival of an Inupiaq Eskimo Skill." *Anthropologica* 31(1):3–24.

Turner, Victor W., and Edward M. Bruner, eds.
1986 *The Anthropology of Experience*. Urbana: University of Illinois Press.

Tuzin, Donald
1984 "Miraculous Voices: The Auditory Experience of Numinous Objects." *Current Anthropology* 25(5):579–96.

Tyler, Stephen A.
1987 *The Unspeakable*. Madison: University of Wisconsin Press.

1986 "Post-modern Ethnography: From Document of the Occult to Occult Document." In *Writing Culture: The Poetics and Politics of Ethnography*. ed. James Clifford and George E. Marcus. Berkeley: University of California Press, pp. 122–40.

Ulin, Robert C.
1984 *Understanding Cultures: Perspectives in Anthropology and Social Theory*. Austin: University of Texas Press.

Ulmer, Gregory
1989 *Teletheory: Grammatology in the Age of Video*. New York: Routledge.

Velikovsky, I.
1960 *Oedipus and Akhnaton*. New York: Doubleday.

Vickers, Adrian
1989 *Bali: A Paradise Created*. Berkeley: Periplus Editions.

Vonnegut, Kurt
1976 *Slapstick*. New York: Dell.

Wagner, Roy

1986 *Symbols That Stand for Themselves*. Chicago: University of Chicago Press.

1981 *The Invention of Culture*. Rev. ed. Chicago: University of Chicago Press.

Ward, Jeffrey J., and Oswald Werner

1984 "Difference and Dissonance in Ethnographic Data." In *Epistemology and Process: Anthropological Views*. ed. R. Rubinstein and R. Pinxten. Ghent: Communication and Cognition Books, pp. 91–116.

Watling, E. F.

1947 *Sophocles: The Theban Plays*. Harmondsworth, England: Penguin.

Westen, Drew

1984 "Cultural Materialism: Food for Thought or Bum Steer?" *Current Anthropology* 25(5):639–53.

Whyte, William Foote

1955 *Street Corner Society*. 2d ed. Chicago: University of Chicago Press.

Wuthnow, Robert, James Davison Hunter, Albert Bergesen, and Edith Kurzweil

1984 *Cultural Analysis: The Work of Peter L. Berger, Mary Douglas, Michel Foucault, and Jürgen Habermas*. Boston: Routledge and Kegan Paul.

Zipes, Jack

1979 *Breaking the Magic Spell: Radical Theories of Folk and Fairy Tales*. New York: Methuen.

Notes on Contributors

MICHAEL V. ANGROSINO is professor of anthropology at the University of South Florida. He has conducted fieldwork in Trinidad, Aruba, and Saba and specializes in oral history research and studies of contemporary Caribbean literary genres. His most recent publication is *Documents of Interaction: Biography, Autobiography, and Life History in the Social Sciences*.

PAUL BENSON is a senior graduate student at the University of Illinois at Urbana-Champaign. His interests, reflected in this text, pertain to the employment of multigenre techniques in the production of ethnography. His area of concentration lies with the cultural studies/humanities project, studying the dialogic nature of discourse and its relations to ideology, gender, and the arts. His fieldwork is being conducted at Chautauqua Institution, an American educational center devoted to the study of religion, science, music, and the arts.

IVAN BRADY is Distinguished Teaching Professor of anthropology and Faculty Exchange Scholar at the State University of New York at Oswego. He is a poet, the author of numerous articles and reviews, and the editor of several books, including *Transactions in Kinship,* two volumes of *A Reader in Culture Change* (with Barry L. Isaac), *Extinction and Survival in Human Populations* (with Charles D. Laughlin, Jr.), and, most recently, *Anthropological Poetics*. For seven years he was book review editor of the *American Anthropologist*. Most of his fieldwork has been concentrated in Polynesia and the American Southwest. He is currently studying the development of critical aesthetics in anthropological experience.

EDWARD M. BRUNER is professor of anthropology and professor of criticism and interpretive theory at the University of Illinois, Urbana-

Champaign. His edited volumes include *Art, Ritual, and Society in Indonesia* (with Judith Becker), *Text, Play, and Story: The Construction and Reconstruction of Self and Society,* and *The Anthropology of Experience* (with Victor W. Turner). He was formerly president of the American Ethnological Society and is now president of the Society for Humanistic Anthropology. He is currently writing a book on tourist performances.

COLLEEN BALLERINO COHEN is associate professor of anthropology and women's studies at Vassar College. She has coauthored articles with Frances E. Mascia-Lees and Patricia Sharpe that have appeared in *American Behavioral Scientist, College English,* and *Signs.* Her article "Olfactory Constitution of the Postmodern Body: Nature Challenged, Nature Adorned" appears in *Tattoo, Torture, Mutilation, and Adornment: The Denaturalization of the Body in Culture and Text* and is part of a continuing research interest in representation and women's experience. She is currently working on an ethnographic study of identity, nationalism, and tourism in the British West Indies.

ROBIN FOX was born in the United Kingdom in 1934, educated at the London School of Economics and Harvard, and is professor of social theory at Rutgers. His books include *The Keresan Bridge, The Tory Islanders, Kinship and Marriage, Encounter with Anthropology, The Red Lamp of Incest, The Imperial Animal* (with Lionel Tiger), and, most recently, *The Search for Society* and a book of essays, drama, and poems, *The Violent Imagination.* He is currently working on law, aggression, ideology, primate sexuality, and the history of ideas.

BRUCE T. GRINDAL received his Ph.D at Indiana University and has done ethnographic field research in West Africa and the American South. In recent years he has written about his field experiences in the literary genres of drama, narrative, short story, and poetry. As one of the pioneers in the humanistic movement in anthropology, he served as editor of the *Anthropology and Humanism Quarterly* from 1976 to 1984 and as president of the Society for Humanistic Anthropology from 1984 to 1985. Currently, he is professor of anthropology and director of the peace studies program at Florida State University.

FRANCES E. MASCIA-LEES teaches anthropology at Simon's Rock College of Bard where she is also co-director of women's studies. Her primary research focus has been on exploring sexual stratification, analyzing evolutionary discourses of human sexual behavior, and articulating the intersection of anthropology and critical theory for exploring representations of women. She is the author of *Toward a Model of Women's Status* and the editor of two collections, *Human Sexuality in Biocultural Perspective* and *Tattoo, Torture, Mutilation, and Adornment: Denaturalization of the Body in Culture and Text* (with Patricia Sharpe). Her most recent articles appear in *American Anthropologist, American Behavioral Scientist, American Literary History, College English, Phoebe: An Interdisciplinary Journal of Feminist Scholarship, Medical Anthopology, Reviews in Anthropology,* and *Signs.* She is currently at work on a book with Patricia Sharpe entitled *On Display: Feminist Ethnographies of Representation and Resistance.*

ROBIN RIDINGTON has a B.A. in History from Swarthmore College and a Ph.D in anthropology from Harvard. He is professor of anthropology at the University of British Columbia. He has done fieldwork with the Beaver Indians (Dunne-za) of British Columbia and with the Omahas of Nebraska. His books include *Trail to Heaven: Knowledge and Narrative in a Northern Native Community* and *Little Bit Know Something: Stories in a Language of Anthropology.* He is writing a book about the Omaha Sacred Pole and its traditions. He is particularly interested in narrative as a medium of anthropological communication.

SUSAN RODGERS is associate professor of anthropology in the Department of Sociology and Anthropology at Holy Cross College. Her 1978 Ph.D. dissertation at the University of Chicago, drawing on 1974–76 fieldwork in Sumatra, concerned Angkola Batak oratory as a cultural text on a changing kinship system. Her current research interests (based on four subsequent field studies in North Sumatra) include the Angkola transition to literacy and particularly their use of ritual guidebooks, fiction, and local histories to rethink society in a literate mode. A related interest concerns tribal arts in modernizing outer island Indonesia.

WILLIAM L. RODMAN is associate professor of anthropology at McMaster University. He received his Ph.D. from the University of Chicago and has conducted thirty-six months of fieldwork on Ambae Island in Vanuatu since 1969. He is the author of a number of publications on colonialism, law, and politics in the South Pacific. At present, however, his main interests include critical approaches to interpretive anthropology, current literary theory, and, especially, the application of fictional techniques to ethnographic narrative.

DAN ROSE is an ethnographer of American life with a focus on the landscape of market culture from the lower class through the upper class. He teaches cultural anthropology at the University of Pennsylvania where he is professor of landscape architecture and of anthropology. His books include *Patterns of American Culture, Black American Street Life, Energy Transition and the Local Community, Rhetorical Architecture Dedicated Prose* (an artist's book), and *The Abyss* (a book of poetry). He edits the Series in Contemporary Ethnography at the University of Pennsylvania Press.

PATRICIA SHARPE is co-director of women's studies and a member of the faculty in literature at Simon's Rock College of Bard. Her interest in narrative theory and the representation of women is reflected in her current project, a book about feminine subjectivity in canonical English novels. Her previous publications include "Sexual Double Cross" and "How *Ida* Been Different: Women Writers and Their Female Characters." She has also coauthored articles that have appeared in *American Behavioral Scientist American Literary History, College English, Phoebe: An Interdisciplinary Journal of Feminist Scholarship,* and *Signs.*

WILLIAM H. SHEPHARD received his Ph.D. from Florida State University and his M.A. from New York University. He is a professional actor, playwright, and director with extensive stage credits in New York, Los Angeles, and regional theaters from Florida to Alaska. He has published articles and poetry in *Anthropology and Humanism Quarterly,* and *The Dionysus Group,* a book concerning his work in New York's alternative theater during the late 1960s, is to be published soon. His most recent accomplishments include recognition from the American College Theater Festival for his direction of Sam Shepard's *The Unseen Hand* and for his new play, *Dreamers,* concerning the cultural conflict between Native Americans and whites in the Northwest Plateau Region. He has been teaching courses in acting, play writing, and performance theory in Washington State University's theater program since 1986.

EDITH TURNER is a lecturer in anthropology at the University of Virginia. Her special field is symbolism and ritual. She has done fieldwork in such widely diverse societies as the Ndembu of Zambia and the Inupiat Eskimos of Northern Alaska. She is the author of *The Spirit and the Drum* and a number of articles. She coauthored with Victor Turner *Image and Pilgrimage in Christian Culture: Anthropological Perspectives.*

Index

DATE DUE
